OAKLAND COMMUNITY COLLEGE

3 2355 00357067 8

D0859928

HD 70 .A78 G85 2009
Guirdham, Maureen.
Culture and business in Asia

Oakland Community College
Highland Lakes Library
7350 Cooley Lake Road
Waterford, MI 48327

DEMCO

culture and business in Asia

INTRODUCTION • THE BUSINESS CULTURES OF FIVE ASIAN COUNTRIES • ANALYSING ASIAN BUSINESS CULTURES • OWNERSHIP, FINANCING AND GOVERNANCE • ORGANIZATION AND MANAGEMENT • BUSINESS STRATEGY AND THE BUSINESS OF SOCIETAL CULTURES • SOCIETAL CULTURES REVISITED • POLITICAL CULTURES AND PERCEIVED POLITICAL ENVIRONMENTS • ECONOMIC CULTURES AND PERCEIVED ECONOMIC ENVIRONMENTS • CONCLUDING REMARKS

culture and business in Asia

Maureen Guirdham

palgrave
macmillan

© M. Guirdham 2009

All rights reserved. No reproduction, copy or transmission of this
publication may be made without written permission.

No portion of this publication may be reproduced, copied or transmitted
save with written permission or in accordance with the provisions of the
Copyright, Designs and Patents Act 1988, or under the terms of any licence
permitting limited copying issued by the Copyright Licensing Agency,
Saffron House, 6-10 Kirby Street, London EC1N 8TS.

Any person who does any unauthorized act in relation to this publication
may be liable to criminal prosecution and civil claims for damages.

The author has asserted her right to be identified as the author of this
work in accordance with the Copyright, Designs and Patents Act 1988.

First published 2009 by
PALGRAVE MACMILLAN

Palgrave Macmillan in the UK is an imprint of Macmillan Publishers Limited,
registered in England, company number 785998, of Houndmills, Basingstoke,
Hampshire RG21 6XS.

Palgrave Macmillan in the US is a division of St Martin's Press LLC,
175 Fifth Avenue, New York, NY 10010.

Palgrave Macmillan is the global academic imprint of the above companies
and has companies and representatives throughout the world.

Palgrave® and Macmillan® are registered trademarks in the United States,
the United Kingdom, Europe and other countries.

ISBN-13: 978-0-230-51808-7 paperback
ISBN-10: 0-230-51808-7 paperback

This book is printed on paper suitable for recycling and made from fully
managed and sustained forest sources. Logging, pulping and manufacturing
processes are expected to conform to the environmental regulations of the
country of origin.

A catalogue record for this book is available from the British Library.

A catalog record for this book is available from the Library of Congress.

10 9 8 7 6 5 4 3 2 1
18 17 16 15 14 13 12 11 10 09

Printed and bound in Great Britain by
CPI Antony Rowe, Chippenham and Eastbourne

HD 70 .A78 G85 2009
Guirdham, Maureen.
Culture and business in Asia

55.00

For Catherine, George and Theo

contents

list of illustrations   xi

preface and acknowledgements   xiv

1   introduction   1
Asian business   1
Asian cultures   2
The study of culture–business relations   3
The methodology of our study   4
The meaning of culture   5
Culture–business links   5
The institutional perspective   6
Business culture   13
Business decision-making   21
Influences on business culture   22
Issues raised by a focus on business culture   23
Conclusion   27
About this book   27
References   28

2   the business cultures of five Asian countries   32
China   33
    Hong Kong special administrative region   44
India   47
Japan   65
Taiwan   77
Singapore   86
Conclusion   92
References   93

3   analysing Asian business cultures   94
Personalism in business control and decision-making   94
Personalism in employment and work relations   97
Hierarchy   98
Status acknowledged by deference   100

	Entrepreneurialism	101
	Attitudes to risk	107
	Innovation and creativity	108
	Corporate governance	110
	Corruption	111
	Personalism in business-to-business relations (B2B)	113
	Contractual relations	118
	Business relations with government	120
	Business culture variety within the country	121
	Negotiation style and approach	122
	Stereotypes of business owners	123
	Change	125
	Conclusion	127
	References	127
4	**ownership, financing and governance**	**132**
	Ownership	132
	Financing	138
	Corporate governance	142
	Conclusion	150
	References	150
5	**organization and management**	**154**
	Work behaviour	154
	Work attitudes, motivations and goals	155
	Working in teams	159
	Workplace cultures	162
	Organizational structures and processes	164
	Decision-making	166
	Control	168
	Managerial values	169
	Management practices and style	172
	Business communication style	177
	Leadership	181
	Human resource management	182
	Diversity management	186
	Conclusion	189
	References	190
6	**business strategy**	**194**
	Business goals	197
	Forward planning	199
	Strategy in domestic markets	200

International business strategy 206
Conclusion 210
References 211

7   dimensions of societal cultures 213
Dimensions of Asian societal cultures 215
Hofstede's values dimensions 216
Schwartz's values dimensions 223
The Chinese Values Surveys 226
The World Values Surveys 227
Critique 229
Conclusion 231
References 232

8   societal cultures revisited 235
Worldviews 235
Traditional societal cultures 240
Collectivism 240
Hierarchy 241
Personal networks 242
Societal groups 243
Age and generation 243
Gender 246
Class and caste 251
Norms 253
Equality norms 253
Ethical norms 254
Modern cultural values 257
Conclusion 260
References 261

9   political cultures and perceived political environments 264
The effects of the political system 265
Media freedom, independence and trustworthiness 269
The strength or weakness of government control 270
Government policies and cultures 277
Institutional integrity, 'straightness', rule of law and corruption 283
Legal environment 284
The role of government in industry and business 288
*Government's role in industrialization, modernization and
   economic reform* 288
Government regulation of business 290
Competition from government-owned businesses 291
The influence of the bureaucracy 292

Conclusion 295
References 296

10   economic cultures and perceived economic environments 299
Compctitiveness 299
Economic freedom 302
Demographics 303
Income, poverty, wealth and their distribution 304
Savings, investment and consumption 305
Industry structure 306
Markets and institutions 307
   Labour markets 309
   Discrimination in labour markets 310
   Financial infrastructure 312
International trade and globalization 314
Economic beliefs and attitudes 316
   Asian economic attitudes 318
   Asian economic cultures 319
Conclusion 323
References 324

11   concluding remarks 327
Suggestions for further research 338
Practical implications 340
Objections 341
Limitations 343
A final word 344
References 344

appendix: a note on the methodology of this study 346
Sampling 351
Data collection 351
Data recording 352
Data interpretation 353
Data analysis 353
Research output 355
Research limitations 355
Interviewee analyses 356
References 358

select bibliography 359

index 363

illustrations

Tables

1.1 Gross Domestic Product (GDP) per capita at purchasing
power parity in US$ 2006 and Human Development
Index (HDI) 2006   24

2.1 A summary of the present study's findings on the elements of
Chinese business culture   47

2.2 A summary of the present study's findings on the elements of
Indian business culture   64

2.3 A summary of the present study's findings on the elements of
Japanese business culture   77

2.4 A summary of the present study's findings on the elements of
Taiwanese business culture   85

2.5 A summary of the present study's findings on the elements of
Singaporean business culture   91

3.1 Personalism in business control and decision-making   95

3.2 Personalism in employment and work relations   98

3.3 Importance of hierarchy   99

3.4 Deference   100

3.5 Entrepreneurialism   101

3.6 Attitudes to risk   107

3.7 Innovation and creativity   109

3.8 Governance   111

3.9 Corruption   112

3.10 Personalism in business-to-business relations (B2B)   113

3.11 Business relations with government   120

3.12 Business culture variety within the country   121

3.13 Negotiation style and approach   123

3.14 Change   126

4.1 Attitudes to business ownership   133

4.2 Ownership distribution of listed companies   134

5.1 Work behaviour of employees in five Asian countries   161

5.2 Decision-making in Asian businesses   166

5.3 Information flows and control systems in China, India and Japan 169
5.4 A comparison of Chinese, Indian and US management values 170
6.1 Business goals in four Asian countries 198
6.2 Attitudes to forward planning in four Asian countries 200
7.1 Corporate debt ratios of four Asian countries and the USA
     compared with their scores on conservatism and mastery 225
7.2 Corporate debt ratio rankings of four Asian countries and the
     USA compared with their rankings on conservatism and mastery 225
7.3 Shifts in values in China, India and USA found by the
     World Values Surveys between 1990 and 2001 (USA 1999) 229
9.1 Perceived voice and accountability indicators for eight Asian
     and two comparison countries 2006 268
9.2 Perceived government effectiveness of eight Asian and
     two comparison countries 2006 271
9.3 Perceived political stability and absence of violence indicators for
     eight Asian and two comparison countries 2006 276
9.4 Policy-continuity related obstacles to doing business perceived by
     business entrepreneurs 281
9.5 Three governance indicators for eight Asian and two comparison
     countries 2006 283
9.6 Percentages of firms rating official corruption-related problems
     above the median level in comparison with other factors
     affecting business 285
9.7 Index of regulations as obstacles for doing business compared
     with other obstacles 291
10.1 Competitiveness of five Asian countries 301
11.1 Elements of the business cultures of five Asian countries from
      Chapters 2 and 3 331
11.2 Elements of the business cultures of five Asian countries from
      Chapters 4, 5 and 6 334
A.1 Function/expertise of interviewees 357
A.2 Type of industry of interviewees' employing organizations 357
A.3 Type of ownership of interviewees' employing organization 357

Figures

1.1 An interpretation of Whitley's (1992) application of
     institutional theory to Asian business systems (p. 86) 9
1.2 Business cultures and patterns of business decisions in Asia 18

1.3 Relationship between the strength and speed of response of factors outside a business decision-maker's control in a decision area and the extent of business culture influence on decisions in that area 19

1.4 Influences on the behaviour of a business decision-maker 21

11.1 Relations among cultures and business decisions suggested by the findings of the present research 339

preface and acknowledgements

A combination of experiences led to the research that forms the core of this book. Helping set up student work experience programmes in Central and Eastern Europe and in Central Asia brought contact with large numbers of business executives in those regions and made me aware of country by country differences in attitudes to a range of aspects of business. Researching for, and writing, books on intercultural communication at work introduced me to the literature on culture and business. Living amongst, and forming friendships with, members of a Chinese banking community in London began a process of studying Asian approaches to business. Finally, several periods of living, working and setting up projects in India gave me the opportunity for extended discussions of my topic with academic experts and business leaders in that country.

My thanks go therefore to all the people who helped me in the course of these learning experiences, but especially to the members and staff, past and present, of the Czech Business Leaders' Forum, the Hungarian Business Leaders' Forum, the Bulgarian Business Leaders' Forum, the Kazakhstan Institute of Management, Economics and Philosophy (KIMEP), the Madras Management Association and the Administrative Staff College of India.

This book could not have been completed without the willing and positive assistance of Nirmala Mary and Jyothi Shenoy Subherwal in searching the literature and analysing the primary research. I am most sincerely grateful to them.

The advice given by Professor G. Pingle, Mr J.N. Amrolia, Mr S. Madhavan, Mrs. S. Hao, Mr. J. Wang and others was invaluable. I give them my warmest thanks.

My grateful thanks are also due to the people who contributed to the primary research with their time, knowledge and experience. They include the following as well as many others whose circumstances made them prefer to remain anonymous: Prem Chandrani, Arun Diaz, Meagan Dietz, Conrad D'Souza, Katsutoshi Endo, Reyad Fezzani, Yasuiko Fujii, Roshal Gonsalves, Hanif Kanjer, Nuno Goncalves Pedro, Taka Hata, Kiyoshi Hayano, Shunji Hidaka, Sue Huang, Rhonda Lam, Injae Lee, Chase Ma, Seon Man Ko, Junko Matsumi, Mikiko Miyaji, Isao Murafuji, John Pexton, Professor Ramachander, B. Samant, B. Santhanam, Zia Shiekh, Mingran Tan, Chua Thian Yee, Wenqing Tian, Anand Vasudevan and Vincent Zhou.

Permission has kindly been granted by the following to use copyright material:

Franklin Allen for Allen, F., Chakrabarti, R., Sankar, D., Qian, J. and Qian, M. (2007) 'Financing Firms in India', *Wharton Financial Institutions Center Working Paper* URL: http://fic.wharton.upenn.edu/fic/papers/06/0608. pdf' Table 8 Ownership Structures of Indian Firms vis-à-vis Other Country Groups. The World Bank for Brunetti, A., Kisunko, G. and Weder, B. (1999) 'Institutional Obstacles to Doing Business: Region-By-Region Results from a Worldwide Survey of the Private Sector', *World Bank Policy Research Working Paper No. 1759*. Appendix Table 7 – Index of obstacles for doing business – regional averages.

Note: This book was written before the upheavals caused by the global financial crisis of 2008 were fully played out. We do not believe that it will alter the main conclusions we drew from the research. To date, the origins of the crisis have been identified with Western practices in banking and other industries, so it may be more likely to reinforce Asian countries' preferences for doing business in a non-Western way. During this period, also, governance issues of a major kind surfaced in Satyam, an iconic Indian company, seeming to support our conclusions on weak corporate governance in that country.

1 introduction

This book discusses relations between culture and business in five Asian countries – China, India, Japan, Taiwan and Singapore. It traces important links but also notes the limits of those links and the operation of other factors influencing business and management in this sample of countries. It draws heavily on qualitative research conducted by the author with help from two other researchers. As a result of this research, particular aspects of both culture and business are the central concern of the book: these are respectively business cultures and business decision-making.

Asian business

The significance of Asian business as a topic probably needs little justifying. The 'unprecedented growth' of China and India for a period from the early 1990s on led to predictions that they would 'dominate the world economy within the next few decades'.[1] In 2006, the United States of America (USA) was richer by about $70 billion a year as a result of its trade with China, despite painful job losses in unskilled industries.[2] China's growth was described as a 'compression of developmental time'. China's $200 billion consumer market was viewed as a principal source of growth for many multinational enterprises and China had become one of the USA's most significant trading partners. Its exports to the USA approached $45 billion and its annual trade surplus with the USA reached over $30 billion by the year 2000.[3] India's sustained growth rate of nearly 10 per cent per annum over several years would astonish if it were not compared with China's, which was a percentage point or two higher. Like China, by around 2005 India had an estimated 200 million consumers with middle-class incomes. At the time of writing, Japan had been the world's second largest economy for more than three decades, but had recently experienced a long period of stagnation and below-trend growth, which cast doubt on a business model previously admired in the West. The East Asian 'tigers', which included Taiwan, Singapore and Hong Kong astounded the world by their phenomenal growth rates from about 1970, then created fears of triggering a world recession by the Asian financial crisis of the late 1990s, and then again impressed by the speed of their recovery.

Asian cultures

China is not only the world's largest country in terms of population, but it is also a country with a highly distinctive cultural heritage. Although both ethnic minorities and religious belief are more common in China than is sometimes recognized, the majority Han population and a social philosophy – Confucianism – rather than a religion have both dominated its traditional culture. Its economic system, around the turn of the second millennium, appears to be in the process of a transition from communism to capitalism. In consequence, questions arise about whether China's culture, too, is changing and if so, in what direction. There are contradictory signs of a shift towards modernism on the one hand and a return to traditional beliefs and ways on the other. In addition, within its post-1997 borders, China embodies both a transitional society and, in Hong Kong, one which seeks to preserve past liberalism in a fundamentally changed context. For a study of culture's relationships to business, China is a valuable, perhaps even an essential, example.

India, the world's next most populous country and its largest democracy, has been largely neglected in past studies of Asian business such as those of Chen (2001)[4] and Whitley (1992).[5] Including it is overdue, not just because, like China, it shows signs of becoming one of the world's great economies, but also because Asia can be misunderstood unless it is included. Historically and culturally its links with countries further East have been strong. Trade between India and China, both overland and by sea, extend back at least two millennia. Its culture, especially in the form of Buddhism, reached all the way to Japan nearly 1500 years ago. Although Buddhism largely disappeared from its country of origin, it remained current in the Japanese version and at the start of the 21st century was experiencing a resurgence in China.[6] In contrast to China, India has a long history of having been conquered and subject to outside influences; it is also, again contrastingly, a country where religion has been central to the culture. It is highly diverse linguistically and in religious terms, as well as ethnically; it, too, constitutes a vital example and a revealing comparison with China.

Of the other three countries in our study, one, Japan, with a population of nearly 200 million has a culture with many idiosyncratic features resulting from its high ethnic homogeneity and past isolation. Its business system, too, has unique features. The combination of a unique culture and business system has great potential for any study of culture and business.

The two smaller economies included in the study earn their place in part precisely because they are small and hence provide a contrast to the three major economies. They are also, themselves, highly contrasting examples. Taiwan, an island off the shore of China, exemplifies a pre-Communist Chinese culture; Singapore's culture is influenced not only by its having been a former British colony, but also by the high and sustained levels of immigration from the rest of Asia that it has maintained since independence and by government policies designed to attract multinational companies.

In sum, any culture–business relationships found to apply to five such different countries have a good chance of being robust.

There are reasons other than Asia's growing economic importance and cultural variety for focusing on it in this study. The phenomenal growth of the 'Asian tiger' economies in the 1980s, a growth that was hard to explain in traditional economic terms, led to the development of an alternative model of economics, institutional theory, which has had a great impact on the social sciences since that time. An outline of the institutional perspective is given later in this chapter. A further reason is the possibility, that has been asserted by scholars, that collectivist cultures, which broadly include Asia's, are more 'effective' at imposing cultural conformity than individualist cultures are and so more closely linked to behaviour. Thus the links between culture and business behaviour may be stronger there than in the more frequently studied individualist countries of the West. Since collectivism predominates in most of the world (the contrasting 'individualist' cultures may represent only a diminishing 17 per cent of the world's population), Asia may exemplify relationships that are rather widespread.

The study of culture–business relations

From early beginnings in the 1970s, the study of links between culture and business has been a significant area of research. In part, its growth is due to early-stage 'globalization', which demonstrated the weakness of universalist normative models originating in the USA, for example by the low success rate of management by objectives in France; in part by Japan's rise, and the interest that aroused in Japanese management practices, which were conspicuously different from Western ones; in part by one path-breaking piece of research, that of Geert Hofstede, whose findings based on a survey of IBM employees in 66 countries pointed clearly to significant differences between cultures and to significant consequences for business and management flowing from those differences;[7, 8] and, finally, in part because practitioners in international business and related fields had long been noting the need to adapt for cultural difference.

This body of existing research means that the present book and study are a contribution to a substantial field. It is a field, however, which according to some leading scholars in the area has reached a kind of impasse. There are now several quantitative studies for researchers to draw on – those of Hofstede (1980) himself, Schwartz (1994),[9] Bond (1988)[10] and the GLOBE project,[11] for example – but there is increasing doubt whether such studies have really accessed the essentials of culture or culture–business relations. The criticism of Fiske (2002)[12] regarding one strand of cultural research, on individualism and collectivism, may apply to most others. Fiske wrote that this research,

> treats nations as cultures and culture as a continuous quantitative variable; conflates all kinds of social relations and distinct types of autonomy; ignores contextual specificity in norms and values; measures culture as the personal preferences and behavior reports of individuals; rarely establishes the external validity of the measures used; assumes cultural invariance in the meaning of self-reports and anchoring and interpretation of scales; and reduces culture to explicit, abstract verbal knowledge.

Again, in the words of Smith (2006), 'Critics...have doubted the value of characterizing the variability of nations in terms of dimensions, and have argued for greater use of more qualitative analyses of culture.'[13] Writing more particularly of the links between culture and management, Chatterjee and Pearson (2006) criticized frameworks that link broad cultural value dimensions with micro-level managerial issues as 'neither taking into account the dynamics of culture nor the imperatives of economic reform agendas. Although the influence of deep-seated and all-pervasive tradition may remain at the core level, the imperatives of economic experimentation and learning continue to dominate at other levels.'[14] London and Hart (2004)[15] advocated the use of qualitative research, rather than traditional quantitative empirical tools, especially for exploring implicit assumptions and examining new relationships, abstract concepts and operational definitions. While the present researchers believe that the advances made by quantitative studies are of the greatest value, they also contend that there is scope for new contributions from qualitative approaches.

The methodology of our study

The main input to this book is a primary research study undertaken by the author and two other researchers. Our response to comments such as those mentioned in the paragraph above was to adopt a qualitative methodology, which is described in the Appendix, for our study of possible links among cultures and businesses in five Asian countries. The method we used was by qualitative analysis of intensive interviews of business decision-makers from (and mainly in) those countries. As Sheer and Chen (2003) explained, this method of intensive interviews is very effective for research aimed at uncovering culturally acquired and shared understandings. 'This method allows for the gathering of rich information from a sample of individuals who have been involved. The method allowed us to approach the problem from an interpretive perspective and study the particular rather than the general to gain insight into the specifics.'[16] The particular interest of Sheer and Chen (2003) was in Sino-Western business negotiations, but a similar case can be made for using qualitative analysis of intensive interviews in the present research. The vast majority of our interviewees were business decision-makers from the country about which they were interviewed. In respect of the relations between business and culture in a given country, business decision-makers from that country can be considered to have privileged access: they are themselves 'members' of that culture and in most cases have had a sufficiently long exposure to experience it and 'feel' it; they are also participant observers, able to see 'from inside' and to interpret with inside knowledge the behaviours of their business compatriots. Many of our interviewees were also alumni of leading Western business schools or had worked in international companies and so had acquired a basis for comparison.

The meaning of culture

The concept of culture used in this book conforms to the position of Adler et al. (1986)[17] who maintained that the idea of culture as a mind-state raises the problem of reductionism and an explanatory cul-de-sac, whereas using social patterns for explanation removes the understanding of culture's determinants. Adler et al. (1986) argued that more progress and better predictions may be made when culture is accepted as an 'observable aspect of human behaviour, manifest in social interaction and tangible objects like organizations, but resting on symbolic frameworks, mental programmes, and conceptual distinctions in people's minds'.

Culture–business links

In focusing on links between culture and business there is no intention of implying that culture alone can explain complex social-political-economic phenomena such as business decisions and practices. Wilkinson (1996) criticized 'culturalist' explanations for organizational behaviour because they involve four fundamental problems: post-hoc rationalization, gross assumptions about causal links, a danger of racism and an absence of historical understanding. Wilkinson also noted that empirical studies that test for causal links between culture and organizational behaviour are in their infancy.[18] Casson and Lundan (1999)[19] pointed out that purely cultural explanations of the national 'economic miracles' of the Asian economies have been challenged by those who criticize the way they ignore standard economic factors. Furthermore, Au and Cheung (2004)[20] found from an analysis of secondary data from 42 countries that intra-cultural variation (ICV) – dispersion of individuals within a culture – explained as much of the influence of job autonomy on organizational and social outcomes as the job

autonomy cultural mean. 'Specifically, the cultural mean and ICV of job autonomy exert different effects on job satisfaction and life satisfaction. The effect of
the cultural mean is positive and that of the ICV is negative.' Findings such as
this suggest that caution is needed in generalizing from cultural means. They also
strengthen the argument for more qualitative research.

There is now, however, a consensus that culture has *an* influence on business
that may be significant. In the words of Steier et al. (2004),[21] 'Culture ... represents an important determinant of firm performance.' In an area of particular
concern to scholars of Asian business, Rhodes (2007)[22] argued that the analysis
of governance should focus on beliefs, practices, traditions and dilemmas; such
phenomena are almost certain to have a substantial cultural component.

The institutional perspective

One set of views on how culture influences economic variables, including business
actions, is based on the institutional perspective. The institutional perspective
developed in response to the growth of the newly industrializing Asian economies
in the 1970s and 1980s, growth which was partially attributed to cultural factors.
Tayeb (2006),[23] for example, argued that in addition to an export orientation and
a positive attitude to foreign direct investment, cultural, political and economic
characteristics, such as public education and a neutral role for religion, were major
reasons behind the success of the Asian tigers (Hong Kong, South Korea, Taiwan,
Singapore, Indonesia, Thailand and Malaysia). As previously noted, the importance of this perspective in modern economics, sociology and political science
provides a reason for studying the culture–business links of the continent. More
generally, Henisz and Swaminathan (2008) argued, 'Institutional characteristics ... influence every aspect of behavior by multinational enterprises, including
their location choice; the organization of their local subsidiary; their choice of
technology, capital and labor staffing; and their sequence of investment.'[24]

There is no single and universally agreed definition of 'an institution' in
the institutional school of thought, but Scott's (1995, 2001) account is widely
accepted. Scott asserted:

> Institutions are social structures that have attained a high degree
> of resilience. [They] are composed of cultural-cognitive, normative,
> and regulative elements that, together with associated activities and
> resources, provide stability and meaning to social life. Institutions are
> transmitted by various types of carriers, including symbolic systems,
> relational systems, routines, and artefacts. Institutions operate at dif-
> ferent levels of jurisdiction, from the world system to localized interper-
> sonal relationships. Institutions by definition connote stability but are
> subject to change processes, both incremental and discontinuous.[25]

The link between culture and institutions in this definition is both implicit and explicit. In using the terms 'symbolic systems, relational systems, routines and artefacts' for the carriers and transmitters of institutions, Scott was consciously or unconsciously echoing the language of at least one form of culture theory, in which culture is transmitted by symbols, shared meanings and rituals. In explicit terms, Scott identified cultural-cognitive components of institutions alongside normative and regulative elements and, in fact, emphasized their importance: 'Rules, norms, and cultural beliefs are central ingredients of institutions.' The cognitive component of a country's institutions reflects the cognitive categories widely shared by the people. Scott (1995) further suggested, 'Cognitive elements constitute the nature of reality and the frames through which meaning is made.' Cognitive programmes affect the way people notice, categorize, and interpret stimuli from the environment. They also affect what people treat as legitimate behaviour. Individuals may comply with cultural rules and conventions out of habit without even being aware that they are complying.[26]

Within Scott's typology, the cultural-cognitive element includes traditions, taken-for-granted rules and conventions, together with preconscious widely accepted customs. The element 'equates to culture defined in terms of socially established structures of meaning that control people's worldviews, what action is possible, and what is less likely to be questioned or even considered'.[27] Actors are constrained by schema, frames and scripts, sometimes without realizing it. The 'structures of meaning' are often socially constructed over time and come to be perceived 'as objective and external to the actors: not as man-made but a natural and factual order'. For example, the hierarchical relations between castes in India would for many centuries have been regarded by most Indians as of a 'natural and factual order'.

The normative element of a country's institutions, according to Scott (2001),[28] concerns expectations about the behaviour of organizations and individuals. These expectations are held by the individuals and organizations of the country. Norms provide conscious choices concerning group and individual roles and the normative system is somewhat political in nature, often associated with the professions. Normative institutions are purposely constructed and include authority systems and roles that occur in response to what is consciously perceived as necessary and proper to direct the behaviour of individuals and organizations. The rules of professions such as accountants and lawyers are examples of normative institutions. The regulative aspects of a country's institutions include laws, regulations and codified government policies.

Of the three elements of the typology, cognitive institutions are most closely associated with culture. However, all these elements of institutions influence one another and interact. For instance, laws on banking are clearly influenced by the religion of the country, so that those applying in Islamic countries are different from those applying in most other countries. Equally, over time, a country's laws can shift the range of rules and conventions that are taken for granted, as in countries where long-standing universal suffrage has been followed by an increase in the cultural commitment to equality in employment.

Institutional theory results in predictions that differ from those of standard economic theory about the kind of business behaviour that maximizes the performance of firms. In the words of Redding (2004),[29]

> " Institutional theory holds that businesses, like other organizations, operate within constraints imposed by society's institutions. More than that, they are initially set up to make use of opportunities determined by the institutional framework. ... The institutional view does not ignore economic theory: within the institutional constraints, it states, organizations act according to standard economic theories. However, the society's institutions, by placing constraints on firms' strategic choices, do become a critical constraint on the long-term performance of an economy. How well or badly firms' strategies accommodate to those constraints also helps decide which will be more or less successful.

There have been several applications of institutional theory to the East Asian economies whose study led to the emergence of the theory. Most widely discussed is that of Whitley (1992),[30] which applied institutional theory in a highly detailed way to analyse three Asian business systems – those of Japan, South Korea and the Chinese diaspora in South East Asia (Taiwan and Hong Kong). Figure 1.1 shows the present author's interpretation of Whitley's model as described on p. 86 of his book.

To enable the reader to understand this better, there follows a simplified account of how this model applies in Japan, tracing it from Whitley's (1992) descriptive account of Japan's business system. In the early 1990s, Japan's business system was marked by a predominance of specialized firms that achieved integration through *keiretsu*. A *keiretsu* is a corporate network with horizontal ownership- and non-ownership linkages. While member companies do not have to buy from other *keiretsu* members, they do give preference to intra-group business.[31] Lifetime employment for core employees was another element of the system; and a third was close involvement of managers in the work of the groups they supervised, though without the need for them to be technically expert in the group's work. These characteristics of Japan's business system reflected a managerial and societal willingness to delegate authority and develop trust relations with non-kin, in contrast to the other Asian societies Whitley studied. Further, levels of trust and interdependence were higher, while the extent to which business relations were personal was lower, than in the other Asian countries (though more personal than in some Western countries). Japan's contemporary institutions, in turn, displayed decentralized authority relations, cooperation between

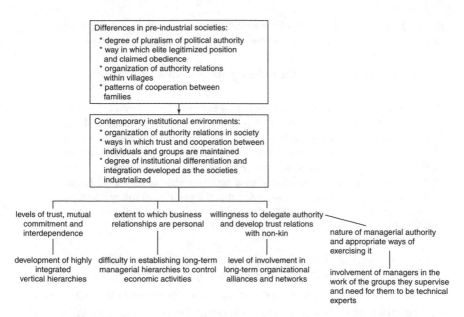

Figure 1.1 **An interpretation of Whitley's (1992) application of institutional theory to Asian business systems (p. 86)**

Source: Based on Whitley, R. (1992) Business Systems in East Asia: Firms, Markets, and Societies, London: Sage, p. 86.

individuals and groups maintained somewhat impersonally through law and a general rule-conforming culture, and a range of institutions and forms (including executive central government, law-making institutions and courts, together with local authorities) developed during industrialization. These modern institutions arose out of Japan's pre-industrial society which exemplified three characteristics: there were plural sources of authority, so that villages, for instance, enjoyed large measures of self-rule, the elite's authority was legitimated by potential coercion (as distinct from moral principle, as in China), and families within villages cooperated throughout the year owing to the demands of rice-based agriculture.

Thus, according to Whitley (1992), the significant ways in which business systems vary are according to the predominant type of firm (generalist or specialist), the strength of high-trust network-type relationships among firms, as opposed to impersonal market relations, and the sources and nature of authority within organizations – in particular, the nature of managerial authority and worker subordination. The advantages of this approach include the point that by identifying

> just three major dimensions of variation in business systems that are of universal significance, Whitley (1992) avoids the gross oversimplification of one-dimensional analysis – such as a distinction between Confucian and non-Confucian countries. At the other extreme, he also

> avoids the proliferation of dimensions that occurs when every country is held to be specific in a different way from every other country.[32]

Whitley's approach disputed the industry-specific view. In this view,

> international differences in industrial systems are purely a reflection of the different composition of industries found in each country. Each industry has its own particular functional logic, which determines the best-practice style of management and the most appropriate pattern of ownership. Thus, economies of scale mean that the steel industry in each country is dominated by a small number of very large firms, while diseconomies of scale mean that the printing industry normally consists of a large number of small firms. In general, each industry has its own distinctive 'recipe'.[33]

Managers are aware of this recipe and willingly conform to it because they accept that it is appropriate for their conditions. In Whitley's (1992) view, on the contrary, the variation in business systems between countries is brought about by their adaptation to different institutions, rather than by their industrial configuration determined by their resources.

Thus Whitley's (1992) analysis of East Asian business systems exemplifies the way that institutional theory in economics stands opposed to classical resource-dependence theory. The supporters of the resource-dependence view criticized it for ignoring standard economic factors. They explained the high growth rates of Asian economies during the 1970s and 1980s, which had led to the emergence of institutional theory, by arguing that an increase in the

> supply of labor to manufacturing industry, driven by a massive shift of population from the countryside to the towns, was a major stimulus to the growth of labor-intensive assembly operations. Trade liberalization and falling international transport costs promoted exports by encouraging foreign multinationals to base offshore processing in Asian countries. High rates of domestic saving, coupled with progressive financial deregulation and increased capital mobility, allowed these investments to be financed at low interest rates.[34]

As Casson and Lundan (1999)[35] argued, however,

> The concept of 'purely economic' factors is questionable. Asian factory workers were far better disciplined in the 1970s than their Western counterparts, and this obviously stimulated productivity growth. High rates of saving are likely to be influenced by family structures and by the obligations that link successive generations of the same family. Thus, both high productivity growth and high savings rates may ultimately have cultural causes.

Tsui-Auch and Lee (2003)[36] studied the contrast between Singaporean and Korean businesses' responses to the Asian financial crisis of the late 1990s. They argued that the findings supported the institutional perspective on Asian capitalism.

> " First, social organization along family and network ties was constantly harnessed by both the state and the family businesses. Secondly, the professionalization of management was aimed not only at yielding efficiency, but also at gaining legitimacy from the state, customers and shareholders. Economic action is, in fact, action embedded in social relations, as institutionalists argue. Third, the business owners' modification of the managerial enterprise model to fit their local contexts demonstrates a capacity to change within the scope of cultural and institutional constraints.

In relation to organizations, the distinction between institutional and classical theories was made clear by Oliver (1997).[37]

> " Institutional theory adopts an open system perspective: organizations are strongly influenced by their environments. But not only are competitive forces and efficiency-based forces at work, socially constructed belief and rule systems also exercise enormous control over organizations – both how they are structured and how they carry out their work. As belief systems and norms vary over time and place, institutional concepts provide a means to study organizational emergence and change.

This opportunity to study organizational emergence and change is missing from a perspective that asserts that there is one best economic model (resource-dependent profit maximization) to which all businesses, being economically rational entities, must converge. To support this perspective, Oliver (1997) brought the concept of agency further forward than it is in some earlier versions of institutional theory: on the positive side, businesses conform to social expectations because doing so allows them to get rewards through increased legitimacy, resources and survival capabilities; on the negative side, economic choices are constrained not only by technological, informational, and income limits but also by institutional factors such as social norms, habits, and customs. Business decision-makers take into account both the opportunities and the constraints provided by the expectations, beliefs and habits of their culture; the present author would add that many are also part of that culture and so are influenced by its expectations, beliefs and habits, sometimes unconsciously, as well as consciously taking them into account.

One important question that the institutional theorists had to answer was how institutions actually affect what people do. How are institutions enacted and reproduced? The explanation given by Scott (1995) was as follows:

> One cognitively oriented view is that a given institution is encoded into an actor through a socialization process. When internalized, it transforms to a script (patterned behavior). When (or if) the actor behaves according to the script, the institution is enacted. In this manner, institutions are continuously (re-)produced. The enactment of an institution externalizes or objectifies it – other actors can see that the institution is in play, and a new round of socialization starts. After some time, the institution (and the resulting patterned behaviour) becomes sedimented and taken-for-granted. Then, it might be difficult for the actors even to realize that their behaviour is in fact partly controlled by an institution. Acting in accordance with the institution is viewed as rational by those who share the institution.[38]

Here, Scott (1995) is at once answering both the 'free will' objections to institutional theory and the objections that actors often believe their acts to be economically rational. The argument used is similar to that widely used for the way that culture exerts its influence.

The approach of Scott (1995, 2001) and Oliver (1997) goes some way towards addressing another weakness of earlier applications of institutional theory, such as that of Whitley (1992). In his distinguished analysis of business systems, Whitley (1992) several times referred to the influence of 'cultural preferences and beliefs' on business. For example, on p. 4, in refuting the economic rationality account, he wrote

> The interdependence of firms' activities and their uncertainty about the future actions means that the results of their decisions are dependent on how they interpret 'what is going on' ... and cannot be reduced to a single, external, system logic. If dominant coalitions change their understandings and priorities, their actions will change and so will market outcomes. Thus *'rational' and efficient structures and practices are dependent on, and vary according to, currently dominant beliefs, priorities and ways of making judgements.*

Again, on p. 45, he wrote

> The comparative analysis of business systems presumes that distinctive ways of organizing economic activities becomes established and effective because of major differences in key social institutions, such as the state, the financial system and the education and training system, *as well as more diffuse factors such as cultural preferences and beliefs.*

On a third occasion, on p. 85, 'The establishment and continued effectiveness of different kinds of business systems, then, are explicable in terms of their interdependence with dominant social institutions, *including established beliefs and values*' (Present author's italics).

Whitley (1992) went on to examine the proposition that 'business systems are interdependent with dominant social institutions' in relation to Korea, Japan and China (as represented by countries such as Taiwan and Singapore, where much of business was carried out by Chinese communities). He found in favour of the proposition and in the course of testing he revealed a great deal about both the institutions and the business systems of those countries. However, despite his emphasis on cultural preferences and beliefs in theory, in practice he focused on them only incidentally. For example, in his chapter on institutional influences on pre-industrial Japan, Korea and China, he discussed 'the major features of their political systems, ... the significant differences in the development of their economic systems, the basis on which ruling elites claimed legitimacy and ... the organization of village communities, especially their authority structures'. These features have implications for 'the organization of authority and subordination relations in different societies, the ways in which trust and co-operation between particular individuals and groups are developed and maintained, and the degree of institutional differentiation and integration which has developed in these industrializing societies'.

It would be hard to maintain that any of the factors in these lists are a direct description of cultural preferences and beliefs or established beliefs and values, however much they may be claimed to reflect them. The result is that Whitley's application of institutional theory to East Asian business largely lacks what is, by his own account as set out above, a key element. In this book it is that institutional element, the cultural-cognitive element of 'established beliefs and values', that will be the main focus, because the individual business decision-maker can only take into account what he or she perceives and is likely only to consider what he or she believes. (As a later section of this chapter explains, the other focus of this book is business decisions rather than the outcomes of those decisions.) Institutional factors or resources may directly impact the outcomes of business decisions, but even these outcomes will only affect future decisions as they are filtered through the minds of decision-makers. Thus perceptions, beliefs and values, those core components of culture, are significant for understanding business decisions.

Business culture

In the words of Hofstede et al. (1990), culture has many 'layers'.[39] Again, Lenartowicz and Roth (2004) asserted, 'Defining the proper level or layer at which culture should be assessed' is fundamental to studies of culture.[40] This book puts forward the suggestion, based on research in five Asian countries, that one level or layer has been neglected to the detriment of the study of Asian business. This is the layer of the business culture of a business community, which may be national, regional or of some other extent.

The term 'business culture' is quite widely used in an undefined, uncritical way in writing about business. The following are some examples:

1. An article of 2004 entitled 'Understanding Korea: John Austin urges the need to take account of Korean business culture', stated, 'Koreans see themselves as being very direct people and they often contrast their approach to that of the "polite" Japanese. Due to the importance attached to relationships, it is more often the dinner, drinks and karaoke following the business meeting that seals the deal.'[41]
2. 'What may be broadly called the "health ideology", which has its origins in the American intellectual class, has spread beyond it to affect much wider masses of people in their values and behavior and has led to global political activism. The business culture has absorbed much of this by instituting "wellness" programs and encouraging "fitness." '[42]
3. 'Business culture emerges over time from the interaction between a company's current management and leadership practices, and from the people management and control systems used by managers and leaders in the course of steering the business in a specific direction to achieve its mission through its chosen business strategy.'[43]
4. 'There is a bonus from the "Commonwealth business culture" provided by the English language, and various legal, commercial, accounting and financial procedures.'[44]
5. 'The entire question of a specifically Chinese business culture may arise because of the multiple forms of business ownership and the incomplete market economy during the transition period of socialism. A company can be state owned, collectively owned (by a local community), privately owned, a joint venture, or an independent foreign enterprise. People in different kinds of companies have different degrees of access to the outside world, different work ethics, and different values and behavioral patterns.'[45]

These examples, which could be multiplied many times over, show the concept of business culture being treated as unproblematic and yet having a wide range of different meanings. Example 1 is typical of many that treat business culture as relating to the surface culture of manners and practices, in other words business etiquette; Example 2 treats it as almost synonymous with the business community; Example 3 as equivalent to organizational culture; Example 4 as consisting of institutions and procedures; and Example 5 approaches the idea that a business culture is composed of group values, behavioural patterns and ethics. Thus it seems that business culture is a concept which is widely applied and even disputed over, as in Example 5, but is used with widely varying meaning.

14 1

INTRODUCTION · THE BUSINESS CULTURES OF FIVE ASIAN COUNTRIES · ANALYSING ASIAN BUSINESS CULTURES
· OWNERSHIP, FINANCING AND GOVERNANCE · ORGANIZATION AND MANAGEMENT · BUSINESS STRATEGY ·

In a number of scholarly articles, too, the term is used but little explored or analysed. Eyjolfsdottir and Smith (1996),[46] in an article entitled 'Icelandic Business and Management Culture', discussed the distinction between national culture and organizational culture. At that point in the article, the context suggested that the term organizational culture was being used as a synonym for business culture. The article went on to acknowledge, 'It has proved useful to make distinctions between national culture and organizational culture within nations that are large and ethnically diverse', but suggested that in Iceland, with its tiny population and ethnic homogeneity, 'a greater degree of uniformity between national and organizational culture will prevail'. In practice, they found that while Iceland matches the national culture dimensions of Scandinavia, using Hofstede's five values, there was a unique aspect to the Icelandic business culture – that of the 'fisherman mentality' which led to higher levels of peer cooperation and lower levels of contact with subordinates than elsewhere in Scandinavia. This research is useful; it provided an early finding on business culture. Unfortunately, however, although the terms business culture, management culture and organizational culture were used, they were neither distinguished nor defined.

Keeley (2001)[47] used the term 'business culture' extensively and found important relations between it and human resource management (HRM); however, only 'culture' was actually discussed and business culture, although one of the central variables in the research, was defined merely as 'business practices and culture (referred to as business culture)'. One article (Bjerke 2000)[48] appeared to use the concept to refer to business-related values and practices, which corresponds in part to the usage in this book; but again the term was left undefined. Bjerke (2000) typified US business culture as characterized by 'the need for progress; the importance of innovation; individualism; action-orientation; the prominence of efficiency, logic and science; informality and equality'. These characteristics appear to be values or ideas closely related to values. In contrast, the characteristics of China's business culture were described in the article as 'power and autocracy, familism, *guanxi*, face and prestige, flexibility and endurance'. Some of these characteristics are value-like, so that familism, for instance, is enlarged on as follows: 'Individuals have a very deep attachment and sense of belonging to social groups.' Others, however, appear more likely to be summary judgements of practices than values: for example, 'power and autocracy' is amplified as, 'Even in modern times Chinese management is a top run, one-man show by an autocratic boss assuming responsibility for all management functions.'

As late as 2003, Berger (2003)[49] treated the concept of business culture as unproblematic and did not define it. The article did, however, agree with the contention that business culture and societal culture are distinct, giving as an example the fact that '...despite a multitude of business schools and training courses to teach Indians how to behave as participants in the global economy, many of the computer professionals in Bangalore succeed in combining such participation with personal lifestyles dominated by traditional Hindu values.'

The literature does yield two definitions of 'business culture', one of which is given in Randlesome et al. (1990)[50] as the following: 'The concept of business culture embraces ... the attitudes, values and norms which underpin commercial activities and help to shape the behavior of companies in a given country.' Later described by one of its authors as a 'more pragmatic definition of business culture and its determinants',[51] it 'further postulates that the business culture of any country grows out of the business environment, past and present, in that country'. The business environment is described as 'taking in the relationship between business and government, business and finance, business and the labor market, and so on'. Unfortunately, in applying the concept of business culture in books on Europe and Germany, the business environment was allowed to represent the business culture and effectively to displace the aspect of 'software of the mind', as Hofstede (1981) described culture. As Kitayama (2002)[52] pointed out, 'Culture is not just "in the head", but it is in the head as well as "out there" in the form of external realities and collective patterns of behavior.' While concentrating only on externalities is in some ways understandable in view of the difficulty of accessing mental software, the result is to add further confusion to the concept.

The other approximation to a definition is given in Deeks (1993):[53]

> " In a business culture it will be business that dictates the whole way of life of a community. The notion of such a culture can be either confined or extended. Confined to the business community itself, it has a similar focus to that of organizational culture, a relatively restricted set of shared values and ways of doing things understood by a discrete group. Extended beyond the business community, business culture may permeate into all aspects of society and, if pervasive enough, become a suitable label with which to characterize a particular nation or a particular historical era.

The notion that culture, any culture, national, organizational, professional or business 'dictates the whole way of life of a community' is surely an overstatement. Culture is an influence on behaviour but there are other influences that may conflict with it. However, the 'confined' notion of business culture as 'a relatively restricted set of shared values and ways of doing things understood by a discrete group' that is 'the business community itself' approaches the concept that underlies this book. Compared with the Randlesome et al. (1990) definition, which treats the 'behavior of companies' as external to business culture, though partially shaped by it, its inclusion of 'ways of doing things' is an advantage. First, it corresponds to accepted anthropological definitions of culture more generally, as in Kroeber and Kluckhohn's (1952)[54] definition, which refers to 'patterns ... of and for behavior'. Second, in the present research it was common for interviewees to talk about things that businesses in a community do when describing that community's business culture.

We turn now to the concept of business culture that has emerged from our research and is used in this book. We define a business culture as 'a set of business-related values, beliefs, attitudes, meanings and practices shared by a business community'. An important element of this definition is the phrase 'shared by a business community'. This distinguishes the business culture concept from organizational or corporate culture, terms which are specific to one organization; from a professional, trade or occupational culture, whose 'community' may overlap with, but is distinct from, the 'business community'; and from a societal, political or economic culture or the culture of any other social grouping, which is not confined to a business community. Business cultures are also distinguished from other kinds by being narrower in the matters to which values, attitudes, beliefs and practices apply – restricted to business-related matters.

In a chapter on organizational cultures, Hofstede and Hofstede (2005)[55] located national and organizational cultures at opposite ends of a continuum along which values dominated at the national end and practices at the organizational end. That is, they contended, differences between national cultures are predominantly differences of values; in national cultures the importance of differences of practices is much lower than values. Differences between organizational cultures, on the other hand, are predominantly differences of practices, while differences of values are less clear-cut. Along their continuum Hofstede and Hofstede (2005) also located social class cultures (values more significant than practices), industry cultures (practices more significant than values) and occupational cultures (both about equally important).

Consistent with the lack of recognition of business culture in academia, Hofstede and Hofstede (2005) did not locate this type on their continuum. From our research, however, it seems appropriate to locate business cultures in about the same position as occupational cultures – a position where values and practices are both, and about equally, important in differentiating one culture from another.

We concluded from our research that the business culture affects the business decisions of members of that culture, as shown in Figure 1.2. Like other forms of culture, the impact of business culture on a business decision-maker's or communicator's thoughts is generally subconscious and unitary. He or she does not normally think, 'What are the implications of our business culture for this decision?', nor, 'What aspect of business culture is most relevant to this decision?' Thus it is just a matter of analytical convenience to distinguish various aspects. However, we discerned three aspects from the series of interviews undertaken for our study, which in turn correspond to those found in the business and management literature. They are as follows: work (or workplace) culture, management culture and ownership culture. Each of these areas is linked

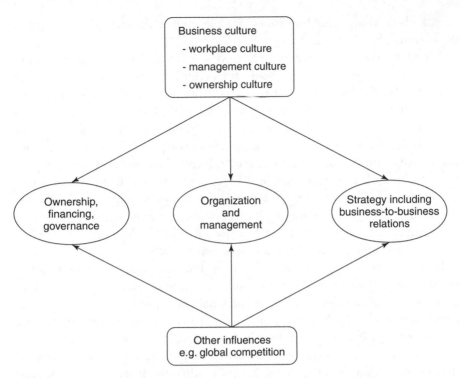

Figure 1.2   **Business cultures and patterns of business decisions in Asia**

to others that will be discussed in their place in the book. For instance, the ownership culture is closely linked to issues of financing and governance. The three aspects of business culture are also interrelated. Thus, the work culture of employees both influences a business community's management culture and is in turn influenced by it.

Our research suggested that the influence of business culture in the five countries we studied was felt for decisions in the areas of ownership, financing and governance, organization and management (within which human resource management is for this purpose subsumed) and strategy, including business-to-business (B2B) relations. Each of these three decision areas is the subject of a chapter of this book. Rather than operations or consumer marketing, for instance, these emerged from our research as the decision areas most closely linked to business culture in the Asian context. While culture and business culture may well influence business operations, the technical orientation of operations perhaps minimizes their influence. Similarly, consumer marketing decisions will be influenced by the decision-makers' beliefs about the consumer, and these beliefs may be sufficiently shared among a business community to constitute part of their business culture. In this exploratory study, however, no clear-cut consensus on a

Nature of Factors Beyond a Business
Decision-Maker's Control

Uncontrollable factors are weak or slow-acting				Uncontrollable factors are strong and quick-acting	
Ownership (concentrated/ distributed)	Governance (strong/weak)	Financing (equity/debt, generated internally/ externally)	Organization and management (impersonal/ personal)	Strategy and business relations	Consumer marketing

DECISION AREAS

Figure 1.3 **Relationship between the strength and speed of response of factors outside a business decision-maker's control in a decision area and the extent of business culture influence on decisions in that area**

national set of beliefs (still less values) relating to consumer marketing emerged. In contrast, business relations between organizations were a clear focus for beliefs and values shared among a business community and so this area will be a focus of the chapter on strategy.

There is, in fact, a certain logic to the possibility that consumer marketing is likely to be less affected by business culture than some other areas. This logic is that the impact of business culture on business decisions is weakest where the factors outside the decision-maker's control are strongest or quickest to affect the decision's outcome. To put this differently, choice should be distinguished from decision; a decision-maker's choices may be rather limited when uncontrollable factors are strong and fast-acting. In the Asian context, those factors are ranged as shown on the continuum in Figure 1.3.

Consumer markets and consumer behaviour are largely outside the control of individual organizations, despite the effects of advertising. The consequences of decisions which do not correspond to the realities of the market are also felt rapidly – which helps explain the high rates of product failure even among consumer businesses that are successful overall. It is true that business decision-makers can attempt to control consumer markets by, for instance, price-fixing cartels and that the business culture may either endorse or reject such behaviour. The more open the competition in a country's consumer markets, however, the less the scope for business culture to affect decisions. With globalization and because most countries are eager to participate in international markets, competition is increasing. The rationale given here accounts for the omission of consumer marketing from this volume.

In Figure 1.3, strategy is positioned to the left of consumer marketing but nevertheless well to the right in the continuum, reflecting the situation of strategy as essentially concerned with differentiating the business's offering, while being constrained by the strong and quick-acting uncontrollable factor of competition. This factor, of course, increased immeasurably and dramatically in those economies of Asia that were opened to the outside world only late in the 20th century.

While B2B marketing is in principle like consumer marketing, the smaller number of buyers gives business decision-makers a greater opportunity for mutually advantageous arrangements (sometimes at the expense of the ultimate customer) allowing more scope for the business culture. Another factor, external to the logic depicted in Figure 1.3, is that B2B relations within a business community generally take place between parties who both or all share the same business culture. This reinforces the effect of that culture. In international B2B, the effect of the business culture of any one of the interacting parties can be weakened and intercultural negotiation is required. This may explain, in addition to other factors analysed elsewhere in this book, the tendency for East Asian businesses, with their strong business cultures, to prefer to do business with others from their own ethnic group or community.

Organization and management is positioned to the left of strategy in Figure 1.3, indicating that the uncontrollable factors in that area are weaker and slower-acting. Where unions are weak (as in many Asian countries) and/or long-term unemployment is high (as in the past in India), there are few constraints on whom to employ in what capacity. In these circumstances the business culture is likely to affect whether a meritocratic system operates, in which high-performing but unrelated individuals can reach the 'top', or a trust-based system in which personal connection or seniority plays a significant part.

Finance, positioned left of organization and management in Figure 1.3, is a market in which business decision-makers are 'buyers'. This gives them more power except under monopolistic or oligopolistic conditions. Power translates into choice, which allows scope for the business culture to have an impact on decisions. A further factor which strengthens decision-makers' choice in the matter of financing, at least for small businesses, is that individuals or families can be their own suppliers, by accumulating start-up or working capital from personal sources.

The factors determining whether business decision-makers have choice in the matter of governance, placed to the left of finance in Figure 1.3, are not intrinsic to the way business is conducted. Unless standards are imposed, usually by government though sometimes by public opinion or activists, governance is an issue of choice. In many Asian countries, lack of strong public opinion on governance, and weak rule of law even where the government has ruled on governance, mean that governance is a matter of choice, and so the business culture has impact.

Finally, the distribution of ownership of non-state-owned businesses is generally a matter of choice for business founders (providing their business is viable) and so the business culture has most impact of all in this area, as its position on the far left of Figure 1.3 indicates.

Business decision-making

The patterns of, for instance, ownership, financing, governance in a country and so on are consequences of large numbers of business decisions; in our view, following our research, these are often influenced by the same business culture. At the same time, we contend, these patterns are themselves outward manifestations of that culture. This dual nature of human products is true of cultural artefacts more generally. The stylistic resemblances of Minoan pots are both the consequences of a large number of decisions made by Minoan potters influenced by their culture and are themselves outward manifestations of that culture. In our research, the first aspect, that of the relationship between business cultures and business decisions, was the focus of our exploration. While business culture may (or may not) influence other aspects of business, such as the response of dealers to a marketing initiative, its impact, if any, is likely to be especially clear in the area of business decision-making.

The model of individual decision-making that informs this book is set out in Figure 1.4, which depicts a set of influences on the behaviour, including decision-making and communication behaviour, of a person engaged in business-related work. Since this was not a primary focus of our research we used a simplified model, but one that incorporated 'culture'. The model shows 'thoughts', which refers to largely conscious mental processes, as first-order influences; thoughts themselves are influenced by conscious and unconscious perceptions, beliefs, attitudes and emotions and these in turn are influenced by genetic make-up, personal experience, and various types or aspects of culture. (Personal experience is also

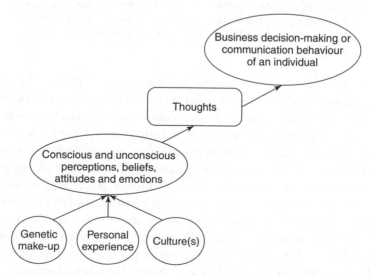

Figure 1.4   **Influences on the behaviour of a business decision-maker**

influenced by culture because culture creates one lens through which an individual sees and interprets his or her experiences.) Cultures are of various types – or, to put it another way, individuals are members of a range of cultures: these include organizational cultures, professional cultures, industry cultures and societal cultures. The business culture of a country or region is a fifth type of culture of which indigenous business decision-makers are members.

We recognize, of course, that business decisions are often, even usually, the product not of one individual's thought processes, but of a 'dominant coalition'. This does not, however, affect the impact of the business culture on decisions except where the members of the dominant coalition are from different cultures. While this is an increasing phenomenon globally, including in Asia, it applies as yet in only a small minority of businesses there; our study was concerned with decision-making in businesses where the members of the dominant coalition are from the 'home' country.

Influences on business culture

Randlesome et al. (1990) considered it 'self-evident' that 'the relationship between business and government, the shape and orientation of the economy, the financial institutions, and the trade unions all exert a profound effect on the business cultures of … countries.' They added

> In other words, the business culture in a particular country grows partly out of what could be called the 'current business environment' of that country. Yet business culture is a much broader concept because alongside the impulses which are derived from the present business environment figure the historical experiences of the business community.

This argument, that the factors listed by Randlesome et al. (1990) influence business culture, is plausible. It must be noted, however, that our research did not provide sufficient grounds for us to draw conclusions about influences on business cultures. Our interviewees did not neatly partition into categories their observations on what made doing business or managing an organization in their country different. These subdivisions, even the separation of the variables (elements) composing business cultures from other variables which are not treated as elements of business cultures, are based on interpretations by the researchers influenced by Western conventions. For further comment on this caution, see the Appendix. For the most part, in the four chapters discussing these variables (societal culture, political culture and environment and economic culture and environment), earlier studies that either suggest a link or an absence of link between these variables and the country's business culture have been drawn on.

The societal culture, more often called the national social culture, has frequently in past studies been identified with those value-dimensions emerging from research by Hofstede (1981),[56] Bond (1986)[57] and Schwartz (1994),[58] which have been widely deployed in further studies because of their claimed capacity to differentiate among cultures in meaningful ways. There certainly seems to be an a priori case for value-dimensions such as individual-collectivism having an influence on business culture and so Chapter 7 examines the Asian business cultures covered in this book in relation to these concepts of culture. In response, however, to the kind of criticism reported by Smith (2006),[59] that dimensions may be of limited value for 'characterizing the variability of nations', Chapter 8 considers societal cultures more broadly in relation to business cultures and decisions. It discusses such matters as culture-wide attitudes to education, religion, morality, gender relations and social divisions.

Chapters 9 and 10 explore the political and economic cultures and environments of business. The interactions between business, culture and environment in these areas are highly complex. For instance, the business culture of East Asia probably helped produce the financial crisis that threatened to engulf the economies of the region in 1997. Part of the response to that crisis was a partial shift in the business culture. Macroeconomic policy reforms after the crisis focused on the financial sector and introduced more liberal policies towards mergers, foreign ownership and bankruptcy, fiscal incentives for asset transfer and revised accounting standards to ease asset valuations; these attracted greater cross-border ownership and equity alliances to benefit from the stock and currency devaluations. The result was an infusion of foreign capital, technical know-how and relational networks (especially from Japan). Changes to the way businesses operated after the crisis included at least some restructuring of unsustainable debt – conversion to equity, extending terms of debt repayment or cutting interest rate below the risk-adjusted cost of capital. There was also a renewed vision that recognized the significance of technology and innovation for continued success.[60] These developments could be described as amounting to a degree of shift in the business cultures of the region.

Issues raised by a focus on business culture

A focus on business culture gives rise to two issues that have been discussed by other sources but need clarification in this context. One is the question of whether cultures are converging, hence reducing the significance of cultural difference; the other is the question of how people become imbued with a business culture.

There has been an extensive debate over whether cultures are converging.[61] This question applies a fortiori in relation to business cultures because globalization impacts business directly through international trade. Undoubtedly there is convergence in many superficial matters and no doubt in some deeper ones. Interviewees in our research gave examples of change that suggest some convergence towards a Western model and emphasized that change was occurring fastest in industries that do business with the West. On the other hand, if cultures are converging there must be a force producing change. One standard answer would be 'stage of economic development'. As Table 1.1 shows, however, our sample of Asian countries includes countries with highly divergent income levels and positions on the United Nations' Human Development Index (HDI) 2006, yet there is no suggestion from the findings that those closest to the West in economic development have business cultures closest to those in the West. Japan, for example, has a highly developed economy and is ranked seventh on the HDI measure, above the UK, and yet our findings showed its business culture to be very different from that of any developed Western country.

A major argument against cultural convergence is that traditionalism and modernity may not be opposed. Strong traditional values, such as group solidarity, interpersonal harmony, paternalism and familism can coexist with modern values of individual achievement and competition. Findings that Chinese subjects in Singapore and China endorsed both traditional and modern values support this argument. The researchers concluded, 'It is also conceivable that just as we talk about Westernization of cultural values around the world, we may also talk about Easternization of values in response to forces of modernity and consumption values imposed by globalization.'[62] Chia et al. (2007)[63] found tentative support for the modernization theorists' proposal that economic development produces socio-economic structures that lead to a convergence of values orientations. However, they also found conflicting results. For example, Hong Kong and Singapore, although developed, open

Table 1.1 *Gross Domestic Product (GDP) per capita at purchasing power parity in US$ 2006 and Human Development Index (HDI) 2006*

	China	India	Japan	Singapore	Taiwan
GDP	5,896 HKSAR 30,822	3,139	29,251	28,077	*
HDI index	0.68 HKSAR 0.96	0.58	0.95	0.94	
HDI rank	81 HKSAR 22	126	7	25	

Note: * Taiwan is omitted from statistics collected by the United Nations.

Source: Based on United Nations Development Program; URL: http://hdr.undp.org/hdr2006/statistics/indicators/133.html.

economies, placed traditional values (self-transcendence and conservation) above the modern values of self-enhancement and openness to change, contrary to modernization theory.

There is reason to believe that deep culture is relatively stable, because a corpus of knowledge and belief that is widely shared across a population creates an inertia – a tendency to reduce deviations from an equilibrium – that attenuates variability over time in values, behavioural norms and patterns of behaviours. Cultural stability helps to reduce ambiguity, and leads to more control over expected behavioural outcomes. Inglehart and Baker (2000)[64] examined cultural change as reflected by changes in basic values in three waves of the World Values Surveys, which covered 65 societies and 75 per cent of the world's population. The data showed that while economic development is associated with shifts away from absolute norms and values towards values that are increasingly rational, tolerant, trusting and participatory, the broad cultural heritage of a society, whether it is Protestant, Roman Catholic, Orthodox, Confucian or Communist, leaves an enduring imprint on values, despite the forces of modernization.

Studies focusing on managers have drawn similar conclusions. Discussing research based on managers in elite MBA programs, Morris et al. (1998)[65] pointed out that while that Asian participants in their study were arguably among the most Westernized members of their societies, yet they still differed quite markedly in their values from the US participants. Hence, they concluded, 'Our data are consistent with the view that even the most cosmopolitan sectors of these societies have not completely converged in their values and managerial behaviors.' Equally, Chia et al. (1997)[66] found that although political and socio-economic factors influenced the values orientations of managers in the China, Hong Kong, Singapore and Taiwan region, economic development level did not fully explain these values; societal context and cultural traditions were also part of the explanation. Refuting the argument that globalization is reducing the distinctiveness of Asian cultures, Chillier and Denis (1997)[67] pointed out that for the Chinese, modernization does not mean Westernization: 'They are not at all inclined to imitate Western life styles and political systems.' They adopt what they consider good in each culture. Finally, a study by Ralston et al. (2008) of managerial work values in the USA, Russia, Japan and China found that 'crossvergence with culture dominant' had more explanatory value than either convergence or divergence. Crossvergence constitutes an integration of influences from culture and economic ideology (such as communism versus capitalism) that results in a unique value system that borrows from both.[68]

The example of Taiwan shows that a 'synthesis' can occur between cultural globalizing forces and organized local responses. The global culture has neither taken over local Taiwanese culture, nor has it faced severe rejection. 'Overall, there is no evidence that the encounter of globalization and localization has ever resulted in serious cultural conflict or clash.'[69] Finally, a case study of a Thai subsidiary of an international corporation found that the notion that the impact of national culture diminishes with 'Western' industrialization carried little weight. Instead, a 'unified and idiosyncratic local business culture' was discovered, in spite of the country having long become a democratic free-market economy underpinned by a cohesive constitutional monarchy.[70]

It is sometimes asserted that computer-mediated communication (CMC) leads to global uniformity but Leung et al. (2005) countered that information and knowledge 'are interpreted through cultural lenses, and the transfer or diffusion of organizational knowledge is not easy to accomplish across cultural boundaries'. It seems likely that Leung et al. (2005) were right to conclude from their literature review that CMC has 'the simultaneous effects of increasing both cultural convergence and divergence', although 'more research is needed before comprehensive theoretical statements can be formulated'.[71]

The second question, how a business culture comes to be embedded in individual decision-makers, can be put in another way: how might a distinctive business culture be spread through a community? There are, fortunately for our theory, many forces at work in Asian countries capable of spreading the local business culture. These include the influence of the family (perhaps the most important of all) and community, education, peers, socialization to work, business networks, media coverage of business (including stories of business 'heroes') and business associations such as Chambers of Commerce.

It has been suggested that cultural values are likely to be more directly influential in Asian societies than Western. Begley and Tan (2001)[72] argued that cultural values may hold sway more powerfully in societies that emphasize conformity rather than those that prize individuality.

> " The literature on shame versus guilt supports this reasoning. In shame-based East Asian cultures, people uphold community norms, draw signals on appropriate behavior from groups and authorities, and seek to blend into the group. In guilt-based Anglo cultures, people are urged to heed their personal consciences, seek independence, and receive approval by standing out from the crowd.

The characterization of cultures as 'shame-based' or 'guilt-based' is probably an oversimplification; in addition, this argument was directed at general societal culture. However, the point that different cultures may influence their members' behaviour to varying degrees could be true (it is untested) and could also be true for business cultures. If so, it might help explain the point made by Whitley (1992) that business systems 'prevalent in East Asian countries ... seem more different from each other and more homogeneous within each society than those apparent in Western European and North American nations'.[73]

Conclusion

This chapter presents the rationale for a study of Asian business that focuses on links between culture and business. The rationale locates such a study within the institutional perspective on economies and organizations. This perspective has been applied previously to Asian business, notably by Whitley (1992), but with a limited emphasis on the cognitive institutions that correspond to culture. Therefore, our study fills a gap in the literature.

The chapter also introduces a layer of culture that has been neglected in earlier research, the layer of business culture, which is defined here as a set of business-related values, beliefs, attitudes, meanings and ways of doing things shared by a business community. The claim of this book is that a country or area's business culture has an influence on business decision-making that is significant enough to merit its study.

About this book

The primary purpose of this book is to set out the findings, conclusions and implications of a qualitative research project into the relations between culture and business in five Asian countries. This chapter, Chapter 1, has explained the initial reasons for the research. These reasons were a perceived gap in the literature and a response to calls from scholars for more qualitative research. The outline of the literature given here also provides a context for the research findings. The previous literature also, of course, influenced the conclusions we drew from those findings.

Chapters 2 and 3 set out the main findings from our qualitative research into the business cultures of China, including Hong Kong, India, Japan, Taiwan and Singapore. Chapter 2 undertakes a basic country-by-country analysis of the main aspects of business culture revealed in the research. An attempt has been made to retain as much as possible of the richness of the original material, to allow readers to judge it for themselves. Chapter 3 supplies a cross-cultural analysis, subdividing the research findings by 'aspects of culture' and comparing the five subject countries on these aspects. Chapter 3 also relates the findings it reports to the (somewhat meagre) previous literature relevant to business culture.

Chapters 4, 5 and 6 explore the findings of the research on the relations between business culture and key areas of business decision-making: ownership, financing and governance in Chapter 4, organization and management in Chapter 5 and business strategy in Chapter 6. These chapters also compare these findings with the findings of previous research on the relations between the broader societal culture and these categories of decision.

Chapters 7, 8, 9 and 10 consider the relations among other 'layers' of culture, business culture and business decision-making.

The final chapter, Chapter 11, sets out the conclusions drawn from the project. In particular it proposes a theory based on our empirical research that major categories of business decisions are influenced by a hitherto neglected 'layer' of culture, the business culture of the country or other distinctive region within a country. Chapter 11 also puts forward suggestions for further research.

The Appendix is an important part of this book. It sets out the methodology. It also justifies what appears to be a new 'paradigm' for research in the area of culture and business, based on the argument that the beliefs of practitioners can themselves be regarded as theories, albeit naïve and untested, of possibly equal value to the untested or partially tested theories of academics and other outside observers.

This organization of the book has resulted in occasional reuse of a quotation from the interviews where the same remark illustrated more than one point.

References

[1] Robbins, J. (2006) *Tiger Economies Go Head to Head*, BBC 2 Programme.

[2] Kynge, J. (2006) *China Shakes the World: The Rise of a Hungry Nation*, London: Weidenfeld.

[3] Chung-Sheng Y., Taylor, G.S. and Tung, W. (2003) 'A cross-cultural comparison of work goals: The United States, Taiwan, and the People's Republic of China', in Alon, I. and Shenkar O. (eds) *Chinese Culture, Organizational Behavior and International Business Management*, Westport, CT: Praeger.

[4] Chen, M. (2004) (2nd edition) *Asian Management Systems: Chinese, Japanese and Korean Styles of Businesss*, London: Thomson.

[5] Whitley, R. (1992) *Business Systems in East Asia: Firms, Markets, and Societies*, London: Sage.

[6] Sen, A. (2005) *The Argumentative Indian: Essays on Indian Culture, History and Identity*, London: Penguin.

[7] Hofstede, G. (2001) (2nd edition) *Culture's Consequences: Comparing Values, Behaviors, Institutions and Organizations*, Thousand Oaks, CA: Sage.

[8] Hofstede, G. (1981) *Cultures and Organizations: Software of the Mind*, London: Harper Collins.

[9] Schwartz, S.H. (1994) 'Beyond individualism/collectivism: New cultural dimensions of values', in Kim, U., Triandis, H.C., Kagitcibasi, C., Choi, S.-C. and Yoon, G. (eds) *Individualism and Collectivism: Theory, Method and Applications*, 85–119, Newbury Park, CA: Sage.

[10] Bond, M.H. (1988) 'Finding universal dimensions of individual variation in multicultural studies of values: The Rokeach and Chinese value surveys', *Journal of Personality and Social Psychology*, 55(6): 1009–15.

[11] House, R.J., Javidan, M., Hanges, P.J. and Dorfman, P.W. (2002) 'Understanding cultures and implicit leadership theories across the globe: An introduction to project GLOBE', *Journal of World Business*, 37(1): 3–10.

[12] Fiske, A.P. (2002) 'Using individualism and collectivism to compare cultures – a critique of the validity and measurement of the constructs: Comment on Oyserman et al. (2002)', *Psychological Bulletin*, 128(1): 78–88.

[13] Smith, P.B. (2006) 'When elephants fight, the grass gets trampled: The GLOBE and Hofstede projects', *Journal of International Business Studies*, 37(6): 915–21.

[14] Chatterjee, S.R. and Pearson, C.A.L. (2006) 'Indian managers in transition: Orientations, goals, values and ethics', in Davis, H.J., Chatterjee, S.R. and Heuer, M. (eds) *Management in India: Trends and Transitions*, New Delhi: Sage.

[15] London, T. and Hart, S.L. (2004) 'Reinventing strategies for emerging markets: Beyond the transnational model', *Journal of International Business Studies*, **35**(5): 350–70.

[16] Sheer, V.C. and Chen, L. (2003) 'Successful Sino-Western business negotiation: Participants' accounts of national and professional cultures', *The Journal of Business Communication*, **40**(1): 50–85.

[17] Adler, N. (1986) *International Dimensions of Organizational Behavior*, Boston, MA: Kent Publishers.

[18] Wilkinson, B. (1996) 'Culture, institutions and business in East Asia', *Organization Studies*, **17**: 421–47.

[19] Casson, M. and Lundan, S.M. (1999) 'Explaining international differences in economic institutions', *International Studies of Management & Organization*, **29**(2): 29–42.

[20] Au, K. and Cheung, M.W.L. (2004) 'Intra-cultural variation and job autonomy in 42 countries', *Organization Studies*, **25**(8): 1339–62.

[21] Steier, L., Chrisman, J.J. and Chua, J.H. (2004) 'Entrepreneurial management and governance in family firms: An introduction', *Entrepreneurship Theory and Practice*, **28**: 295–303.

[22] Rhodes, R.A.W. (2007) 'Understanding governance: Ten years on', *Organization Studies*, **28**(8): 1243–64.

[23] Tayeb, M. (2006) 'India: A non-tiger of Asia', in Davis, H.J., Chatterjee, S.R. and Heuer, M. (eds) *Management in India: Trends and Transition*, New Delhi: Response Books.

[24] Henisz, W. and Swaminathan, A. (2008) 'Institutions and International Business', *Journal of International Business Studies*, **39**(4): 537–9.

[25] Scott, W.R. (1995 and 2001) *Institutions and Organizations*, Thousand Oaks, CA: Sage.

[26] Kshetri, N. and Dholakia, N. (2005) 'E-commerce patterns in South Asia: A look beyond economics', *Journal of Asia Pacific Business*, **6**(3): 63–79.

[27] Ahlstrom, D. and Bruton, G.D. (2002) 'An institutional perspective on the role [of] culture in shaping strategic actions by technology-focused entrepreneurial firms in China', *Entrepreneurship: Theory and Practice*, **26**(4): 53–69.

[28] Scott, W.R. (1995 and 2001) *Institutions and Organizations*, Thousand Oaks, CA: Sage.

[29] Redding, G. (2004) 'The Capitalist business system of China and its rationale', *Asia Pacific Journal of Management*, **19**: 2–3. (Internal references omitted).

[30] Whitley, R. (1992) *Business Systems in East Asia: Firms, Markets, and Societies*, London: Sage.

[31] Aggarwal, R. and Mellen, L.E. (1997) 'Perspective on Japanese finance for portfolio investors', *Review of Business*, **18**, June 22.

[32] Ibid.

[33] Spender, J.C. (1989) *Industry Recipes: The Nature and Sources of Managerial Judgement*, Oxford: Blackwell.

[34] Ibid.

[35] Casson, M. and Lundan, S.M. (1999) 'Explaining international differences in economic institutions', *International Studies of Management & Organization*, **29**(2): 29–42.

[36] Tsui-Auch, L.S. and Lee, Y.-J. (2003) 'The state matters: Management models of Singaporean Chinese and Korean business groups', *Organization Studies*, **24**(4): 507–34.

[37] Oliver, C. (1997) 'Sustainable competitive advantage: Combining institutional and resource-based views', *Strategic Management Journal*, **18**(9): 697–793.

[38] Scott, W.R. (1995 and 2001) *Institutions and Organizations*, Thousand Oaks, CA: Sage.

[39] Hofstede, G., Neuijen, B., Ohayv, D.D. and Sanders, G. (1990) 'Measuring organizational cultures: A qualitative and quantitative study across twenty cases', *Administrative Science Quarterly*, **35**(2): 286–317.

[40] Lenartowicz, T. and Roth, K. (2004) 'Culture assessment revisited: The selection of key informants in IB cross-cultural studies', *Management International Review*, **44**(1): 23–51.

[41] Austin, J. (2007) 'Understanding Korea: John Austin urges the need to take account of Korean business culture', *New Zealand International Review*, **32**(January/February).

[42] Berger, P.L. (2003) 'The cultural dynamics of globalization', in Berger, P.L. and Huntington, S. (eds) *Many Globalizations: Cultural Diversity in the Contemporary World*, New York: Oxford University Press.

[43] 'Measuring diversity', Workinfo.com, URL: http://workinfo.com/free/downloads.

[44] West, K. (1994) *Britain, the Commonwealth and the Global Economy*, London: The Round Table.

[45] Yan, Y. (2003) 'Managed globalization: State power and cultural transition in China', in Berger, P.L. and Huntington, S.P. (eds) *Many Globalizations: Cultural Diversity in the Contemporary World*, Oxford: Oxford University Press.

[46] Eyjolfsdottir, H.M. and Smith, P.B. (1996) 'Icelandic business and management culture', *International Studies of Management & Organization*, **26**(3): 61–73.

[47.] Keeley, T.D. (2001) *International Human Resource Management in Japanese Firms: Their Greatest Challenge*, Basingstoke: Palgrave.

[48] Bjerke, B. (2000) 'A typified, culture-based, interpretation of management of SMEs in Southeast Asia', *Asia Pacific Journal of Management*, **17**: 103–32.

[49] Berger, P.L. (2003) 'The cultural dynamics of globalization', in Berger, P.L. and Huntington, S. (eds) *Many Globalizations: Cultural Diversity in the Contemporary World*, New York: Oxford University Press.

[50] Randlesome, C., Brierley, W., Bruton, K., Gordon, C. and King, P. (1990) *Business Cultures in Europe*, Oxford: Butterworth-Heinemann.

[51] Myers, A. and Randlesome, C. (1997) 'Cultural fluency: Results from UK and Irish survey', *Business Communication Quarterly*, **60**(3): 9–22.

[52] Kitayama, S. (2002) 'Culture and basic psychological processes – toward a system view of culture: Comment on Oyserman et al. (2002)', *Psychological Bulletin*, **128**(1): 89–96.

[53] Deeks, J. (1993) *Business and the Culture of the Enterprise Society*, London: Quorum Books.

[54] Kroeber, A. and Kluckhohn, C. (1952) *Culture*, New York: Meridian Books.

[55] Hofstede, G. and Hofstede, J. (2004) *Cultures and Organizations: Software of the Mind; Intercultural Cooperation and Its Importance for Survival*, New York: McGraw Hill.

[56] Hofstede, G. (1981) *Cultures and Organizations: Software of the Mind*, London: Harper Collins.

[57] Bond, M.H. and Hwang, K.K. (1986) 'The social psychology of Chinese people', in Bond, M.H. (ed.) *The Psychology of the Chinese People*, Hong Kong: Oxford University Press.

[58] Schwartz, S.H. (1994) 'Beyond individualism/collectivism: New cultural dimensions of values', in Kim, U., Triandis, H.C., Kagitcibasi, C., Choi, S.-C. and Yoon, G. (eds) *Individualism and Collectivism: Theory, Method and Applications*, 85–119, Newbury Park, CA: Sage.

[59] Smith, P.B. (2006) 'When elephants fight, the grass gets trampled: The GLOBE and Hofstede projects', *Journal of International Business Studies*, **37**(6): 915–21.

[60] Wang, J. and Gupta, V. (2003) 'Post-crisis management: A study of corporate restructuring in Asia', *Journal of the Academy of Business and Economics*, **2**(2): 209–17.

[61] Ralston, D.A., Holt, D.H., Terpstra, R.H. and Kai-Cheng, Y. (2008) 'The impact of national culture and economic ideology on managerial work values: A study of the United States, Russia, Japan, and China', *Journal of International Business Studies*, **39**: 8–26.

[62] Leung, K., Bhagat, R.S., Buchan, N.R., Erez, M. and Gibson, C.B. (2005) 'Culture and international business: Recent advances and their implications for future research', *Journal of International Business Studies*, **36**: 357–78. (Internal references omitted).

[63] Chia, H.-B., Egri, C.P., Ralston, D.A., Fu, P.P., Kuo, M.-H. C., Lee, C.H., Li, Y. and Moon, Y.-L. (1997) 'Four tigers and the dragon: Values differences, similarities, and consensus', *Asia-Pacific Journal of Management*, **24**: 305–20.

[64] Inglehart, R. and Baker, W.E. (2000) 'Modernization, cultural change and the persistence of traditional values', *American Sociological Review*, **65**: 19–51.

[65] Morris, M.W., Williams, K.Y., Leung, K., Larrick, R., Mendoza, T.M., Bhatnagar, D., Li, J., Kondo, M., Luo, J.-L. and Hu, J.-C. (1998) 'Conflict management style: Accounting for cross-national differences', *Journal of International Business Studies*, **29**(4): 729–47.

[66] Chia, H.-B., Egri, C.P., Ralston, D.A., Fu, P.P., Kuo, M.-H. C., Lee, C.H., Li, Y. and Moon, Y.-L. (1997) 'Four tigers and the dragon: Values differences, similarities, and consensus', *Asia-Pacific Journal of Management*, **24**: 305–20.

[67] Chillier, C. and Denis, J.-E. (1997) 'Advertising in China: Trends, constraints, and implications for foreign firms', URL: http://market.unige.ch/docs_online/papers_Denis/199722.pdf.

[68] Ralston, D.A., Holt, D.H., Terpstra, R.H. and Kai-Cheng, Y. (2008) 'The impact of national culture and economic ideology on managerial work values: A study of the United States, Russia, Japan, and China', *Journal of International Business Studies*, **39**: 8–26.

[69] Hsiao, H.-H. (2002) 'Coexistence and synthesis: Cultural globalization and localization in contemporary Taiwan', in Berger, P.L. and Huntington, S.P. (eds) *Many Globalizations: Cultural Diversity in the Contemporary World*, New York: Oxford University Press.

[70] Andrews, T.G. and Chomprusi, N. (2001) 'Lessons in "cross-vergence": Restructuring the Thai subsidiary corporation', *Journal of International Business Studies*, **32**(1): 77–93.

[71] Leung, K., Bhagat, R.S., Buchan, N.R., Erez, M. and Gibson, C.B. (2005) 'Culture and international business: Recent advances and their implications for future research', *Journal of International Business Studies*, **36**(4): 357–79.

[72] Begley, M. and Tan, W.-L. (2001) 'The socio-cultural environment for entrepreneurship: A comparison between East Asian and Anglo-Saxon countries', *Journal of International Business Studies*, **32**(3): 537–53.

[73] Whitley, R. (1992) *Business Systems in East Asia: Firms, Markets, and Societies*, London: Sage.

2 the business cultures of five Asian countries

This chapter will draw on a study of Asian business decision-making conducted by three researchers including the author during 2006, 2007 and 2008. (The methodology of the study is described in the Appendix.) Seventy-five interviews, all undertaken by the author, took place in Hyderabad (India), Taipei (Taiwan), Singapore, Hong Kong (China), Mumbai (India), Beijing (China), Tokyo (Japan), London and Chennai (India). Interviewees were asked what they considered to be the main distinguishing characteristics of the way business is conducted and organizations are managed in their country. The interviews were unstructured to give interviewees scope to express their own opinions and introduce any aspects they thought relevant. As the interview series progressed (locations are given above in chronological order), points made in earlier interviews were raised towards the end of the interviews and discussed with succeeding interviewees. Most importantly, if the term 'business culture' had not been used explicitly by the interviewee (many did), they were asked if their country had a distinctive business culture. Our findings from this research reflect the views of 75 Asian business executives about their own country's business cultures.

One conclusion from our study was that while there are commonalities which distinguish the business cultures of all the five Asian countries covered from those of the West, there are also important differences within the region as well as variations in the way the 'same' aspect of culture is played out from country to country. At the same time, business cultures cohere in a way that is lost in a thematic analysis. This chapter will therefore attempt an outline of the business cultures of China, India, Japan, Taiwan and Singapore, based on the comments of the business decision-makers we interviewed.

Most of the elements of the business cultures of the five countries set out in this chapter are those mentioned spontaneously in five or more instances in our study, in accordance with the criterion required by the qualitative research methodology we used for the study, which is described in the Appendix. A further few elements, marked with a double asterisk in the text (**) and by italics in the tables, did not meet this criterion, being mentioned spontaneously in fewer than five instances. A justification for including them, subject to drawing attention to their weaker status, is given in the Appendix.

China

Networks, weak governance and corruption distinguished the way business was done in China, according to our research, while deference to superiors, hierarchy and, in the private sector, lack of planning, marked internal organization. The reality of government control over business was much weaker than the way it was portrayed in the West.

- China's business culture was seen as marked by overt signs of deference.

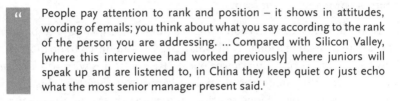

> " People pay attention to rank and position – it shows in attitudes, wording of emails; you think about what you say according to the rank of the person you are addressing. ...Compared with Silicon Valley, [where this interviewee had worked previously] where juniors will speak up and are listened to, in China they keep quiet or just echo what the most senior manager present said.[i]

'Most subordinates self-censor though they will occasionally feed an idea in to a boss in such a way that the boss can take the credit.'[ii] More positively, one interviewee spoke in terms of respect rather than deference: 'In Chinese companies execution is very good. This is because of the high respect for the team leader which means everybody acts promptly and thoroughly, even if they disagree with the decision.'[iii] The importance attached to rank and position had been noted and adjusted for by international companies working in China: 'MNCs [multinational companies] have two business cards. On one they elevate the individual's title to gain entry. Before you will get in to see someone in an SOE [state-owned enterprise], they will want to see your title to ensure you are senior enough.'[iv]

- In Japan, as will be discussed, the person receiving deference might have little real power; high levels of deference did not necessarily equate to a high power-distance organizational culture. In China, however, both deference and hierarchy were very important: 'The most distinctive feature of Chinese business is hierarchy.'[v] 'In China, power wins every argument. ...Chinese businesses are less bound and hierarchical than Korea's, but close to that extreme.'[vi] In SOEs, 'Everything goes up to the boss for approval', and, 'They [managers]

[i] Mainland Chinese, Consultant, international management consultancy
[ii] Ibid.
[iii] Mainland Chinese, General Manager, Chinese chemical state-owned enterprise and international energy MNC
[iv] Mainland Chinese, General Manager, Chinese state-owned enterprise
[v] Ibid.
[vi] China, Expatriate, Senior Consultant, international management consultancy

will make unrealistic promises to keep the boss happy.'vii A particular feature of China's hierarchical business culture was the importance of the Chairman (or occasionally Chairwoman). This applied to both SOEs and private companies. The Chairman provided the strategic vision and the long-term aspirations. He might be an owner (private) or a government appointee (SOE): 'The CEO's [Chief Executive Officer's] job is to please this guy.'viii The CEO had some countervailing power, however, because he or she usually had expertise that the Chairman lacked. Nevertheless, 'The CEO accepts and implements the Chairman's decisions – s/he is the West's equivalent of a COO [Chief Operations Officer]. The Chairman switches both the CEO and the other members of the management team.'ix

- Business-to-business (B2B) relations in China were described as interpersonal rather than inter-organizational. At its weakest, this amounted to no more than in many countries. As one interviewee put it, 'Relationships with other organizations are often personal – for example, playing golf together; this is especially true for salespeople.'x However, this understates the phenomenon, which included *guanxi*, a more structured and sophisticated version of networking: 'Relationships are important in business in all countries, but in China their impact is deeper and wider and the phenomenon is a more sophisticated one – there is a structure of different kinds of relationship.'xi Several respondents brought out the significance of *guanxi* more fully. *Guanxi* was pervasive within China: '*Guanxi* affects everybody.'xii *Guanxi* modified or undermined profit maximization or other business objectives which are regarded in the West as normal: 'It means personal factors are put over business considerations.'xiii How *guanxi* functions varied across Chinese communities: 'I am Chinese, but when I first went to the mainland for business, I had to learn what was expected in PRC [the People's Republic of China].'xiv Finally, a corollary of B2B personalism in China as elsewhere in Asia was the relatively low importance of contracts. 'The contract does not seal the deal. It is a "guide". It's the relationship that counts. For instance in the power sector, one party will finance another, help out over the tariff when it rises.'xv One interviewee warned against a common misunderstanding of *guanxi*: 'I think the concept that *guanxi* is essential to operating in China is not accurate. Don't think of *guanxi* as this "strategic

---

vii Mainland Chinese, Financial Controller, Chinese venture firm
viii China, Expatriate, Senior Consultant, international management consultancy
ix China, Expatriate, Consultant, international management consultancy
x Mainland Chinese, Consultant, international management consultancy
xi Hong Kong Chinese, CEO, Chinese consulting firm
xii Mainland Chinese, Partner, international accounting firm
xiii Mainland Chinese, Senior Manager, Human Resource Management, Chinese state-owned enterprise
xiv Hong Kong Chinese, CEO, Chinese consulting firm
xv China, Hong Kong, Expatriate, General Manager, energy MNC

34   2

INTRODUCTION · **THE BUSINESS CULTURES OF FIVE ASIAN COUNTRIES** · ANALYSING ASIAN BUSINESS CULTURES · OWNERSHIP, FINANCING AND GOVERNANCE · ORGANIZATION AND MANAGEMENT · BUSINESS STRATEGY ·

advantage" that one must have to compete/survive but think of *guanxi* as a "relationship" because that is the direct meaning of the word.[xvi]

- *Guanxi* operated within organizations as well as between them and could be applied to gain access to decision-makers:

> " A good approach is to make yourself well known to and trusted by the decision-makers' subordinates. They may bring your issue before him with a favourable report, or when your issue is brought to him he will consult them and get a favourable report, or at least he will know already who you are. So I start from the grass roots. This makes it harder for the decision-maker to pull the wool over your eyes but you have to know which subordinates have *guanxi* with him.[xvii]

However, the significance of *guanxi* in corporate decision-making should not be exaggerated. For example, in employee selection its effects varied:

> " The effectiveness of *guanxi* in getting a job is not significantly different from networking for a job in the Western market. It would range across the different business structures, being more effective if the company is smaller and your '*guanxi*' or 'network' can make the direct decision, to less effective in bigger companies where there is a more structured HR [Human Relations] approach.[xviii]

- Weak governance was a noted feature of China's business culture, in some cases amounting to corruption despite attempts by the government to stamp it out. In some opinions, not abiding by the law was seen as an inevitable consequence of the situation: 'It is very hard not to break the law in China, because there are so many, often contradictory, laws. This means that businesses are at the mercy of Party or other officials.'[xix] Good relations with local authorities were essential; the fines were heavy and the regulations were strict and detailed: 'It is impossible to keep them all, so all businesses break them. Good relations mean you will be warned [before punitive action is taken].'[xx] Weak governance was seen by some, however, as consistent with the culture, rather than an inevitable response to circumstances: 'There is an embedded resistance in the Chinese people to the rule of law. They ask, "How can I bribe officials?" "How can I leverage my position?" '[xxi]

[xvi] Mainland Chinese, Sales and Marketing, Chinese consumer manufacturing
[xvii] Hong Kong Chinese, CEO, Chinese consulting firm
[xviii] Mainland Chinese, Sales and Marketing, Chinese consumer manufacturing
[xix] Hong Kong Chinese, Banker, international bank
[xx] Hong Kong Chinese, failed entrepreneur in China, Financial Controller, international consumer goods company manufacturing in China
[xxi] China, Singaporean Chinese, CEO, Thai MNC, business services

Agency costs could be high. 'Investors need to make sure their interests are aligned with those of the ruler of the company or they may get burned. They need a good exit strategy. Books are not always of the clearest transparency. In SOEs, the government has the last say.'[xxii] In the privatized former SOEs, 'Staff are not working towards the benefit of the shareholders, but to please the boss; keep the boss happy.'[xxiii] The 'boss' would generally be a political appointee. 'In the giant SOEs the ambitions of the Chairman (who is also the corporate strategist and chief decision-maker) will be political and he will be being groomed for a political post such as Governor. He brings political connections and access to money to the business.'[xxiv]

In SOEs, there was little or no accountability.

> " Many small SOEs went out of business but there was no compensation for their creditors. The big ones are not accountable because they are very profitable from monopoly profits in an expanding market. Media coverage brings some limited accountability. For example, China Mobile, subjected to adverse publicity, started to use consultants and recruit overseas.[xxv]

Trade creditors spoke of experiencing the lack of respect for laws and rules in Chinese business. For instance, an interviewee from a Japanese trading company said

> " The SOEs break the rules – in fact they have no written rules. For instance, they will pay for goods with letters of credit, then find some minute difference from the contract and say they will not pay. They will pay in the end, because otherwise we would not deal with them again and they need us, but it wastes a lot of time.[xxvi]

In this respect a Taiwanese interviewee who did business in China likened the country to Taiwan 50 or 60 years before:

> " The people work hard, seek prosperity, but there is a lot of cheating – for instance, one outsourcer I know found that the quantity of rice reportedly being supplied to provide their workers' meal [for which the outsourcer paid] was more than three times what a large portion each would require.[xxvii]

[xxii] China, Expatriate, Senior Consultant, international management consultancy
[xxiii] Mainland Chinese, Financial Controller, Chinese venture firm
[xxiv] Mainland Chinese, Senior Manager, Human Resource Management, Chinese SOE
[xxv] Mainland Chinese, Financial Controller, Chinese venture firm
[xxvi] Japanese, Team Manager, Marketing Analysis, Japanese trading company
[xxvii] Taiwanese, Finance and Accounting, manufacturing

Although China was 'increasingly close to using international accounting standards and having appropriately trained accountants',[xxviii] Chinese businesses were seen to have little respect for or understanding of the purpose of professional standards in accounting:

> Chinese companies, both private companies and SOEs, especially provincial ones, see accountants as service providers who should do what they want because they are being paid. They can't see any value added from the service and use accountants only because the law requires them to. They are very price conscious and can be concerned with the accountants being 'flexible'. There is no understanding or respect for professional standards. When there are issues they may say, 'We can hire someone else to do the work.'[xxix]

This attitude was so pervasive that working in China was risky for the international accountancy firms. 'There are some good companies but they vary widely. The best international accountancy firms research extensively before taking on a client to ensure they have integrity.'[xxx]

- Interviewees broadly agreed that corruption was common ('Corruption is rampant'),[xxxi] but opinions differed on its causes and the current trend. One Chinese interviewee attributed corruption (and much else) to the stage of economic development. Another argued that most official corruption was 'for the sake of officials' children or their concubines'.[xxxii] A third said the cause was the lack of any impersonal system of government in China, so that everything depended on the personality: 'A dictatorship depends on the dictator.' Past prosecutions for corruption seemed 'to have an aura of being part of a political struggle – for example to get rid of someone who was blocking someone else's path'.[xxxiii]
As far as the trend was concerned, one interviewee judged that the system had checks and balances to deal with corruption.[xxxiv] To another, recent prosecutions seemed to have an 'aura of sincerity', and to be likely to improve the situation because the 'guys at the top' were serious about it and secure and strong enough to tackle high-ranking officials and their children.[xxxv] Conflicting with these positive views was the opinion that the situation was

---

xxviii Hong Kong Chinese, failed entrepreneur in China, Financial Controller, international consumer goods company manufacturing in China
xxix Mainland Chinese, Partner, international accounting firm
xxx Ibid.
xxxi Mainland Chinese, General Manager, international business information hardware manufacturer
xxxii Mainland Chinese, Partner, international accounting firm
xxxiii Hong Kong Chinese, CEO, Chinese consulting firm
xxxiv China, Hong Kong, Expatriate, General Manager, energy MNC
xxxv Ibid.

worsening: 'The drive against corruption is weak and itself undermined by corruption. Punishments are slight. Insider traders, who made ten million yuan, were fined 200,000.'[xxxvi]

- Views varied on Chinese attitudes to risk. Some Chinese saw their compatriots as reckless: 'They'll make a 20 million dollar decision on the basis of a talk with friends, or anecdotal information, or to maintain their *guanxi*: feasibility studies are done after the decision is made, to justify it. It's just paper.'[xxxvii] However, someone else did not consider that they are risk takers: 'The Chinese are cautious, risk averse. The gamblers are exceptions.' Others considered that the Chinese are gamblers but only because they have nothing to lose.

> They have to fight for any chance in life. They don't gamble for fun, like in Las Vegas; they gamble to have any hope of a decent life. They hope to change their fate and stop worrying. Many people on top salaries (2000 dollars a month) are on the brink of bankruptcy. One serious illness is all it would take. Medical expenses are very high; insurance does not cover the cost of drugs; this explains the high savings rate.[xxxviii]

Others argued that the Chinese 'handle' risk: 'China has a benchmarking culture. This is one way to handle risk. Unlike Japan and Korea, they don't throw money at either problems or opportunities.'[xxxix]

- In contrast to these divided views on risk, there was a consensus that innovation was low in Chinese businesses. The Chinese, by their own account, were 'fast followers' rather than innovators.[xl] A Chinese venture capitalist saw the semiconductor and internet proposals put to him as innovative only in the Chinese context, though responding to the fast-moving Chinese consumer taste in electronics meant that in mobile phones, for example, they might occasionally come out with something new.[xli] SOEs were seen as good at copying but as using their monopoly at the expense of innovation for the whole industry. China Mobile's strategy in the data services market, for instance, was to encourage service providers, then regulate the market and squeeze margins, which was profitable for them but suppressed innovation among private companies.[xlii]

Some explanations given for the low rate of innovation were situational, such as that the Chinese were faced with such high growth in demand that

---

[xxxvi] Mainland Chinese, General Manager, international business information hardware manufacturer
[xxxvii] Hong Kong Chinese, Banker, international bank
[xxxviii] Mainland Chinese, General Manager, international business information hardware manufacturer
[xxxix] China, Expatriate, Senior Consultant, international management consultancy
[xl] Mainland Chinese, General Manager, Chinese state-owned enterprise
[xli] Mainland Chinese, Financial Controller, Chinese venture firm
[xlii] Mainland Chinese, Consultant, international management consultancy

there was a temptation, to which the private companies were most vulnerable, to go for speed – for example, by building an 'old technology' polluting ship rather than wait for a new technology clean one.[xliii] Others admitted the situational influence but doubted whether it was the whole cause, arguing that although as yet they had had no real need to innovate, there were doubts about their ability: their talent was too much 'inside the box'.[xliv]

- Contrary to the prevalent Western view that the 'dictatorship of the Party' allowed the Chinese government to implement its policies virtually unopposed, Chinese interviewees were more conscious of its weaknesses and internal divisions, while acknowledging that the capacity of officials to interfere with individual businesses remained very great. While SOEs were strongly influenced by government, even they were not entirely under its control. An instance was in the area of safety and environmental standards: 'The government is now telling businesses in the state industries to improve standards on safety, the environment etc. The government is trying to give the right message, but China is more decentralized than Russia.'[xlv] Outside of strategic industries, there were often minimal controls. 'For example, anybody who wants to could build a polyester plant. Our company found customers coming from nowhere; they could get a massive loan, build a plant using basic technology and meet a local market need. An example would be a local textile mill to serve a local market.'[xlvi]

One cause of government weakness in policy execution was internal to the government itself. 'The Chinese government is not a monolith. Government officials' thoughts are fluid – they are afraid, especially that they don't understand the implications of what they are being asked. They say "No" because it is safer.'[xlvii] Consequently, government decision-making was often 'inconsistent, raw or primitive'.[xlviii] Government control went in cycles.

> " Take the textile industry, for instance. The government promoted and controlled the industry; control was about managing demand and keeping the value chain co-ordinated so costs would not rise through one weak link. Then they realized 'letting go' would bring in private money and initiative, and so enhance growth. They let it go for about ten years. That led to excesses, such as state-owned banks being over-exposed, which threatened the financial structure, and led to corruption and environmental damage. Therefore they switched back to 'consolidation'.[xlix]

[xliii] China, Hong Kong, Expatriate, General Manager, energy MNC
[xliv] China, Expatriate, Consultant, international management consultancy
[xlv] Ibid.
[xlvi] China, Hong Kong, Expatriate, Asia Product Manager, energy MNC
[xlvii] Mainland Chinese, General Manager, international business information hardware manufacturer
[xlviii] Ibid.
[xlix] China, Hong Kong, Expatriate, Asia Product Manager, energy MNC

On the other hand, some ministries were considered competent and effective: 'The Ministry of Commerce, which has a lot of decision-making power over trade, regulation of markets, or NDRC, which is the policy-setting mechanism for a lot of strategic industries, are staffed by high-quality technocrats with more detailed industry knowledge than their Western counterparts.'[l]

- There was a strongly held view that Chinese businesses were averse to forward planning. For instance, when would-be entrepreneurs approached a venture capitalist, they usually had no business plan: 'The Chinese hate doing business plans – they say, "The future will change so why should I plan?" '[li] 'Private companies, in Southern China, started by people with no more than primary school education up to 30 years ago, have no strategy or formal planning.'[lii] Another way of looking at this was to say that the Chinese operate by trial and error: 'The Chinese approach is trial and error. Not scientific.'[liii] This approach was contrasted with that of the French, for instance, who wanted 'long discussion and research' before taking action. For example, the Chinese subsidiary of a French manufacturer had a strong position in the high-end product market but no offering in the third level; the Chinese managers drew up a plan to launch an affordable third-level brand, recruit 200 dealers (this would be only 10 per cent of the total) and support them only with minimum back up; it was considered a small investment. 'We would find an agency, design a logo and off we go.'[liv] The French headquarters wanted the answers to how this would affect their existing market and what message it would send to other markets. So they researched it; the studies took one month, after which they went ahead.[lv]

- The Chinese approach to negotiating was an overall one, not line by line.

> " On their core issues they won't give an inch; the rest they don't want to negotiate at all and will concede to save time. This leaves their opposing negotiator perplexed. Is it because they don't understand the issue? Or because they consider their position so robust that the downside potential is unimportant? Or because they intend to cheat?[lvi]

Any deal had to 'make rational sense' to the Chinese. Any deal had also to 'offer a clear commercial benefit for all companies and individuals'. For example, an oil company found that a proposal to build a refinery in a given city was welcomed by the mayor, whose consent was vital. This was because it would lead

---

[l] China, Hong Kong, Expatriate, Asia Product Manager, energy MNC
[li] Mainland Chinese, Financial Controller, Chinese venture firm
[lii] Ibid.
[liii] Hong Kong Chinese, Banker, international bank
[liv] Mainland Chinese, Marketing Manager, consumer MNC
[lv] Ibid.
[lvi] Hong Kong Chinese, Banker, international bank

to benefits for the city such as a government bonus granted to cities attracting foreign direct investments and a tax credit for the city.[lvii] 'Making rational sense' and 'offering a clear commercial benefit' are expectations that could be interpreted in some cases as rent-seeking: 'In the less developed provinces, good relationships [especially with politicians] have to be bought.'[lviii]

In negotiations, the Chinese preference for personalism in business surfaced again:

> It is necessary to pave the way to the first negotiation; to see them many times without an agenda. This can take six months or a year. Whole meetings take place without the substantive issue being discussed. This applies particularly to the older Chinese. The younger ones have been more exposed to Western ways.[lix]

On the other hand, important though it was for trust to develop before bargaining begins, this did not imply that the Chinese approach to negotiations was 'win-win': 'They pay lip service to win-win but to me they are still win-lose.'[lx] 'They know the concept and pay lip service to it but in the long term they go for win-lose.'[lxi] 'The concept of win-win is advanced. It is just becoming known. Some highly educated officials understand it, but it is not forged into people's second nature. It is intermittent.'[lxii]

Within this constraint, however, the Chinese were seen as having a sense of 'fair play' by those who had dealings with them.

> For example, as borrowers, they will acknowledge that the lender is at more risk than they are, and will say 'I won't cheat you' and mean it. They are attracted to value-enhancing investors, especially those with expertise in accounting, marketing, and technical systems and will give them a better deal.[lxiii]

'If you have a good relationship (and that's a big "if"), the Chinese will not screw you to the extent that you lose everything. They look for good relations.'[lxiv]

- **In China, organizational decision-making was influenced by *guanxi*: '*Guanxi* works within organizations as well as between them'.[lxv] 'People want to have

[lvii] China, Hong Kong, Expatriate, General Manager, energy MNC
[lviii] Hong Kong Chinese, Banker, international bank
[lix] Hong Kong Chinese, CEO, Chinese consulting firm
[lx] China, Expatriate, Consultant, international management consultancy
[lxi] Mainland Chinese, Consultant, international management consultancy
[lxii] Mainland Chinese, General Manager, international business information hardware manufacturer
[lxiii] Hong Kong Chinese, Banker, international bank
[lxiv] Ibid.
[lxv] Hong Kong Chinese, CEO, Chinese consulting firm

personal closeness to the decision-maker, even if not equal. The motive is self-protection: if something happens and you have *guanxi* with them, they will be flexible.'[lxvi] Another effect of the culture was the centralization of all power: in the case of one Chinese family business, 'No one but the owner took any decisions – there was no delegation; he took the decision even on how much to spend on an office chair; he lacked trust in the ability and the loyalty of the staff.'[lxvii] A third aspect was the preference for personal rather than impersonal instruction and guidance: 'Daily execution on the ground is by guidance from managers rather than detailed procedural manuals.'[lxviii]

- **Our Chinese interviewees made no spontaneous references to the bases for employment or promotion, although when asked directly one interviewee suggested that the differences from the West were not marked. However, there was a broad preference for the interpersonal over the impersonal. Loyalty within a firm was not to the company or an individual's own career but to another individual. 'If s/he leaves, they become discontent, may try to leave themselves.'[lxix] Efficiency depended on the individual manager in China, even in a professional accountancy firm, in spite of the fact that the organization was staffed by professional accountants, who started from the same educational level, received the same training and used the organization's procedural manual just as they did in Los Angeles or London.

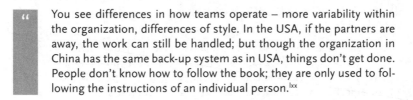

> You see differences in how teams operate – more variability within the organization, differences of style. In the USA, if the partners are away, the work can still be handled; but though the organization in China has the same back-up system as in USA, things don't get done. People don't know how to follow the book; they are only used to following the instructions of an individual person.[lxx]

- **Some interviewees thought entrepreneurialism in China was high naturally but suppressed by adverse conditions, especially the rules on migration and travel;[lxxi] for others, levels of entrepreneurship were high but this was again a function of stage of economic development.[lxxii] The entrepreneurs of South China were seen by some as rational risk takers: 'The founders of private companies in Southern China, started almost immediately the economy opened up by people with no more than primary school education, are not risk averse.'[lxxiii]

[lxvi] Mainland Chinese, Partner, international accounting firm
[lxvii] Mainland Chinese, General Manager, international business information hardware manufacturer
[lxviii] Mainland Chinese, Consultant, international management consultancy
[lxix] Mainland Chinese, Partner, international accounting firm
[lxx] Ibid.
[lxxi] China, Expatriate (British), General Manager, energy MNC
[lxxii] Hong Kong Chinese, CEO, Chinese consulting firm
[lxxiii] Mainland Chinese, Financial Controller, Chinese venture firm

In the view of another interviewee the Chinese are optimists.[lxxiv] On the other hand, the Western assumption that entrepreneurs are usually risk takers seemed not to be part of the Chinese business culture. Instead, explanations such as lack of alternatives were given: 'The opportunity costs for many are not high; they have little to lose and the upside is enormous',[lxxv] or an argument was made that many entrepreneurs were protected from risk: 'Some [entrepreneurs] are children of party cadres, having protection against real risk.'[lxxvi]

- **Two Chinese interviewees (out of 20) thought the differences among different types of Chinese business made it wrong to think in terms of an overall business culture. Instead, one interviewee considered, 'There are three kinds of businesses on mainland China, with different cultures: these are SOEs, high-tech start-ups and more traditional private businesses.' To another, the significant breakdown was between 'SOEs, those that have been privatized, private local Chinese companies, private overseas Chinese companies and private foreign companies. All of these have different characteristics in business operation, staff and internal culture.'[lxxvii] These typologies differed from those in most published accounts by Western observers, where the distinction drawn is between SOEs, TVEs and hybrid firms. (TVEs, town-and-village enterprises, are collectively owned, with community members being the owners. These collective owners do not, however, have shares in a formal sense and are permitted to participate in the TVE on the basis of their residency, a right that is mandated by the community government. Hybrid firms include Sino-foreign joint ventures, Sino-Sino joint ventures and partnerships between state, collective, and private ownership forms.)[1] Even when specifically asked about them, respondents were not familiar with these categories. The hybrid firms were seen as a minor category.

The perceived differences among the three types of businesses that were recognized (SOEs, high-technology start-ups and more traditional private businesses) were these:

1. SOEs had a 'communist culture', even when they were listed. They were strongly influenced by government. Their CEOs were government officers. As noted above, there were 'agency costs'. Some of the consequences of this mindset were perceived as the following:
   - Everything went up to the boss for approval. This led to delays.
   - They would make unrealistic promises to keep the boss happy – they would promise that software would be up and running in three months when it

---

[lxxiv] Hong Kong Chinese, CEO, Chinese consulting firm
[lxxv] Ibid.
[lxxvi] Ibid.
[lxxvii] Mainland Chinese, Sales and Marketing, Chinese consumer manufacturing company

must take six. *'What happens when they don't have it up and running in 3 months?'* 'But that's not now.'

- A Chief Financial Officer (CFO), for instance, would commission millions of yuans worth of software but specify it badly so three years later it would fail. That did not matter to him, though, because by then the CFO had moved on. In the meantime he gained prestige from having set up a big project.
- There were multiple layers of holding companies below the government. No one knew who had responsibility.

2. Private companies, of which the main examples were in Southern China, were predominantly in low-technology industries where they competed on price and sold through other companies' brands, both Chinese and international. (Some of these, such as the often-cited village which manufactured 80 per cent of the buttons in the world market, were known formally as TVEs or 'Town and Village Enterprises' but, as noted above, the term was not used by any interviewee nor readily understood when used by the interviewer.)

3. Start-ups were built round a 'new' idea; the founders got support from a venture capitalist and were 'globally more efficient', although averse to forward planning; they were flexible, well-educated, often returnees from the USA, particularly Silicon Valley. Internet start-up founders were often single, educated and successful. Applicants to one respondent's venture capital company, which specialized in technology, often had long experience in the area: 'Semi-conductor applicants will be 40 plus, internet applicants 30 plus.'[lxxviii]

Hong Kong special administrative region

Although Hong Kong has not been a separate country since it was returned to China in 1997 when Britain's lease on it ended, its history was so different from that of the rest of the country that in general culture and, especially, in business culture, significant differences were to be expected and some were, in fact, identified. 'Integration is happening: both "sides"are trying to copy the other's best practice; but it is a slow process.'[lxxix]

- 'Business efficiency [in Hong Kong] is as high as anywhere in the world. It is a very fast moving world in a rapidly changing environment.'[lxxx] 'Things that are impossible in other parts of China are possible in Hong Kong.'[lxxxi] A similar point was made by a business entrepreneur who compared Hong Kong with

---

[lxxviii] Mainland Chinese, Financial Controller, Chinese venture firm
[lxxix] Hong Kong, Finance and Accounting, financial services
[lxxx] Ibid.
[lxxxi] Ibid.

Singapore: 'You can get more done in two days in Hong Kong than in a month in Singapore [specifically in terms of raising money and doing deals]; company valuations in Hong Kong are 20 times earnings, in Singapore they are three times.'[lxxxii] A utility, China Light and Power (CLP), was first described in terms of efficiency: 'CLP is a forward-looking company. It works for efficiency enhancement.'[lxxxiii]

Individual employees in Hong Kong, as well as businesses, were said to pride themselves on their efficiency and hard work. 'Hong Kong Chinese are more efficient than mainland Chinese – more demanding on themselves, less reliant on their family background. This comparison is based on the top tier PRC students.'[lxxxiv] 'Hong Kong people "treasure efficiency". They have a "can do" spirit.'[lxxxv] 'People work long hours and work hard to get the job done. This is in contrast to Japan, where they do long hours but don't necessarily work hard. They [Hong Kong people] have a strong work ethic. They are adaptable, too – it's in the DNA'.[lxxxvi] There was a negative side: 'There is a lot of within-company competition and fighting at an individual level.'[lxxxvii]

- Another, possibly linked, aspect of Hong Kong business was that the city was a centre where people were 'conscious of being a link between mainland China and the rest of the world.'[lxxxviii] One Hong Kong interviewee's entire business was

> bridging between partners – foreign companies from the USA or Europe – and mainland Chinese, which in itself shows that there are cultural differences that need to be bridged. The partners often disagree on small things. Then, because they are suspicious of one another, things can quickly go from bad to worse.[lxxxix]

An American woman entrepreneur based in Hong Kong said

> Hong Kong is a hub; it's the best place in Asia to find merchandise suppliers; the people here are very good at doing trade – they have local contacts in China. You can do on-the-ground research in China, or use the internet or go to trade shows, but it is hard to find out which are any good; the best way to find suppliers of the right quality

---

lxxxii Singapore, Indian, Entrepreneur, internet-based business service
lxxxiii Hong Kong, Public Affairs Manager, Hong Kong utility company
lxxxiv Hong Kong, Finance and Accounting, financial services
lxxxv Hong Kong, Public Affairs Manager, Hong Kong utility company
lxxxvi Hong Kong, Finance and Accounting, financial services
lxxxvii Ibid.
lxxxviii Ibid.
lxxxix Hong Kong Chinese, CEO, Chinese consulting firm

and reliability and flexibility is through middlemen in Hong Kong; it's better here in Hong Kong.[xc]

This focus on China was reflected in the fact that in half of the interviews done in Hong Kong, the interviewees chose to talk about mainland China rather than Hong Kong itself.

- In Hong Kong, the business benefits of being, by Asian standards, a low-corruption society were emphasized, as they were in Singapore. 'Hong Kong's turnover in listings [share volumes traded as a result of companies listing there] is above Shanghai's. Companies are attracted to clear rules and fair regulators.'[xci] 'Hong Kong is Westernized in many ways. The legal system, the civil service and the police are all straight.'[xcii] One ethnic Chinese interviewee was eager to explain how corruption control came about:

It was only quite recent, since 1972 or 1973; I attribute the change to press freedom and one determined British Governor, who set up a system of investigation using outsiders – British were brought out – and started by tackling the most senior civil servants. It helps that Hong Kong civil servants are well paid, though that is not in itself enough.[xciii]

Another interviewee, though, thought it was an attribute of the society: 'HK people are fair.'[xciv]

- **Hong Kong businesses shared the familism of other Asian businesses.

Hong Kong family businesses are marked by big families, networks, similar controlling styles. Compared to MNCs, they don't give their people discretion or leeway; they are not multicultural but dominated by ethnic Chinese; as a result companies backed by Chinese capital are less efficient; it is an organizational culture issue.[xcv]

'In Hong Kong family businesses, even when they are listed businesses, the main control remains with family members. It shows in close monitoring of all processes and subordinates; delegation is not easy. The younger generation do delegate – professionalization is occurring.'[xcvi]

Table 2.1 summarizes these findings on Chinese business culture.

[xc] China, Expatriate, entrepreneur
[xci] Hong Kong, Finance and Accounting, financial services
[xcii] China, Expatriate, General Manager, energy MNC
[xciii] Hong Kong Chinese, CEO, Chinese consulting firm
[xciv] Hong Kong, Public Affairs Manager, Hong Kong utility company
[xcv] Hong Kong, Finance and Accounting, financial services
[xcvi] Ibid.

Table 2.1 **A summary of the present study's findings on the elements of Chinese business culture**

Elements of Chinese business culture	Perceived characteristics
Personalism in business control and decision-making	High – *guanxi* operates within organizations
Personalism in B2B	B2B depends on personal networks, *guanxi*
Status acknowledged by deference	High deference to superiors
Hierarchy	High – hierarchy very important
Governance	Weak
Corruption	Official corruption endemic
Attitudes to risk	Some gamblers; others rational risk-handlers
Innovation and creativity	Low (but fast copiers)
Business relations with government	Government not dominant except in SOEs, not monolithic
Business strategy	An aversion to forward planning and preference for trial and error
Approach to negotiating	Holistic, rational, personal
Personalism in employment and workrelations	*Mixed, but China not a meritocracy*
Personalism in business control and decision-making	*High*
Entrepreneurialism	*High but restricted*
Different types of businesses have different cultures	*SOEs – 'communist culture'; low-tech private businesses; efficient high-tech businesses*
Distinctive elements of Hong Kong's business culture	**Perceived Characteristics**
Governance	Strong
Corruption	Low
Employee motivations and behaviour	Highly efficient
Special features	Bridge between China and the rest of the world
Personalism in business control and decision-making	*High but changing with incoming professionalization*
Personalism in employment and work relations	*HKSAR meritocratic except in the SME sector where familism prevails*
Innovation and creativity	*Low (but highly efficient)*
Change	*The people cope well with change*

India

The predominance of family ownership and control was what most distinguished Indian business according to our research, and it brought consequences for governance and professionalism. Corruption flowed from both familism and the role of government. India's unique social culture influenced some work attitudes and employment relations.

- Indian business was repeatedly described by our interviewees as family business. This applied even to MNCs. 'The most important point', as one Indian interviewee put it, 'is that Indian business is family business. 90 per cent are. We have almost no corporate corporations – corporations owned by institutional investors. All our businesses have faces'.[xcvii] '70 per cent of Indian business is family-owned.'[xcviii] 'The strongest influence on India's business culture is the family.'[xcix]

> They [the founding family] still hold on to the purse strings, which is understandable because it is their money. Even in listed companies they will have 70 to 80 per cent of the shares. Unlike in Australia and other European countries, for instance, where at least 25 per cent must be in public hands in many cases in India it is only 8 to 10 per cent. So public listing does not necessarily change the style of doing business.[c]

Family ownership could restrict business ambitions. As one of our interviewees who came from a family business explained, 'We are not hyper-competitive. We've done fairly well even so. With fewer than ten shareholders there is not the pressure to expand.'[ci] Another interviewee, accounting for the business not expanding in India outside the State where it was founded, said, 'Because we were only two brothers, we could not manage everything.'[cii]

Many respondents considered that family ownership had undermined professionalism in the past but that that was changing: 'The private businesses have a focus on control. The majority are family owned or controlled. The family is in the driver's seat, even within joint ventures. They went through a rough phase – not wanting outside influence.'[ciii] 'It [family ownership] also leads to them employing people they feel comfortable with rather than on merit. This started to impact performance once Indian business was less insulated from the global economy. Many family businesses recognized this and started delinking ownership and management, hiring professionals.'[civ] The consequences

[xcvii] Indian, Chairman, family-owned business group, Indian MNC industrial goods manufacturer
[xcviii] Indian, Consultant, former CEO Indian subsidiary, US MNC industrial goods manufacturer
[xcix] Indian, independent business consultant and academic
[c] Ibid.
[ci] Indian, Senior General Manager and family member, family-owned business, consumer goods manufacturer
[cii] Indian, Chairman and family member, family-owned business group, Indian MNC industrial goods manufacturer
[ciii] Indian, Finance and General Management, Indian MNC heavy industry
[civ] Indian, Consultant, Former CEO Indian subsidiary, US MNC industrial goods manufacturer

of personalism in business management might be extreme. Siphoning off of money by the family accounted for some business failures.

'In family businesses there is no clear distinction made between business money and family money. It works both ways; in the early days the family will take no salary or expenses; later the most lavish personal expenditure, for example on weddings, will be paid for from business funds.'[cv] As this quotation from an interview suggests, Indian family businesses were often affected by serious governance problems. 'Decisions are not necessarily in the best interest of the business. For example, a family might incur debt to set up a business; later, business funds will be used to make an acquisition in their personal names – this allows them to pay off their debt. The legality, especially of the tax implications, is ignored.'[cvi] 'The tone in such businesses is set by family ownership – they still have to generate personal funds for the family.'[cvii] Employees colluded in this for two reasons. One was acceptance of the situation: 'There is a recognition that the family has a huge personal stake. "Appeasement" is not quite the word, but you could say the company executives "appease" the family. The top executives work to satisfy the family.'[cviii] The second reason for employees to collude was obligation: 'Relationships can over-ride business ethics or performance management. For instance a family-owned company might be a benign dictatorship, there could be paternalism, giving the employee's family support over weddings, health, housing; in return there could be "no questions asked" if doubtful practices are engaged in.'[cix]

On the other hand, our research found, awareness of governance issues was widespread in the Indian business community, including in family businesses. In some cases, standards, it was claimed, were always high:

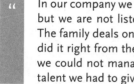

> In our company we follow all the rules of listing, Clause 49 and so on, but we are not listed. We separated ownership from management. The family deals only with corporate overall issues. Crucial areas. We did it right from the start partly because we were only two brothers, we could not manage everything. We also realized that to get good talent we had to give them the opportunity to rise in the business.[cx]

More generally, the opening up of the Indian market to global forces brought change: 'Liberalization is now 15 years old. Levels of corporate governance

[cv] Indian, independent consultant and academic
[cvi] Indian-American, CEO, international internet-based business services
[cvii] Ibid.
[cviii] Indian-American, CEO, international internet-based business services
[cix] Indian, Consultant, former CEO Indian subsidiary, US MNC industrial goods manufacturer
[cx] Indian, Chairman, family-owned business group, Indian MNC industrial goods manufacturer

have risen steadily during that period. There is substantial transparency and compliance now.[cxi]

- Manager–subordinate relations within family businesses were described as 'master–servant' in nature.

> In family businesses this applies even to the very top managers. Indian companies are still run like a family fiefdom. An employee's time is never his own. A friend of mine was Chief Operating Officer (COO) of a very large Indian MNC. The Chief Executive Officer (CEO) would ring him up on Saturday to go to watch cricket with him. There was no question of saying 'No'.[cxii]

'15 years ago, no subordinate would leave the office until the boss did. This is changing, but quite slowly.'[cxiii] 'Indian bosses are autocratic and Indian subordinates are subservient.'[cxiv] 'I have trouble stopping my excellent secretary from standing all the time in my presence.'[cxv] 'The usual managerial climate is Theory X.'[cxvi] (Theory X assumes that workers have no intrinsic work motivations and must be provided with extrinsic rewards or punishments to work well. Theory Y assumes the opposite.)

> There will be very little opposition to a senior manager's point of view from his subordinates. There is a lot of deference. You can see it in the body language. There might be some discussion if the manager is only one rung up but if he is two rungs up there will be none.[cxvii]

One effect of this high power distance was to prevent timeliness in decision-making.

> Critical decisions do not get taken. There is an expression: 'Taking the boss's permission twice'. For instance, the owner announces that they will give a 30 per cent bonus. The MD (Managing Director) does not query it [but he also does not act on it]. He goes away and works out the cost implications. Then he brings those back to the boss and asks his permission again. But if it goes wrong and the decision turns out to be a bad one, the MD is still in the firing line.[cxviii]

[cxi] Indian, Senior General Manager and family member, family-owned business, consumer goods manufacturer

[cxii] Indian, Senior Consultant, Indian business services (banking operations and technology)

[cxiii] Indian, Senior Manager, private Indian bank

[cxiv] Indian, Senior Consultant, business services (banking operations and technology)

[cxv] Indian, Economist, former Entrepreneur, senior academic

[cxvi] Indian, Product Manager, Indian business services (IT management)

[cxvii] Indian-American, CEO, international internet-based business services

[cxviii] Ibid.

50 2

INTRODUCTION · **THE BUSINESS CULTURES OF FIVE ASIAN COUNTRIES** · ANALYSING ASIAN BUSINESS CULTURES · OWNERSHIP, FINANCING AND GOVERNANCE · ORGANIZATION AND MANAGEMENT · BUSINESS STRATEGY ·

- Indian family businesses, like elsewhere, had a succession problem, but they also had a tendency to split: 'Indian family businesses have a problem of keeping the group intact after the third generation. Usually when they split momentum is lost, there is no longer a critical mass. Often the cause is ego or hubris – they believe themselves better than their brother(s).'[cxix]

- Although one respondent claimed that nearly all recruitment in India was merit-based,[cxx] a more common view was that management in Indian companies was 'still very personalized'.[cxxi] 'The number of companies (outside IT) where an individual employee can succeed independently can be counted on one hand. Most graduates will apply to a company where their father or another relative has connections.'[cxxii] Equally, in family businesses, 'Performance evaluation and rewards are driven by the personality of the top man. Which of three candidates obtain a scholarship to Harvard depends on his choice.'[cxxiii]

- Employees in India expected that a wide range of their needs and wants would be met by the company and most companies accepted this and operated accordingly. 'People tend to be soft.'[cxxiv]

> " There is a recognition that businesses have to deal not only with people's socio-economic situations but also with their habits [and in these there are regional variations of emphasis within India]. For example, in Chennai, lunchtime is sacrosanct. We respect that. In Bengal, the family's health is all-important. We have to recognize that if there is a clash between the personal and the commercial – a sick mother or a presentation – the personal has priority. If we were to ignore it, it could lead to labour unrest. People do expect that the company will take care of them – will pick up the tab. This will include taking care of their parents.[cxxv]

'Entitlements are high, including retirement benefits, subsidized housing, assured medical benefits, index-linked benefits, opportunities to go abroad, educational loans, promises of a job for the son.'[cxxvi] Meeting these employee expectations affected business costs. 'Many companies do not work in terms of salary or even package but C2C – cost to company. Salary in India is often as

---

cxix Indian, Consultant, former CEO Indian subsidiary, US MNC industrial goods manufacturer
cxx Indian, Human Resources Senior Manager, Indian industrial goods manufacturer
cxxi Ibid.
cxxii Indian, Marketing Consultant and Academic
cxxiii Ibid.
cxxiv Indian-American, CEO, international internet-based business services
cxxv Ibid.
cxxvi Indian, Marketing Consultant and Academic

little as 25 per cent of C2C.[cxxvii] However, except in SMEs (small and medium enterprises), the cost in management time was contained:

> " The high level of employee perks do not really represent a problem. You build it into your wage bill; it need not take management time because you outsource it; it has advantages of building solidarity and loyalty. Employees see it as an entitlement, an employer's obligation to train, develop their career, give fringe benefits such as soft housing loans. It is a function of doing business in a poor country, where the level of public goods is low. Competitive pressure for labour maintains it nowadays.[cxxviii]

Employers had also to cope with their employees' 'batch' mentality. A batch is a cohort of individuals who were in the same year in university or started employment in the formal sector at the same time. Each individual's expectations were that s/he would be treated at least as well as the other members of his or her batch well into their careers. This applied even after a change of employer. For instance, a manager reported receiving strong objections from an employee because, having joined the company from another, he discovered that someone who joined from the same company six months later was taken on at a higher salary. The complaint was widely regarded as legitimate because they were in the same batch.[cxxix]

Two factors could modify this 'soft' relationship with employees. One was the state of the employment market. In bad times, employees were forced to lower their expectations. 'Earlier employees were "nowhere". People would be threatened with firing overnight. This reflected the job market.'[cxxx] The other factor was a tendency for non-Indian organizations to chip away at what they saw as excessive employee privileges. One manager for a Western company with a subsidiary in India reported the following,

> " Last night I was coming home with Siram at midnight after work when he turned to me and said, 'You know this new guy we've employed. Well, he lives 35 kms from work and he's finding the journey difficult.' The point is, they expect us to sort it out. They'll take a job which involves moving their entire family a thousand miles and without even asking expect the company to make all the arrangements and pay for it. They don't even mention it. Where in the U.K. you wouldn't mention it because you know you'll have to deal with it without involving the company, in India they don't mention it because they take it for granted that the company will deal with it.[cxxxi]

---

cxxvii Indian, Business Development and Strategy, Indian engineering and construction
cxxviii Indian, CEO, Indian subsidiary of a French-owned MNC industrial goods manufacturer
cxxix India, Expatriate, CEO MNC, internet-based business services
cxxx Indian, Entrepreneur, Indian internet-based business services
cxxxi India, CEO MNC, internet-based business services

52 2

INTRODUCTION · **THE BUSINESS CULTURES OF FIVE ASIAN COUNTRIES** · ANALYSING ASIAN BUSINESS CULTURES · OWNERSHIP, FINANCING AND GOVERNANCE · ORGANIZATION AND MANAGEMENT · BUSINESS STRATEGY ·

At a later interview, this manager reported that he was in the process of nego-tiating a reduction in the number of days of holiday entitlement for employees in the Indian subsidiary.

In return, as it were, for 'soft' treatment by their employers, Indians were expected to be, and generally were, very hard-working people. 'The work-life balance does not exist. They will go the extra mile. It is true that there are many holidays and that Saturday working is going. However, private sector employees often work through holidays.'[cxxxii] 'People do not distinguish clearly between work and private life. They carry work home, their families adapt; on vacation they stay in touch with work; it is acceptable to be called back from vacation.'[cxxxiii]

 It is accepted that you will get work calls while you are on holiday – everything except your wedding and your father's funeral. A super-ior will call up for help with finding a file, and you don't mind. You think, 'He's seth' – boss. There is a limit but it goes well beyond that accepted in the West.[cxxxiv]

One interviewee accounted for this level of work commitment by saying that it originated in the competitiveness of Indian life. 'So many people are scram-bling for a living. It was enforced by the environment and somewhere along the way it became cultural.'[cxxxv] However, there were two qualifications: 'The regions differ from one another significantly in terms of work ethic',[cxxxvi] while in the large cities, 'Employee motives are to make money. There is a talent shortage and salaries are rocketing.'[cxxxvii]

One interviewee offered an explanation for the apparent contradiction of employees having high expectations of what their employer would do for them but also expecting to contribute beyond the normal in the West.

 In India, staff spend 50 per cent of their time at work. Therefore it is more important to them than in countries [he cited the USA] where they work less. The effect is a high work commitment and strong work ethic but also high expectations of how they will be treated.[cxxxviii]

- Corruption in the older companies was taken for granted in India. '15 per cent of the purchase value is the kick-back in stationery purchases for

---

[cxxxii] Indian, Entrepreneur, Indian internet-based business services
[cxxxiii] Ibid.
[cxxxiv] Indian, Lawyer, Deputy CEO, Indian educational not-for-profit
[cxxxv] Indian, Entrepreneur, Indian internet-based business services
[cxxxvi] Ibid.
[cxxxvii] Indian, Finance and General Management, Indian MNC heavy industry
[cxxxviii] Indian, Product Manager, Indian business services (IT management)

businesses.[cxxxix] 'All they (the founding families of large, often publicly listed, businesses) care about controlling is Purchasing and Finance. They take no interest in the other departments. The reason is obvious.'[cxl] 'One owner was only interested in the number of loaded vehicles entering the company's warehouses. That was because his cut came from a percentage – a kind of royalty – on each load.'[cxli]

> " The founders of the older companies…were particularly interested in Purchasing and Finance so the family could take money out. For example, the family would take out a massive loan for project finance; the equity stake was much smaller; project costs would be inflated to recover their input well before the project was completed. The banks found this difficult to combat: if they foreclosed, the [court] cases could go on for 15 or 20 years. The steel sector had a lot of these problems – businesses felt safe in defaulting on these loans; the banks would keep doing financial restructuring to keep them 'evergreen' to avoid writing them off as bad debts. The situation was only resolved by the expansion of the economy which enabled the projects to become earning assets.[cxlii]

Corruption in officialdom was equally or more pervasive. 'It's there. You build it into your budgets.'[cxliii] 'There is corruption everywhere. You still need licences for power, land, clearances. The only solution is to make it transparent, but that will only happen if you have a better supply-demand balance and our population pressures undermine that. There are also vested interests.'[cxliv] 'Official corruption is inescapable. For example I have recently been setting up a hospital, a charity, for which I needed 22 licences; for 21 of them I had to pay bribes to officials.'[cxlv] The growth of the large family businesses was attributed to their ability to practise corruption under the socialist regime: 'They knew how to press the right buttons in government.'[cxlvi]

There was a suggestion that the corruption was cultural: 'Givers are as responsible as takers for Indian corruption. The average Indian hates to queue, is always willing to pay a small bribe to get to the front, has no sense of the British type of "fair play".'[cxlvii] 'Bribery often comes mainly from people

cxxxix Ibid.

cxl Indian, Economist, former Entrepreneur, senior academic

cxli Indian, Business Development and Strategy, Indian engineering and construction

cxlii Indian, Finance and General Management, Indian MNC heavy industry

cxliii Indian, Senior General Manager and family member, Indian family business, consumer goods manufacturer

cxliv Indian, Chairman and family member, family-owned business group, Indian MNC industrial goods manufacturer

cxlv Indian, Senior Consultant, business services (banking operations and technology)

cxlvi Indian, Finance and General Management, Indian MNC heavy industry

cxlvii Indian, Senior Consultant, business services (banking operations and technology)

54 2

INTRODUCTION • THE BUSINESS CULTURES OF FIVE ASIAN COUNTRIES • ANALYSING ASIAN BUSINESS CULTURES • OWNERSHIP, FINANCING AND GOVERNANCE • ORGANIZATION AND MANAGEMENT • BUSINESS STRATEGY •

wanting to bend the rules and so offering rather than people demanding. It is called "speed money" because they want to speed things up.'[cxlviii]

One interviewee suggested that the trend in official corruption was favourable, as might be expected 17 years after the ending of the 'licence raj': 'It is easing. Corruption is less than it was.' There was also widespread agreement that the newer industries, such as business process outsourcing [BPO] and biotechnology, were immune: 'It [corruption] is not really there, because the Government has kept its hands off and imposed limited licensing. And they started with a zero tax regime. Also most of those in these industries are young Indians educated in the West, who won't go along with it.'[cxlix] On the other hand, the revenue departments continued to give trouble:

> The revenue departments of government interfere with business. They are oppressive. An example would be that an official will 'black-mail' a business over a cost item that could be either revenue expenditure [operating cost] or capital expenditure: unless they pay a bribe, he will force them to put it in the more disadvantageous category.[cl]

'Where it does exist, it is worse than in China, where a single pay-off clears it; in India it is every layer in the hierarchy; the sheer number of licences required is the nightmare'.[cli]

- Some widely accepted characteristics of India's business culture were attributed to its social culture or religious basis:

> An important part of the national business culture comes from the impact of Hinduism – the fact of no fixed ideology, that Hindus are not people of the book; it means they are flexible but there are no rules. Time is seen as cyclical, not as a linear progression. Thus there is no adhering to time commitments; people commit in hope rather than expectation or intention. This is a major problem. Indians themselves learn to adjust; for instance they won't anticipate that a delivery will come until it is actually there. It extends beyond just time commitments to, for example, contract violations: there is a lack of realism, a lot of wishful thinking.[clii]

> Delivery delays are here to stay in this country. It's our cultural orientation to the way we look at time. If an Indian has an appointment, he doesn't make any real effort to get there on time, nor does he call to say he's delayed. Instead, he reasons: 'She should know that the traffic is bad in the city.'[cliii]

cxlviii Indian, Finance and General Management, Indian MNC heavy industry
cxlix Indian, Entrepreneur, Indian internet-based business services
cl Indian, CEO, family-owned business, advertising
cli Indian, Entrepreneur, Indian internet-based business services
clii Indian, Economist, former Entrepreneur, senior academic
cliii Indian, Product Manager, Indian business services (IT management)

'Indians don't think through whether they can deliver. It is understood in business that you must build in two to three weeks extra for delivery on any contract. Our company used to differentiate themselves by delivering on time; now it is a little less distinctive.'[cliv]

Truthfulness too,

> means something different – not only will people avoid telling bad news, they do not see a promise as a binding commitment; contracts are entered into lightly with no real intention of performing – this is partly because they are unenforceable because of the huge delays in the Indian courts. People resort to violence or the threat of it to get what they are contractually entitled to – this applies particularly in real estate deals.[clv]

'When Indians are given an unrealistic deadline they accept out of courtesy – afraid the other person will be offended if they say "No". They let problems escalate out of fear of authority.'[clvi] 'Indians have a big problem in saying "No". They also don't "raise a red flag" when things start to go wrong. Then when the crisis arrives, they offer an excuse.'[clvii]

- Unique to India was a concern with the impact on business of social divisions based on a rural division of labour and reinforced by religion. The phenomenon was caste. 'In the private sector, caste dominates promotion – members of the owner's or founder's community get promoted ahead of others,' was one comment.[clviii] 'There are companies that there is no point in applying to if you are not a member of the right caste. For example, in the pharmaceutical industry, the Reddy company really only employs members of the Reddy caste,' was another.[clix] Others included the following: 'In smaller cities, caste is very important. For instance the Marwari community in Orissa acts together to preserve its dominance. The community provides financing for purchasing land linked to mineral wealth.'[clx]

> The caste system still has an influence. Though it was based on skills that are unrelated to those of today, there is a hangover, in parents thinking that there is only one thing that their children should be doing. If they are Brahmins, the child must be a professional – nothing arts-related or acting.[clxi]

[cliv] Indian, Entrepreneur, Indian internet-based business services
[clv] Indian, Economist, former Entrepreneur, senior academic
[clvi] Indian, Product Manager, Indian business services (IT management)
[clvii] Indian, Entrepreneur, Indian internet-based business services
[clviii] Indian, Economist, former Entrepreneur, senior academic
[clix] Indian, Administrative Assistant, Indian hotel business, qualified research chemist unable to obtain relevant work
[clx] Indian, Finance and General Management, Indian MNC heavy industry
[clxi] Indian, CEO, Indian educational not-for-profit

56 2

INTRODUCTION • THE BUSINESS CULTURES OF FIVE ASIAN COUNTRIES • ANALYSING ASIAN BUSINESS CULTURES • OWNERSHIP, FINANCING AND GOVERNANCE • ORGANIZATION AND MANAGEMENT • BUSINESS STRATEGY •

> Caste is losing its relevance but ironically, the reservation system, whereby 27 per cent of places at university and in public sector jobs are reserved for 'Dalits' [formerly outcastes] or scheduled tribes, is keeping it alive. It provokes a backlash. The recent threat to extend it to the private sector would have been a disaster – if we are to compete globally, we must appoint on merit.[clxii]

- Indian business culture was viewed as changing. The aspect of change most emphasized was professionalization of the management of family businesses. 'Now with the openness and competitiveness of the market they have had to professionalize. Before they made plenty of mistakes but if they had the licences and permits, they were ok; now there is no room for errors.'[clxiii]

Other aspects of change were caste, efficiency, criteria for success and adoption of Western ways. In fact the term 'caste' was rarely used, preference being given to 'community'. Caste (or community) was described as 'not really an issue in the big cities. The talent shortage means businesses are mainly meritocracies now'.[clxiv] 'India is changing – as tenure in jobs decreases, efficiency increases. A deadline orientation is coming in. Western-facing industries are changing fastest.'[clxv] 'In big business, performing in terms of delivering on time matters a lot. The value of time is prominent. This links across to market awareness, which in Mumbai is very high.'[clxvi]

> " Hopefully the Indian business culture is evolving, through the competitive pressure brought by freedom of entry, especially to foreigners. In some ways this creates new problems, for instance, with women getting in on the act. Gender discrimination and sexual harassment are serious. There is a shift from socialism: now the measure of success is turnover, where it used to be the number of employees.[clxvii]
>
> Indian owners are starting to use consultants and talk to bankers. It is only over the last five years and it is the impact of globalization. The Indian social culture is impinging less. The global business culture is starting to percolate into India, especially in Bombay. In the BPO industry, staff are not only trained to a neutral accent, but also to Western ways of approaching things. That's because of who their clients are. Also, though, as Indian companies acquire overseas companies, they have to staff them with locals, even at the top, so Indian headquarters staff have to learn to work with them. They need to learn. Of course, the top management of the subsidiary will have to adapt to Indian ways.[clxviii]

clxii Indian, Business Development and Strategy, Indian engineering and construction
clxiii Indian, Consultant, former CEO Indian subsidiary, US MNC industrial goods manufacturer
clxiv Indian, Finance and General Management, Indian MNC heavy industry
clxv Indian, Entrepreneur, Indian internet-based business services
clxvi Indian, Finance and General Management, Indian MNC heavy industry
clxvii Indian, Economist, Entrepreneur, senior academic
clxviii Indian-American, CEO, International internet-based business services

- **Entrepreneurialism was present in the business culture of India ('The private sector companies are driven by entrepreneurial instinct and talent'[clxix]), but until the liberalization of the economy in the 1990s, the degree of entrepreneurialism varied by class and region within the country:

> " Indians are entrepreneurial in the sense that the majority would like to own their own business. Less so in the South, where most career ambitions are to have a successful professional life. In the North, owning a trading business is a common career ambition, but they do it by incremental steps – branching out with support from their family. In East India, they work to live, instead of living to work. They enjoy culture, sport; they are more laid-back.[clxx]

In India, the middle classes were described as not aspiring to be entrepreneurs but to draw a salary. 'Most Indian business schools have no course on entrepreneurship.'[clxxi] While some middle-class Indians run businesses, these are usually small and not very profitable. 'To be middle class is to draw a pay packet weekly or monthly, rather than daily or hourly.'[2] 'Many who started new businesses came from money.'[clxxii]

Another view was that Indians are entrepreneurial 'but it was stifled by 50 years of socialist thinking'.[clxxiii] Liberalization in the 1990s led to a flowering of entrepreneurial energy:

> " Two sunrise industries sprang up. One was the IT industry. The other was infrastructure development. Once infrastructure development was privatized, the private sector poured billions of dollars into ports, power, airports, etc. These are mainly new entrants such as GMR or GVK, one-time SMEs whose owners raised huge amounts of money; the private airline industry is another example. These developments show that there is a lot of entrepreneurial spirit in India. Now, after several years of good growth, the young have enormous confidence (apart from those at subsistence level). The scale and size of what they are willing to undertake is very great. Take the steel industry. The government-owned steel company grew very slowly up to 3½ to 4 million tons of output; in three years one private company has grown to the same level and will expand to 12 million tons by 2010. This was unthinkable five years back. Indian companies are bidding for major infrastructure projects abroad – Istanbul's new airport is being built by an Indian company. India's entrepreneurs have confidence in their ability to get things done.[clxxiv]

[clxix] Indian, Finance and General Management, Indian MNC heavy industry
[clxx] Indian, Successful Entrepreneur, Indian internet-based business services
[clxxi] Ibid.
[clxxii] Ibid.
[clxxiii] Indian, Senior Consultant, business services (banking operations and technology)
[clxxiv] Indian, Human Resources, Senior Manager, Indian listed manufacturer

58   2

INTRODUCTION · **THE BUSINESS CULTURES OF FIVE ASIAN COUNTRIES** · ANALYSING ASIAN BUSINESS CULTURES · OWNERSHIP, FINANCING AND GOVERNANCE · ORGANIZATION AND MANAGEMENT · BUSINESS STRATEGY ·

'The entrepreneurial spirit of India has been set free by liberalization.'[clxxv]

Elements of India's social culture were mentioned as influences on entrepreneurialism: 'There has been a community element in entrepreneurialism in India – some have a business background: the Andhras in Andhra Pradesh, the Chettiars in Tamil Nadu, the Marwari in Maharashtra. However, this does not preclude people from other communities, and increasing numbers of communities are getting involved in business.'[clxxvi]

> A large number of people in India are not risk takers. There are certain pockets. Some communities – Chettiars, Syrian Christians, Reddys in the South, Banias and Marwaris from the North, Modis and Patels from Gujarat, Sindhis from the West. Perhaps 200 to 300 families. Indians are excellent traders, but many businesses do not expand beyond a small enterprise – perhaps four shops. Admittedly the lack of infrastructure creates problems for small businesses wanting to scale up. It is very difficult to run a business in, say, both Chennai and Mumbai. Another thing is – not fatalism, but a sense derived from religion (both Hindu and Moslem) that 'this is what is given'.[clxxvii]

When asked about risk taking, our interviewees in India were ambivalent: 'It varies.'[clxxviii] '60 to 70 per cent of people are risk avoiders. It is an individual, not a cultural thing.'[clxxix] 'People are not either risk averse or risk takers.'[clxxx]

- **There was also some ambivalence in the views we found in India on the innovativeness and creativity of its business culture. The most positive statement was that India 'is chaotic but its chaos is orderly and creative'.[clxxxi] A more specific judgement was, 'Indian business does not display really original ideas. In the pharmaceutical industry, for instance, they specialize in bulk drugs, not new drugs; in IT, Infosys is very successful but does not have the originality of Microsoft. Indians are good at problem-solving rather than invention.' Whether this lack of innovation was intrinsic to the Indian business culture, however, was unclear even to the speaker:

> It may be due to the environment, though. Indians do much better in the US context. In India, a lot of energy goes into managing the system, leaving little [energy] for real creativity. For instance, in academic life, in engineering, even the leading Indian institutions do not have top-class facilities. ... People develop their problem-solving skills

[clxxv] Indian, consultant
[clxxvi] Indian, Human Resources, Senior Manager, Indian listed manufacturer
[clxxvii] Indian, consultant
[clxxviii] Indian-American, CEO, International internet-based business services
[clxxix] Indian, Economist, Former Entrepreneur, senior academic
[clxxx] Indian, CEO, Indian educational not-for-profit
[clxxxi] Indian, CEO, Indian subsidiary of a French-owned MNC industrial goods manufacturer

by finding ways to beat the system. It helps make them adaptable. On the negative side, though, too much energy goes into it, thus reducing creativity.[clxxxii]

- **In India, we were told, 'Corporate governance is always an issue although it is starting to change. In the 1990s, the stockmarket was marked by improper practices such as firms doing IPOs [initial public offerings] without any accountability.'[clxxxiii]

> " Until the very recent past it [governance] was just lip service. This still applies in family businesses. Now there is a serious attempt by the authorities to make it work – regulations, Clause 49, audit committees etc. Companies must have 50 per cent non-executive directors. The Managing Director and the Director of Finance must certify that accounts are a true record. But many non-executive directors are 'friends'.[clxxxiv]

- **In India, interpersonal relations between organizations were important:

> " A lot depends on relationships...there is no sitting at home to do business deals – face-to-face means a lot – we socialize over business. If you go back a long way, you have a basis for doing business. If someone you knew in one organization moves to another organization, you have the basis for doing business with the second organization but you might have lost the basis for doing business with the first organization.[clxxxv]

One consequence of personalism was an absence of impersonal criteria for business decisions:

> " Indians assume that things are decided on a discretionary basis, which may or may not be favourable to themselves, not on the basis of universally applicable laws or systems. For instance the granting of a loan by a bank is decided without any standard process but on the basis of personal judgement, not of the individual but of an introduction from someone, contacts or bribery.[clxxxvi]

Subcontracting, which was an established practice in India earlier than in the West, was often not done on strictly business criteria. 'A business might set up a

---

clxxxii Indian, Finance and General Management, Indian MNC heavy industry
clxxxiii Indian, Finance and General Management, Indian MNC heavy industry
clxxxiv Indian-American, CEO, International internet-based business services
clxxxv Indian, Senior Manager, private Indian Bank
clxxxvi Indian, Economist, Former Entrepreneur, senior academic

60   2

INTRODUCTION · THE BUSINESS CULTURES OF FIVE ASIAN COUNTRIES · ANALYSING ASIAN BUSINESS CULTURES · OWNERSHIP, FINANCING AND GOVERNANCE · ORGANIZATION AND MANAGEMENT · BUSINESS STRATEGY ·

new factory and subcontract its operation to a cousin's business.[clxxxvii] However, there was a difference of emphasis from a *guanxi* system: 'With Indians, the relationship builds over time (but unlike in Far East, is not a pre-requisite); with Americans, it's the same at the end as the beginning – the relationship quotient is low.'[clxxxviii]

Thus, in India's business culture, good personal relations were not seen as essential before business took place but they smoothed the process and they facilitated later operations.

- **On the subject of government-business relations, our interviewees emphasized the capacity of Indian state governments to either encourage development or impede it by, for instance, anti-business policies in communist-run states or social engineering policies such as job reservation. 'This has got worse as the government's positive discrimination in favour of lower-caste people has increased.'[clxxxix] 'In Bengal and Kerala, the communist governments have driven out business so their growth rates are low relatively. They are now trying to catch up. Similarly, Tamil Nadu's economy suffered because the DMK [the governing party] drove out the Brahmins.'[cxc]

- **Two Indian interviewees suggested that Indian businesses and their cultures, should be subdivided, in one case into 'modern' versus 'traditional' companies, in the other into public sector companies, older private sector companies, which still dominated the economy, and new technological start-ups.

> " Large public sector companies have a different culture from large private sector companies. The public sector companies are driven by government policy – high level government directives. The decision-making is not primarily commercial. The spectrum of employees involved in, for instance, large public sector projects are the senior crowd who have worked in the company for 20 or 25 years. To them, the organization is the be-all and end-all. Their vision is narrow – they have had no opportunity to see outside. In the public sector, career growth cannot be accelerated; they have three times the number of employees they need to do the work. They also have a customary way of doing things. There is no room for creativity. In contrast, the private sector companies are driven by entrepreneurial instinct and talent. The private sector companies encourage originality. This goes beyond the technology sector. For instance, people who bring growth rise fast within the ICICI bank.[cxci]

[clxxxvii] Indian, consultant and academic.
[clxxxviii] Indian, Successful Entrepreneur, Indian internet-based business services
[clxxxix] Indian, Administrative Assistant, qualified research chemist unable to obtain qualification-related employment
[cxc] Indian, Business Development and Strategy, Indian engineering and construction company
[cxci] Indian, Economist, Former Entrepreneur, senior academic

The culture of the very small minority of businesses in the high-technology field was generally different.

> The most noticeable difference [in comparison with working for a Danish, US and UK companies in their respective countries] is that in Indian high-technology companies you are given a chance to contribute – to run everything. In other countries if you are young, it is seen as too risky to let you do that. Here they are willing to risk it based on your profile – your education and experience.[cxcii]
>
> Another difference is that here a big-name company will give a small start-up a chance. Reputation does not play a key role. This is because the market is very young – only the leaders are making moves. They will try you on a small basis, because they are early adopters of new technology, which is risky anyway, so they won't mind a start-up. They don't consider that past performance tells you much about how things will go this time. Also they know they have more power with a start-up, who will be more dependent on them, and they are willing to use it to get the best deal or the best service.[cxciii]

'Hi-tec staff welcome innovation. They respond to solid reasoning. They can be motivated by situations; in our start-up, they suffered delayed salary, no bonuses; openness with them kept them working. They are often committed to self-development and self-improvement.'[cxciv]

- **Our research found that relationships at the work place in India were informal; managers shared their experiences with subordinates and peers. This informality could be quite extended. One expatriate manager in India commented that if there was any email correspondence from applicants for a position – for instance, with Human Relations (HR) over salary details – Indians used text language in their emails. 'So "you" becomes "u". It's all very informal. And that, of course, gets HR wondering whether they are going to be able to write in the house style when they're on the job.'[cxcv]

Indians in general could feel uncomfortable contradicting another person. Although they are 'generous with advice',[cxcvi] they 'have a big problem in saying "No" '.[cxcvii] Therefore, if Indians perceived a bias or particular preferred response, they would provide it to avoid the discomfort of disagreeing; often, the person

---

cxcii Indian, Product Manager, Indian business services (IT management)
cxciii Ibid.
cxciv Ibid.
cxcv India, Expatriate (British), CEO MNC, internet-based business services
cxcvi Indian, Economist, Former Entrepreneur, senior academic
cxcvii Indian, Successful Entrepreneur, Indian internet-based business services

62 2

INTRODUCTION · THE BUSINESS CULTURES OF FIVE ASIAN COUNTRIES · ANALYSING ASIAN BUSINESS CULTURES · OWNERSHIP, FINANCING AND GOVERNANCE · ORGANIZATION AND MANAGEMENT · BUSINESS STRATEGY ·

who disagreed with another would begin a response in very positive terms and gently disagree in a subtle way that was meant to avoid offence. When combined with Indians' deference towards superiors, this trait could lead to their accepting entirely unrealistic orders: 'Negotiating realistic resources upfront is impertinence.'[cxcviii] On the other hand, at least in the high-technology sector, interpersonal communication could be very direct. In the words of a British expatriate manager,

> They will overtly criticize others. Where I would say, 'He seems to be struggling a bit,' if I said anything, they will say, 'He's no good.' Complaints and requests are made without any attempt to soften them. I get emails from very junior staff saying, 'Dear Brian, The food's no good.' Requests are usually in the form 'Do the needful,' without any attempt to soften such as 'please'.[cxcix]

- **In India, typical comments on the approach to negotiating were as follows:

> Indians love negotiating, bargaining. Not so much in Mumbai, where time is more valuable. But in the smaller towns, it is their sport, their pastime. Calcutta is the most extreme for this. There is no 'getting to yes'. They aim to win, even in procuring services, where it is obvious that the provider will be demotivated if you have struck too hard a bargain.[cc]

Indians 'look for opportunities to bargain in any situation'. For example, their approach was contrasted with that of the Americans and Europeans when they have a complaint with a supplier.

> The US market is most patient, then Europe, India least. They will go straight to the CEO to raise their concerns and will immediately stop payment. In comparison, in Germany, the client would keep close contact with the support engineers, then move up the hierarchy to the project manager; when Indians react, it's noise. They drag up every issue that's arisen, even if it was solved months ago – they are negotiating, looking for something more than just getting the problem put right.[cci]

Table 2.2 summarizes these findings on Indian business culture.

cxcviii Indian, Senior Consultant, business services (banking operations and technology)
cxcix India, Expatriate (British), CEO MNC, internet-based business services
cc Indian, Successful Entrepreneur, Indian internet-based business services
cci Indian, Product Manager, Indian business services (IT management)

Table 2.2 **A summary of the present study's findings on the elements of Indian business culture**

Elements of Indian business culture	Perceived characteristics
Personalism in business control and decision-making	High – widespread familism and some casteism; Business goals often include raising personal funds for the founding family; Basis for decision-making top down; Restricted within-company information flows
Personalism in employment and work relations	High familism and some casteism; 'Soft culture'; High expectations on both sides
Status acknowledged by deference	Extremely high deference to owners; high to superiors
Hierarchy	High; boss–subordinate relations 'master–servant'
Corruption	Widespread except in high-technology businesses
Business norms	Impact of Hinduism: time not linear; delays routine
Work communication issues	Aversion to giving bad news
Change	Globalization reducing impact of traditional culture
Governance	*Weak but being seriously addressed by government*
Personalism in B2B	*Personal relationships are important but not a guanxi system*
Business relations with government	*State governments more relevant than central government*
Different types of businesses have different cultures	*Public sector businesses 'not primarily commercial'; older private businesses have family business characteristics; high-tech businesses 'modern'*
Negotiation style and approach	*Hard bargaining; the aim is to beat the other side*
Entrepreneurialism	*Medium – occurs in certain communities; also now sometimes in young not from business backgrounds*
Attitudes to risk	*An individual, not a cultural, matter*
Innovation and creativity	*Low (but good problem-solvers)*

Japan

The aspect of the business culture of Japan most emphasized by our respondents was the internal organization and decision-making processes of companies. Another major theme was change to the traditional structures and market relationships of companies, though opinions differed on how effective, extensive and long-lasting this change would be.

- Japanese employees perceived their organizations as like families or communities. Lifetime employment was being reduced but was still fairly common. 'When a graduate joins a company, it is like joining a family. As in a family, you don't want to effect radical change and you don't seek quick promotion or large salary hikes.'[ccii]

> " In a Japanese company, everybody knows everyone else and what everyone is doing. When I started work for M. Company, ten years ago, I slept in an M. Company dormitory with other employees and we talked business into the small hours. We would also go away for weekends together and talk business with older people and younger people. We played tennis and golf together too.[cciii]

'Those who enter the workplace at the same time are strongly tied – they are called "doki".'[cciv] 'Many people don't make a clear distinction between work and private life. There is an expression, "Nomunication". Nomu means drink.'[ccv]

> " Japanese organizations are community-style, not functional-style. In the big Japanese companies, even the retired people are still involved. We hold events for them, keep in touch with them; occasionally, when an issue arises, we might say, 'Mr. A. (who is retired) knew all about that.' And we go to his house and talk to him. Also, when someone has moved on from one part of the company, they go back to the events of that part. For instance, in two days' time, the factory where I was manager 20 years ago will have a gathering for 2300 employees; I will be there.'[ccvi]

- There was an emotional element to the Japanese management culture, which made adjusting to economic realities difficult:

> " Following the bursting of the bubble, with companies in trouble, life time employment (LTE) had to go; wages were sticky, so the only way was to

---

[ccii] Japanese, Finance and Accounting, education
[cciii] Japanese, Audit, venture capital
[cciv] Japanese, Human Resources, business services
[ccv] Japanese, Audit, venture capital
[ccvi] Japanese, Operations Management, Japanese consumer durables manufacturer

fire people. In a way this was normalization – life time employment really only came in during the 1950s, although it started in the Meiji era [19th century]; however, in people's minds it was strongly associated with Japan's growth and success; ending it was especially traumatic.[ccvii]

Change had occurred, because it had to:

HR used to be a key vehicle for corporate policy. It had the right to deploy people around the company – it would consult with line managers but ultimately had the power. This followed from the LTE policy which makes human resources the most important company asset. When the bubble burst, LTE ended, HR lost its power. There is some hire and fire now.[ccviii]

Despite such changes, however, the culture itself – the values – survived: 'In Japan, the culture underlying seniority and LTE (lifetime employment) still applies. The union system is still within-enterprise.'[ccix] 'The impact of enterprise unions is that strikes are rare and the approach is cooperative; the union brings employee complaints to management's attention, but also convinces employees not to do things that would damage "our company". In return, management provides reasonable levels of disclosure to unions.'[ccx]

- Like families, our interviewees reported, Japanese companies did not allocate individuals to closely defined roles: 'Japanese companies do not have a role culture. Responsibilities are not allocated out to roles or positions. There is a lot of overlap.'[ccxi]

When I worked for an American company it was split up by functions – it was a silo-based company. In a way that reflected professionalism: 'I'm a finance professional and I leave marketing to the marketing professionals.' But in Japanese companies, people are not so specialized. It does have some drawbacks. You can get duplication. And because there is so much to learn, it takes up to two years before a new employee becomes effective.[ccxii]

When Japanese companies, under the pressure of globalization, tried to introduce divisionalization, there was some resistance based on Japanese employee

---

[ccvii] Japanese, Finance and Accounting, banking
[ccviii] Ibid.
[ccix] Japanese, Operations Management, Japanese consumer durables manufacturer
[ccx] Ibid.
[ccxi] Japanese, Finance and Accounting, education
[ccxii] Japanese, Audit, venture capital

attitudes. For instance, when the Japanese subsidiary of a large MNC was being asked to divisionalize, a problem arose: 'This will be demotivating for the existing workforce, for whom it is important to be working for the company, not a division, and it will make hiring difficult for the same reason.'[ccxiii] There was a suggestion that Western management systems might conflict with Japanese business culture.

> I disagree with this approach. It is still very difficult to fire people. We have to keep the 'entire person' in our enterprise. We need to admire our employees, encourage them, not tell them they have failed to reach their target. People have a negative response to criticism – they become demotivated; we would have to move them to another place, they become isolated, their output goes down. Our Japanese employees are vulnerable-minded; criticism is too direct a way for them.[ccxiv]

- Deference was very marked in Japanese organizations:

> You can watch it in a restaurant in the evening. Six or seven salary men will be dining at a round table. Within a minute, you can tell who is the senior guy by the way all the others are silent if he even starts to open his mouth and the way they laugh at his jokes. They younger ones, the rookies, will never speak at all unless spoken to. If the younger shows enough respect, the older will say, 'Let us speak frankly,' but the younger still knows he mustn't. No first names are ever used at work; occasionally the rookies will be given a nickname. In this so-called socialising after work, now that I am getting older, senior, I no longer have to keep offering food and drink to seniors.[ccxv]

'In terms of respect within traditional Japanese companies, even a one year age gap is very significant. The younger person will call the older by the honorific suffix "-san", the older will use the familiar "-kun".'[ccxvi] Some believe this to be changing, 'Now respect has to be earned',[ccxvii] but in the older companies, the old culture survives, as a previous paragraph noted.

Japanese deference, however, need not imply that the senior has any real power. As one interviewee explained,

> The CEO – the top guy – is a balancer. He is not expected to show vision or decide strategy; he should suppress his own ideas and accept all opinions; what they do is what the consensus says they

ccxiii Japanese, Human Resource Management, business services
ccxiv Japanese, Operations Management, Japanese consumer durables manufacturer
ccxv Japanese, Strategic Management, business services
ccxvi Japanese, Human Resource Management, business services
ccxvii Japanese, Finance and Accounting, banking

> should do. On the other hand, the CEO takes responsibility. In times of trouble, even if no decision of his [*sic*] brought about the trouble – there were no decisions which corresponded to his value system – he is a representative guy, so he resigns.[ccxviii]

When the CEO did want to take action, he might not be supported.

> When in 2007 the CEO of a Japanese camera manufacturer wanted to bring in shared service Head Office departments, I was brought in as a consultant. I found from interviews with key people – Vice-Presidents – that there was a complete lack of positive opinion but they would prefer no change. They added, 'In this company we don't have to listen to what the CEO says.'[ccxix]

Another interviewee put the point more succinctly: 'Japanese CEOs tune all the engines; in a big Western company like GE [General Electric] the CEO *is* the engine.'[ccxx] Illogical though this dis-equation of status and power may seem to a Westerner, there is a logic: high status compensates for having responsibility without power. When the interviewer asked, *'Why would anyone want to get to the top of a company?'* the answer was

> Good question, especially as their pay is only a little above middle managers. And a new law means that for the first time directors can be held liable for corporate debts and so bankrupted; this has created a market for directors' insurance. But they are respected, honoured even, while they are in post.[ccxxi]

Decision-making was bottom up.

> It is known as the *ringi* system. A junior writes a proposal with persuasive arguments and passes it to his peers and boss, who stamps his approval and passes it on to his peers and boss until it reaches the CEO. The CEO gives the final stamp of approval and in doing so is influenced mainly by which middle managers approved – whether they are people whose judgement he trusts. Usually he approves. If the idea is not well received by a manager he may reject it, modify it or return it to its originator for modification (most likely the last). The process is long and troublesome but when a decision is made, people are committed to it and action follows fast.[ccxxii]

[ccxviii] Japanese, Finance and Accounting, education
[ccxix] Japanese, Strategic Management, business services
[ccxx] Japanese, Audit, venture capital
[ccxxi] Japanese, Finance and Accounting, education
[ccxxii] Ibid.

68 2

INTRODUCTION • **THE BUSINESS CULTURES OF FIVE ASIAN COUNTRIES** • ANALYSING ASIAN BUSINESS CULTURES • OWNERSHIP, FINANCING AND GOVERNANCE • ORGANIZATION AND MANAGEMENT • BUSINESS STRATEGY •

- Consensus was a central value for the Japanese.

> The Japanese are not good at doing deals. One reason is that consensus is essential. There is a longer approval cycle. A negotiator will have only limited discretion and when he or she refers back, it is not to one individual with more discretion but to make sure everybody is well informed and approves the deal.[ccxxiii]
>
> Management meetings take place but have no purpose; their agenda will be very broad and no decisions will be made. In a fast-growing venture company, a charismatic leader does all the talking; in a traditional company, there will be no clear conclusion reached. Key people in middle management will coordinate to get the CEO to agree to their consensus opinion. Decisions lack logic. They are decided by gut feel, atmosphere and a desire not to rock the boat.[ccxxiv]

- In both Japanese society and business there was a strong feeling in favour of equality. 'Previously all the members of a cohort of graduates would have the same salary five years after entry.'[ccxxv]

> Japanese junior salarymen tolerate near-impossible working conditions because they all know their turn will come (even though for most it won't). This is because the Japanese education system is not competitive – everyone is taught to think they are equal, so they have no reason to think they won't reach the top.[ccxxvi]

'Everyone at the bottom believes he (usually) or she is leading the company.'[ccxxvii]

- Most traditional Japanese businesses had not been primarily concerned with making profits. 'Pressure to maximize shareholder returns has only surfaced recently.'[ccxxviii] They tended to have other values or goals. For instance, the 'Sony spirit', according to the company's website, thrived on exploring the unknown and hoped to serve mankind through scientific and technological innovation; to achieve this, 'all members of the Sony family pull together to overcome difficulties, finding joy in creative work and pride in contributing their talents'. One interviewee worked for a traditional company that had had the same 'mission' statement since its foundation early in the 20th century. He explained the way these kinds of goals got implemented: 'Once these principles are fully

---

[ccxxiii] Japanese, Marketing Manager, Western MNC telephony manufacturer
[ccxxiv] Japanese, Strategic Management, business services
[ccxxv] Japanese, Human Resource Management, business services
[ccxxvi] Japanese, Finance and Accounting, education
[ccxxvii] Ibid.
[ccxxviii] Ibid.

understood, everybody should act according to their own judgement. We have autonomous, decentralized management while insisting on the principles. We believe that if we do our best, we can break through anything.[ccxxix]

- Japanese businesses based their decisions on thorough research and information gathering. 'To validate the use of Chinese suppliers, the Japanese will visit the factory eight times for a week at a time; the Europeans will go to the factory once for one day.'[ccxxx] 'In non-Japanese companies, the senior guys will take a decision with limited information in order to be timely; they will take the risk; in Japan the information for decision-making must be as complete as possible.'[ccxxxi] 'Japanese clients are very slow to make decisions; the US are fastest; Europeans in between.'[ccxxxii] 'The Japanese are perfectionist in preparation; this makes them good at manufacturing but perhaps too slow for financial markets.'[ccxxxiii]

- Consistently with their emphasis on thoroughness, Japanese companies approached strategy with detailed forward planning. 'The Japanese are good at forward planning in detail. The Japanese in general are detail-oriented, meticulous, and good with their hands.'[ccxxxiv] 'The Japanese combine detailed planning with trial and error.'[ccxxxv] However, there was criticism of their strategic vision as well as comments on their cultural difficulty in pursuing some strategies: 'Most companies here do not work in terms of function and have no realistic strategic vision.'[ccxxxvi] 'Japanese are not strong in module manufacturing – they want an integrated approach – this is due to culture; they can see the logic of competition, cost cutting through outsourcing, so they do it, but it goes against the grain.'[ccxxxvii] The comment in the paragraph above, 'The Japanese are perfectionist in preparation...' ended with the statement, 'This is uncertainty avoidance.'

- Some interviewees attributed Japanese thoroughness to risk aversion, which was widely described as a characteristic. 'Japanese companies are risk-averse. Because after World War II companies grew fast, there was no real need for radical decisions; their goal became to avoid mistakes.'[ccxxxviii]

> In Japan, risk-consciousness is always high; in London, people strike a risk-return balance. This makes London a better place for financial serv-

ccxxix Japanese, Operations Management, Japanese consumer durables manufacturer
ccxxx Japanese, Sourcing and Procurement, French MNC business services
ccxxxi Japanese, banking
ccxxxii Japanese, Sourcing and Procurement, French MNC business services
ccxxxiii Japanese, Finance and Accounting, banking
ccxxxiv Japanese, Audit, venture capital
ccxxxv Japanese, Finance and Accounting, education
ccxxxvi Japanese, Strategic Management, business services
ccxxxvii Japanese, Finance and Accounting, education
ccxxxviii Japanese, banking

70　2

INTRODUCTION · THE BUSINESS CULTURES OF FIVE ASIAN COUNTRIES · ANALYSING ASIAN BUSINESS CULTURES · OWNERSHIP, FINANCING AND GOVERNANCE · ORGANIZATION AND MANAGEMENT · BUSINESS STRATEGY ·

ices. ... Japanese attitudes to risk lie behind the land price bubble of the 1980s; people and lenders believed that land was a risk-free investment, that the price of land would never go down. They did learn from the bursting of the bubble; yield is now used as the basis for valuations.[ccxxxix]

- The views of our interviewees on innovation in Japanese business were largely negative. Typical comments included the following: '60 to 70 per cent of new service businesses are copies, perhaps with some tweaking, though on the technology side, some products are new in global terms. The Japanese consumer is an eager buyer of new technology products.'[ccxl]

> We don't have enough experimentation, despite our bad experiences since 1990. There is a lack of thought leadership. Business Schools just import ideas from the USA and UK. For instance 6-sigma is really quality circles which the Japanese invented but it was turned into a concept in the USA. We are not good at formalising ideas; if we put forward ideas and they are criticized, we lose face so we self-censor.[ccxli]

'We have to say the right thing or nothing. The effect is a lack of brainstorming; creativity is harmed.'[ccxlii] 'Development of innovative ideas was not much needed in the past. Now it is, the education system has to change.'[ccxliii] There was a suggestion that innovation and creativity were alien to Japanese corporate culture as well as its societal culture: 'Companies are having to adopt new values such as innovation and creativity while retaining their core values.'[ccxliv] This need was depicted as imposing so much strain that management consultants, not often used, were being employed more frequently.

- In contrast to the Indian attitude, in Japan keeping promises and fulfilling or over-fulfilling on undertakings were seen as normative.

> A thing that is important here is to deliver on your commitments. To promise to deliver by a certain date and then not do so is not tolerated. So people are cautious about the promises they make. For instance, suppliers dream of getting a contract with [European] Company X because of its huge volume sales. Japanese suppliers might be selected for their technological edge but their delivery schedule when they quote will be 50 per cent longer than, say, the American competition's. But if they still get the contract it will be delivered when they say

[ccxxxix] Japanese, Finance and Accounting, banking
[ccxl] Japanese, Audit, venture capital
[ccxli] Japanese, Human Resource Management, business services
[ccxlii] Japanese Product Manager, Western MNC pharmaceuticals manufacturer
[ccxliii] Japanese, banking
[ccxliv] Japanese, Human Resource Management, business services

it will, whereas the Americans will probably come back with delivery delays and excuses.[ccxlv]

The Japanese saw their business culture as committed to quality and contrasted this with the approach of the Chinese:

> " Another thing is attention to detail. As suppliers they [the Japanese] expect close contact with the customer. They will send an engineer along with the first few shipments in case of problems; in contrast the Chinese, once they ship it out of the window, it's no longer their concern. The Japanese try to prevent trouble; the Chinese are quick to react when there is trouble, but they don't work to prevent it.[ccxlvi]

'To compete, the Japanese, like the Germans and the Finns, rely more on providing expertise, higher quality, more service; not so much on price and not on bribery.'[ccxlvii]

- The high-context, low-key style of work communication in Japan was emphasized as if it reflected deeper cultural values: 'If a Japanese person states something, it is important; Americans speak out all their thoughts, so it is hard for Japanese to know what is important and what is not. Japanese communication proceeds gradually from the edge towards the core.'[ccxlviii] 'Face to face interaction is very important.... We drink toasts; wine helps build a positive feeling!'[ccxlix] 'One Japanese can and will guess what another one wants to say without him saying it. Western people cannot understand this. Japanese never say directly what they think. ...Japanese will guess what other people think from a few words and accommodate, behave in a civilized way.'[ccl]

> " People, including juniors, are generally attuned to reading atmosphere and context and adapting. Bosses don't quarrel openly, especially not in front of others. However, others may detect that there is hidden conflict and they will try to make it right. Acting maturely, adjusting to atmosphere used to be considered one of the most important work skills; it is becoming less common now. Conflict is always avoided.[ccli]

- There was general agreement that Japanese business and society needed to change. 'With globalization, the old Japanese way cannot survive. We have high productivity, but our GDP [gross domestic product] per capita is $30,000,

---

[ccxlv] Japanese, Marketing manager, Western MNC telephony manufacturer
[ccxlvi] Ibid.
[ccxlvii] Ibid.
[ccxlviii] Japanese, Human Resource Management, business services
[ccxlix] Japanese, Operations Management, Japanese consumer durables manufacturer
[ccl] Japanese, Finance and Accounting, education
[ccli] Japanese Product Manager, Western MNC pharmaceuticals manufacturer

China's is $2,000. And we have to trade – we can't go back to being isolated like in the Edo period.[cclii] The process of change was seen as having started and as having affected both the internal management of companies and their business relations.

> " The *keiretsu* system had to go during the troubles of the 1990s. Instead of using the same suppliers who were members of the *keiretsu*, we had to go for the lowest price. For instance, Mitsui Bank was our only bank; now we use HSBC, Mitsubishi and other banks as well. ... I think the big Japanese companies have over-destroyed long-term relationships.[ccliii]
>
> In the years up to 2002, the structure of some Japanese companies shifted to one where rewards follow responsibilities, to job-based from post-based. Often the firms that changed their structure introduced MBO [management by objectives]. The fact that previously their staff had no experience of setting targets or giving feedback led to difficulties, so, after 2002, those companies worked on improving these systems to make them work better in the Japanese context.[ccliv]

At the same time, these companies introduced a competency framework to complement the targets built into MBO with an emphasis on processes.

> " The competencies their staff had were not always what were needed in the new context. For instance, previously, salespeople did not have to find new customers but, with the breakdown of the *keiretsu* system, they had to. This applied, for instance, to the banks. Previously, their salespeople would simply call on a customer to say 'hello'; now they had to research the customer and find bank offerings that correspond to the customer's needs.[cclv]

The consequences of these changes were not always welcome: 'It's a chaotic situation. In some of the bigger companies, the traditional culture has almost collapsed.'[cclvi] 'Japanese companies need to find new growth; this calls for a shift from incrementalism to radicalism over the next five to ten years. They are likely to converge on global norms. However, this will probably cause them to experience internal conflict.'[cclvii] One example of such internal conflict arose when companies tried to fill the vacancies caused by the ten-year gap in recruitment that resulted from companies not hiring during the recession of the

---

[cclii] Japanese, Team Manager, Marketing Analysis, Japanese trading company
[ccliii] Ibid.
[ccliv] Japanese, Human Resource Management, business services
[cclv] Ibid.
[cclvi] Ibid.
[cclvii] Japanese, banking

1990s. As the economy expanded again after 2000, the companies made mid-career hires which caused problems, 'because the incomers had been socialized to the culture of another organization and found it extremely difficult to adjust. Also the culture of the hiring organization had to be made explicit and written down, which was never done before'.[cclviii]

The traditional culture of Japanese companies was so strong that change produced an effect

> equivalent to culture shock: managing in a Japanese company now is difficult; on the one hand you have to imbue your staff with the importance of harmony and respect; on the other hand you have to build an aggressive and competitive team. The manager has to be like an army chief. This is because of globalization and Asian competition.[cclix]

Change that disturbed Japan's egalitarian social model was particularly problematic:

> There is a shift towards less equality of outcomes in favour of equality of opportunity on the European model. However, although there are visible changes in the society, only 10 per cent of individuals are affected and there is already a backlash. There are more people who are afraid that if our society becomes unequal they will go to the bottom than there are people who are frustrated because they believe they would go to the top.[cclx]

- **In Japan, although familism was less marked than in India or Hong Kong (or Taiwan), the importance of personal relations within business organizations was stressed. Here, though, they were mainly based on intensive intra-organizational relations built up over time instead of, as elsewhere, extra-organizational links such as family or community. In Japan, contrasting with large Japanese companies' increasingly impersonal business-to-business practices, intra-organizational arrangements remained interpersonal, despite changes over recent years. 'When a graduate joins a company, it is like joining a family.'[cclxi] 'The CEO is like the father of a family. He needs to be popular.'[cclxii] 'Most Japanese company directors are employees, friends of the CEO, friends who can't say "No". They behave like family members.'[cclxiii] These practices had negative consequences: 'The companies do not use their strengths. This

---

[cclviii] Japanese, banking

[cclix] Japanese, Team Manager, Marketing Analysis, Japanese trading company

[cclx] Japanese Strategic Management, business services (1)

[cclxi] Japanese, Finance and Accounting, education

[cclxii] Japanese, Human Resources, business service (1)

[cclxiii] Japanese, Finance and Accounting, education

74 · 2

INTRODUCTION · **THE BUSINESS CULTURES OF FIVE ASIAN COUNTRIES** · ANALYSING ASIAN BUSINESS CULTURES · OWNERSHIP, FINANCING AND GOVERNANCE · ORGANIZATION AND MANAGEMENT · BUSINESS STRATEGY ·

affects their performance in both the domestic and the international markets. Decisions are not based on a system but on personal relationships.[cclxiv] There were also consequences for corporate governance.

- **The Japanese held negative views on the entrepreneurialism of their people.

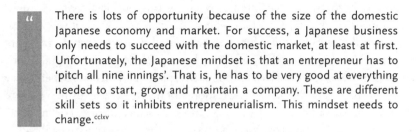

> There is lots of opportunity because of the size of the domestic Japanese economy and market. For success, a Japanese business only needs to succeed with the domestic market, at least at first. Unfortunately, the Japanese mindset is that an entrepreneur has to 'pitch all nine innings'. That is, he has to be very good at everything needed to start, grow and maintain a company. These are different skill sets so it inhibits entrepreneurialism. This mindset needs to change.[cclxv]

- **Governance only surfaced as an issue in Japan in response to specific questions, but there was an awareness of problems and an agreement that standards were not adequate. 'There is less understanding about [business] compliance overall. Many areas that are black and white in the West are grey in Japan.'[cclxvi] '[Governance is] not good. [There are such problems as] cross-shareholding in *keiretsus*, hostile acquisitions, triangle mergers. [Companies] try to be safer by asking friends to hold shares. ... So they try to hide trouble from the CEO.'[cclxvii]

> One SME where I am a director because we are its venture capitalists introduced a new [non-executive] director. When I asked who he was, the CEO said, 'He is my main customer's Purchasing Director.' People were comfortable with the old way of not having non-executive directors.[cclxviii]

'We have a lot of discussion about who is the owner of the company. Shareholders? The employees think it is their company – after all, they give more to it than just money, like shareholders. The managers think it is their company – after all, they run it.'[cclxix]

- In contrast to the negative view of governance, corruption was not seen as a problem: 'There is not a lot of corruption despite some insider trading scandals recently. Most behaviour is governed by common sense.'[cclxx]

[cclxiv] Japanese, Strategic Management, business services
[cclxv] Japanese, Audit, venture capital
[cclxvi] Ibid.
[cclxvii] Japanese, Finance and Accounting, education
[cclxviii] Japanese, Audit, venture capital
[cclxix] Ibid.
[cclxx] Japanese, Sourcing and Procurement, French MNC business services

- **In Japan, interviewees were not inclined to emphasize the limiting of trust in doing business to those with whom there was a personal connection, though relationships remained important. For about 50 years after the Second World War, Japanese businesses were intensively networked with other businesses in *keiretsu* or *kaisha*, but the personal aspect of these links may not have been very strong. The impression given was that intensively cultivating business contacts might yield a competitive advantage in Japan, whereas in '*guanxi*' cultures it was a necessity. When dealing with suppliers for an internet food-delivery company in Japan, we were told, 'The important thing is to have human relationships, especially with the farmers and food processors who produce the speciality foods as it is their rarity that makes people want them.'[cclxxi] One respondent described the business culture as follows: 'We have a wet culture or you could say a sticky culture. For instance, when a venture capital company exits, the people at the client company will say, "I know your fund has to leave but could you stay on the board?"'[cclxxii]

- **The prevalent view in Japan on business-government relations was that the less government intervention the better.

> It's not like Singapore or Taiwan; just export guarantees, that kind of thing. Business does not want close relations with government – they take too long to decide things. The exception is the agricultural sector businesses – there are subsidies; also there is government support for alternative energy suppliers; but oil, machinery, manufacturing, are almost completely independent.[cclxxiii]

- **The approach to negotiations in Japan was one of 'win-win': 'The Japanese seek long-term relationships in negotiations.'[cclxxiv]

> It's the relationship. If I lose this time but win next time and maybe the time after, that's acceptable. Also I will be concerned not to make the other person lose face. These attitudes can be a problem in negotiating internationally, where the other party's attitude is deal by deal. They can also be a problem internally, leading to compliance issues.[cclxxv]

The need for everybody to approve deals, based on the cultural imperative of consensus was seen as disadvantageous in gaining business: 'There is quite a concern now about the need to empower subordinate negotiators.'[cclxxvi]

Table 2.3 summarizes these findings on Japanese business culture.

[cclxxi] Japanese, General Management, retail
[cclxxii] Japanese, Audit, venture capital
[cclxxiii] Japanese, Team Manager, Marketing Analysis, Japanese trading company
[cclxxiv] Japanese, Finance and Accounting, education
[cclxxv] Japanese, Audit, venture capital
[cclxxvi] Japanese, Marketing Manager, Western MNC telephony manufacturer

Table 2.3 **A summary of the present study's findings on the elements of Japanese business culture**

Elements of Japanese business culture	Perceived characteristics
Personalism in employment and work relations	Organizations are communities of their employees. In big companies, appointment is merit-based but promotion is seniority-based
Organizational structure	Not a role culture; staff are generalists rather than specialists
Status	Deference to seniors and superiors is very high
Hierarchy	Power distance is low – status and power are not coequivalent
Basis for decision-making	Consensus; information is widely dispersed
Business goals	Often not primarily financial returns to owners
Business strategy	Forward planning is thorough but strategic vision may be lacking
Attitude to risk	Risk averse
Innovativeness	Low (except in technological products) but good modifiers
Business norms	Delivering on undertakings is normative; egalitarianism
Business communication style	Low-key, high context, conflict avoided
Change	Need for change is widely recognized; some is happening but there is resistance.
Personalism in business control and decision-making	*High – personal relations outweigh systems*
Entrepreneurialism	*Low*
Governance	*Weak*
Corruption	*Low*
Personalism in B2B	*B2B relationships even within keiretsu are mainly inter-organizational though there are elements of personalism.*
Business relations with government	*Minor*
Negotiation style and approach	*Negotiations are part of a relationship – balanced approach*

Taiwan

Although Taiwanese businesses compete very successfully round the world, it was the characteristics traditionally associated with the Chinese family-owned business that received most attention from our interviewees: the importance of personal relationships, pride in ownership, face concerns, entrepreneurialism and intense competitiveness were all emphasized.

- The importance of personal relationships was strongly emphasized.

> For traditional Taiwanese businesses, mutual trust of contacts and reputation are key. Everything depends on a close relationship with both business partners and customers. For instance, they will supply a stable quantity at a given price, no matter what is happening in the wider market. This means at times they are making less money than they could, or even losing, at others they are protected from losing their customers to price competition.[cclxxvii]

'*Guanxi* is most important.'[cclxxviii]

> Unlike in the USA, for instance, where people who do business together over a period may start to socialize together, in Taiwan people who know one another socially may decide to do business together. ... Business relations are essential but if they go wrong there is no real recourse, so they dare not trust strangers.[cclxxix]

In addition to the importance of personal contacts for business generally, they were seen as essential for any deal or negotiation: 'The first step in any deal is the relationship, which can only come about through a contact. Who you know.'[cclxxx]

> In a negotiation, price is not determinate, nor is any other material factor; instead there must be a link – people with the same background, classmates – leading to understanding. The location of negotiations is very important. A lot of business is done in the 'social' clubs which are a feature of the Taiwanese business community; these clubs control admissions – there are clubs for Chinese, Japanese, locals.[cclxxxi]

Even in the technological sector, which in some ways had a different culture from the traditional businesses, personal connections were used, for instance, for financing: 'The capital markets favoured technological business; nevertheless high tech entrepreneurs would usually go into partnerships with people they knew, such as classmates; in such businesses no one was dominant.'[cclxxxii]

- Ownership of a business was described as a central value for many Taiwanese. Its importance was linked to the desire for control and to distrust of outsiders, but went beyond these factors to a core aspect of identity. 'The Taiwanese

---

[cclxxvii] Taiwanese, Partner, Taiwanese venture capital
[cclxxviii] Taiwan, Expatriate, Human Resource Management, banking
[cclxxix] Taiwanese, Product Manager, Taiwanese consumer goods manufacturer
[cclxxx] Taiwanese, Finance and Accounting, manufacturing
[cclxxxi] Taiwan, expatriate banker
[cclxxxii] Taiwanese, Partner, venture capital

only trust themselves or their immediate family. Family businesses often resist expanding through distrust of outsiders. This accounts for the many SMEs (small and medium enterprises).[cclxxxiii] 'Everything is done by the owner, not the CEO or any other manager, through social contacts. No matter how senior a negotiation counterpart, or how big his organization, he will be treated as inferior if he is not the owner. He will need an introduction through a contact.'[cclxxxiv]

> There is huge pride in ownership, pride in being a smart businessman, pride in being self-made: it shows in company names, marketing communications, the tone of ads; it emerges during negotiations. Even in extreme situations, when the business is losing money, reserves are almost gone, it is unable to meet tight capital requirements and lacking expertise, the owners are still stubborn: they prefer to go bankrupt than sell. If negotiations are opened, for example by a bank, the owner treats you as an employee and therefore inferior.[cclxxxv]

'The founders and owners of a business retain power even if the company is listed.'[cclxxxvi] 'There has been M&A (merger and acquisition) activity over the last three years, but it meets with seller resistance; owners would prefer to go bankrupt. They say it is better to be the head of a chicken than the tail of a bull.'[cclxxxvii]

The owners of traditional family businesses wanted to hand the business down in the family[cclxxxviii] but ownership brought a problem of succession planning which was often poorly resolved. 'Succession is a big problem. The issue of who will gain power hangs over the business for a long time; often these empires are divided among founders' sons, limiting growth. One example is S., which was split among the family and the business suffered.'[cclxxxix] In contrast, however, the owners of the newer high-technology businesses 'want to get out, having made their pile, in 10 to 15 years'.[ccxc] 'There are two kinds of local business: old-industry businesses are hierarchical and formal; new businesses try to stay lean and the CEO delegates.'[ccxci]

- Face concerns influenced Taiwan's business culture, as shown in comments such as, 'Taiwanese have high expectations of how they will be treated,

---

cclxxxiii Taiwanese, Senior Vice President, Finance and Accounting, fund management
cclxxxiv Taiwan, expatriate banker
cclxxxv Ibid.
cclxxxvi Taiwanese, Finance and Accounting, manufacturing
cclxxxvii Taiwanese, Senior Vice President, Finance and Accounting, fund management
cclxxxviii Taiwanese, Finance and Accounting, manufacturing
cclxxxix Taiwanese, Partner, Taiwanese venture capital
ccxc Taiwanese, Finance and Accounting, manufacturing
ccxci Ibid.

especially with regard to "face" ',[ccxcii] and, 'They are very willing to sue, often for bizarre things, such as a bank owing a dollar on a closed account; this is motivated by indignation and driven by pride; it is not as a way to make money.'[ccxciii] Face issues affected how the Taiwanese negotiated: 'Taiwanese business people are street-wise, used to getting their price. They don't believe in win-win outcomes of negotiations; they must feel they won – that is more important than whether they actually did get the best deal.'[ccxciv] On the other hand, within the restricted trusted circle, negotiations could lead to very long-term arrangements: 'Oral agreements can run for many years, perhaps adjusted annually, to such an extent that it makes valuing the business difficult.'[ccxcv]

- The professional culture of many Taiwanese businesses was an engineering culture. They were not driven either by marketing or by finance.

> " The build-up of the Taiwanese economy depended on the fact that Taiwanese businesses were efficient, with a focus on production and process engineering, not design or marketing. There are tens of thousands of engineers with MScs. Electronic engineering is the Number One option; this is not a function of the child's interests, but the result of social pressure. So businesses' professional cultures are those of professional engineers. Modern Taiwanese business suffers from this bias – more creativity is needed.

- Competition among Taiwanese businesses was seen as intense; the terms 'hyper-competitive' and 'over-competitive' were introduced by interviewees. One divided Taiwanese businesses into two kinds: the traditional and the newer high-technology businesses, 'But both are hyper-competitive. An example is Foxconn, the largest EE [electronic equipment] business in Taiwan; its CEO is known as GOD. He runs the business on a military model and eliminates competitors through M&A [mergers and acquisitions]. Weakening the competition reduces transaction costs. He employs 200 to 300 lawyers to fight patents in Taiwan, where patent law is strong.'[ccxcvi]

Competitiveness was seen as an attribute of the societal culture. It created problems for business:

> " The Taiwanese are over-competitive. It is second nature to them. This starts in school. ... Big businesses are riven by intense competition among small groups; this is a recognized problem. They are also more ruthless towards other Taiwanese than

[ccxcii] Taiwan, Expatriate, banker
[ccxciii] Taiwan, Expatriate, banking
[ccxciv] Taiwan, Expatriate, Human Resource Management, banking
[ccxcv] Taiwan, Expatriate, banking
[ccxcvi] Taiwanese, Partner, Taiwanese venture capital

towards foreigners. These divisions...exist in our mentality. They [Taiwanese] are polite but prefer foreigners. (The prejudice against 'foreign devils' has gone.)[ccxcvii]

- Entrepreneurialism was a strong feature of Taiwanese business culture, commented on by most interviewees, and given the status of a tradition, a source of national pride. 'The traditional Taiwanese business has an entrepreneurial boss/owner, whose success comes from hard work and dedication.'[ccxcviii] 'Initially Taiwan was an OEM (original equipment manufacturing) centre for mainly US companies; our businesses made modifications, found niche markets. Our business people were creative and not risk averse.'[ccxcix] 'You can see it [entrepreneurialism] in the predominance of SMEs in the economy.'[ccc] One interviewee explained, however,

> " A study found that there are two main reasons why Taiwanese start businesses. (1) Many find it difficult to find a normal job. It is the default option, for instance for Chinese economic migrants who do not speak Taiwanese. (2) Salaries in the traditional companies are low – wealth distribution is extremely unequal. So they start a business and treat their own employees the same way.[ccci]

- In part, Taiwanese entrepreneurialism was attributed to a positive attitude towards taking risk: 'The Taiwanese are entrepreneurial and not risk averse – they enjoy taking risks. For instance, the stockmarket is very volatile, more than that of other emerging markets, yet there are large numbers of participants – 70 per cent of trades by volume are by individuals against 20 per cent in the USA.'[cccii] 'The Taiwanese have a gambling mentality.'[ccciii] There was an alternative view: 'The people are risk averse, but many feel they have nothing to lose.'[ccciv] In the technology sector, on the other hand, 'It is a competence story. They feel they have an outstanding technical competence that will support a business, so they don't perceive it as risky.'[cccv] Equally as important as tolerating risk, though, was a Taiwanese capacity for handling it effectively. For example, many new businesses were actually spin-offs from larger companies. 'The parent company, or rather its founders in their personal capacity, will support this entrepreneurship by investing, looking to make money when it becomes

---

[ccxcvii] Taiwanese, Senior Vice President, Finance and Accounting, fund management
[ccxcviii] Taiwanese, Partner, Taiwanese venture capital
[ccxcix] Taiwanese, Finance and Accounting, manufacturing
[ccc] Taiwan, Expatriate, Human Resource Management, banking
[ccci] Taiwanese, Product Manager, Taiwanese consumer goods manufacturer
[cccii] Senior Vice President, Finance and Accounting, fund management
[ccciii] Taiwan, Expatriate, Human Resource Management, banking
[ccciv] Taiwanese, Product Manager, Taiwanese consumer goods manufacturer
[cccv] Ibid.

an IPO.[cccvi] Risk was reduced because they were able to choose a time when capacity was tight, so the new venture was likely to have a market; second, as industry insiders they recognized opportunities with good potential and could make accurate valuations. Other new ventures – in the technology industry in particular – were started by the children of rich industrialists, using family money.

- In the past, a third factor supporting entrepreneurialism in Taiwan was government support, but recent changes meant that its role was less taken for granted, less part of the business culture, than in, for instance, Singapore. 'Industrialization was encouraged by government. Infant industries received government subsidies so they were price-competitive. This was their USP (unique selling point).[cccvii]

> Our first businesses were largely focused on the domestic market; they were supported by the government as infant industries with an import tax. For instance Wong of Formosa Plastic started as a trader importing wood, then got into manufacturing plastic as a domestically produced substitute which meant he benefited from an import tax protection. The company is now a petro-chemicals conglomerate, Taiwan's largest business.[cccviii]

The semiconductor industry, so significant for Taiwan's development, was promoted by the government. In service industries too, the government took the lead. 'There was a wave of new banks started 15 years ago, with Government approval; mainly by companies from related industries like insurance. Now consolidation is starting, with mergers and taking advantage of a new law allowing holding companies for banks.[cccix] 'Up to 1990, the government had a strong industrial policy looking to import substitution. However, with democracy came a lack of political direction for industry, which led to "economic chaos", demonstrating the dependence up to then of the business sector on government leadership.[cccx]

- There were differences of perception about the level of innovativeness in Taiwanese businesses. On the one hand, one historical account suggested that creativity was among the factors that led to the growth of the Taiwanese economy in the 1960s and 1970s: in addition to the comment above that 'Initially ... our business people were creative', there was the comment, 'The people were innovative'; on the other hand, there was a view that in the past,

---

[cccvi] Taiwanese, Partner, Taiwan venture capital
[cccvii] Taiwanese, Senior Vice President, Finance and Accounting, fund management
[cccviii] Taiwanese, Partner, Taiwanese venture capital
[cccix] Taiwanese, Finance and Accounting, manufacturing
[cccx] Taiwanese, Partner, Taiwanese venture capital

'Creativity was not a priority – that has been changing over the last five years.'[cccxi] Similarly, there were divergent views on whether creativity in Taiwan was adequate for the demands of the modern economy: 'Modern Taiwanese business suffers from this bias – more creativity is needed.' 'Innovation comes only from a joint effort of local business with foreign companies, especially US companies.'[cccxii] Japanese managers going to Taiwan were briefed that the educational system made staff good at learning but not creative compared with Japan.[cccxiii] Against this negative view, there was an opinion that newer businesses were 'fast-growing, ambitious, creative',[cccxiv] and the consolatory idea that the Taiwanese were 'very good at reverse engineering and introducing useful modifications'.[cccxv]

- Judgements on Taiwanese governance varied from, 'There are loopholes',[cccxvi] to the view that there were high levels of 'embezzlement'.[cccxvii] Political corruption was considered endemic and damaging. An example of a loophole in governance was given: a motherboard fabricator used its muscle both as a major purchaser of components and a shareholder to influence board decisions in its favour in the component supplier.[cccxviii] 'Embezzlement' was the term applied to distortion of profits in the local companies; this occurred despite government regulations which required external directors in businesses whose capital exceeded a low figure. Nevertheless, local businesses found the Taiwanese environment highly regulated and attempted to reduce this pressure by investing in China: 'Taiwan is a highly regulated environment; in China regulations depend on who you are. So the Taiwanese see it as more responsive.'[cccxix]

More concern was expressed about political corruption. 'It poisons the atmosphere.'[cccxx] A 'major motive' for trying to gain wealth was to emigrate due to discontent with Taiwan, including corruption.[cccxxi] A non-Taiwanese banker working in Taipei said that for some deals, interaction with the political world was essential and that the wives of ministers were 'important' because of their intermediary role in corruption. As a counter-corruption measure, the international bank he represented would not allow Taiwanese politicians to open

---

[cccxi] Senior Vice President, Finance and Accounting, fund management
[cccxii] Ibid.
[cccxiii] Taiwan, Expatriate (Japanese), Human Resource Management, banking
[cccxiv] Taiwanese, Finance and Accounting, manufacturing
[cccxv] Taiwanese, Partner, Taiwanese venture capital
[cccxvi] Ibid.
[cccxvii] Taiwanese, Finance and Accounting, manufacturing
[cccxviii] Taiwanese, Partner, Taiwanese venture capital
[cccxix] Taiwan, expatriate banker
[cccxx] Senior Vice President, Finance and Accounting, fund management
[cccxxi] Taiwan, expatriate banker

accounts. The judicial system was described as 'as bad as anywhere in terms of favouring the powerful', but very strict for everyone else.[cccxxii]

- **Taiwanese familism did not necessarily lead to strongly marked hierarchical organization, we found. The work culture in one business, Foxconn, was described as militaristic, but this was in contrast to most others; the people were described as 'happy-go-lucky' and more independent than the Japanese; the notably high staff turnovers might point to high levels of staff discontent, but many were attributed to staff setting up business for themselves and being backed by their former employers, which instead suggested that relations were cordial. Decision-making was centralized, but a Japanese expatriate interviewee said that suggestions that the Taiwanese do not share expertise with subordinates was exaggerated.[cccxxiii] Deference, too, was less marked than in Japan or China: 'Formality is not high. There is often a first-name basis for the boss, though not for the President.'[cccxxiv]

- **It was in Taiwan that the aspect of 'face' received most comment: 'Taiwanese have high expectations of how they will be treated, especially with regard to "face".'[cccxxv] 'When their [Taiwanese business executives'] negotiating position is unsustainable, "face" enters – it is unbearable for them to be exposed as needing to co-operate. Exposing their face can lead to closing the door permanently.'[cccxxvi]

- **In Taiwan, different kinds of businesses were seen by some interviewees as having somewhat different cultures, although not to the extent of negating the underlying business culture. In the case of Taiwan, the distinction was drawn between traditional businesses founded up to 200 years ago, in sectors such as banking and real estate, and those in the technology sector, founded with government support in the 1970s and 1980s, often by returnees from the USA.

> " The traditional Taiwanese business has an entrepreneurial boss/ owner, whose success comes from hard work and dedication. These are largely focused on the domestic market, and were supported initially by the government as infant industries with an import tax.[cccxxvii]
>
> Taiwanese businesses are mainly of two kinds – there are two different stories: those founded up to 200 years ago, operating mainly in banking, finance and real estate, and those whose founders went to the USA in the late 70s and 80s, came back and started technology businesses with government support.[cccxxviii]

[cccxxii] Taiwan, Expatriate banker
[cccxxiii] Taiwan, Expatriate, Human Resource Management, banking
[cccxxiv] Taiwanese, Partner, Taiwanese venture capital
[cccxxv] Taiwan, Expatriate, Management, banking
[cccxxvi] Taiwan, Japanese Expatriate banker
[cccxxvii] Partner, Taiwanese venture capital
[cccxxviii] Taiwanese, Product Manager, Taiwanese consumer goods manufacturer

Table 2.4 **A summary of the present study's findings on the elements of Taiwanese business culture**

Elements of Taiwanese business culture	Perceived characteristics
Personalism in business control and decision-making	High in older businesses; pride in business ownership is a key value
Personalism in B2B	B2B and financing depend on personal networks, *guanxi*
Governance	Weak
Corruption	Political corruption endemic
Entrepreneurialism	High
Attitudes to risk	Not risk averse; risk handlers
Innovation and creativity	Views vary (but good at reverse engineering)
Business relations with government	Government previously led business, not now
Approach to negotiation	Link essential
Business goals	In older companies dynastic goals reflect pride in ownership; in high-technology businesses the goals are making money and moving on
Professional culture	Engineering
Competitiveness	Both individuals and businesses are hyper-competitive
Personalism in employment and work relations	*High in older companies, low in newer technology-based companies*
Hierarchy	*Medium-high in older companies, lower in newer technology-based companies*
Status acknowledged by deference	*Relatively low*
Face issues	*Important*
Different types of businesses have different cultures	*Some elements of culture vary in different types of businesses (traditional – banks, real estate – and technology-based)*
Change	*Change meets resistance, but CFOBs* are being professionalized*

Note: *Chinese family-owned businesses.

- **The distinction in Taiwan between the old-established companies and the new businesses in the technology sector surfaced again in the area of work and employment relations:

> In the old, well-established companies, if you are not related to the founder, there is a fairly low ceiling, though there is relative security of employment. In the technology sector, they recruit mainly from graduates of three engineering universities in a 'Silicon Valley' setup. The average duration of employment is three years. Promotion is

merit-based – they try to emulate the Western model. There are high rewards, including options, but very long hours (you are always on call) and little security. You could get called to the CEO's office and be given 30 minutes notice.[cccxxix]

Traditional businesses were characterized by 'early entry of employees'. 'Promotion is based on seniority and depends on trust; ... loyalty rather than ability are rewarded, but there are no shares for non-family employees, though there could be a big bonus decided by the whim of the boss.'[cccxxx]

Table 2.4 summarizes these findings on Taiwanese business culture.

Singapore

Government leadership, a high level of immigration attracted by the openness of the economy and its domination by MNCs most strongly affected the way business was done in Singapore, our research found.

- More than anywhere else, there was an emphasis in Singapore on the role of government in business and the effect of this on Singaporean business attitudes. 'The Singapore government drives a lot of things.'[cccxxxi] 'The Government fosters an environment for entrepreneurs with grants, loans and advice.'[cccxxxii]

There is government support for SMEs and start-ups to succeed – a government culture in favour of entrepreneurship. The so-called SPRING loans are one example. The culture is 'parental' – there is no money for free; you have to participate, be motivated, invest yourself. It's like dealing with your father. Help comes with a message; it's an educational process. For instance, most government loans require an asset pledge; they differ from bank loans in lower interest rates and less track record needed.[cccxxxiii]

The last statement was made by a Singaporean entrepreneur. Others were less positive about the effect of government support on entrepreneurship: 'The government spends to support but has no idea how to spend the money; there are too many committees.'[cccxxxiv] Other negative consequences of the Singapore

cccxxix Taiwanese, Product Manager, Taiwanese consumer goods manufacturer
cccxxx Taiwanese, Partner, Taiwanese venture capital
cccxxxi Singaporean, Finance and Accounting, education
cccxxxii Ibid.
cccxxxiii Singaporean, Finance, Banking; Entrepreneur, food and beverages
cccxxxiv Singapore, Indian, Entrepreneur, internet-based business service

government's leadership in business were also observed: 'Singaporean business-men wait for government to tell them what to do.'[cccxxxv] 'The government sector competes directly with the private sector for markets and resources such as talent.'[cccxxxvi]

On the other hand, there were plaudits for the government's policy of attracting MNCs and its effectiveness in implementing that policy 'The government is good at getting MNCs to come to Singapore.'[cccxxxvii]

> Singapore is a meritocracy. It attracts talent – the government welcomes international companies so long as they stay out of Singaporean politics; the companies are then a magnet for talent, which in turn is a magnet for the companies. Singapore does not practise labour protectionism unlike, say, Thailand or most other Asian countries; Singaporean businesses recruit internationally, other Asian businesses internally (mainly for language and familiarity reasons, not kinship); those foreigners recruited to other Asian countries often fail, leading to reinforcement of the policy and practice.[cccxxxviii]

'Singapore is positioned to be a place for expatriates. It is safe, clean, attractive – a decompression chamber for Asia. This positioning has worked quite well. In comparison, Shanghai and Tokyo are very different cultures, Hong Kong is polluted.'[cccxxxix]

- Another aspect of Singapore's business culture was also seen as benefiting the economy. This was its high level of governance, as attested by several independent measures. 'Corruption comes from a culture that the rules of the game can be bent. This is one of the few places in Asia where this culture is not established.'[cccxl] Good governance applied in the bureaucracy, bribery, adherence to the rules and the nature of competition. 'The bureaucracy is transparent and limited.'[cccxli] 'In 15-and-a-half years I have not been asked for or offered a bribe and do not know anyone who has.'[cccxlii] 'The rules are clear, people are aware of them and play by them.'[cccxliii] 'There is a level playing field – for instance the level of bank fees are the same for everyone.'[cccxliv] The international perception of Singapore's good govern-

---

[cccxxxv] Singaporean, Finance and Accounting, education
[cccxxxvi] Ibid.
[cccxxxvii] Ibid.
[cccxxxviii] Singaporean, Human Resources, business services
[cccxxxix] Singaporean, Human Resources, business services
[cccxl] Singaporean, CEO, Thai MNC, business services
[cccxli] Singaporean, Finance, Banking; Entrepreneur, food and beverages
[cccxlii] Ibid.
[cccxliii] Ibid.
[cccxliv] Ibid.

ance was seen as a business advantage: 'Middle Eastern countries are now looking to Singaporeans for services such as airport and water management. There is a perception that Singaporean companies and individuals have high quality standards and are honest.'[cccxlv] These perceptions were simply taken for granted by other business executives in Asia: 'Singapore's rich-poor gap is equally wide [as India's], though its society is more egalitarian. But *enforcement* is more effective in Singapore; they throw the book at corruption. For example an Army officer was cashiered and jailed for taking a $15 bribe.'[cccxlvi]

- The one negative consequence of Singapore's policy of attracting MNCs was to reduce the attractions of entrepreneurship to young graduates. In any case, it was considered, Singapore lacked an entrepreneurial culture. 'Singaporeans are not entrepreneurs. They only create SMEs out of necessity. 70 per cent of businesses are Chinese-owned. SMEs form business clusters geographically to serve the immediate community.'[cccxlvii]

The Singapore environment makes it superficially easy to set up a company: there is excellent infrastructure, such as private airlines, Changi [international airport], communications (though these are not quite as good as Japan or Korea); ground transport is excellent, the tax regime is benign, there is cheap unskilled labour, for several years office space was cheap compared, for instance, with Hong Kong, liquidity is high and yet there are no great entrepreneurs. Last year's award for entrepreneurialism was won by a baker.[cccxlviii]

'The emphasis on educational success – the system still has streaming – leads to a lack of entrepreneurial spirit.'[cccxlix]

Not everyone agreed that the Singapore environment made it easy to set up a business. 'Being an entrepreneur in Singapore is a tough proposition. The domestic market is too small and there are barriers to entry: what is important is a business network.'[cccl]

- Apparently linked in interviewees' minds to the question of entrepreneurialism was the issue of innovativeness, which extended not only to being creative but also to accepting new ideas. 'If there were no international companies, there would be no innovation.'[cccli] 'There is a problem in Singapore of gaining accept-

cccxlv Singaporean, Human Resources, business services
cccxlvi Indian, Senior Consultant, business services (banking operations and technology)
cccxlvii Singaporean, CEO, Thai MNC, business services
cccxlviii Singapore, Indian, Entrepreneur, internet-based business service
cccxlix Singaporean, Finance and Accounting, education
cccl Ibid.
cccli Ibid.

88   2

INTRODUCTION · **THE BUSINESS CULTURES OF FIVE ASIAN COUNTRIES** · ANALYSING ASIAN BUSINESS CULTURES · OWNERSHIP, FINANCING AND GOVERNANCE · ORGANIZATION AND MANAGEMENT · BUSINESS STRATEGY ·

ance for innovative ideas. To solve it the government has tried hiring Westerners. It doesn't work because there is a mismatch in communication.[ccclii] 'Singaporeans are not innovative but so what? Japanese aren't either but they are successful.[cccliii] Nevertheless, it was asserted that there were a few businesses which were innovative, such as Creative Technology, which made sound blasters, and OSIM which made a success of lifestyle products such as a massage chair.[cccliv]

- The character of the people in the local business community was emphasized in Singapore. 'They are astute; they have faced lots of adversity, Singapore has no natural resources, they went through the Japanese occupation.[ccclv] 'They don't give you a second chance. There is low tolerance for mediocrity or failure.[ccclvi] The members of the Singaporean business community, were described as 'astute, calculative.' 'They might not want to do business with you if they are not satisfied with what's in it for them.[ccclvii] 'Failure is not tolerated.[ccclviii] 'They have zero tolerance for bad ideas.[ccclix] 'Their work ethic is weaker than Tokyo; they have got the work/life balance right.[ccclx] On the negative side, 'Singaporeans are too disciplined to be dynamic', said a Hong Kong commentator,[ccclxi] while another thought, 'Singaporeans can be "not savvy" – for instance in their dealings with China. This is the result of being "led by the nose" by government.[ccclxii]

- **Doubt was expressed by two Singaporean interviewees about there being a distinctive Singaporean business culture. This doubt originated in the fact that Singapore's business community was quite diverse. The view was that the culture was Asian, not specifically Singaporean. 'Most businesses are owned and run by first generation migrants from India or, especially, China.[ccclxiii] 'Singapore is a melting pot. This is dangerous – easily misunderstood: on the surface Singaporeans are Westernized; but their value systems are related to their experience as an individual or as a family. They give off a misleading message. This "dualism" is a by-product of modernization.[ccclxiv] 'Singapore is an immigrant nation from all over South East Asia, especially South China.[ccclxv] To an Indian entrepreneur based in Singapore, this predominance of South

ccclii Singaporean, CEO, Thai MNC, business services
cccliii Ibid.
cccliv Singaporean, Finance and Accounting, education
ccclv Ibid.
ccclvi Singaporean, Finance, Banking; Entrepreneur, food and beverages
ccclvii Ibid.
ccclviii Singaporean, Finance and Accounting, education
ccclix Singaporean, Finance, Banking; Entrepreneur, food and beverages
ccclx Singapore, Indian, Entrepreneur, internet-based business service
ccclxi Hong Kong, Public Affairs Manager, Hong Kong utility company
ccclxii Singaporean, Human Resources, business services
ccclxiii Singaporean, Finance and Accounting, education
ccclxiv Singaporean, CEO, Thai MNC, business services
ccclxv Singaporean, Human Resources, business services

DIMENSIONS OF SOCIETAL CULTURES · SOCIETAL CULTURES REVISITED · POLITICAL CULTURES AND PERCEIVED POLITICAL ENVIRONMENTS · ECONOMIC CULTURES AND PERCEIVED ECONOMIC ENVIRONMENTS · CONCLUDING REMARKS

2

89

East Asians meant that the culture was 'alien': 'The Chinese are aligned with the culture. For example there are issues about how to deliver messages to suppliers and partners. I need to polish what I want to say. It must be genuine but the presentation must be appropriate for the culture.'[ccclxvi] These denials that there is a distinctive Singaporean business culture were, however, contradicted by descriptions, sometimes from the same interviewee, of unique characteristics for the way business was done or organizations were managed in the country.

- **Singapore was positioned as a modern economy but the SME sector was traditional. 'Singapore is a meritocracy – in marked contrast to Malaysia or China.'[ccclxvii] In the SME sector, however, because meritocracy did not apply, the 'biggest challenge' for these businesses was

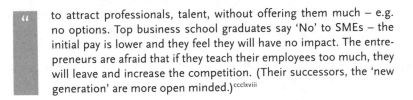

> to attract professionals, talent, without offering them much – e.g. no options. Top business school graduates say 'No' to SMEs – the initial pay is lower and they feel they will have no impact. The entrepreneurs are afraid that if they teach their employees too much, they will leave and increase the competition. (Their successors, the 'new generation' are more open minded.)[ccclxviii]

- **Singapore was found to be subtly different from the rest of East Asia with regard to business-to-business relations. As the following statements show, personal connections and reciprocal obligations were less of an issue and the lack of them need not constitute a barrier to entry. 'In Singapore, there are start-up difficulties in that you need to know the right agencies – suppliers, contractors. "Who is reliable?" There is no single source of this information; on the other hand, unlike in much of Asia, it is not essential to have a local partner.'[ccclxix] In Singapore's SME sector, 'Trust is based on your track record, historical dealings, oral understandings, ability to deliver, not on a contract; however, because these businessmen are very careful about costs, if you offer a favourable price, they will try you out on a small basis.'[ccclxx]

- **In Singapore, the business culture that was described was that of the local businesses rather than the MNCs. The difference between traditional and technology-sector business was much less emphasized mainly because the number of indigenous high-technology businesses that could be named were

ccclxvi Singaporean, Finance, Banking; Entrepreneur, food and beverages
ccclxvii Singaporean, Human Resources, business services
ccclxviii Singaporean, Finance and Accounting, education
ccclxix Singaporean, Finance, Banking; Entrepreneur, food and beverages
ccclxx Singaporean, Finance and Accounting, education

90   2

INTRODUCTION · **THE BUSINESS CULTURES OF FIVE ASIAN COUNTRIES** · ANALYSING ASIAN BUSINESS CULTURES · OWNERSHIP, FINANCING AND GOVERNANCE · ORGANIZATION AND MANAGEMENT · BUSINESS STRATEGY ·

Table 2.5 **A summary of the present study's findings on the elements of Singaporean business culture**

Elements of Singaporean business culture	Perceived characteristics
Governance	Strong
Corruption	Low
Entrepreneurialism	Low
Innovation and creativity	Low (but MNCs bring innovation)
Government role and style	Role of government central
Domestic market size awareness	High awareness of small domestic market
Business owners' character	Astute; not savvy; culture Asian not specifically Singaporean
Special features	A magnet for talent
Personalism in business control and decision-making	*Low – meritocracy except in the small and medium enterprise (SME) sector*
Personalism in employment and work relations	*Meritocratic except in the SME sector where familism prevails*
Attitudes to risk	*Singaporean Chinese are risk takers; MNC employees are not*
Different types of businesses have different cultures	*MNCs international, local businesses Asian*
Change	*Change meets resistance in the SME sector*

very few: the two mentioned previously, Creative Technology and OSIM, which is successful in lifestyle products such as a massage chair, were the only two. Instead, a distinction was drawn between MNCs and SMEs, while only the latter were regarded as having a Singaporean business culture. 'Singapore's business culture is based on history – most businesses are owned and run by first generation migrants from India or, especially, China. In these, there is an emphasis on trust, sincerity. ... They are mostly in low barriers-to-entry traditional businesses; though the well-established network through distributors constitutes some. The other main sector is MNCs.[ccclxxi] In Singapore, attention was drawn to the 'very different' cultures of MNCs and local businesses – international versus Asian. Differences of these kinds would probably apply elsewhere, but the importance of MNCs was perceived as greater in Singapore.

Table 2.5 summarizes these findings on Singaporean business culture.

[ccclxxi] Singaporean, Finance and Accounting, education

Conclusion

This chapter has presented a country-by-country analysis of the elements of the five business cultures identified in the present study.

The predominant characteristics of mainland Chinese business cultures were high levels of deference shown towards people of status; the importance of hierarchy; *guanxi*, which is a highly developed system of relationship 'networking' combined with a preference in favour of personal and interpersonal communications and transactions rather than impersonal; the operation of *guanxi* within as well as between organizations; weak governance and persistent corruption; a tendency towards entrepreneurialism, which may or may not be cultural, but is often frustrated by the environment; attitudes to risk taking that ranged from reckless to risk averse; a low level of innovation and creativity but a high propensity for 'fast-copying'; complexity in the role and influence of government; an aversion to forward planning; a distinctive approach to negotiating.

Hong Kong interviewees emphasized three aspects of their business culture that differentiated it from the Chinese mainland: its efficient, dynamic business climate; its people's consciousness of being a link between China and the rest of the world; and its being by Asian standards a low-corruption society.

The main distinguishing characteristics of India's business culture, according to the present study, were as follows: employer-employee relations are personal and expectations on both sides are high; the personal often takes priority over the demands of business and merit; there is limited separation of work and private life; Indian business is family business, even in the case of listed MNCs; decision-making is top down; manager–subordinate relations are master–servant; interpersonal relations are important both within and across organizations but there is no *guanxi* system; Hinduism impacts on time orientation and attitudes to truth; caste influences employment relations; corruption in officialdom and the older companies is taken for granted; India's business culture is changing.

The present study found that Japanese people perceived their organizations as like families or communities; Japanese companies do not have a role culture – responsibilities are not allocated out to roles or positions; status and power are not coequivalents in Japanese businesses and high deference may be shown to a position-holder who has little real power; in both Japanese society and business there is a strong feeling in favour of equality; most traditional Japanese businesses have not been primarily concerned with making profits; Japanese business decisions are based on thorough research and information gathering; the Japanese see themselves as risk averse; consensus is a central value; Japan's high-context and low-key business communication style reflects deeper cultural values; and there is widespread recognition of the need for Japanese business and society to change.

The main features of Taiwanese business culture as described by respondents in Taiwan included close and personal relations with business partners and business customers; business ownership is a very important value linked to family control and decision-making but also to dynastic goals (except in the new high-technology businesses); face is important; the predominant professional culture is an engineering one; Taiwanese business is 'hyper-competitive'; the Taiwanese are entrepreneurial; the recent loss of government support for industry is felt strongly; views on the creativity of Taiwanese business vary; governance is weak and political corruption rampant.

Some doubt was expressed about their being a distinctive Singaporean business culture, with one-third of interviewees saying 'No', largely on the grounds that Singapore was a nation of migrants. Nevertheless, respondents had clear ideas on what made doing business or managing in Singapore 'different', and some of these differences were not repeated elsewhere in the sample. These features were a high awareness of the small size of the local market; the significant role of government and the dependence of business on it; low entrepreneurialism; change focusing on professionalization; a low tolerance for failure; owners' business character as astute, calculative and cost conscious; Singapore as a magnet for talent; Singaporeans' reputation for quality and honesty but not being savvy in dealings with China.

Previous studies have commented on some of the aspects described in this chapter, though generally without identifying them with business culture.

References

[1] Boisot, M. and Child, J. (1996) 'From fiefs to clans and network capitalism: Explaining China's emerging economic order', *Administrative Science Quarterly*, **41**(1): 600–28.
[2] Banerjee, A.V. and Duflo, E. (2007) 'What is middle class about the middle classes around the world?' URL: http://econ-www.mit.edu/files/2081.

3 analysing Asian business cultures

Chapter 2 described elements of the business cultures of five Asian countries country by country. This chapter will begin to compare our findings for the five countries on the major elements identified (omitting one or two that receive detailed coverage later in the book), and also compare them with related findings from previously published studies. Summaries are given in the tables within each topic (Tables 3.1 to 3.14). (Where the table shows no entry, there were no findings from our research for that country on that element.) The topics are organized in the sequence of internal practices within the business, then external relations of the business, concluding with some general topics that may relate to either of these. Further discussion of our findings will form part of Chapters 4 to 10.

Personalism in business control and decision-making

The determination of founding families to retain control, even of listed companies, was one of the most pervasive aspects of Asian business cultures that emerged from our research. As Chapter 2 showed, it was found to be equally as strong in India as East Asia. The contrast with Anglo-American (especially US) business cultures, as they are conventionally understood, was marked: for instance, there were few occurrences of the mindset of serial entrepreneurialism, where, following a successful start-up and sale the proceeds are reinvested in a new business, or following failure, and even bankruptcy, the individual starts over. Insofar as this mindset was found, it was among the founders of high-technology businesses many of whom had US experience and may have been 'infected' with the US business culture.

Allocation of managerial responsibility within the firm in all the countries except Singapore, where pride was expressed in being a meritocracy, was strongly influenced by personal considerations. (Even in Singapore, the same applied to the SME [small and medium enterprise] sector.) Variations were found among the countries, however, in the form that intra-organizational personalism took. In the family businesses of India and Taiwan, which in both countries dominated the economy despite the presence of 'modern' institutions such as joint stock

Table 3.1   *Personalism in business control and decision-making*

	China	India	Japan	Taiwan	Singapore
Personalism in business control and decision-making	*High – guanxi operates within organizations HKSAR. High but changing with incoming professionalization*	High familism, some casteism	*High – personal relations outweigh systems*	High – pride in business ownership is a key value	*Low – meritocracy except in the small and medium enterprise (SME) sector*

companies, the main manifestation of personalism was that only those with close connections to the founder family were trusted with decision-making or control. In mainland China, the Chinese family business was only a nascent phenomenon, although it seemed likely that the same characteristics might manifest themselves in due course. At the time of the study, personalism in China was mainly manifested in *guanxi* which operated within as well as between organizations. In Japan, instead of familism in the sense of founding families retaining control and attracting loyalty, the organizations themselves functioned like families.

On the predominance of family business and its corollary of lack of delegation to non-family, Budhwar (2003) commented that compared with the USA, the gap between ownership and management was less in **India** and that 'today's proprietor-manager' had still to shake off his [*sic*] trading and speculative background. Indians were disposed to hierarchical relationships; a power-based hierarchy existed in most Indian organizations. Management was often autocratic, based on formal authority and charisma. Decision-making was very centralized, with much emphasis on rules. Expert power was frequently relegated in favour of position power. It was difficult for non-family members to advance into upper management positions, particularly in private businesses. However, Budhwar (2003) pointed out, there was a conflict of management cultures in India, due to the influence of Western business educational models that conflicted with tradition. 'These two sets of values co-exist and are drawn upon as frames of reference depending on the nature of the problems that managers face.'[1] Kumar (2007) found that in the Indian bureaucracy, 15 years of liberalization and more than 50 years of democracy did not bring about differences in hierarchical tendencies: younger employees who had joined the bureaucracy less than 2 years previously and older employees who had joined roughly 25 years earlier displayed similarly 'hierarchical' attitudes. Employees in the Indian bureaucracy continued to be dependent on their superiors and conscious of the status of their superiors. However, these employees did not feel the need to develop a personalized relationship with their superiors. Further, employees in higher management depended less on their superiors and were less conscious of the status of their superiors than those at supervisor level. Although this study dealt with the bureaucracy, the same tendencies were reported for traditional businesses, though perhaps in a weaker form.[2]

The views expressed in our interviews on the predominance of familism in **Taiwan** agreed with those of Liu (2000) who wrote

> " Regardless of size or scale, Taiwanese enterprises cannot be separated from the family: the latter is always the foundation of the former, and the Chinese family still has a strong effect on how contemporary Taiwanese businesses are initiated, organized, and expanded. In this sense, the enduring organizational form of Taiwanese enterprises is the family business, which is something else that economic globalization has not fundamentally altered. Just the reverse, in fact: under globalization, there is growing recognition of family business as a unique and effective organizational form and management setting.[3]

Redding (1990) accounted for familism within businesses in part as allowing costs to be lower by requiring less internal auditing and reporting. On the other hand, Redding (1990) suggested, most family businesses remained small because personalized control could not be widely extended in the same way as systematic or procedural control. Such businesses commonly restricted the information available to non-family managers to ensure that they remained dependent. This limited the non-family members' effectiveness and so reinforced the preference for involving only 'trusted' executives in decisions. Goal setting was regarded as an internal family affair and was not done in collaboration with all those doing the work. There were dangers in all this: without goals that were mutually agreed upon objectives, workers might lose interest and become less motivated. Without a clear division of labour, clearly set tasks and job specifications, work efforts could lack focus and time be wasted as people worked out for themselves how best to do their work.[4]

With growth, Redding (1990) conceded, family businesses ultimately considered professional management, but the making of deals was still handled by the family in the traditional way. This could lead to power conflicts between the professionals and the family entrepreneurs. Professionals still tended to be excluded from the inner circles of management. Since family owners usually retained control over pay increases and other crucial personnel matters, professional managers might also lack real authority within the workforce. Also, with less formal management control systems, objective assessment of employee performance might be lacking and top management might only pay special attention to loyalty or other less professional attributes. Redding (1990) argued that firms with such unstable means of control could not meet global competitive standards.[5]

A more culture-oriented explanation of familism and personalism in business than that of Redding (1990) was supplied by Bjerke (2000) who commented that in cultures where it obtained, individuals had a very deep attachment and sense of belonging to social groups. Family included clan, people who shared a sur-name, a home village, region or education. The effect of familism was that family and non-family members differed both in attitude and behaviour.[6] The outcome could be that these businesses suffered from an 'endemic lack of trust'.[7]

Steier et al. (2004) concluded from a symposium on family firms that they might be more complex than non-family firms.

> There is likely interplay between family culture, family business culture [here meaning the organizational culture of a family business], and the extant culture [the culture of the surrounding society] that affect the goals, strategy, structure, and performance of a family firm. The relationship among family members and between family members and non-family members in a business may run the entire spectrum of stewardship at one end and agency at the other, depending on the life cycle stage one examines. Succession provides an important mechanism for organizational renewal. Finally, the contributions of family firms to innovation and economic development may depend on their orientation and relative size. While entrepreneurial families may have advantages in innovation and new venture development and contribute significantly to it, dominant family firms that pursue political rent seeking may inhibit it.

Steier et al. (2004) made three observations regarding family versus non-family firms based on their findings in an exploratory study. First, family involvement did not appear to impact short-term performance either positively or negatively; second, strategic planning seemed to enhance the performance of both family- and non-family firms; third, non-family firms derived greater benefit from the stra-tegic planning process, presumably because of more pervasive agency problems.[8]

Personalism in employment and work relations

Employment and work relations were most strongly emphasized as aspects of the business cultures of India and Japan, although personalism in this area was recog-nized as a characteristic of many businesses in all five countries.

Budhwar (2003) confirmed the priority given to the personal in business in **India**, arguing that apart from merit, relations mattered a lot and change that affected relationships adversely was not easily accepted, as a result of which optimum performance was very rarely achieved.[9] In similar vein, Kanungo and Mendonca (1994) pointed out that since Indians were socialized in an envir-onment that valued strong family ties and extended family relationships, they

Table 3.2 **Personalism in employment and work relations**

	China	India	Japan	Taiwan	Singapore
Personalism in employment and work relations	*Mixed, but China not a meritocracy; HKSAR meritocratic except in the SME sector where familism prevails*	*In traditional businesses, personalism prevails and work relationships are all-embracing; the modern private companies use merit-based systems. 'Soft' culture.*	*Organizations are communities of their employees. In big companies, appointment is merit-based but promotion is seniority-based.*	*High in older companies, low in newer technology-based companies*	*Meritocratic except in the SME sector where familism prevails*

were more likely to develop strong affiliative tendencies or greater dependence on others. In the work context, interpersonal relationships were more salient to them and, as a result, their job-related decisions might be influenced more by interpersonal considerations than by task demands.[10]

Hierarchy

The autocratic, top-down style of management in Chinese and Indian businesses and the contrasting consensus approach in Japan were noted in Chapter 2. Selmer et al. (1994) wrote of **China**:

> The hierarchical structure of interpersonal relationships dictates authoritarian patterns of interactions between superior and subordinates. Subordinates are expected to be submissive and relatively passive in hierarchical relations. Proper social distance between individuals is maintained, since improper familiarity might threaten the notion of inequality and diminish perceived status differences. However, traditionally, it is a benevolently authoritarian leadership modeled after the family head who manages his household. Chinese employees seem to prefer such a paternalistic authoritarian style, through which a benevolent and respected leader is not only considerate of his [sic] employees, but also takes skilled and decisive actions. ...The decision-making process is typically not participative, since open debates about his leadership tend to be viewed as a threat to the leader's status or as a challenge to his authority.

> Subordinates assume that the leader has thought of everything, and they are expected to follow decisions and instructions from the top without question. Centralized decision making preserves the leader's superior image and is a relevant adaptation to the expectations of employees, coinciding with the predominant Chinese values of respect for authority, conformity, and hierarchical submission.[11]

Despite the importance of hierarchy in its organizations, the culture of **India** does not support hierarchy through a moral basis for command and obedience in the manner of Confucianism. Indeed, despite the rank ordering of society in the caste system, it is debatable whether Indian culture supports unquestioning obedience at all, as Sen (2005) suggested in *The Argumentative Indian: Writings on Indian Culture, History and Identity*.[12] A more plausible influence on Indians' submission to hierarchy is their recognition of power engendered by a recent history of high levels of unemployment, including graduate unemployment, and a fairly recent history of colonialism. This view is supported by the substantially different employee attitudes we found from our study in the information technology (IT) sector, where talent shortages rather than unemployment were prevalent.

Lincoln et al. (1986) observed that in terms of authority relationships, managers in **Japan** were more remote than their US counterparts, fitting the high power distance and respect for hierarchy characteristic of Japanese society.[13] Judging from the present study, however, Lincoln et al. (1986) mistook deference towards high-status individuals with acceptance of influence. In Japanese business, the two are not always, or perhaps usually, coextensive. Apart from the contradiction provided by our findings, Lincoln's conclusions seem based on a misreading of Hofstede's (1980) findings: Japan was ranked only seventeenth/eighteenth on power distance out of 74 countries and scored only 50, whereas the highest-scoring country (Malaysia) scored 104.[14] Consistent with statements by our interviewees, Lee et al. (2000) concluded from a literature review that participation of workers and middle management had been important for Japanese firms and

Table 3.3 **Importance of hierarchy**

	China	India	Japan	Taiwan	Singapore
Importance of hierarchy	High – hierarchy very important	Boss–subordinate relations are 'master–servant'	Low power distance – status and power are not coequivalent	*Medium-high in older companies, lower in newer technology-based companies*	

that it was the relationships between management levels ('middle up-down management') that were most important. Employees were appreciated as assets. In addition, consensus building and group loyalty were emphasized as important principles in Japanese management. Finally, corporate values seemed to guide a Japanese firm's organization.[15]

Redding (1990) argued that a fundamental requirement for businesses to survive and prosper was vertical cooperation. In Chinese family-owned businesses (CFOBs) in **South East Asia**,

> Vertical cooperation is realized through hierarchy, which is informal and personal in nature. At the top of the hierarchy is the founding family, the key stakeholder. Discipline within the hierarchy is based around Confucian paternalism, a cultural value that applies not only to family members but also to some degree to all employees. Subordinates exhibit often unquestioning obedience, a willingness to work hard and loyalty; higher levels within the hierarchy behave responsibly towards their subordinates.

Achieving vertical cooperation through paternalistic hierarchy could produce weaknesses; ambitious and able individuals might become demotivated or not attracted to the business, leading to a talent shortage; factions and cliques formed around particular figures in the hierarchy; individuals might devote more energy to cultivating the right people than performing well on the job.[16] There was a suggestion from our interviews that in most family-owned businesses in **Taiwan**, this picture overstresses hierarchy and the unquestioning obedience of staff.

Status acknowledged by deference

In our study we found that deference to people of status was common to China, India and Japan but that its significance varied. In China and India, status was linked to power; in Japan, on the contrary, deference was offered as a kind of compensation to office holders who had substantial responsibility but not

Table 3.4 **Deference**

	China	India	Japan	Taiwan	Singapore
Status acknowledged by deference	High deference to superiors	Extremely high deference to owners; high to superiors	Very high deference to seniors and superiors	*Relatively low*	

commensurate power or reward. Businesses in Taiwan, despite sharing many of the characteristics of Asian family businesses, including personalism, were described as low in deference and formality.

Only in relation to **India** could we find comments on deference in the literature:

> To Indians, in general, a position of power is synonymous with special privileges. The norms, systems and processes of the ordinary folk do not apply to the high and mighty. So deep-rooted is this belief that if a security guard so much as asks a man clad in spotless whites for his identity card, he stands to lose his job. 'Do you know who I am?' is a standard phrase employed to throw one's weight around in this country. In a Western country, so used are they to treating everyone as equal before the law that they actually do not understand the question or its implied threat. Many of our politicians have had a rude shock when faced with this reality abroad.[17]

Entrepreneurialism

Our interviews suggested that high levels of entrepreneurialism were only seen as a significant part of the business culture in Taiwan, while a lack of entrepreneurial spirit, despite government encouragement for entrepreneurs, was noted in Singapore. In China, views on entrepreneurialism were mixed, and a distinction was drawn between starting a business and entrepreneurialism in the sense of willingness to take risks.

A cultural explanation for attitudes to entrepreneurship in **China** has been supported in the literature. Ahlstrom and Bruton (2002) wrote, 'A richer understanding of Chinese entrepreneurship is possible if the cultural, largely informal, normative and cognitive institutions and the enabling role they can play in commercial activity is considered.'[18] Other explanations of entrepreneurialism in China have been political rather than cultural. Zhang (2007) concluded that entrepreneurialism is structurally as well as culturally influenced from findings that entrepreneurs in the

Table 3.5 **Entrepreneurialism**

	China	India	Japan	Taiwan	Singapore
Entrepreneurialism	*High but restricted*	*Medium – occurs in certain communities; also now sometimes in young not from business backgrounds*	*Low*	High	Low

sense of business founders who were mainly independent of government support occurred more in some areas of China than others. Founders of TVEs (town and village enterprises) did not generally exhibit entrepreneurialism in that sense; they were strongly supported by and linked to local government. The areas where relatively independent entrepreneurs emerged were those where central and local government allowed space for social actors and a market economy was developing.[19] A study based on questionnaires completed by 53 small firms in the electronics industry may help explain the disjunction between entrepreneurialism and risk tolerance reported in our study. It concluded that Chinese private entrepreneurs not only had a strong propensity for risk taking and innovation, but also that their profit-maximizing orientation and hard-budget constraints encouraged more proactive moves in their investment decisions. However, the researcher noted,

> During our interviews with Chinese private business owners, we found a common fear: that in the absence of adequate legal protection of private property rights, they are constantly concerned about possible hostility directed against them in a future political campaign and about the possible appropriation of their assets. Consequently they are reluctant to make long-term investments in the growth of their enterprises.[20]

A broad-based study of top managers from over 3500 Chinese firms, including both state-owned and non-state-owned enterprises, found that firm performance was closely related to how entrepreneurial the managers' attitudes were. These findings were robust no matter what the managers' perception of their environment – whether they evaluated the firm's current and future business prospects, availability of financial resources and projected sales revenue as favourable, neutral or unfavourable. Entrepreneurial orientation was measured by six items that tapped into attitudes towards innovativeness, risk-taking propensity and proactiveness. Such a finding is universal in nature – that is, the link between managers' attitudes and firm performance should be non-specific to the Chinese culture. On the other hand, the attitudes themselves could well be affected by culture.[21]

Dana (2000) concurred in the opinion expressed in our interviews that a combination of historical factors, including the caste system, British occupation, cultural values and government regulations stifled entrepreneurialism in **India** until recently.[22] Asserting that India's entrepreneurs would be effective in the right circumstances, the country's chief economic planner said in a published interview, 'The good news is we don't have to worry about industry: give them a competitive market, reasonable macroeconomics, and deliver the infrastructure, and our entrepreneurs know what to do.'[23]

In **India**, unlike China, entrepreneurialism does not conflict with the beliefs of most of the population. This applies especially among the young. Citing the example of a 28-year-old Bangalore woman who 'set up her own business, but also maintains traditional values such as worshipping in the puja room at home and serving tea to her parents', a BBC programme asserted, 'With more than half its population under the age of 25, India has seen a massive rise in the number of young entrepreneurs.' On the other hand, the cultural values of familism and deference to the wishes of older family members can present an obstacle to entrepreneurialism. Although both know-how and the legal system may prove obstacles to the hoped-for transformation of Bangalore into the Silicon Valley of Asia,

> The biggest hurdle for Indian entrepreneurs may be cultural. 'Most people prefer a safe job at one of the big services firms, since that is what their parents and future in-laws want', says Ashish Gupta of Helion Ventures. 'Our middle class is adaptive, not innovative,' says Subroto Bagchi founder of MindTree Consulting, a start-up backed with venture capital.[24]

Entrepreneurialism in **Japan,** already low at 7 per cent in 1970, declined to only 4 per cent by 2002, the lowest among industrialized countries. Our findings suggested that the blame lay in part with the business culture. Previously the country's societal culture has been blamed, a suggestion disputed by Yasuda (2002) who argued that the higher rate of business start-ups during Japan's era of rapid growth demonstrated that this explanation was wrong. Instead, it could be explained by Japan's aging population and the seniority principle, which meant that the income gap between salaried and self-employed was strongly in favour of the former by the time they have accumulated the kind of experience that they could use to start a business.[25] Feigenbaum and Brunner (2002), on the other hand, allocated a role to the societal culture but as one variable among others. These included the difficulty of financing a start-up in a way that provided a strong foundation for future growth, the problems that Japanese start-ups faced in obtaining the human resources that they needed and the way that Japanese institutions crippled start-ups with their procurement policies. The cultural attitudes that most affected entrepreneurialism in Japan, according to Feigenbaum and Brunner (2002), were those towards failure; these explained 'the bias toward the aversion of risk rather than the management of risk'. This, they said, applied to all the relevant players.[26]

Supporting the viewpoint of our interviewees that entrepreneurialism was central to the business culture of **Taiwan** is the fact that it has an unusually high level of self-employment for a country at its stage of development.

> This derives from macro-level opportunities in the market on the demand side including the shift from manufacturing to service industries; while gender, ethnicity, personal ties and the type of human

> capital on the supply side, including individual attributes that aid in the acquisition of social capital, such as kinship networks, geographical origins, or previous work experience, determine one's entry into self-employment. Past government policies to encourage small businesses eases the entry into self-employment and the business culture encourages the notion that 'black hands (i.e., blue-collar workers) becoming bosses (by becoming self-employed)' is a viable path of upward mobility for manufacturing workers.[27]

Taiwanese entrepreneurialism has been linked to a Chinese culture that runs counter to Confucian orthodoxy while endorsing the Confucian contempt for law. Lam et al. (1994) argued that Confucianism was hostile to entrepreneurship, as shown by the way merchants, the historical equivalent of business executives, were allocated the lowest rung in society, by a rigidity in social relations which discouraged flexibility and initiative, by an emphasis in education on rote learning of classics rather than any applied studies and by siphoning off of talent into the bureaucracy where official purposes were elevated above those of the economy. On the other hand, the Confucian stress on education did provide the society as a whole with a disciplined, hard-working workforce, which served the needs of entrepreneurs.[28] However, Lam et al. (1994) also argued that although Confucian orthodoxy formed one pole of Chinese culture, this had other dimensions. A pole which included Taoist, Buddhist and other subcultures that are, in Western terms, counter-cultures, challenged orthodox Chinese culture.

> " Whereas Confucianism stresses order and authority, the heterodox cultures reject the primacy of central authority and legitimize rebellion as a means to escape domination. They idealize egalitarian values, despise formal education and the pretensions of those who think themselves to be the moral and intellectual betters of the common man, and place great faith in elixirs and in magical slogans as formulas for political success.

Chinese entrepreneurs in Taiwan have often come from families that belonged to these counter-cultures and so were 'divorced' from the overall Chinese social hierarchy and freed from the constraints of orthodoxy. This left them at liberty to 'challenge segments of industry dominated by vulnerable large-scale enterprises, question the established order of brand name products and "pirate" know-how and technology'. When the product was relatively simple to manufacture (or the 'pirate' was an OEM [original equipment manufacturer] supplier to the firm that owned the rights) and protected only by legally registered trademarks, patents and copyrights, and especially when it commanded a premium for a foreign brand name, Taiwanese entrepreneurs would copy it. They were protected from the possibility of 'whistle-blowing' because their employees were, unlike themselves, constrained by

104 3

INTRODUCTION • THE BUSINESS CULTURES OF FIVE ASIAN COUNTRIES • ANALYSING ASIAN BUSINESS CULTURES
• OWNERSHIP, FINANCING AND GOVERNANCE • ORGANIZATION AND MANAGEMENT • BUSINESS STRATEGY •

Confucian orthodoxy, and so would place loyalty to their 'boss' above government-mandated law.[29]

The exigencies of survival between patriarchal orthodoxy on the one hand and state bureaucratic orthodoxy on the other gave to Chinese, and particularly Taiwanese, entrepreneurship a 'guerrilla' character. This type of entrepreneurship also formed a self-identity that was set against the state orthodoxy and reinforced the Confucian contempt for law, thus leading to past infringements of intellectual property and copyright laws.[30] On the other hand, Berrell and Wrathall (2007) asserted that Taiwan had experienced success in building new norms for intellectual property (IP) protection, which suggested that cultural values supporting IP piracy could be overcome if sufficient facilitating factors were present in the political, business and social environment.[31]

Chou (2003) related the prevalence of SMEs in Taiwan, where they comprised 98.1 per cent of all enterprises, to research showing that the Taiwanese had the inclination to become bosses.[32] Other research suggested that in addition to the family ethic, in Taiwan motives for family enterprise included tax avoidance and reducing labour disputes. In small enterprises, unpaid family workers were one of the major sources of labour. The owner's wife was often in charge of some important aspects of the business. In larger enterprises, recruitment of family members could help businesses avoid tax without being detected. In high-technology industries, the greatest concern was to stabilize the core workers and to stimulate their potential. Therefore, these companies often provided large amounts of job training and very high bonuses.[33]

Dahles (2002), commenting on entrepreneurialism in **Singapore**, wrote that Singaporeans 'do not rank among the world's most daring and innovating business leaders'.

> Local entrepreneurs – if they do not give up the ambition of running a private enterprise altogether – generally prefer to avoid risk where possible. Their choice to play the role of subcontractor to both foreign MNCs [multinational companies] and domestic GLCs [government-led companies] shows such an inclination. Another strategy of risk-avoidance is to confine business activities and partnerships to familiar domains and established ties. Research on 'enterprising culture' among the three major ethnic groups in Singapore – Chinese, Indian, and Malay – concludes that close-knit ethnic and family ties dominate the organization of small-scale businesses in Singapore at large. The perception that it is safer to work in an environment of shared cultural values seems to have engendered intra-ethnic networking. Among the Chinese, in particular, sentimental or moral reasons may encourage the strengthening of ethnic ties stretching as far back as their ancestral 'hometown' in China (qiaoxiang) through economic investments. However, one should not jump to the conclusion

> that ethnic ties necessarily engender intra-ethnic networking or that shared ethnicity and culture create a low-risk business environment. There is fierce competition among Chinese entrepreneurs for government concessions in Malaysia, and business activities in China turned out to be high-risk and loss-making ventures for many a Singapore-Chinese entrepreneur.[34]

Previous research in **East Asia** found a clear link between Asian attitudes to starting a business and culture-level values of social status, the shame associated with failure, the importance of work and the value of innovation. High culture-level value attached to social status was the only one of these four values that was linked to a positive interest in entrepreneurship, but several negative relationships to culture-level factors were found. The perceived feasibility and desirability of becoming an entrepreneur was lower in cultures which emphasized shame in the case of failure, possibly because such a value may induce greater scrutiny of entrepreneurial prospects. A high importance attached to work similarly led to a low assessment of entrepreneurial feasibility. Since new business ventures are risky, people in societies that place a very high value on work, acutely aware that venture failure means loss of work, may be especially conservative in assessing their feasibility. Finally, negative relationships were found between the value placed on innovation and the feasibility of starting a new business, relationships which can be understood in terms of risk aversion. Singaporean and Indonesian informants stated that they would only start a business if it were a sure thing, a perspective that emphasizes feasibility. To innovate, they would seek the protective walls of a larger company. Based on their argument that cultural values may hold sway more powerfully in East Asian 'shame-based cultures' than in Anglo-Saxon 'guilt-based cultures', Begley and Tan (2001) considered it follows that decisions about starting a business might be more subject to normative cultural beliefs in East Asian than Anglo-Saxon countries.[35]

A similar conclusion that would endorse a finding of relatively low levels of entrepreneurialism in Asia came from a study that identified cultural distance from the USA as a predictor for lower levels of three variables previously found to be linked to entrepreneurialism: internal locus of control, risk-taking propensity and energy. Since the cultural distance of Asia from the USA was high on most dimensions, these findings would support a conclusion of low predicted entrepreneurialism there.[36]

Finally, Begley et al. (2005) found little support from research in 13 Anglo-Saxon, East Asian and South Asian countries for hypotheses that perceived environmental munificence and carrying capacity were influential in how feasible or desirable starting a business was thought to be in the East Asian or South Asian regions. Measures consisted of perceived financing available, supportive government regulation, market opportunities, access to support services, supply of skilled labour, connections needed and competitive conditions. Only supply of skilled labour in South Asia correlated positively.[37] This absence of a link between positive attitudes towards entrepreneurship and the perceived environment supports a view that cultural factors are a stronger influence.

Attitudes to risk

As Chapter 2 noted, the Chinese interviewees in this study varied in their views of the country's business risk attitudes, with descriptions varying from 'reckless' and 'gamblers' to 'cautious, risk averse'; handling risk with a benchmarking culture was also mentioned. Japanese companies were regarded as always conscious of risk and as risk avoiders. In contrast, the Taiwanese 'enjoy taking risks' and their success in building up their economy in the 20th century was partly attributed to this characteristic; they also managed risk – for example, the riskiness of many new ventures was reduced by their being spin-offs from established companies. Indians expressed ambivalence in regard to the risk-taking propensity of their business culture; this ambivalence was not found in earlier research, such as a study that measured managerial risk propensity among 285 Indian managers in India and Singapore and found that managers in India were significantly more willing than managers in Singapore to take risks.[38]

To Dahles (2002) risk aversion in **Singapore** appeared widespread:

> Risk aversion is expressed in a general preference for being an employee rather than an employer, a professional rather than a business leader. There is a fear of losing out (*kiasu*), a risk-avoiding attitude that seems to be pervasive in the Singaporean culture, though a part was played by historical factors. These include the legacy of the colonial state under which Chinese immigrants were barred from non-commercial activities as well as political measures taken by the Singaporean government against the vested interests of the Chinese business community in the early days of the city-state.[39]

Research by Sheedy (2001) showed widespread speculative behaviour by corporate treasurers in Hong Kong and Singapore, often with inadequate controls, suggesting a risk-taking approach to financial matters.[40] However, later research by

Table 3.6 **Attitudes to risk**

	China	India	Japan	Taiwan	Singapore
Attitudes to risk	Some are gamblers; some rational risk-handlers	*An individual, not a cultural, matter*	Risk averse	Not risk averse and able to handle risk effectively	*Singaporean Chinese are risk takers; MNC employees are not*

Sheedy (2004) among post-graduate finance students in Australia, Hong Kong/ China and Singapore found that students in Hong Kong/China and Singapore were *more* risk averse than their Australian counterparts and concluded that national attitudes to risk do not explain the speculative behaviour of corporate treasurers in Hong Kong and Singapore.[41] Our interviews suggested a more nuanced picture: 'The Chinese, who are 70 to 80 per cent of the Singaporean business community, are risk takers, but employees in multi-national companies are risk averse.'[i]

Our study found that institutional factors in Asia can break the link between entrepreneurialism and a positive attitude to risk taking. We found, for instance, that Chinese entrepreneurs' links to local governments often take the risk out of entrepreneurship there, while Singaporean entrepreneurs often enter mature industries where the risks are known and limited. In the words of Feigenbaum and Brunner (2002) these start-ups, like most of Japan's, are 'not entrepreneurial'. 'These startups address well-developed needs with products and services that are not substantially innovative. ... Most restaurants, retail stores, and IT contractors fall into this category. Such startups do not need to invest much in research and development.'[42]

Innovation and creativity

Overall, we found highly negative judgements on the innovativeness of their countries' businesses from the Asian business decision-makers in our study, as Table 3.7 indicates. These judgements were major elements of the business cultures revealed in China, Japan, Taiwan and Singapore; in India the assessments either emerged spontaneously from only a minority of interviews or only in answer to questions from the interviewer.

The rather low level of innovativeness (except for technological products) perceived by our interviewees in **Japan** provides a different emphasis to two sets of two case studies, which themselves had divergent findings. One study of two large, traditional Japanese corporations found that such businesses could be very effective in innovating. The two corporations 'simultaneously created new service markets and established a dominant position in the competitive fields of the internet and mobile communications in Japan'. To do so they accepted new organizational bodies imbued with an entrepreneurial spirit, supported by different types of personnel, and then continuously promoted entrepreneurial strategies. They also succeeded in integrating these strategies with those of their existing organizational bodies.[43] On the other hand, another set of two case studies of Japanese organizations found that barriers of inertia impeded the pursuit of strategies of

---

[i] Singaporean, Finance, Banking; Entrepreneur, food and beverages

108   3

INTRODUCTION · THE BUSINESS CULTURES OF FIVE ASIAN COUNTRIES · **ANALYSING ASIAN BUSINESS CULTURES**
· OWNERSHIP, FINANCING AND GOVERNANCE · ORGANIZATION AND MANAGEMENT · BUSINESS STRATEGY ·

Table 3.7 **Innovation and creativity**

	China	India	Japan	Taiwan	Singapore
Innovation and creativity	Low (but fast copiers) HKSAR Low (but highly efficient)	*Low (but good problem-solvers)*	Low except in technological products; good modifiers	Low (but good at reverse engineering)	Low (but MNCs bring innovation)

technological innovation and internationalization in such businesses. 'Embedded internal network connections and knowledge-sharing routines between central R&D [Research and Development] and other divisions are inappropriate for the revised strategy. Existing external connections, with preferred suppliers and customers within *keiretsu* structures, and close relationships with existing R&D partners retard these firms' strategic flexibility.'[44] Whitley (2007) noted that large Japanese pharmaceutical companies tended to have 'rather passive' connections with the formal research system except through the recruitment of new graduates, and in that sense were 'relatively separate from generic knowledge production'. The result was that innovations 'build on continuous group learning in and between network members, and so tend to follow particular technological trajectories that do not devalue current organizational capabilities'.[45]

An exploratory survey of 40 firms from 3 innovative sectors – high-technology manufacturing industries, knowledge intensive business services and creative content industries – found a favourable perception of **Singapore** as an innovative city. It also found that excellent infrastructure and intellectual property right protection was related to businesses' decisions to locate innovative activities in Singapore. Thus, while the population may not be culturally creative or innovative, as our interviews suggested, other factors may compensate.[46]

In the context of an Asian country not included in our sample, South Korea, Fukuyama (1995) argued that in low trust societies, the lack of trust led to bottlenecks in sharing socially useful knowledge and less transparency in business transactions, resulting in stunted innovation by firms. Diffusion of scientific and technological knowledge could be seriously blocked by the lack of trust. The costs of innovation may be high because of the high transaction costs incurred. Efforts to generate new knowledge may be too difficult in a low trust society. While the causes of low levels of societal trust may differ – Korea's was ascribed to historical facts such as the severe control of the Japanese colonial government, war with North Korea, one civil revolution and two military coups d'etat over five decades – the negative outcome for innovation may be similar for the other Asian restricted-trust societies.[47]

Corporate governance

Weak corporate governance was a common theme for the two 'Confucian' societies in our study, Taiwan and China, different though their business systems were. In contrast, in Singapore and Hong Kong, interviewees were not only proud of their strong governance but also considered it a business advantage in their particular economic situations. The opportunities for expropriation arising in family businesses and business groups were emphasized in Taiwan, while in China, weak rule of law generally left owners of businesses to act as they pleased, with little concern for governance issues. These perceptions were largely consistent with previously published findings.

Noting that Taiwan, China and Hong Kong were at different stages of economic development and had vastly different development strategies and political economies, Liu (2000) pointed out that nevertheless Chinese business culture was 'one common thread' among them. These three economies all faced some level of ownership concentration, with possible negative consequences for corporate governance. In Taiwan and Hong Kong, family-owned but listed companies dominated the stock exchange, while in China the recent corporatization of state-owned enterprises still left the state with significant blocks of ownership.[48]

Despite signs of change, particularly in the government's determination to impose rules, in India, we were told, 'Corporate governance is always an issue.'[ii] An investigation of corporate governance in **India** found that regulation had taken on a strict form without any commensurate conviction on the part of corporate leadership. Equally, institutional investors such as mutual funds and pension funds were not active in monitoring company management or the pattern of debt and equity holdings; nominee directors from financial institutions had in fact restricted their interventions to safeguard their institutional interest in the companies.[49]

One reflection of weak corporate governance in India was shown by bank lending practices. Bhati (2006) observed that a social risk evaluation was more appropriate for risk evaluation and reduction by banks in India, because instrument-based methods used variables that could not be accurately measured by banks in emerging economies.[50] However, a different explanation was provided by our respondents:

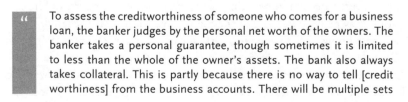

> To assess the creditworthiness of someone who comes for a business loan, the banker judges by the personal net worth of the owners. The banker takes a personal guarantee, though sometimes it is limited to less than the whole of the owner's assets. The bank also always takes collateral. This is partly because there is no way to tell [credit worthiness] from the business accounts. There will be multiple sets

---

[ii] Indian, Finance and General Management, Indian MNC heavy industry

110   3

INTRODUCTION • THE BUSINESS CULTURES OF FIVE ASIAN COUNTRIES • **ANALYSING ASIAN BUSINESS CULTURES** • OWNERSHIP, FINANCING AND GOVERNANCE • ORGANIZATION AND MANAGEMENT • BUSINESS STRATEGY •

Table 3.8 **Governance**

	China	India	Japan	Taiwan	Singapore
Governance	Weak HKSAR Strong	*Weak but being seriously addressed by government*	Weak	Weak	Strong

 of books – one for the owner, which you won't see, one for the tax man, one for the creditor.[iii]

The present study found that while governance issues were not a major element of the business culture of **Japan**, there was an awareness of its weaknesses. According to Yafeh (2000) Japan's governance mechanisms traditionally relied on monitoring by large shareholders and banks as opposed to American-style corporate governance, in which hostile takeovers and managerial incentive schemes played a major role. Although there is substantial evidence on the effectiveness of the Japanese system, there is also evidence on its significant shortcomings, concurring with the findings of the present study.[51]

Corruption

Even more than weak governance, corruption was seen as a major problem in China, India and Taiwan, but not in Hong Kong, despite signs that it was increasing there, nor in Singapore and Japan.

Statistics show that corruption presents a serious social problem in **China**. In 2006, China was ranked joint 72nd least corrupt by Transparency International (TI) with a score of 3.5 out of 10, where TI considered the problem to be serious in any country with a score below 5.0. (Hong Kong was rated 14th. In Asia, only Singapore and Japan were ranked higher than Hong Kong.) In the early 1980s, there were more than 20,000 estimated cases of corruption under investigation in China each year. By 1996, this number had increased to 46,314. In Guangdong, a southern province of China, a Chinese survey released in 1991 showed that 84.5 per cent of respondents had learned about corruption from personal experience. In 1989, a study in Guangzhou, the capital city of Guangdong, found that 73.1 per cent of respondents reported having difficulty in getting government officials to handle a request unless they were given a favour.[52]

According to D'Souza (2003) what the West 'misconstrues' as bribery is often reciprocal gift-giving. 'Gift-giving is seen as an act of reciprocity, and often

---

iii Indian, Senior Consultant, Business Services (banking operations and technology)

misconstrued as bribery by Westerners, yet it appears to be an important constituent of the Asian culture and can be seen as a form of relationship investment, that if cultivated well, can uplift interactions between businesses.'[53] Lee and Oh (2007), with possibly greater realism, classified China's corruption as high in pervasiveness but low in arbitrariness; India's as the reverse, and Japan's, Singapore's and Hong Kong's as low in both.[54] Arbitrariness is more damaging to business than pervasiveness; if the amount needed is known and the certainty that if the bribe is paid the service will follow, business can adjust, though of course it increases costs and so reduces competitiveness; however, if corruption is arbitrary, uncertainty increases and may act as a disincentive to investment. In relation to another issue that vexed the West in its dealings with China, intellectual property protection, Ahlstrom and Bruton (2002) noted that there was now nominal protection of intellectual assets in China, but these regulations were not widely enforced; judgements were based on connections of lawyers with judges and enforcement was spotty.[55]

Fears were growing that *Hong Kong's* low-corruption status might be progressively undermined by its growing links to China. Both objective measures and perceptions of corruption increased dramatically during the 1990s. The moral constraints on corruption which were in place before 1997, it is suggested, were progressively displaced by the uncertainty about the future and the temptation of earning quick money. Opportunities for corruption increased due to the growing presence of mainland Chinese investments in Hong Kong and the unremitting social and economic interactions across the SAR (Special Administrative Region) border with the mainland. Moreover, Hong Kong business-persons became more liable to bribery owing to their gradual acculturation or adaptation to the 'corrupt business culture'[sic] of the Mainland.[56] However, Hong Kong had improved its TI ranking from 18th in 1996 to 14th in 2006. One form of corruption that has attracted the attention of observers of Asian business and politics is cronyism. For instance, Khatri et al. (2006) focused on cronyism as a 'purported primary contributor' to the Asian financial implosion of 1997 because of the reportedly widespread practice whereby executives in Asian financial institutions funded questionable business transactions by family and friends. Cronyism is a reciprocal exchange transaction where party A shows favour to party B based on shared membership in a social network, at the expense of party C's equal or superior claim to the valued resource. It is a form

Table 3.9 **Corruption**

	China	India	Japan	Taiwan	Singapore
Corruption	Official corruption high. *HKSAR* low	Widespread except in high-technology businesses	*Low*	Political corruption endemic	Low

of corruption. Cronyism may be motivated either by instrumental factors or by relational factors, such as affection or loyalty. Cronyism is not *guanxi*, in which obligations are inherited,[57] whereas cronyistic obligations generally do not pass from generation to generation. Second, *guanxi* may lead to favouritism, but it is not itself favouritism. Cronyism, on the other hand, is the act of favouritism itself. Finally, unlike cronyism, the benefits derived from *guanxi* do not necessarily come at the expense of other parties. Nevertheless, exchange transactions based on *guanxi* can involve cronyism.[58]

Personalism in business-to-business relations (B2B)

The present study identified the building, maintenance and use of personal networks (*guanxi*) for business purposes as a 'major' element of the business culture of China and Taiwan, as Chapter 2 showed. The picture was less clear-cut in India, Japan and Singapore.

The topic of *guanxi* has been of considerable interest to outside observers of **China**, and has been described before. For example, to Ahlstrom and Bruton (2002), this Chinese 'system' of interpersonal networking, literally 'connection' or 'relationship', 'involves a flexible, but relatively permanent, set of exchange relationships based on reputation and trust, that provides access to resources and information over an indefinite period of time. *Guanxi* also involves mutual obligations that need to be reciprocated and maintained between individuals.'[59] Bjerke (2000) described it as a series of interlocked networks; it tended to be less emotional than utilitarian, as our own study also found. 'In the West, there is business first, then the networking; in Asia, there is networking first, then the business.'[60] As might be expected, different kinds of relationship within a *guanxi* network allowed or required different obligations. For example, in Hong Kong, 'costly' favours were more likely to be sought from family members than classmates, club members or family friends. Chow and Ng (2004) found evidence in

Table 3.10   **Personalism in business-to-business relations (B2B)**

	China	India	Japan	Taiwan	Singapore
Personalism in B2B	B2B depends on personal networks, guanxi	*Personal relationships are important but not a guanxi system*	*B2B relationships even within keiretsu are mainly inter-organizational though there are elements of personalism*	B2B and financing depend on personal networks, guanxi	

Hong Kong that the size of individuals' *guanxi* networks was linked to their social 'face'.[61] While the results of a study of supplier search mechanisms in mainland China found that industrialization and modernization had reduced the importance of traditional forms of *guanxi*, such as family and community connections, it also showed that these had been replaced by business connections;[62] *guanxi* had changed its form but retained its importance.

Kipnis (1997) added that *guanxi* could be understood as personalized trust forming the basis for transactions in circumstances where contract law and the courts were unreliable;[63] Xin and Pearce (1996) also pointed to the role of personal relationships or *guanxi* in overcoming the deficiency of legal institutions, while Zhou et al. (2008) found that far from the growth of the market economy reducing the relationship basis for transactions in favour of contracts, growing asset specificity and uncertainty linked to marketization had increased it.[64] In certain areas of China, unofficial guidelines could become so widely employed that they got enacted as official rules by Beijing; this meant that alliances with powerful organizations in these areas could be fruitful.[65] Ahlstrom and Bruton (2002) asserted that high-technology entrepreneurs in China needed *guanxi* to attain legitimacy. They faced an environment that had yet to fully legitimize their activities. (The government's repeated attempts to restrict its citizens' access on the internet were given as an example.) Chinese entrepreneurs had three ways to create legitimacy: forming industry alliances in combination with undertaking pro-social initiatives; aligning with firms in another industry that are already publicly listed; and using existing regional connections. All these methods were likely, in the Chinese context, to require them to build and maintain *guanxi*. The *guanxi* 'system' means that helping out other organizations leads to them being under normative pressure to be grateful and willing to reciprocate.[66] Xin and Pearce (1996), too, found that the development of private firms in China was significantly dependent upon their use of *guanxi* as a substitute for formal institutional support.[67] Child and Warner (2003) noted that both SOEs (state-owned enterprises) and private firms depended on *guanxi* to develop their external networks and to acquire business opportunities. Personal relationships substituted for contracts, although Chinese partners in joint ventures with foreigners usually accepted and often welcomed the more impersonal approach. The inward transfer of 'global' management practices was occurring, especially in such joint ventures.[68]

Park and Luo (2001) found that smaller firms made greater use of *guanxi* to compensate for their lack of organizational connections to the remnants of the state planning system. Horizontal cooperation was a fundamental requirement for businesses to survive and prosper in the absence of integration within larger groups or organizations; such cooperation was brought about by making deals with similar businesses. These deals were based on trust rather than formal contracts, which significantly reduced transaction costs, including legal costs. Trust-based deal-making gave the CFOBs speed and flexibility, which amounted to a key competitive advantage. Although *guanxi* is a personal, not an organizational, asset, having owners or senior managers with *guanxi* affected firm performance. It reduced uncertainty, improved the performance of interprovince export ventures, was positively related to sales stability and may have had a positive impact on efficiency and growth. However, there are costs attached to using *guanxi*: costs of the resources devoted to establishing and maintaining the networks of connections. 'These include entertainment expenses and the cost of gifts, but they also involve senior management time, which has a very real opportunity cost.'[69]

In broader economic terms, *guanxi* had both positive and negative effects. It helped overcome the perceived risk for Hong Kong businesses of investing in China. Their investments were a major boost to the development of labour-intensive industry along the South Coast.[70] On the other hand, an analysis of trading relations in China's automobile industry showed that rather than open markets, transactions predominantly took place between 'particularistic networks of trading between institutionally tied actors'. Markets exhibited a dualism in which actors not sharing particularistic ties were discriminated against. The author considered this pattern strong enough to 'derail the rational development of the industry by sustaining a "cellular" pattern of industrial development' and argued that it was modern industrial sectors that were most adversely affected by this pattern of trading.[71] Again, crony capitalism, which led to soft loans being made to the personal contacts of bankers, has been blamed for the Asian financial crisis of the 1990s; though not *guanxi* itself, the two are linked. 'Implicit government guarantees and poor banking supervision led to poor decisions about credit allocation in Asia's banking-dominated financial systems.'[72]

Conflicting with our findings on business relations in **India**, which were that personal contacts are not essential before business can be done, but tend to develop over time, Bandyopadhyay and Robicheaux (1995) argued that relationalism may not develop over time as one expects in the West. This argument was based on their unexpected finding that relationalism was not greater among established dealers than among new ones. This result

> " might be based upon characteristics of the Indian culture. ... In India, a high degree of trust, solidarity and mutually may be required to initiate any viable business relationship. It may be that no business relationship can be established in India without high levels of these relational attributes. Without these, communication and trade may be impossible. Whereas in the west, relationalism initially may be low and build over time, in India it may have to be high from the outset of a business relationship.[73]

The explanation of this difference of findings may be that the extent of personalism in Indian business-to-business relations varies by company location, size of company and industry. In some industrialized and urbanized areas of India, such as Chennai, a shift away from reliance on personalized trust has been documented.[74] Impersonal contractual relationships, law and governmental bureaucracy to a considerable extent replaced the need to establish trust through enduring personal ties. Equally, larger firms supplying finished products in higher-income markets were able to rely to a significant extent, on the one hand on institutionalized sanctions backed by law and, on the other, on the dependence of smaller firms upon them. In both cases there was little need for trust: the larger firms had confidence in the institutionalized sanctions to which their trading partners were subject, or in some cases in the incentives which inhered in their interdependence. Even these larger firms, however, sought to personalize transactions, especially to smooth difficulties over delivery times and payments schedules. 'Delayed payments are a characteristic problem of Indian industry. Extended credit terms are very general and create particular difficulties for smaller firms whilst often benefiting larger ones; and personalising relationships is an important means of managing credit transactions.' Among SMEs, transactions were still secured by personal trust, usually dependent upon either 'specific character assessment', through the experience of repeat transactions or collaboration and through third-party assessment, or 'generic character assessment', where awareness of individuals' caste, religious, or regional background entered into the thinking of those involved.

In the garment industry of Ahmedabad, contract enforcement with suppliers and dealers depended heavily on personal trust.

> Personal trust is based sometimes on caste connections, or on experience of collaboration ('process trust'), and third-party monitored reputation (or 'specific character assessment') – where the 'third-parties' are manufacturers or traders in a different line from the one in which the principal is operating – in a context in which 'reputational jeopardy' is significant. There may also be resort to 'danda' – physical violence. There was no evidence at all of the existence of the kind of 'extended trust', reflected in the development of co-operative relationships between firms, that is supposed to be characteristic of successful industrial districts.

In the software industry, there was a 'striking combination' of formal contract and institutionally backed sanctions and incentives with trust built through personal connections.[75] This last pattern corresponds to the one that predominated in our findings on business culture, although our research was not confined to the software industry but broadly based. Possibly here the culture is in advance of the wider reality.

Further evidence on Indian attitudes to personalism in business relations was supplied by Allen et al. (2007) who found from a study based on 112 SMEs in

116   3

INTRODUCTION • THE BUSINESS CULTURES OF FIVE ASIAN COUNTRIES • **ANALYSING ASIAN BUSINESS CULTURES**
• OWNERSHIP, FINANCING AND GOVERNANCE • ORGANIZATION AND MANAGEMENT • BUSINESS STRATEGY •

two Indian cities that Indian owners' preferred methods of resolving business disputes were personal. 'Mediation of mutual friends or business partners' was most favoured, closely followed by 'negotiate and settle out of court'; well behind these were 'mediation of a non-governmental body such as a trade union', 'going to court' and (least preferred by far) 'government mediation'. While availability of some methods may be reflected in these preferences, as may the delay factor involved in using Indian courts, the strong preference for personal methods of dispute resolution remains clear.[76] A final point that emerged from our own research was the continuing importance of political connections in India: 'An entrepreneur usually still needs political backing, most importantly to acquire land for premises.'[iv] To a great degree these connections with politicians were seen as corrupt: 'Big business has a strong influence and obtains advantages through its political contacts, buying up land and coal mines very cheaply through influence, gaining concessions in Special Economic Zones. Even when contracts go out to tender, big businesses can rig the bidding through purchasing bureaucrats and politicians.'[v]

Our interviews in **Taiwan** revealed the importance of social networking there. Much business was done in social clubs. These have 'controlled admissions – Chinese, Japanese, local', which tended to reinforce any tendencies for business-to-business relations to be ethnically based.[vi] This phenomenon was noted previously by Barton (1983) who wrote

> Business people appear to work assiduously at networking in Southeast Asia, through a high degree of socializing in voluntary associations, secret societies, clubs and charitable institutions.[77] These might serve as 'functional substitutes' for more formal sources which would be used in Western countries. For instance, firms seeking information about the financial health of a client firm, and therefore its capacity to pay, would rarely use professional credit rating agencies because the ratings were based on publicly available company reports that were themselves regarded as unreliable. Credit rating information could be more reliably obtained through informal sources such as personal contacts.

Liu (2000) observed

> Traditional practices still prevail in Taiwan's business world, and ... Taiwanese businessmen still conduct much of their business through *guanxi* (a network of personal relationships and connections) and *xinyong* (personal reliability, trustworthiness). This personalized

---

[iv] Indian, Marketing Consultant and Academic
[v] Indian, Equity Analyst
[vi] Taiwan, Expatriate Banker (Japanese)

business culture is not limited to developing business connections and partnerships; it also contributes to Taiwanese entrepreneurship and management style...[78]

Taiwanese *guanxi*, in the view of Kienzle and Shadur (1997), could be based on family, race, religion, profession or simply long-term assiduous cultivation of powerful contacts, but also through close links between enterprises owned by a single family.[79] A study of 250 business relation dyads in Taiwan showed that *guanxi* was extremely important, whereas factors such as similarity of age, gender, religion, education and occupation were not.[80] Past research found that maintaining good *guanxi* was ranked as the most important business activity,[81] but findings from an exploratory study of SMEs in the clothing and textiles industry in Taiwan may give a better perspective on the function of *guanxi*. This research suggested that to counteract competitive pressure from globalization and Chinese low-cost products, business decision-makers emphasized horizontal and vertical industry networking but only in combination with other strategies. These other strategies included leadership with a technical and innovative motivational style of management, an organizational culture that underpinned continuous improvement, both original equipment manufacture and original design initiatives, specialist staff recruitment, a presence in key overseas markets and integrated IT.[82] Chung (2006) also argued that even in relation to East Asia, *guanxi* networks were overemphasized in the literature on business organizations. Case studies of five major Taiwanese business groups suggested instead that the influences of *guanxi* were clear when markets were tightly controlled. At that time, personalistic networks were the core capabilities underpinning diversification. 'However, as groups grew and institutions developed, the significance of political *guanxi* diminished and the decision-making of diversification strategy became hinged mainly upon the resources the firm accumulated over time.'[83]

Contractual relations

A corollary of B2B personalism in Asia was the relatively low importance of contracts. This was true in the small business sector of **China**, as the following comment about contracts showed:

> They tend not to read them, or if they read them, to understand them. It is important they understand, even if you are not going to abide by them exactly; so we go through them item by item. Contracts may include concepts they do not understand. One example would be 'management fee'. Our agents insisted on profit base, even though it was clearly disadvantageous for them.[vii]

[vii] China, Expatriate, entrepreneur

118   3

INTRODUCTION • THE BUSINESS CULTURES OF FIVE ASIAN COUNTRIES • **ANALYSING ASIAN BUSINESS CULTURES** • OWNERSHIP, FINANCING AND GOVERNANCE • ORGANIZATION AND MANAGEMENT • BUSINESS STRATEGY •

It also applied in big business deals in China, as the quotation in Chapter 2 on guanxi in the power sector showed. However,

 It is not true that, as some have suggested, the Chinese treat contracts cynically at the time of signing as something that they can renegotiate; it's more that they live more in the present than lawyers do, and can't see why it should not be renegotiated when circumstances change. If things start falling apart, they try to fix the problem.[viii]

'You do document things. Anything signed 10 or 15 years ago would look/be completely different.'[ix]

In contrast, although still entailing a low value for contracts, in **India** the view was that contracts are 'entered into lightly with no real intention of performing as the quotation in Chapter 2 relating to real estate deals showed. Another explanation for contracts lacking force in India was the social culture based in Hinduism: 'There is a lack of realism, a lot of wishful thinking which leads to contract violations.'[x] The law and the minutiae of a written contract were not the guiding principles of relationships in **Japan**, but rather something to fall back on reluctantly if business people could not act reasonably and fairly of their own accord. Under such a view, litigation served only to make society more confrontational, less harmonious and less orderly.[84] In **Taiwan**, 'Agreements lack detailed clauses – what matters is the principle not the letter of the law. Documents are thin.'[xi] Reliance on contracts hampered Singaporeans in doing business elsewhere in Asia: 'Singaporeans are not good at dealing with the mainland Chinese because they rely overmuch on contracts. Compare this with the Taiwanese, who are best at dealing with Chinese.'[xii]

One conclusion that might be drawn from the foregoing discussion is that networks in emerging Asian economies act to supplement or replace weak formal institutions, whether legal, financial or, as in India's case, bureaucratic or governmental. This argument carries the implication that if economic development is accompanied by strengthening of formal institutions, such as new legal structures and commercial arrangements, the role of networks is likely to diminish.[85] Nevertheless, our findings suggested, the force of cultural preference is likely to impede or delay the bringing about of such a change.

[viii] Ibid.
[ix] Ibid.
[x] Indian, Economist, Former Entrepreneur, senior academic
[xi] Taiwan, Expatriate (Japanese), General Management, banking
[xii] Singapore, Finance and Accounting, education

Business relations with government

As Table 3.11 shows, business relations with government were significant elements of the business cultures of China, Taiwan and Singapore. In India, our interviewees stressed the impact of the governments of India's 28 states. In Japan there was little recognition of the important role that other sources suggested had been played by the bureaucracy in guiding business. These attitudes were in marked contrast to both Taiwan and Singapore: in Taiwan, the ending of the earlier positive government direction of industry was regretted, while in Singapore its continuation was broadly welcomed.

The role of government in business in **China** has been a focus of academic interest. An empirical examination of the attitudes of managers and managerial students found that the Chinese respondents gave more prominence to government as an organizational stakeholder than either Australian or Indonesian respondents.[86] Law et al. (2003) noted that, since 1978, China's national (that is, central) government had continuously delegated its authority to local governments to implement and, at times, interpret national policies. Local governments could exercise discretion in setting taxes, specifying entry barriers and creating administrative red tape for businesses operating within their jurisdictions. Some local governments functioned as 'economic warlords' and protected firms that they owned from those they did not own. Firms needed to maintain good relationships with local governments to operate successfully.[87] Boisot and Child (1996) commented that the devolution of power from the central government had reduced the importance of regulatory institutions, allowing traditional (culturally related) institutions, such as feudal-type transacting, to reassert themselves. Private firms in China had to perform a number of functions that government, legal institutions or established commercial traditions typically accomplish in mature economies. Connections with local government officials were needed to minimize the threat of interference in the form of excessive fees and sudden arbitrary regulatory changes.[88]

Table 3.11 **Business relations with government**

	China	India	Japan	Taiwan	Singapore
Business relations with government	Government not dominant except in SOEs, not monolithic	*State governments more relevant than central government*	*Minor*	Government previously led business, not now	Role of government central

Business culture variety within the country

In China and India there was a minority view taken by two respondents in each country that the differences between the cultures of different kinds of businesses were so great that it was wrong to think of a national business culture.

Child and Warner (2003), after stating that it was impossible to characterize a Chinese corporate culture owing to rapid change and the variety of types of enterprise, referred to the 'two contrasting types of firm that are likely to have long-term prominence within the system'. These were SOEs, which it was official policy to maintain at least within strategic sectors of the economy, and private firms. SOEs, owing to their large size, the legacy of government administration and some influences from Chinese culture, tended towards bureaucratic behaviour. Power distance was large. There was little delegation and a strong emphasis on vertical links within hierarchies. In private firms, information flows were in the upward direction and decision-making was restricted to family members; employees' loyalty was more important than their performance. Both traditional SOEs and private firms exhibited corporate cultures that reflected paternalistic cultural values. In traditional SOEs, the 'residual of the iron rice-bowl' model persisted, though under increasing threat from restructuring. (This Mao-era model provided lifetime employment and guaranteed welfare benefits including housing, health care, education and generous, early pensions.) SOEs' culture was one of

 top-down leadership and authority, collectivism and mutual dependence, with an emphasis on conformity and attachment to the organization based on moral rather than material incentives. ... Loyalty to superiors and to the work unit has been complemented by

Table 3.12 **Business culture variety within the country**

	China	India	Japan	Taiwan	Singapore
Different types of businesses have different cultures	*SOEs – 'communist culture'; low-tech private businesses; efficient high-tech businesses*	*Public-sector businesses 'not primarily commercial'; older private businesses have family business characteristics; high-tech businesses 'modern'*		*Some elements of culture vary in different types of businesses (traditional – banks, real estate – and technology-based)*	*MNCs international, local businesses Asian*

> employment protection and the provision of welfare benefits. This moral contract is now fast breaking down as SOEs either reform or go bankrupt. There is little evidence as yet of what the corporate culture of reformed SOEs may turn out to be, though case studies suggest it will combine an emphasis on personal achievement with a strong collective spirit.
>
> In the private sector, most firms are still small and their culture is very centred on the owner. ... Within private firms, ... workers do not normally participate in decision making, even on questions concerning benefits. In the typical urban private firm, employees can be divided into two groups. The first comprises local people and externally recruited university graduates. These people generally hold better positions in the firms, enjoy superior wages and benefits and stay with the firm longer. They are regarded as long-term primary members of the corporate collectivity and are likely to identify with its culture. The second group consists of migrants from rural areas, who occupy a much more marginal position.[89]

Other writers have taken a different view from Child and Warner on the existence of a distinctive business culture in **China**. Selmer et al. (1994) considered that the influence of Chinese culture on management practices was so significant that a Chinese managerial system was distinctly identifiable. They wrote

> " Despite the growth in size and complexity of modern industrial firms, Chinese business organizations commonly display a conservative and security-centered approach to internal management. ... Another common feature among all Chinese organizations, whether they are small traditional family businesses or large modern corporations, is that the power of decision making is centralized, usually in a single dominant owner, manager, or founder.[90]

Negotiation style and approach

As Table 3.13 shows, our research found that the Chinese approach to negotiation and the Taiwanese insistence on a prior link were important aspects of their business cultures. Our findings further suggest that there were substantial differences in the approach to negotiation in two other Asian countries: Indians love to bargain, while to the Japanese, a negotiation is only part of a long-term relationship. (This topic was not raised in Singapore.)

Tinsley and Pillutia (1998) found that differences in the negotiating behaviour of Hong Kong Chinese and Americans could be predicted from each culture's value profile, based on the cultural values in the Schwartz and Sagiv (1995)[91] typology (self-enhancement versus self-transcendence and conservatism versus openness to change). Negotiation strategies, they argued, are selected because, as they 'fit' with the cultural

Table 3.13 **Negotiation style and approach**

	China	India	Japan	Taiwan	Singapore
Negotiation style and approach	Holistic, rational, interpersonal, not unfair but there is no 'getting to yes'	*Hard bargaining; the aim is to beat the other side*	*Negotiations are part of a relationship – balanced approach*	A link is a pre-condition The aim is to win; face issues are paramount	

values, they are more effective than other strategies. These selected strategies then become normative, as cultural members are prone to use these effective strategies more frequently. Tinsley and Pillutia (1998) found that *Hong Kong* Chinese negotiators' counterparts espoused significantly higher levels of an equality norm than their US counterparts, who in turn gave more support to a joint gain outcome.[92]

Stereotypes of business owners

Each country's business culture, except that of Japan where owners of businesses seemed to have a low profile, included stereotypes of business owners. In China they were seen as highly money-oriented: 'The Chinese are money-oriented. They are happy to work with you even if you unintentionally upset them, so long as there is money to be made. They are the easiest to do business with.'[xiii] 'The Chinese are very cost conscious and smart investors.'[xiv]

> The more successful they are, the more they worry about money, especially tax; they aim for a foreign passport. They are vulnerable. ... So they keep a low profile: never get into the 'top ten' lists, avoid media coverage, go to Hong Kong for listing. The political landscape may change overnight with a domino effect – therefore they seek a quick return and to get out.[xv]

Money orientation was far more strongly emphasized as a characteristic of business owners in China than in the other four countries: possibly awareness of this characteristic may be greater in a country with Confucian and

---

[xiii] China, Expatriate, entrepreneur
[xiv] China, Expatriate (British), General Manager, energy MNC
[xv] Hong Kong Chinese, Banker, International Bank

Communist anti-business traditions. Some other qualities, some positive, some not, were also mentioned: 'They are trustworthy ... unlike Egyptians. They want to do a good job. They are happy to work on a fixed-price basis.'[xvi] 'Their weakness is in service to customers: failing to offer a free tyre check to customers for other products; not suggesting winter tyres in the North East; this weakness is especially true in rural areas. They are resistant to change, not always ambitious'.[xvii] The stereotypes of business owners in the other countries were more varied: 'Indians are smart, argumentative, both between themselves and with us, fast-thinking. Their entrepreneurs are better communicators than either Koreans or Chinese.'[xviii] 'Taiwan's business owners are solution-oriented and pragmatic; they like to figure out a way to do things.'[xix] In the technology sector, Taiwanese businesses have to be, and are, fast, efficient and sophisticated. 'If Dell, for instance, goes to a Taiwanese manufacturer with a concept, within two months it can be distributed globally. The trick is co-ordination.'[xx] '[In Singapore] many entrepreneurs are ill educated (even illiterate) – they concentrate on practicality and are not interested in things of no immediate benefit. For instance, they will not adopt "knowledge management" but basic IT is ok because its benefits are obvious. Their attitude is a cap on growth.'[xxi]

An Indian management academic and business leader, in a highly critical comment, described his compatriots as prone to 'defection orientation' – a tendency to compete (try to win and not to cooperate) even when cooperating (trying to maximize profit) would obviously be the best strategy. 'Defection is our national trait. ... Be it our company law or criminal law, we thrive on finding loopholes in these laws.' It also led to a lack of systems orientation and standardization. As an example,

> " our speed breakers come in all shapes and sizes and if they account for a disproportionately large percentage of all road accidents in India, it is nobody's concern. Our road signs, when they are there, are standardized neither in their content nor in their position and not even in their enforcement. Our vehicle number plates are tolerated in any language. Our road dividers could be anything ranging from slabs of stone or cement to tin barrels and plain boulders. ... The fact is that we need to cooperate first to standardize anything. This will, in turn, generate cooperation from the 'standardized' system as it benefits all.[93]

[xvi] China, Expatriate, entrepreneur
[xvii] Mainland Chinese, Marketing Manager, consumer MNC
[xviii] China, Expatriate (British), General Manager, energy MNC
[xix] Taiwan, Japanese Expatriate Banker
[xx] Taiwanese, Product Manager, Taiwanese consumer goods manufacturer
[xxi] Singaporean, Finance and Accounting, education

Bjerke (2000) typified **South East Asia's** entrepreneurs as displaying flexibility and endurance: management 'may appear like a mess: there is often no formal personnel management to speak of, constant supervision of staff is common and expected, they do not believe in advertising and promotion, there are few standardized trademarks or displays, they do little market research, or organization of logistics – they are traders at heart. They are good at finance. They rarely apply formal long-term planning, but have a long-term orientation in persevering on the basis of a steady accumulation of small returns; their goals are dynastic; they replace strategy with flexibility; they are adaptive and pragmatic, but not creative and innovative; they are cautious about accepting risk; they are religious or superstitious'.[94]

Change

It was in India and Japan that change and the need for change were seen as major features of the business culture. In China, although change was not emphasized, possibly because the pace and duration of change had been such as to dull sensibilities, it was noticed. 'The Chinese are coping with enormous change, but they are good at the necessary mental adjustments.'[xxii] The businesses of Singapore and Taiwan, however, were seen as resistant to change: '[For outsiders] doing business in Singapore demands flexibility – Singaporeans are resistant to change. Developing business there takes time. This is good training for managing relationships with MNCs.'[xxiii] 'The Taiwanese dislike change. Local businesses often fail in fast-changing environments.'[xxiv] Nevertheless, in Taiwan, change was occurring, especially by the professionalization of the management of family businesses. The response of one well-known Taiwanese company (Acer) to the challenge of succession planning in a family business was to employ professional managers.[xxv]

A large-scale survey in **China** found that openness to change was related to modernization: change was more salient for employees in joint ventures and reformed enterprises than for those in state-owned enterprises; in more developed regions change had higher salience and valence; senior managers regarded change as more salient and they were less sceptical about change than their subordinates; employees in organizations with flexible cultures were less sceptical about change and regarded it as both more important and more useful.[95] Ability to cope with change is often a strength of CFOBs, according to Redding (1990).

[xxii] China, Expatriate (British), General Manager, energy MNC
[xxiii] China and Malaysia, Business Development, International MNC, energy
[xxiv] Taiwan, Expatriate banker
[xxv] Taiwanese, Partner, Taiwanese venture capital

Table 3.14 **Change**

	China	India	Japan	Taiwan	Singapore
Change	*The people cope well with change*	Globalization is reducing the impact of traditional culture	Need for change – some happening	*Change meets resistance, but CFOBs are being professionalized*	*Change meets resistance in the SME sector*

This is because their concentrated and simple decision-making structure allows flexibility, speed and the opportunity to move ahead based on the intuitive decisions of the entrepreneurs. Given the central monopoly over information, one or a few key figures probably have superior business intuitiveness. These individuals often started the business from scratch and have experience in every aspect of the business.[96]

Chatterjee and Heuer (2006) described **India** as on the threshold of a major transformation in its business culture: 'Family dominated business conglomerates and large public sector enterprises continue to dominate the Indian economy, but these are beginning to give way to innovative, globally oriented corporate players – particularly within the booming Information Technology (IT) industry.' On the other hand, these authors considered, 'Several "traditional" characteristics of Indian management remain in place – notions of authority and hierarchy, the role of familial networks, indigenous ethical-philosophical frameworks and community boundaries, the importance of continuity and stability in institutional and individual norms and practices, and, finally, a general acceptance of ambiguity.' Their conclusion: 'It is possible and plausible to suggest that India is moving towards developing a unique "hybrid" form of management that seems to remain grounded in selected traditional patterns of behaviour, while accepting many of the best practices of global management systems.'[97] Chatterjee and Pearson (2006) reported that a survey of senior Indian executives found that undoubtedly traditional values still dominated the consciousness of Indian society and institutions, but 'surprisingly' many managers were able to work with global values at their individual levels of work ideology by successfully building and relying on 'meso' level work value sets.[98]

Despite the experience of prolonged recession starting in 1990 and a subsequent widespread recognition of the need for change, a report found that the conservatism of **Japan** and the strength of its 50-year-old traditional approach which prized social cohesion above shareholder returns meant that the transformation of its business model could only happen slowly and with much debate.[99]

Liu et al. (2006) reported that although most public companies in **Taiwan** were still controlled by families, the CEO (Chief Executive Officer) position had been shifting towards non-traditional, professional relationships, albeit somewhat tentatively. Privately held firms, in contrast, were not hiring more unrelated CEOs.[100] This suggested that corporate governance in Taiwan was being influenced by the institutional pressure of the initial public offering (IPO) in spite of cultural preferences that might militate against such a reduction of family control over their firms.

Conclusion

This chapter has analysed the findings of the present study by aspect of business culture instead of country by country as in Chapter 2. An attempt has been made to compare and so reveal similarities and differences among the countries in the sample.

The large number of categories that we have preserved in our analysis means that our account lacks parsimony and elegance. However, in this, the first real attempt to 'capture' and compare business cultures, it seems more important to retain richness than to create a model. Summaries of our findings are given in Tables 11.1 and 11.2.

The chapter also compares findings and conclusions from previous studies with our findings on the different elements of business cultures in the five countries. While few of these acknowledged that they were discussing business culture, we considered that their findings and comments were relevant. Even taking this 'generous' approach to relevance in the literature, the amount available was limited, suggesting that some of the elements we identified have been little researched in the past. Comparisons with our own findings showed up both agreement and disagreement.

References

[1] Budhwar, P.S. (2003) 'Culture and management in India', in Warner, M. (ed.) *Culture and Management in Asia*, London: Routledge Curzon.

[2] Kumar, M.R. (2007) 'Assessment of hierarchical tendencies in an Indian bureaucracy', *International Journal of Public Sector Management*, **20**(5): 380–91.

[3] Liu, L.S. (2000) 'Corporate governance development in the Greater China: A Taiwan perspective', in Li, J.T., Tsui, A.S. and Weldon, E. (eds) *Management and Organizations in the Chinese Context*, New York: Macmillan.

[4] Redding, S.G. (1990) *The Spirit of Chinese Capitalism*, New York: Walter de Gruyter.

[5] Ibid.

[6] Bjerke, B. (2000) 'A typified, culture-based, interpretation of management of SMEs in Southeast Asia', *Asia Pacific Journal of Management*, **17**: 103–32.

[7] Harriss, J. (2003) 'Widening the radius of trust: Ethnographic explorations of trust and Indian business', *Journal of the Royal Anthropological Institute*, **9**(4): 755–73.

[8] Steier, L.P., Chrisman, J.J. and Chua, J.H. (2004) 'Entrepreneurial management and governance in family firms: An introduction', *Entrepreneurship: Theory and Practice*, **28**(4): 295–303.

[9] Budhwar, P.S. (2003) 'Culture and management in India', in Warner, M. (ed.) *Culture and Management in Asia*, London: Routledge Curzon.

[10] Kanungo, R.N. and Mendonca, M. (1994) 'Introduction: The need for indigenous management in developing countries', in Jaeger, A.M. and Kanungo, R.N. (eds) *Management in Developing Countries*, London: Routledge.

[11] Selmer, J., Kang, I.-L. and Wright, R.P. (1994) 'Managerial behavior of expatriate versus local bosses', *International Studies of Management & Organization*, **24**(3): 49–63.

[12] Sen, A. (2005) *The Argumentative Indian: Writings on Indian Culture, History and Identity*, London: Penguin.

[13] Lincoln, J., Hanada, M. and Mcbride, K. (1986) 'Organizational structures in Japanese and US manufacturing', *Administrative Science Quarterly*, **31**(2): 338–64.

[14] Hofstede, G. (1980) *Culture's Consequences: Comparing Values, Behaviors, Institutions and Organizations*, Thousand Oaks, CA: Sage.

[15] Lee, J., Roehl, T.W. and Choe, S. (2000) 'What makes management style similar and distinct across borders? Growth, experience and culture in Korean and Japanese firms', *Journal of International Business Studies*, **31**(4): 631–52.

[16] Redding, S.G. (1990) *The Spirit of Chinese Capitalism*, New York: Walter de Gruyter.

[17] Raghunathan, V. (2006) *Games Indians Play: Why We Are The Way We Are*, London: Penguin Books.

[18] Ahlstrom, D. and Bruton, G.D. (2002) 'An institutional perspective on the role [of] culture in shaping strategic actions by technology-focused entrepreneurial firms in China', *Entrepreneurship: Theory and Practice*, **26**(4): 53–69.

[19] Zhang, J. (2007) 'Business associations in China: Two regional experiences', *Journal of Contemporary Asia*, 1 May.

[20] Tan, J. (1996) 'Regulatory environment and strategic orientations in a transitional economy: A study of Chinese private enterprise', *Entrepreneurship: Theory and Practice*, **21**: 31–44.

[21] Chow, I.H. (2006) 'The relationship between entrepreneurial orientation and firm performance in China', *SAM Advanced Management Journal*, **71**(3): 11–20.

[22] Dana, L.P. (2000) 'Creating entrepreneurs in India', *Journal of Small Business Management*, **38**(1): 86–91.

[23] Zainulbhai, A.S. (2007) 'Clearing the way for robust growth: An interview with India's chief economic planner', *McKinsey Quarterly Online*, http://www.mckinseyquarterly.com/ Clearing_the_way_for_robust_growth_An_interview_with_Indias_chief_economic_planner_2067.

[24] *The Economist*, 15 December 2007, 'Indian start-ups: Entrepreneurial push', p. 76.

[25] Yasuda, T. (2002) 'Japan's entrepreneurs face rough road', *Asia Times Online*, URL: www.atimes.com/ japan_econ/DF21.

[26] Feigenbaum, E.A. and Brunner, D.J. (2002) *The Japanese Entrepreneur: Making the Desert Bloom*, URL: www.stanford-jc.or.jp/research/publication/books/cover&file/EAF_DJB.pdf.

[27] Yu, W.-H. and Su, K.-H. (2004) 'On one's own: Self-employment activity in Taiwan', in Arum, R. and Muller, W. (eds) *The Re-emergence of Self-Employment*, Princeton, NJ: Princeton University Press.

[28] Lam, D., Paltiel, J.T. and Shannon, J.H. (1994) 'The Confucian Entrepreneur? Chinese culture, industrial organization and intellectual property piracy in Taiwan', *Asian Affairs, an American Review*, **20**(4): 205–17.

[29] Ibid.

[30] Ibid.

[31] Berrell, M. and Wrathall, J. (2007) 'Between Chinese culture and the rule of law: What foreign managers in China should know about intellectual property rights', *Management Research News*, **30**(1): 57–76.

[32] Chou, W.-C.G. (2003) 'Culture and management in Taiwan', in Warner, M. (ed.) *Culture and Management in Asia*, London: Routledge Curzon.

[33] Wang, H.R. (2001) 'Familism or enterprise? The conflict between social value and market principle', in Chang, W.N. (ed.) *The Enterprise Structure in Taiwan and Competitiveness*, Taipei: Lian-Jing.

[34] Dahles, H. (2002) 'Transborder business: The "Capital" input in Singapore enterprises venturing in ASEAN and beyond', *Journal of Social Issues in Southeast Asia*, **17**(2): 249–73.

[35] Begley, M. and Tan, W.-L. (2001) 'The socio-cultural environment for entrepreneurship: A comparison between East Asian and Anglo-Saxon countries', *Journal of International Business Studies*, **32**(3): 537–54.

[36] Thomas, A.S. and Mueller, S.L. (2000) 'A case for comparative entrepreneurship: Assessing the relevance of culture', *Journal of International Business Studies*, **31**(2): 287–301.

[37] Begley, M., Tan, W.-L. and Schoch, H. (2005) 'Politico-economic factors associated with interest in starting a business: A multi-country study', *Entrepreneurship Theory and Practice*, **29**(1): 35–55.

128   3

INTRODUCTION · THE BUSINESS CULTURES OF FIVE ASIAN COUNTRIES · **ANALYSING ASIAN BUSINESS CULTURES**
· OWNERSHIP, FINANCING AND GOVERNANCE · ORGANIZATION AND MANAGEMENT · BUSINESS STRATEGY ·

[38] Williams, S. and Narendran, S. (1999) 'Determinants of managerial risk: Exploring personality and cultural influences', *The Journal of Social Psychology*, **139**(1): 102–25.

[39] Dahles, H. (2002) 'Transborder business: The "capital" input in Singapore enterprises venturing in ASEAN and beyond', SOJOURN: *Journal of Social Issues in Southeast Asia*, **17**(2): 249–73.

[40] Sheedy, E.A. (2004) 'Do attitudes to risk vary by country?', URL: http://ssrn.com/abstract=626581.

[41] Sheedy, E.A. (2001) 'Corporate use of derivatives in Hong Kong and Singapore: A survey', *Macquarie Applied Finance Centre Research Paper No. 23*, URL: www.mafc.mq.edu.au.

[42] Feigenbaum, E.A. and Brunner, D.J. (2002) *The Japanese Entrepreneur: Making the Desert Bloom*, URL: www.stanford-jc.or.jp/research/publication/books/cover&file/EAF_DJB.pdf.

[43] Kodama, M. (2003) 'Strategic innovation in traditional big business: Case studies of two Japanese companies', *Organization Studies*, **24**(2): 235–68.

[44] Collinson, S. and Wilson, D.C. (2006) 'Inertia in Japanese organizations: Knowledge management routines and failure to innovate', *Organization Studies*, **27**(9): 1359–87.

[45] Whitley, R. (2007) *Business Systems and Organizational Capabilities: The Institutional Structuring of Competitive Competences*, Oxford: Oxford University Press.

[46] Wong, P.K., Ho, Y.P. and Singh, A. (2005) 'Singapore as an innovative city in East Asia: An explorative study of the perspectives of innovative industries', *World Bank Policy Research Working Paper No. 3568*, URL: http://ssrn.com/abstract=712606.

[47] Fukuyama, F. (1995) *Trust: Social Virtues and the Creation of Prosperity*. New York: Free Press.

[48] Liu, L.S. (2000) 'Corporate governance development in the Greater China: A Taiwan perspective', in Li, J.T., Tsui, A.S. and Weldon, E. (eds) *Management and Organizations in the Chinese Context*, New York: Macmillan.

[49] Khan, M.A.A. (2006) 'Corporate governance and the role of institutional investors in India', *Journal of Asia-Pacific Business*, **7**(2): 37–54.

[50] Bhati, S. (2006) 'Trust between branch managers and loan officers of Indian banks', *International Review of Business Research Papers*, **2**(4): 51–8.

[51] Yafeh, Y. (2000) 'Corporate governance in Japan: Past performance and future prospects', *Oxford Review of Economic Policy*, **16**(2): 74–84.

[52] Chan, K.-M. (2001) 'Uncertainty, acculturation and corruption in Hong Kong', *International Journal of Public Administration*, **24**(9): 909–28.

[53] D'Souza, C. (2003) 'An inference of gift-giving within Asian business culture', *Asia Pacific Journal of Marketing and Logistics*, **15**(1/2): 27–38.

[54] Lee, S.-H. and Oh, K.K. (2007) 'Corruption in Asia: Pervasiveness and arbitrariness', *Asia Pacific Journal of Management*, **24**: 97–114.

[55] Ahlstrom, D. and Bruton, G.D. (2002) 'An institutional perspective on the role [of] culture in shaping strategic actions by technology-focused entrepreneurial firms in China', *Entrepreneurship: Theory and Practice*, **26**(4): 53–69.

[56] Cheung, A.B. and Sing, M. (2001) 'Post-transition Hong Kong', *International Journal of Public Administration*, **24**(9): 843–4.

[57] Dunfee, T.W. and Warren, D.E. (2001) 'Is *guanxi* ethical? A normative analysis of doing business in China', *Journal of Business Ethics*, **32**: 191–204.

[58] Khatri, N., Tsang, E.W. and Begley, T. (2006) 'Cronyism: A cross-cultural analysis', *Journal of International Business Studies*, **37**(1): 61–75.

[59] Ahlstrom, D. and Bruton, G.D. (2002) 'An institutional perspective on the role [of] culture in shaping strategic actions by technology-focused entrepreneurial firms in China', *Entrepreneurship: Theory and Practice*, **26**(4): 53–69.

[60] Bjerke, B. (2000) 'A typified, culture-based interpretation of management of SMEs in Southeast Asia', *Asia Pacific Journal of Management*, **17**: 103–32.

[61] Chow, I.H.S. and Ng, I. (2004) 'The characteristics of Chinese personal ties (*guanxi*): Evidence from Hong Kong', *Organization Studies*, **25**(7): 1075–93.

[62] Millington, A. and Eberhardt, M. (2006) '*Guanxi* and supplier search mechanisms in China', *Human Relations*, **59**(4): 503–31.

[63] Kipnis, A.B. (1997) *Producing Guanxi: Sentiment, Self and Subculture in a North China Village*, London: Duke University Press.

[64] Zhou, K.Z., Poppo, L. and Yang, Z. (2008) 'Relational ties or customized contracts? An examination of alternative governance choices in China', *Journal of International Business Studies*, **39**: 526–34.

[65] Xin, K.R. and Pearce, J.L. (1996) '*Guanxi*: Connections as substitutes for formal institutional support', *The Academy of Management Journal*, **39**(6): 1641–58.

[66] Ahlstrom, D. and Bruton, G.D. (2002) 'An institutional perspective on the role [of] culture in shaping strategic actions by technology-focused entrepreneurial firms in China', *Entrepreneurship: Theory and Practice*, **26**(4): 53–69.

[67] Xin, K.R. and Pearce, J.L. (1996) '*Guanxi*: Connections as substitutes for formal institutional support', *The Academy of Management Journal*, **39**(6): 1641–58.

[68] Child, J. and Warner, M. (2003) 'Culture and management in China', in Warner, M. (ed.) *Culture and Management in Asia*, London: Routledge Curzon.

[69] Park, S.H. and Luo, Y. (2001) '*Guanxi* and organizational dynamics: Organizational networking in Chinese firms', *Strategic Management Journal*, **22**: 455–77.

[70] Davies, H., Leung, T.P., Luk, S.T.-K. and Wong, Y.H. (2003) '*Guanxi* and business practices in the People's Republic of China', in Alon, I. and Shenkar O. (eds) *Chinese Culture, Organizational Behavior and International Business Management*, Westport, CT: Praeger.

[71] Lee, K.-P. (2007) 'Clans for markets: The social organization of inter-firm trading relations in China's automobile industry', *The China Quarterly*, **192**: 827–54.

[72] Pomerleano, M. (1999) 'The East Asia crisis and corporate finances: The untold micro story', *World Bank Policy Research Working Paper No. 1990*, URL: http://papers.ssrn.com/sol3/papers.

[73] Bandyopadhyay, S. and Robicheaux, R.A. (1995) 'Working with dealers in India', *Journal of Managerial Issues*, **7**(4): 379–402.

[74] Harriss, J. (2003) 'Widening the radius of trust: Ethnographic explorations of trust and Indian business', *Journal of the Royal Anthropological Institute*, **9**(4): 755–73.

[75] Ibid.

[76] Allen, F., Chakrabarti, R., Sankar, D., Qian, J. and Qian, M. (2007) 'Financing Firms in India', URL: http://fic.wharton.upenn.edu/fic/papers/06/0608.pdf.

[77] Barton, C. (1983) 'Trust and credit: Some observations regarding business strategies of overseas Chinese traders in South Vietnam', in Lim, L.Y.C. and Gosling, L.A.P. (eds) *The Chinese in South East Asia, Vol. 1*, Singapore: Maruzen Asia.

[78] Liu, L.S. (2000) 'Corporate governance development in the Greater China: A Taiwan perspective', in Li, J.T., Tsui, A.S. and Weldon, E. (eds) *Management and Organizations in the Chinese Context*, New York: Macmillan.

[79] Kienzle, R. and Shadur, M. (1997) 'Development in business networks in East Asia', *Management Decision*, **35**(1/2): 33–52.

[80] Farh, J.L., Tsui, A.S., Xin, K. and Cheng, B.S. (1998) 'The influence of relational demography and *guanxi*: The Chinese case', *Organization Science*, **9**(4): 471–88.

[81] Davies, H., Leung, T.P., Luk, S.T.-K. and Wong, Y.H. (2003) '*Guanxi* and business practices in the People's Republic of China', in Alon, I. and Shenkar O. (eds) *Chinese Culture, Organizational Behavior and International Business Management*, Westport, CT: Praeger.

[82] Chen, J. and Parker, D. (2007) 'Taiwan's textile and clothing SME response to globalization', *Journal of Asia-Pacific Business*, **8**(2): 89–111.

[83] Chung, C.-N. (2006) 'Beyond *guanxi*: Network contingencies in Taiwanese business groups', *Organization Studies*, **27**(4): 461–89.

[84] Parry, C.J.D. (2006) 'The importance of wa when doing business in Japan', *Journal of Asia-Pacific Business*, **7**(3): 105–15.

[85] Ahlstrom, D. and Bruton, G.D. (2002) 'An institutional perspective on the role [of] culture in shaping strategic actions by technology-focused entrepreneurial firms in China', *Entrepreneurship: Theory and Practice*, **26**(4): 53–69.

[86] Cummings, L.S. and Guthrie, J. (2007) 'Managerial attitudes toward stakeholder salience within selected Western Pacific-Rim economies', *Journal of Asia-Pacific Business*, **8**(1): 7–29.

[87] Law, K.S., Tse, D.K. and Zhou, N. (2003) 'Does Human Resource Management matter in a transitional economy? China as an example', *Journal of International Business Studies*, **34**(3): 255–65. (Internal references omitted).

130   3

INTRODUCTION · THE BUSINESS CULTURES OF FIVE ASIAN COUNTRIES · **ANALYSING ASIAN BUSINESS CULTURES**
· OWNERSHIP, FINANCING AND GOVERNANCE · ORGANIZATION AND MANAGEMENT · BUSINESS STRATEGY ·

[88] Boisot, M. and Child, J. (1996) 'From fiefs to clans and network capitalism: Explaining China's emerging economic order', *Administrative Science Quarterly*, **41**(1): 600–28.

[89] Ibid.

[90] Selmer, J., Kang, I.-L. and Wright, R.P. (1994) 'Managerial behavior of expatriate versus local bosses', *International Studies of Management & Organization*, **24**(3): 49–63.

[91] Schwartz, S.H. and Sagiv, L. (1995) 'Identifying culture-specifics in the content and structure of values', *Journal of Cross-Cultural Psychology*, **26**(1): 92–116.

[92] Tinsley, C. and Pillutia, M.M. (1998) 'Negotiating in the United States and Hong Kong', *Journal of International Business Studies*, **29**: 711–27.

[93] Raghunathan, V. (2006) *Games Indians Play: Why We Are The Way We Are*, London: Penguin Books, 16–17.

[94] Bjerke, B. (2000) 'A typified, culture-based, interpretation of management of SMEs in Southeast Asia', *Asia Pacific Journal of Management*, **17**: 103–32.

[95] Lau, C.-M., Tse, D.K. and Nan, Z. (2002) 'Institutional forces and organizational culture in China: Effects on change schemas, firm commitment and job satisfaction', *Journal of International Business Studies*, **33**: 533–50.

[96] Redding, S.G. (1990) *The Spirit of Chinese Capitalism*, New York: Walter de Gruyter.

[97] Chatterjee, S.R. and Heuer, M. (2006) 'Understanding Indian management in a time of transition', in Davis, H.J., Chatterjee, S.R. and Heuer, M. (eds) *Management in India: Trends and Transition*, New Delhi: Response Books.

[98] Chatterjee, S.R. and Pearson, C.A.L. (2006) 'Indian managers in transition', in Davis, H.J., Chatterjee, S.R. and Heuer, M. (eds) *Management in India: Trends and Transition*, New Delhi: Response Books.

[99] *The Economist*, 30 November 2007.

[100] Liu, Y., Ahlstrom, D. and Yeh, K.S. (2006) 'The separation of ownership and management in Taiwan's public companies: An empirical study', *International Business Review*, **15**(4): 415–35.

4 ownership, financing and governance

This chapter, like the two that follow, describes the patterns of business resulting from business decisions in the five Asian countries we studied. In the case of the present chapter, the patterns are those of the ownership, financing and governance of businesses. These three topics are related. Concentrated ownership, as in a family firm, tends to restrict the available sources of finance to family funds, reinvested profits, trade credit and a limited range of debt financing; dispersed ownership, as in a joint stock company, not only widens the available range of equity financing but also the types of debt financing accessible to the business. Concentrated ownership limits the range of stakeholders affected by the firm's governance practices – where there are no minority shareholders, one major governance issue is eliminated, although just because the creditors of the business may in those circumstances be a more significant factor in its financing, their stake in its governance could be correspondingly greater. In Asia, governance issues often arise in businesses that were once family-owned but have been turned into joint stock companies without the founding family relinquishing its control. However, these relationships are not necessarily obvious. For example, in Taiwan, family-run companies with higher control by the family were found to perform better on governance than those with lower control.[1]

Ownership

Our research found that in three out of five countries ownership of a business was highly valued for giving control, and that founding families (and the state in China) had contrived to retain large measures of control even after listing their businesses. In China and Taiwan, the status of a business owner outweighed that of even the CEO of a large multinational ('Ownership is very important. The CEO is just an employee.'[i]), but that was less true elsewhere. In Singapore: 'When an owner meets with the CEO of a MNC [multi-national company] there must be a matching of status but size of company is very important';[ii] the dominant attitude among the SMEs

---

[i] China, Expatriate, Senior Consultant, International Management Consultancy
[ii] Singaporean, Finance and Accounting, Education

(small and medium enterprises) and even big business owners was determination to retain control: 'They won't let go of control, even when they are listed; their impulses are dynastic.' In India, control linked to present or past ownership was valued for providing personal funds for the family. Only in Japan was the status of ownership less significant, at least of listed companies: 'In the large [Japanese] corporations, employees are more important than shareholders, while their CEOs have high status and respect relative to owners of SMEs.'[iii] The pendulum in Japan had swung so far under its 'employee sovereignty' model[2] that only after its economic crisis of the 1990s were shareholders able to exert any real influence. Even then, a 2008 case where foreign shareholders attempted, but failed, to influence the composition of a company's board showed that shareholder control in Japan was still limited. These findings suggest the attitudes to business ownership shown in Table 4.1.

Patterns of ownership revealed by past studies of Asian businesses exposed both variation within Asia and difference from those of other parts of the world, including the Anglo countries. Table 4.1 shows a comparison, taken from five sample studies, of the distribution of ownership of listed companies. Indian, Chinese and East Asian patterns were compared with two samples from a broad cross-country survey, which may be taken as representing an average, though of course one that is affected by the Asian patterns themselves.

Table 4.2 shows the ownership distribution of listed companies. The most noticeable figures in Table 4.2 are the following:

- The very low percentages of listed company shares that are widely held in East Asia, China and India, and the fact that of those few widely held shares a relatively high proportion was held by corporations rather than individuals, so possibly indicating cross-shareholdings;
- The unsurprisingly high percentage of listed company shares held by the government in China;
- The extremely high concentration of listed company shares owned by families or individuals in India and the high level in East Asia.

Table 4.1   **Attitudes to business ownership**

Attitudes to business ownership	China	India	Japan	Taiwan	Singapore
Family control important – outsiders distrusted	X	X	–	X	x
Family control important – financial reasons	–	X	–	–	–
Family control important – pride and status of owner	–	–	–	X	–

[iii] Japanese, Finance and Accounting, Education

Table 4.2 **Ownership distribution of listed companies (Percentages)**

	Widely held	State/ government held	Family/individual held	Widely held by financial institutions	Widely held by corporations
Global sample of large firms (1999)[a]	24.0	20.2	34.8	8.3	3.7
Global sample of medium firms (1999)[b]	10.7	16.2	52.5	6.3	2.7
East Asia excluding Japan[c]	3.1	9.4	59.4	9.7	18.6
China[d]	0.4	60.0	13.6	1.8	24.3
India (2007)	1.8	0.3	81.1	0.2	15.4

Notes: [a]La Porta, R., Lopez-de-Silanes, F. and Shleifer, A. (1999) 'Corporate ownership around the world', *Journal of Finance*, 54: 471–517.
[b]Ibid.
[c]Claessens, S., Djankov, S. and Lang, L.H.P. (1998) 'Corporate growth, financing, and risks in the decade before East Asia's financial crisis', *World Bank Policy Research Working Paper No. 2017*, URL: http://papers.ssrn.com/sol3/papers.
[d]Allen, F., Qian, J. and Qian, M. (2005) 'Comparing China's financial system', URL: http://ssrn.com/abstract=439820.

Source: Allen, F., Chakrabarti, R., Sankar, D., Qian, J. and Qian, M. (2007) 'Financing firms in India', URL: http://fic.wharton.upenn.edu/fic/papers/06/0608.pdf.

Taken together with the fact that the proportion of listed companies in Asia, though growing, is low by Western standards, these figures help confirm the findings of our research that Asian business cultures support business ownership as a value. This preference survives even though it is linked to economic crises of the recent past and to cases where family disputes led to poor company performance. Evidence for the link to recent economic crises comes from data for 5550 firms in nine Asian countries for the period 1988–96 which showed that owners' preferences for retaining control were partly responsible for the East Asian financial crisis of the 1990s. Though the corporate sector in the early years of the period was 'vibrant',

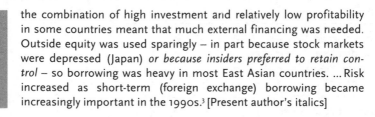

> the combination of high investment and relatively low profitability in some countries meant that much external financing was needed. Outside equity was used sparingly – in part because stock markets were depressed (Japan) *or because insiders preferred to retain control* – so borrowing was heavy in most East Asian countries. ... Risk increased as short-term (foreign exchange) borrowing became increasingly important in the 1990s.[3] [Present author's italics]

An example of the sometimes-unfortunate consequences of family control was given by Brown (2002): bickering among Yeo family members contributed to the

134   4

INTRODUCTION • THE BUSINESS CULTURES OF FIVE ASIAN COUNTRIES • ANALYSING ASIAN BUSINESS CULTURES
• OWNERSHIP, FINANCING AND GOVERNANCE • ORGANIZATION AND MANAGEMENT • BUSINESS STRATEGY •

takeover of Yeo Hiap Seng (Singapore) by Ng Teng Fong. Brown argued, 'Family control and finance were at the heart of Chinese business impermanence.' This weakness led to recurring instability across Chinese enterprises. Despite this negative consequence, Brown (2002) commented, the 'primacy of the family' is a continuing feature of Chinese family businesses.[4] The same is true of India, even though its stock market is far more established than China's and the tendency for its businesses to split greater, as noted in Chapter 2.

In **China**, by the end of the 20th century, reform of the communist economy had produced a situation of a range of firms with contrasting ownership structures.[5] Figures for 2004 from China's National Bureau of Statistics showed, however, that state-owned enterprises (SOEs) accounted for only 1.8 per cent of enterprises, just over 10 per cent of industrial output and just under 10 per cent of employment; whereas the equivalent figures for private businesses were 65 per cent, 22 per cent and 34 per cent respectively. (These figures excluded the substantial contribution on all three measures of businesses funded in part or whole by Hong Kong, Macau, Taiwan or foreign sources.) Collective enterprises represented only 4.4 per cent of output and 7 per cent of employment, which may explain why our interviewees showed little awareness of them. Clearly, with the exception of key strategic industries, by the start of the 21st century, China's economy was dominated by private business. Nevertheless, the Chinese state, as the 'owner' of the SOEs that monopolized several important industrial sectors, displayed the same reluctance to cede the control of companies to the market after listing as was shown by founding families of other businesses both in China and elsewhere in Asia. In 2005, as Table 4.2 shows, 60 per cent of the shares of Chinese listed companies were estimated to be in the hands of government. Only 23 per cent for China Mobile Communications, 21 per cent for China Telecom and 10 per cent for Petro China were allowed to 'free float'.[6]

There is wide variety in the ownership of businesses in **India**. In addition to government-owned enterprises and very large private sector firms, both listed and unlisted, there are also a great many joint sector companies (jointly owned by the government and the private sector), family-owned conglomerates, foreign-owned subsidiaries, multinational corporations and small businesses.[7,8] Despite this surface variety, however, our respondents were emphatic that Indian business was family business. In findings that suggest a link between Indian business-ownership patterns and the Indian business culture revealed by our research, Allen et al. (2007) found from a sample of over 850 Indian listed firms over the period 1995–2004 that equity ownership was highly concentrated within the founder's family and/or the controlling shareholder. There was a lack of publicly available firm-level data on non-listed firms in India, but a survey of 213 entrepreneurs and executives showed that in 85 per cent of the firms the largest owner was the founder's family, and over half of the firms had unlimited liability. 'When asked how the owners (with unlimited liability) would protect their personal assets in case of business failure, 151 out of 157 respondents would negotiate with lenders for an extension; only 22 respondents said they would also file for personal bankruptcy.' This finding, too, is consistent with ours on both personalism and control preference in Indian business culture.[9]

India provides other important examples of the Asian-business cultural preference for retaining control. Cross-shareholding between two firms is common. For example, in 2000, the ownership structure of the Tata Group, one of the oldest and largest groups in India, showed signs of both 'pyramid' and 'cross-shareholding' structures in group firms. (A 'pyramid' denotes a hierarchical chain by which a family controls a firm, and 'cross-shareholding' happens when a controlled firm owns any shares in its controlling shareholder or in the firms along that chain of control.) Tata Investment Corporation Ltd held 9.8 per cent in Tata Chemicals Ltd and 6.14 per cent in Tata Tea Ltd, while Tata Chemicals Ltd held 15.37 per cent in Tata Investment Corporation Ltd directly. Tata Tea held 4.21 per cent in Tata Chemicals Ltd and Tata Chemicals Ltd held 7.68 per cent in Tata Tea Ltd In sum, major affiliates controlled smaller affiliates by owning them singly or jointly and the chairperson controlled all these firms with nil investment of the Tata Group's total equity. The Tata family owned equity in core affiliates (i.e., Tata Industries Ltd and Tata Sons Ltd) which were not limited firms; the majority of the stakes in these two firms were held by 66 philanthropy trusts mainly headed by Tata family members.[10]

In contrast to China and India, until **Japan's** recession of the 1990s, ownership of many listed companies there was so organized as to allow the management 'a relatively high degree of independence from the influence of the shareholders'.[11] (Only approximately 20 per cent of listed companies in Japan have a founding family member actively involved in the business.) This managerial independence was achieved through the institution of the *keiretsu*. Member companies in a *keiretsu* business group held each other's equity for long-term purposes and did business with each other, in some cases on a close, in others on an arms' length basis. The *keiretsu* groups accounted for a large proportion of capitalization on the Tokyo Stock Exchange.[12] A listed company in Japan on an average had more than 12,000 owners. However, a major portion of these shares was held by a limited number of key shareholders who were mostly important business partners, especially banks, insurance companies and other companies in the same corporate group so that effective ownership was highly concentrated.

> " Cross-shareholding is a symbol of a long-lasting relationship between the two parties, and consequently the shares in this arrangement are normally not sold off without the agreement of the issuer. This has created not only a concentrated, but also a stable ownership structure for Japanese companies. Mainly due to this ownership structure, hostile take-overs have been rare in Japan. Moreover, in such an arrangement, each party refrains from intervening in the management of its counterpart by exercising their shareholder rights, because it may invite a retaliatory intervention by the counterpart.[13]

136 4

INTRODUCTION • THE BUSINESS CULTURES OF FIVE ASIAN COUNTRIES • ANALYSING ASIAN BUSINESS CULTURES
• OWNERSHIP, FINANCING AND GOVERNANCE • ORGANIZATION AND MANAGEMENT • BUSINESS STRATEGY •

Isobe et al. (2006) showed that horizontal *keiretsu* membership had a negative effect on firm profitability, increased the gap between targeted and realized returns (the outcome-aspiration gap) and did not enable member firms to reduce risks by smoothing profitability.[14] Since these 'economically rational' explanations for the attractions of *keiretsu* membership fail, the alternative of a culture-related factor enters the picture. Japan's risk-averse business culture may be linked to the *keiretsu* group system: one of the system's attractions to Japanese businesses was that a member company in a *keiretsu* group faced less bankruptcy risk than other companies, since in case of trouble it would be rescued by other *keiretsu* members. Similarly, if a Japanese bank failed, other banks and financial institutions would be expected to participate in the rescue operation.[15]

Equity cross holdings lead to positive feedback loops which can raise companies' price-earnings (PE) ratios and so boost their share price. Aggarwal and Mellen (1997) offered an example:

> " Consider equity cross holdings where company A owns company B's shares and company B owns company A's shares. Let's say for some reason, maybe for good performance, company B's shares go up. Since company A owns some of company B's shares, company A's shares would also go up to reflect the higher value of company B's shares. However, because company B owns some of Company A's shares, Company B's shares would go up again and so forth in a self-reinforcing positive feedback loop.

High Japanese PE ratios meant that in the past the acquisition of foreign technology and other assets was relatively inexpensive for Japanese companies.

Our research found that membership of a *keiretsu* might be a diminishing aspect of Japan's business culture. Possibly the changes predicted by Yoshikawa and Phan (2001) were coming about: they forecast that changes in ownership structure and institutional expectations would force firms to focus on maximizing shareholder value even where the interests of other stakeholders were more emphasized. Their paper predicted that the loss of competitiveness and the prolonged poor performance of firms could change institutional norms to emphasize asset efficiency and transparency rather than stability and business ties.[16] Changes certainly took place after Japan's prolonged economic downturn, with cross-shareholdings being unwound and domestic financial markets becoming more developed, but although Japanese PE ratios fell, they remained high by international standards, suggesting that the conservative Japanese business culture still held sway.[17]

Dana (1998) linked Japan's 'unique business sector' to its Confucian-based culture, which while it 'does not encourage entrepreneurialism per se, ... does inspire values such as diligence, frugality and hard work. Central to the Japanese belief system are the concepts of obligation, indebtedness and loyalty, all of which reinforce harmony for the common good'. These values underpinned the various systems of business alliances in which most firms continued to participate, despite the reduced importance of the *keiretsu* and the fact that they came under strain in times of economic downturn. Other forms of alliance included the *sanchi* (a grouping of small businesses in a similar line of business), *kyodukumiai* (a cooperative of small businesses) and *shita-uke gyosha* (subcontract system). The significance of these alliances lay in the predominance of the small business sector in Japan.

> 99 per cent of the firms in Japan are small: the self-employed and their unpaid family workers are nearly a third of the labour force in Japan (compared with ten per cent or less in the USA) and most are involved in inter-firm linkages. Japan has more small businesses per capita than any other big industrial economy. Over six million small businesses employ 75 per cent of the population. Since the 1980s, most Japanese investment projects abroad have been undertaken by small- and medium-sized firms.[18]

Taiwan's businesses are kept small in part by culture dynamically interacting with different organizational forms, according to Lam et al. (1994). Corresponding to the findings of our own study, Lam et al. (1994) argued that patriarchal behaviour, attributed to Confucianism, drove talented and innovative individuals from existing businesses; that in middle-sized firms, pay was relatively low and other rewards like stock options were not offered; and that owners of businesses themselves often encouraged the managers of divisions to spin it off both with capital from themselves personally and with contacts from the old business. The rationale for this last process was that the original owner gained a stake in a business which was set up in favourable conditions and was headed by a highly motivated new owner. For all these reasons, Taiwanese businesses, except those closely linked to government, usually remained small; to compensate for the loss of economies of scale from which the integrated firm of the West benefits, they evolved a form called a *jituan gongsi*, or 'group corporation', which was made up of independently owned and capitalized small firms and relied on *guanxi*. These small Taiwanese businesses avoided the agency costs associated with the managerial revolution, while paying a price in lack of professionalism.[19]

Financing

Financing of business in Asia, in comparison with the West, was and, despite pressures in the opposite direction, continued into the 21st century to be, far more by debt than equity, far less by raising capital on stock markets than by borrowing, either from financial institutions or from personal sources. This applied even to India, which had had a stock market for over 50 years. In China, stock markets only came into existence in 1980 and in most of South East Asia they were small and illiquid. While these facts were undoubtedly related to stage of economic development, they also corresponded to the distrust for impersonal business methods, the preference for personal relationships in all aspects of business and the control-retaining orientation of the founders of businesses, which were aspects of many Asian business cultures.

Allen et al. (2005) judged that the most successful part of **China**'s financial system, in terms of supporting the growth of the overall economy, was a non-standard sector that consisted of alternative financing channels, governance mechanisms and institutions. This 'non-standard sector' was largely composed of the direct or indirect personal contacts of the founders of private businesses, as Chinese business culture would predict.[20] Evidence from surveys reported in Allen et al. (2005) showed that Chinese start-ups relied heavily on funds from their founders' families and friends, with some role played by banks. Another source of 'seed capital' included illegal channels, such as smuggling, bribery, insider trading, speculation during the early stages of the development of financial and real estate markets and other underground or unofficial businesses.[21] Retained earnings were also important, amounting to 60 per cent of funds after the seed capital stage. During growth, financing was more likely to come from trade credit and private credit agencies (PCAs) than banks. These PCAs ranged from 'shareholding cooperative enterprises run by professional money brokers, lenders and middlemen, to credit associations operated by a group of entrepreneurs (raising money from group members and from outsiders to fund firms, *zijin huzushe*), from pawnshops to underground private money houses'.

Further evidence that Chinese private sector financing patterns reflect cultural preferences came from a survey which found that 100 per cent of Chinese entrepreneurs regarded the loss of reputation in the event of business failure as their major concern, whereas only 60 per cent were greatly concerned about the economic losses involved.[22] Again, it has been shown that courts play little part in resolving business-related disputes in China. A survey reported in Cull and Xu (2005) found that firms in most regions and cities relied on courts to resolve less than 10 per cent of these disputes; although the figure was slightly higher in the coastal and more developed areas, even there it never exceeded 20 per cent.[23] While other factors may also be involved here, this points to the Chinese cultural preference for resolving issues interpersonally, sometimes with the use of a mediator known to the parties.

Although the venture capital market was growing in China, it remained small in comparison with that of Japan and India, which were respectively the first and second largest in the world in 2001. Our own research showed that Chinese entrepreneurs may have lacked understanding of the requirements of these impersonal funders, for instance, in their resistance to forward planning. **India** was more sophisticated in this area; its business culture placed less emphasis on personalism in business-to-business transactions.[24] Nevertheless, there were industries in India where personal methods of financing operated. The diamond industry was one. As Govind Kakaria of Sheetal Group expressed it, 'If the businessman is a "man of words" and has good creditworthiness, he can also borrow from traders themselves. The best part about this industry is that most of the people keep their words. Money lending of crores takes place without any documentation!'[25] However, as Kakaria's words suggested, this type of arrangement was exceptional for India.

Although the size and importance of India's stock markets grew significantly after 2000, they did not play a dominant role in resource allocation and providing external financing to firms. External financing was dominated by banking and alternative sources, rather than market sources. Following the deregulation and financial liberalization of the early 1990s, the entry of non-state owned banks and competition stimulated the growth of the banking sector, which maintained a low level of non-performing loans (NPLs) and a high level of efficiency, in part due to stringent lending standards.[26] The three most important financing channels for Indian firms during their start-up and growth periods were founders' family and friends, trade credits and loans from financial institutions, including state-owned banks and banks specialized in lending to small- and medium-sized firms, according to a survey of Indian SMEs. However

> " credit availability is not uniform...and the market for bank credit is clearly relationship-driven. Over 70 per cent of the respondents said that their firms had to meet an operating/profitability criterion to obtain their largest loans, while the median 'monitoring' frequency of the banks (bank staff contacting a borrower about the loan) is once per quarter.[27]

As these findings suggest, firms' financing decisions are, of course, influenced not only by their own preferences but also by what the market makes available. In India, for instance, the venture capital industry showed restricted growth up to 2000 due to conservative government policies, limitations on the availability of funds and lack of an adequate equity market infrastructure to facilitate the exit process. A study of the industry by Mitra (2000) concluded, 'Overall, investment activity has been conservative, concentrating mostly on start-ups and later stage financing. The private funds have displayed the most conservatism, with negligible investments in seed-stage financing, focussing instead mostly on safer ventures in, for instance, consumer-related products.' These findings are consistent with our own, which found that India's business culture was ambivalent about entrepreneurialism and risk.[28]

Even in **Japan**, where the stock market came into being as early as 1880, the shares of listed companies were narrowly distributed until the country's economic crisis of the 1990s and Japanese industry was financed primarily by what legally were bank loans in the form of short-term indebtedness. In the view of Herbig (1995), however, these loans 'economically ... are an equity investment in the business. ... This means that corporate objectives are to minimize the cost of capital, not maximize profit'.[29] Suzuki and Cobham (2005) argued that on the surface the later 1990s saw a significant shift in corporate financing from external to internal finance through reinvested profits and later through a reduced need for finance in the era of slow growth in the economy; within external finance, the proportion of bank finance decreased from very large to marginal; and bond financing replaced direct finance as deregulation and internationalization of the financial system allowed large corporations to use bonds, especially the Eurobond.[30] They showed, however, that the old biases persisted: their study of Japanese business financing after the Asian financial crisis of the 1990s concluded that despite giving an initial impression of a transformation of the Japanese financial system from a 'bank-based' system to a 'high internal finance' system, there had been no fundamental shift in the nature of investment financing in Japan. Instead, economic and banking conditions in the period had produced the appearance of change.[31] This finding echoed that of another study covering the period before 1997.[32] Again, an examination of the ownership structures of 247 large Japanese manufacturers during the fiscal years 1996–98 found that simple principal-agent representations understated the complexity of the relationship between ownership and financial performance. The relationship between the firm's investment behaviour and financial performance and the equity stakes of a particular category of investor, whether foreign investors, investment funds, pension funds, banks and insurance companies, affiliated companies or insiders, was highly complex.[33]

Problems of access to capital for small firms in Japan were formerly overcome or reduced through the institution of the *keiretsu*. These were often centred round a bank and although the law limited that bank's share to 5 per cent, it often controlled the member firms through administrative power. The reduced importance of these groups after 2000 'may leave a gap which start-ups and small businesses will struggle to fill. Government initiatives to try to fill the gap are having only limited impact'.[34]

A combination of the business and economic cultures of South East Asia including **Taiwan** made the region 'unique' according to Wang and Gupta (2003), who argued that this lay behind the financial crisis of 1997, when a number of debt-ridden South East Asian corporations nearly collapsed. The uniqueness consisted in a combination of the businesses' heavy reliance on debt capital, supported by a high level of trust and personal relationships among the organizations, together with the governments' practice of leaving the monitoring of the loans to the banking sector, where 'personal relationships, corruption, government pressures and guarantees and inadequate information guided decision-making'. Prior experience that could be used to guide liberalization by the government and adaptation to liberalization and pursuit of globalization initiatives by the organizations was lacking.

Firms in the region enjoyed easy access to financing in the years up to the Asian financial crisis of the 1990s. Sources of finance, some of which would not be legal in Western countries, included the transfer of shares between company subsidiaries, stock market listings, loans from offshore and domestic banks, joint venture partners, internally generated profits, state finance and family-owned finance companies. As a result of this ease of financing, South East Asian firms expanded into diverse low-margin or loss-making businesses and markets for which they lacked the in-house skills for product and process development and market expansion.[35] In addition, risk appraisal in finance – forecasting interest rate changes, inflation prospects and anticipated revenues – was often ignored because 'business simply floated on great inflows of capital'. The result was 'often disastrous'. For example, the Summa Bank suffered huge losses.[36]

The crisis led to some reform, including more liberal policies towards mergers, foreign ownership and bankruptcy, fiscal incentives for asset transfers and revised accounting standards to ease asset valuations; these attracted greater cross-border ownership and equity alliances to benefit from the stock and currency devaluations. The result was an infusion of foreign capital, technical know-how and relational networks, especially from Japan. The businesses, too, made some changes after the crisis. There was at least some restructuring of unsustainable debt – conversion to equity, extending terms of debt repayment or cutting interest rates below the risk-adjusted cost of capital. The lenders adopted the 'London approach', which seeks to avoid liquidation of viable debtors by providing them with continuing financial support to minimize losses to creditors. Some companies also displayed a renewed vision, recognizing the significance of technology and innovation for continued success.[37] These reforms could be considered conservative in view of the size of the crisis, and their limited nature points to the continued influence of the old business culture.

Corporate governance

Corporate governance, narrowly understood, is 'structured around multiple factors including the involvement of investors and debtors (external governance), supervision by the board of directors, and compensation systems (internal governance). Each factor's function is affected by other or exogenous factors including competition in the product market'.[38] More broadly, governance is an issue of equitable treatment of all the stakeholders in a business, including customers and the wider community. In this section, the narrower issues are discussed first.

In what may be an indication of the strength of business cultures in many countries, the Organisation for Economic Co-operation and Development noted in 2003 that

> a widening gap is opening up between laws and implementation in many countries. Improving corporate-governance laws and regulations has proved to be easier than enforcing the laws and regulations. The consequence is that minority shareholders continue to be exploited when controlling shareholders and management strip assets from the company, through abusive self-dealing, pay themselves excessive compensation, engage in insider trading or act in their own interests to the detriment of the company. Bank governance is not strong enough to ensure the stability of the financial system and creditors, including banks, are often plagued by bad debts.[39]

These statements could be applied to several Asian countries. It would be only a slight exaggeration to say that the business cultures of Asia traditionally left business owners with few decisions to make about governance. A pattern of behaviour that paid almost no attention to stakeholders other than the owners themselves, or, in the case of Japan, employees, was, in the way of things strongly influenced by culture, considered the natural order.

Evidence that in **East Asia** a culture of large shareholders treating even publicly listed companies as personal fiefdoms, as our research discovered in India, came from a World Bank Policy Research Working Paper in 1999. Using data for more than 2000 companies from nine East Asian economies, Claessens et al. (1998)examined the interactions among ultimate ownership, group affiliation and corporate diversification. They found that in developing economies, where external markets for finance were less developed, allocating resources within business groups was associated with higher market valuations, and diversifying was beneficial, suggesting that both practices were positive for the firms' performance. However, in more developed economies, group-affiliated firms that diversified within the group destroyed value. Nevertheless, group-affiliated firms in developed East Asian countries were found to be equally likely to diversify in this way, despite the destruction of value. Claessens et al. (1999) suggested that this value-destroying diversification might occur because controlling shareholders used diversification to expropriate other shareholders. Their findings rejected the hypothesis that they did it to reduce risk.[40]

In 2006, evidence emerged that the practices similar to those of business groups elsewhere in East Asia were beginning to emerge in **China** despite its relatively recent capitalist history. Results were obtained suggesting that Chinese business groups, which include those formed from SOEs with government encouragement, had control mechanisms derived from pyramid ownership structures that enabled the dominant owners to expropriate value from minority shareholders or tunnel corporate resources for their own interest.[41] While amendments to China's Company Law and Securities Law in 2005, modelled on countries with more developed capital markets, gave some hope that issues of corporate governance, such as the lack of protection for minority shareholders, the paucity of independent directors, the absence of transparency and inadequate financial disclosure were finally being addressed, the issue of weak enforcement remained.[42] In China there were also structural and regulatory impediments to good governance that might, in conjunction with the culture that the 'top man' ruled by fiat, frustrate the often-good intentions of executives. In the words of Orr (2005), while many individual Chinese Chief Financial Officers (CFOs) and Chief Executive Officers (CEOs) were committed to good corporate governance, the 'strong, dominant personalities' that ran many Chinese companies were prone

> to make management decisions instinctively, with little input from other senior executives or outside directors. The few independent directors tend to have less weight in corporate governance. A related problem is the issue of capital structure. Many enterprises that were once entirely in government hands have a fairly small free float. ... Most of the remaining shares are now in unlisted holding companies ultimately controlled by the central government. Another challenge related to corporate governance is the growing role of regulatory authorities. The financial sector's regulator, which is considered to be on the leading edge, has become clearer about rules and responsibilities and is increasingly effective in carrying out enforcement. But in energy, power, and telecommunications – where regulators play an important role in other countries – the regulators are less effective and their powers more modest.[43]

Alternative financing channels and informal governance mechanisms to some degree substituted for formal mechanisms to support corporate governance as well as overall economic growth in China, Allen et al. (2005) argued 'Perhaps the most important corporate governance mechanism is competition in product and input markets.'[44] Competition is encouraged when entry barriers are low, as they were in China. An examination of entry barriers and governance across 85 countries found that countries with heavier regulation of entry had higher government corruption and larger unofficial economies.[45] According to Allen et al. (2005), other important governance mechanisms were reputation, trust and relationships. Cultural and religious beliefs were important for the development of institutions, legal origins and investor protection. The article continued

> The above factors are of particular relevance and importance to China's development of institutions. Without a dominant religion, one can argue that the most important force in shaping China's

144 4

INTRODUCTION · THE BUSINESS CULTURES OF FIVE ASIAN COUNTRIES · ANALYSING ASIAN BUSINESS CULTURES · OWNERSHIP, FINANCING AND GOVERNANCE · ORGANIZATION AND MANAGEMENT · BUSINESS STRATEGY ·

> social values and institutions is the set of beliefs first developed and formalized by Kongzi (Confucius). This set of beliefs clearly defines family and social orders, which are very different from western beliefs on how legal codes should be formulated. Using the World Values Survey conducted in the early 1990s, LLSV (1997b)[46] found that China has one of the highest levels of social trust among a group of 40 developed and developing countries. We interpret high social trust in China as being influenced by Confucian beliefs … reputation and relationships make many financing channels and governance mechanisms work in China's Hybrid Sector.

Other effective governance mechanisms in China, according to Allen et al. (2005) included the fact that many Chinese businesses were wholly family-owned and controlled (so that investor protection of minority shareholders was not an issue), and the importance of trade credits in financing firms. Because cooperation among different suppliers was necessary and all suppliers benefited from the firm doing well, 'Cooperation and mutual monitoring can ensure payments as long as funds are available despite the lack of external monitoring and contract enforcement.'[47]

A more negative conclusion was drawn about a 'fundamental dilemma' that China's political culture created for corporate governance. This dilemma 'stems from the state policy of maintaining a full or controlling ownership interest in enterprises in several sectors', which led to the use of that control for purposes such as maintaining urban employment levels and politically motivated job placement. This in turn set up a 'conflict of interest between the state as controlling shareholder and other shareholders'. The need to provide for the special circumstances of state-sector enterprises then distorted China's Company Law. To the detriment of minority shareholders, private-sector enterprises were made to follow rules that made sense only in a heavily state-invested economy.[48]

Hong Kong Special Administrative Region (SAR) was until 1997 a common-law country with its legal roots in Britain, but Hsu (1999) pointed out that other and different kinds of forces were at work in law.

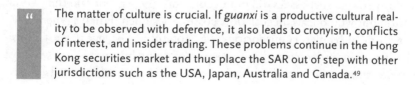

> The matter of culture is crucial. If *guanxi* is a productive cultural reality to be observed with deference, it also leads to cronyism, conflicts of interest, and insider trading. These problems continue in the Hong Kong securities market and thus place the SAR out of step with other jurisdictions such as the USA, Japan, Australia and Canada.[49]

Hsu (1999) regarded much of the law as 'toothless' 'because it does not sufficiently criminalize wrong behaviour'. Article 109 of the Basic Law of the Republic of China Hong Kong SAR, which took effect at the handover of Hong Kong to China in 1997, guaranteed that Hong Kong would retain its form of capitalistic, democratic government for 50 years after the 1997 handover and mandated that the HKSAR provide 'an appropriate economic and legal environment for the maintenance of the status of Hong Kong as an international financial center'. However, Hsu (1999) argued that under colonialism the legal order was a patchwork in which laissez-faire and cronyist elements flourished and that the historical weakness of consumer protection in Hong Kong and the power of the Hong Kong banking 'cartel' continued. For example, the Code of Banking Practice was voluntary – not mandatory but hortatory. 'Not all banker-customer relationships are regarded as fiduciary'.[50]

Our study suggested that in **India** corporate governance regulation was taken seriously by the authorities but that some family businesses dragged their feet. This point is supported by a finding that institutional investors reported that their role in assisting better management practices, productivity, efficiency and effective functioning was limited and unsatisfactory.[51] Furthermore, Allen et al. (2007) reported that in India both the dividend ratio and valuations of listed firms were much lower compared with similar firms operating in countries with strong investor protection, but similar to those listed firms in countries with weak protection, suggesting that the protection in principle provided by the law was ineffective in practice. 'Despite its English common-law origin, strong legal protection provided by the law and a democratic government, corruption within India's legal system and government significantly weaken investor protection in practice.' As a result, 'Informal governance mechanisms based on trust, reputation and relationships are much more important than legal remedies in resolving disputes and enforcing contracts'. For example, when asked about the consequences of delay of (or non-) payments and breach of contracts, espondents ranked loss of future business opportunities, reputation and personal assets as main concerns, while fear of legal remedies was the least important. When asked who would be the best mediator for disputes (multiple choices allowed), 46 per cent of the respondents specified 'mutual friends and business partners' and 26 per cent specified a non-government organization like a trade association as their choice, and only 20 per cent of respondents chose 'going to courts.' When asked how a firm ensured payments, 53 per cent of the respondents screened their business partners carefully so that such issues did not occur, while 59 per cent said they would go to courts but would leave negotiation possibilities open. Finally, when asked about government regulatory authorities (e.g., obtaining a licence to start a business), the survey indicated corruption was part of doing business. The two most common methods to overcome corruption were bribes and using friends of government officials.[52]

Chakrabarti (2005), too, commented negatively on India's corporate governance: 'Concentrated ownership of shares, pyramiding and tunnelling of funds among group companies mark the Indian corporate landscape. Boards of directors have frequently been silent spectators with the Department for Industry nominee directors unable or unwilling to carry out their monitoring functions.'

146   4

INTRODUCTION • THE BUSINESS CULTURES OF FIVE ASIAN COUNTRIES • ANALYSING ASIAN BUSINESS CULTURES
• OWNERSHIP, FINANCING AND GOVERNANCE • ORGANIZATION AND MANAGEMENT • BUSINESS STRATEGY •

He added, though, that after liberalization serious efforts were directed at over-hauling the system and that there was a move towards market-based governance of Indian banks.[53]

Like our interviewees, another author noted that at the start of the 21st century there were signs of a shift in India's corporate structures, attributed not only to economic changes but also to a cultural change in the part of Indian society represented by its former large family businesses. The loosening of family and kinship organization amongst these elite families, with an increasing incidence of cross-caste marriage amongst children who had very often lived for long periods in the United States, led to a move away from a heavy reliance upon 'selective trust', deriving from networks grounded in close kin groups, to a greater reliance on formal institutions of corporate governance. As a result, the highly centralized decision-making by senior family members, organizational informality and reliance on personal loyalty and seniority rather than on competence, was progressively replaced by the use of professional executives.[54] A historical analysis also concluded that there was evidence of a change with positive results for governance. In each period, shifts in institutional and legislative frameworks gave rise to different forms of business ownership. These shifts occurred as political values changed. The result was an amalgamation of diverse coexisting ownership models, with 'evidence of evolution towards more balanced values'.[55]

In **Japan**, the business culture-based preference for working within long-term relationships was reflected in the way that as late as 2008, most directors of even the largest companies were managers of the company, even though large Japanese corporations were mostly set up as stock companies. Out of more than 6000 of the largest corporations that had sufficient capital for listing (one billion yen or more), 99 per cent were stock companies, of which approximately 40 per cent were actually listed on the stock market. Despite the resulting need for external accountability, the directors of Japanese firms were usually promoted from within the company, after having worked there for many years. 'In most cases, they continue to be managers, working within the hierarchy of the company.'[56] Thus the board members of a Japanese company were relatively homogeneous, with a shared set of experiences and organizational culture, in contrast to the Anglo-American practice of having mainly external directors intended to bring a range of experience and attitudes to the policy-making of the company. Another contrast follows: Japanese boards were mainly involved in strategic and management decision-making, whereas the function of Anglo-American boards is to guide policy, appoint CEOs and other senior officers and exercise a general supervision.

By the mid-1990s, it had become apparent that the Japanese corporate-governance system was failing to provide the separation of management from monitoring (including the introduction of outside board members), active information disclosure or adequate protection of minority shareholders' rights. Under pressure from government and foreign shareholders, companies began to introduce changes. However, the adoption of better governance practices was voluntary and Japanese companies' attitudes towards reform were quite diverse, ranging from actively receptive to very cautious. One change that was widely adopted was the executive officer system. This system makes a distinction between executive officers in charge of operating divisions and board members with monitoring responsibilities; it was first introduced by Sony in 1997, and was subsequently introduced by other companies in many industries. In the companies most actively reforming, corporate accounting standards and disclosure requirements were also progressively reformed so as to harmonize Japanese practices with those internationally accepted. In addition, in many of these companies there was a significant reduction in cross-shareholdings between Japanese companies and their creditor banks, while the percentage of shares held by non-affiliated shareholders increased substantially. (This in turn raised awareness among Japanese companies for the need to defend against hostile takeovers and led to some rethinking of the 'unwinding of cross shareholding'. However the broad pattern was as stated.)[57]

Even by 2002, however, half of all listed companies continued to maintain cross-shareholdings, remained dependent on bank loans for financing and retained old hiring practices. Such companies tended to lag in performance compared with those that made significant governance reforms, especially by increased information disclosure.[58] Demonstrating the continuing strength of the traditional business culture, the appointment of external directors proved unpopular among Japanese companies and was not widely adopted.[59] By 2007, only one-third of Japanese companies had outside directors, and these were usually in a small minority; moreover, one survey found that 30 per cent came from partner companies, 18 per cent from other companies in the same *keiretsu*, 16 per cent from a parent company and 5 per cent from the company's 'main bank'. In other words, most external directors were not really 'independent', and there were doubts about how effectively they would challenge board decisions.

One Japanese reform may have actually increased governance problems there. Previously Japan had a ban on holding companies which protected it from the governance problems (common in other Asian countries) of conflicting interests between parents and subsidiaries. Following the lifting of the ban on holding companies, more companies adopted a vertical structure with a holding company at the top. At the same time, the continuing presence of listed subsidiaries, a practice said to be unique to Japan, may have made the consequent governance problems there more acute than elsewhere.[60] A further problem was the continuing situation in which Japanese corporate managers had little incentive for increasing shareholder value, as shown by an analysis of monetary incentives offered to presidents of Japanese companies on the Tokyo, Osaka and Nagoya stock exchanges between 1990 and 2003. Contrary to a popular perception that Japanese corporate governance was converging towards the US style, these findings showed Japanese companies moving away from the US style in the area of monetary incentives for corporate managers. Japanese corporate managers, unlike their US counterparts, received little boost in their personal wealth by delivering excellent business results; but conversely, they received little punishment for extremely poor results.[61]

In **Taiwan**, companies have two-tier Boards, an arrangement modelled on the German system. In principle, this system separates the Board's strategic planning role from its monitoring role. However, Her and Mahajan (2005) found evidence that in Taiwan the business culture undermined the system. Family ties between the monitoring Board members and the CEOs undermined internal monitoring; even without majority ownership, family control of the internal monitoring mechanism impeded governance.[62]

A study of the role of non-executive directors (NEDs) in quoted, family-controlled firms in **Singapore** (Roberts, 2007) led to a critique of the 'suspicious and hostile' perspective of family control and argued that, despite the reality of family power and control, NEDs achieved effective influence by defending the collective interest against the 'damaging intrusion' of 'family altruism and managerial opportunism'.[63] This argument, that governance in family firms may be more effective than is generally believed, could apply more widely than just to Singaporean businesses.

In a possible sign of change in governance in East Asia, a literature review on internal auditing found in 2006 that there had been a 'paradigm shift' in the activities performed by internal auditors. A more dynamic regulatory environment in Asia Pacific, together with the increasing complexity of business transactions and significant advances in information technology, had resulted in opportunities and challenges for internal auditors which led to an update of the professional practices framework.[64]

On the broader issues of corporate governance, however, such as taking account of stakeholders, including the wider community or the environment, conformity or even awareness was very low in Asia, our study suggested. The findings of other studies tend to support this conclusion. A study that compared Asian with US and European business found that while corporate reputation in Asia was increasingly being managed strategically at the highest corporate levels, executives there were more focused on using corporate reputation to derive tangible business benefits than their peers in America and Europe. 'Corporate social responsibility and the broader range of stakeholders beyond customers and shareholders do not feature strongly in the corporate reputation agenda of Asian executives.' The survey results indicated that Asian executives were more concerned with customers, shareholders and bottom-line performance than with 'softer' areas such as community relations and internal communications.[65] Equally, a survey of enterprise managers and local government officials in six Chinese cities demonstrated relatively high environmental awareness but a reluctance to implement environmental protection policies at the cost of sacrificing the rate of economic growth.[66]

Another study based on interviews with managers in Sino-foreign joint ventures found that to Chinese business managers the concept of 'stakeholder' was unknown and unclear. Some concepts related to governance such as 'moral legitimacy' seemed to be alien to the interviewees and only power was consistently shown to be salient. The study further found that groups external to the business but without direct power over it were seen as of no consequence and that the position of owners, managers and employees was considered so obvious as to be unworthy of extra thought as to prioritization. The external stakeholders who were acknowledged were the government, the 'market' and the banks. In all the joint ventures in the study, the Chinese partner was an SOE, and in these the government received prioritization as a stakeholder 'because it was the regulator, resource and special-exception provider and auditor, rather than because there was any "passion" for "maximizing shareholder wealth."' The study concluded

By and large, the interviewees seemed to see their responsibility as internal to the business, and defined stakeholders accordingly. Nevertheless, discussion on stakeholders generally and stakeholder prioritization was not readily or voluntarily forthcoming. It was made clear to the researchers that a number of interviewees found this topic 'not interesting' and 'not important'.[67]

Conclusion

Both the present study and other research show that business-ownership patterns in Asia reflect the business culture of familism and preference for retaining founder control. These patterns and preferences have knock-on effects on both financing and governance. Financing decisions, however, are also affected by the institutional environment, especially weaknesses and gaps in financial infrastructures. Governance in some countries is increasingly affected by government regulation where it is enforced, but the strength of the culture is shown in the way new regulations are obeyed only half-heartedly.

References

[1] Yeh, Y.H., Lee, T.S. and Woidtke, T. (2001) 'Family control and corporate governance: Evidence from Taiwan', *International Review of Finance*, 2: 21–48.
[2] Miyajima, H. (2005) 'The performance effects and determinants of corporate governance reform in Japan', URL: http://ssrn.com/abstract=818347.
[3] Claessens, S., Djankov, S. and Lang, L.H.P. (1998) 'Corporate growth, financing, and risks in the decade before East Asia's financial crisis', *World Bank Policy Research Working Paper No. 2017*, URL: http://papers.ssrn.com/sol3/papers.
[4] Brown, R.A. (2002) *Chinese Big Business and the Wealth of Asian Nations*, New York: Palgrave.

150 4

INTRODUCTION • THE BUSINESS CULTURES OF FIVE ASIAN COUNTRIES • ANALYSING ASIAN BUSINESS CULTURES • OWNERSHIP, FINANCING AND GOVERNANCE • ORGANIZATION AND MANAGEMENT • BUSINESS STRATEGY •

[5] Child, J. and Tse, D.K. (2001) 'China's transition and its implications for international business', *Journal of International Business Studies*, **32**(1): 5–22.

[6] Orr, G.R. (2005) 'What executives are asking about China', McKinsey Quarterly OnlineURL: http://www.mckinseyquarterly.com/What_executives_are_asking_about_China_1478.

[7] Gollakota, K. and Gupta, V. (2006) 'History, ownership forms and corporate governance in India', *Journal of Management History*, **12**(2): 185–98.

[8] Thomas, A.S. and Philip, A. (1994) 'India: Management in an ancient and modern civilization', *International Studies of Management & Organization*, **24**(3): 18–27.

[9] Allen, F., Chakrabarti, R., De, S., Qian, J. and Qian, M. (2007) 'Financing firms in India', URL: http://ssrn.com/abstract=898066.

[10] Ibid.

[11] Yasui, T. (1999) 'Corporate governance in Japan and its relevance to the Baltic Region', *Workshop on Corporate Governance in the Baltics (Vilnius, 21–22 October)*, URL: http://www.oecd.org/dataoecd/8/25/1931660.pdf.

[12] Aggarwal, R. and Mellen, L.E. (1997) 'Perspectives on Japanese finance for portfolio investors', *Review of Business*, **18**.

[13] Yasui, T. (1999) 'Corporate governance in Japan and its relevance to the Baltic Region', *Workshop on Corporate Governance in the Baltics (Vilnius, 21–22 October)*, URL: http://www.oecd.org/dataoecd/8/25/1931660.pdf.

[14] Isobe, T., Makino, S. and Goerzen, A. (2006) 'Japanese horizontal *keiretsu* and the performance implications of membership', *Asia Pacific Journal of Management*, **23**(4): 453–66.

[15] Aoki, M. and Patrick, H. (eds) (1994) *The Japanese Main Bank System: Its Relevancy for Developing and Transforming Economies*, New York: Oxford University Press.

[16] Yoshikawa, T. and Phan, P.H. (2001) 'Alternative corporate governance systems in Japanese firms: Implications for a shift to stockholder-centered corporate governance', *Asia Pacific Journal of Management*, **18**(2): 183–205.

[17] Aggarwal, R. and Mellen, L.E. (1997) 'Perspectives on Japanese finance for portfolio investors', *Review of Business*, **18**.

[18] Dana, L.P. (1998) 'Small but not independent: SMEs in Japan', *Journal of Small Business Management*, **36**(4): 73–7.

[19] Lam, D., Paltiel, J.T. and Shannon, J.H. (1994) 'The Confucian entrepreneur? Chinese culture, industrial organization and intellectual property piracy in Taiwan', *Asian Affairs, an American Review*, **20**(4): 205–17.

[20] Allen, F., Chakrabarti, R., Sankar, D., Qian, J. and Qian, M. (2007) 'Financing firms in India', URL: http://fic.wharton.upenn.edu/fic/papers/06/0608.pdf.

[21] Allen, F., Qian, J. and Qian, M. (2005) 'Comparing China's financial system', URL: http://ssrn.com/abstract=439820.

[22] Ibid.

[23] Cull, R. and Xu, C. (2005) 'Institutions, ownership, and finance: The determinants of reinvestments of profit among Chinese firms', *Journal of Financial Economics*, **77**: 117–46.

[24] Nair, V.V. (2002) 'India second largest market for VC funding', *Hindu Business Line*, 16 April.

[25] Sabharwal, M. (2006) 'Bank loan becomes the back-bone of the diamond sector', September/October.

[26] Allen, F., Chakrabarti, R., De, S., Qian, J. and Qian, M. (2007) 'Financing firms in India', URL: http://ssrn.com/abstract=898066.

[27] Ibid.

[28] Mitra, D. (2000) 'The venture capital industry in India', *Journal of Small Business Management*, **38**(2): 67–79.

[29] Herbig, P. (1995) *Marketing Japanese Style*, London: Quorum Books.

[30] Suzuki, K. and Cobham, D.(2005) 'Recent trends in the sources of finance for Japanese firms: Has Japan become a "high internal finance" country?' Discussion Paper Series, Heriot-Watt University 26–9.

[31] Ibid.

[32] Corbett, J. and Jenkinson, T. (1997) 'How is investment financed? A study of Germany, Japan, the United Kingdom and the United States', *The Manchester School*, **65** (Supplement), 69–93.

[33] Gedajlovic, E., Yoshikawa, T. and Hashimoto, M. (2005) 'Ownership structure, investment behaviour and firm performance in Japanese manufacturing industries', *Organization Studies*, **26**(1): 7–35.

[34] Tsukahara, O. (2006) 'SME financing in Japan', URL: http://www.fsa.go.jp/frtc/20061205/08.pdf.

[35] Wang, J. and Gupta, V. (2003) 'Post-crisis management: A study of corporate restructuring in Asia', *Journal of the Academy of Business and Economics*, 2(2): 209–17.

[36] Brown, R.A. (2002) *Chinese Big Business and the Wealth of Asian Nations*, New York: Palgrave.

[37] Wang, J. and Gupta, V. (2003) 'Post-crisis management: A study of corporate restructuring in Asia', *Journal of the Academy of Business and Economics*, 2(2): 209–17.

[38] Nitta, K. (2007) 'Developing the research frontier in corporate governance analysis', *Research Institute of Economy, Trade and Industry of Japan*, URL: http://www.rieti.go.jp/en/projects/cgp/columns.html.

[39] *The Observer*, May 2003.

[40] Claessens, S., Djankov, S. and Lang, L.H.P. (1998) 'Corporate growth, financing, and risks in the decade before East Asia's financial crisis', *World Bank Policy Research Working Paper No. 2017*, URL: http://papers.ssrn.com/sol3/papers.

[41] Lu, Y. and Yao, J. (2006) 'Impact of state ownership and control mechanisms on the performance of group affiliated companies in China', *Asia Pacific Journal of Management*, 23(4): 485–503.

[42] Feinerman, J.F. (2007) 'New hope for corporate governance in China?' *The China Quarterly*, **191**: 590–612.

[43] Orr, G.R. (2005) 'What executives are asking about China', *McKinsey Quarterly Online*, 3, URL: www.mckinseyquarterly.com/article.

[44] Allen, F., Qian, J. and Qian, M. (2005) 'Comparing China's financial system', URL: http://ssrn.com/abstract=439820.

[45] Djankov, S., La Porta, R., Lopez-de-Silanes, F. and Shleifer, A. (2002) 'The regulation of entry', *Quarterly Journal of Economics*, **117**: 1–37.

[46] La Porta, R., Lopez-de-Silanes, F., Shleifer, A. and Vishny, R. (1997) 'Trust in large organizations', *American Economic Review (Proceedings issue)*, **87**: 333–8.

[47] Allen, F., Qian, J. and Qian, M. (2005) 'Comparing China's financial system', URL: http://ssrn.com/abstract=439820.

[48] Clarke, D.C. (2003) 'Corporate Governance in China: An overview', URL: http://ssrn.com/abstract=424885.

[49] Hsu, B.F.C. (1999) *Laws of Banking and Finance in the Hong Kong SAR,* Hong Kong: Hong Kong Open University Press and Hong Kong University Press.

[50] Ibid.

[51] Khan, M.A.A. (2006) 'Corporate governance and the role of institutional investors in India', *Journal of Asia-Pacific Business*, 7(2): 37–54.

[52] Allen, F., Chakrabarti, R., Sankar, D., Qian, J. and Qian, M. (2007) 'Financing firms in India', URL: http://fic.wharton.upenn.edu/fic/papers/06/0608.pdf.

[53] Chakrabarti, R. (2005) 'Corporate governance in India – evolution and challenges', URL: http://ssrn.com/abstract=649857.

[54] Harriss, J. (2003) 'Widening the radius of trust: Ethnographic explorations of trust and Indian business', *Journal of the Royal Anthropological Institute*, 9(4): 755–73 and in Harriss, J. (ed.) *Power Matters; Institutions, Politics and Society in India*, 169–92.

[55] Gollakota, K. and Gupta, V. (2006) 'History, ownership forms and corporate governance in India', *Journal of Management History*, 12(2): 185–98.

[56] Yasui, T. (1999) 'Corporate governance in Japan and its relevance to the Baltic Region', *Workshop on Corporate Governance in the Baltics (Vilnius, 21–22 October)*, URL: http://www.oecd.org/dataoecd/8/25/1931660.pdf.

[57] Nitta, K. (2007) 'Unwinding of cross-shareholding and beyond', *Research Institute of Economy, Trade and Industry*, URL: http://www.rieti.go.jp/en/projects/cgp/columns.html.

[58] Miyajima, H. (2005) 'The performance effects and determinants of corporate governance reform in Japan', URL: http://ssrn.com/abstract=818347.

[59] Yasui, T. (1999) 'Corporate governance in Japan and its relevance to the Baltic Region', *Workshop on Corporate Governance in the Baltics (Vilnius, 21–22 October)*, URL: http://www.oecd.org/dataoecd/8/25/1931660.pdf.

[60] Nitta, K. (2007) 'Developing the research frontier in corporate governance analysis', *Research Institute of Economy, Trade and Industry of Japan*, URL: http://www.rieti.go.jp/en/projects/cgp/columns.html.

152   4

INTRODUCTION • THE BUSINESS CULTURES OF FIVE ASIAN COUNTRIES • ANALYSING ASIAN BUSINESS CULTURES • **OWNERSHIP, FINANCING AND GOVERNANCE** • ORGANIZATION AND MANAGEMENT • BUSINESS STRATEGY •

[61] Kubo, K. (2008) 'For whose benefit are Japanese companies run?' *Research Institute of Economy, Trade and Industry*, URL: http://www.rieti.go.jp/en/projects/cgp/columns.html.

[62] Her, M.M. and Mahajan, A. (2005) 'Family control, two-tier Boards and firm performance: Lessons from the Taiwanese experience', *Journal of Asia-Pacific Business*, **6**(2): 69–89.

[63] Roberts, J. (2007) ' "Helping the family": The mediating role of outside directos in ethnic Chinese family firms', *Human Relations*, **60**(2): 285–314.

[64] Cooper, B.J., Leung, P. and Wong, G. (2006) 'The Asia Pacific literature review on internal auditing', *Managerial Auditing Journal*, **21**(8): 822–44.

[65] Lines, V.L. (2004) 'Corporate reputation in Asia: Looking beyond bottom-line performance', *Journal of Communication Management*, **8**(3): 233–45.

[66] Tong, Y. (2007) 'Bureaucracy meets the environment: Elite perceptions in six Chinese Cities', *The China Quarterly*, **189**: 100–21.

[67] Jackson, J. and Li, M. (2003) 'Stakeholder prioritization in Sino-foreign joint ventures', in Alon, I. and Shenkar, O. (eds) *Chinese Culture, Organizational Behavior and International Business Management*, Westport, CA: Praeger.

INTRODUCTION • THE BUSINESS CULTURES OF FIVE ASIAN COUNTRIES • ANALYSING ASIAN
CULTURES • OWNERSHIP FINANCING AND GOVERNANCE • ORGANIZATION AND
MENT • BUSINESS STRATEGY • DIMENSIONS OF SOCIETAL CULTURES • SOCIETAL
CULTURES REVISITED • POLITICAL CULTURES AND PERCEIVED POLITICAL ENVIRONMENTS •
ECONOMIC CULTURES AND PERCEIVED ECONOMIC ENVIRONMENTS • CONCLUDING REMARKS

5 organization and management

In all the five countries of our research, the internal functioning of a business, which is the subject of this chapter, was a topic that surfaced very readily in answer to our opening question about key differences in business and management. Our analysis of our interviews revealed work behaviour, workplace cultures, organization structures and processes, managerial values, management practices and styles, business communication styles, leadership and human resource management as important elements of Asian business cultures.

Work behaviour

Successful management depends on an understanding of the behaviour of people at work, including that of owners and managers themselves. Four aspects raised by our interviewees were how hard-working employees are, their work motivations, goals and attitudes and their propensity for team working. Interviewees frequently described the working populations of these Asian countries as 'hard working'. This behaviour was, however, differently attributed in different countries. In **China** employees were seen as working hard partly out of fear, though this was a new phenomenon:

> Chinese employees' attitudes are to stick it out, accept hierarchy and heavy workload and accept that personal rights – even a sick child – come behind public duty and so the job. Previously their attitude was based on a moral duty and national pride; now it is fear. The employer's obligations to the employee have diminished. There is now no secure net of support. People can be laid off without compensation and pensions are not enough to live on. All this follows the major lay-offs of the [19]90s.[i]

Another explanation for the industriousness of Chinese people was low expectations: 'They will work hard to help their parents. If they can afford to get married,

---

[i] Mainland Chinese, Consultant, International Management Consultancy

they are satisfied. They will go on working hard.'[ii] As noted in Chapter 2, these attitudes – the fear, the moral duty, the low expectations – might all be shifting among the young in the big cities, though it was too soon to say whether this was going to be a widespread or long-lasting change. In *Hong Kong*, however, the people continued to be very hard working and the motivation for this was intrinsic: that they 'treasure efficiency'.[iii]

In **India**, insecurity based on recent experience of high unemployment levels even among graduates probably underlay the prevalent long-hours culture. 'We have a longer hours culture even than Asia – Singapore, for example.'[iv] 'In India, staff spend 50% of their time at work. The effect is a high work commitment, strong work ethic (but also high expectations of how they will be treated).'[v] In **Taiwan**, workers were 'driven by insecurity'[vi] and the high savings rate was cited as evidence.

Working hard may be related to societal cultures in the form of organizational citizenship behaviour. This is 'individual behavior that is discretionary, not directly or explicitly recognized by the formal reward system, and that in the aggregate promotes the effective functioning of the organization.' A study found that in **China** this construct included several behaviours that did not apply in the West: maintaining interpersonal harmony, self-training, protecting and saving company resources, keeping the workplace clean and participating in social welfare activities.[1] A survey of Chinese supervisors and subordinates found that traditionalists and women were motivated towards organizational citizenship behaviour by the values they had come to endorse through socialization concerning their role in society; for them citizenship behaviour was not dependent on whether they perceived the organization as 'fair'. Citizenship behaviour depended on justice perceptions only for the minority of less traditional, male, Chinese workers. The authors concluded that whether they felt they had been treated fairly did not strongly affect the work behaviour of the majority of Chinese.[2]

Work attitudes, motivations and goals

Overall, as Chapter 2 suggested, our research found rather negative beliefs about worker attitudes in **China**: employees were either still operating in a 'quasi-communist' satisficing mode or, among the urban young, were infected by a 'get-rich-quick' approach. *Hong Kong* employees, on the other hand, were described as responding well to managers who showed that they saw their value, and who 'give them exposure, allow them to develop. They value the chance to gain confidence

---

ii Chinese, Consultant, International Business Information Technology Consultancy
iii Hong Kong, Public Affairs Manager, Hong Kong Utility Company
iv Indian, CEO, Family-owned business, Advertising
v Indian, Product Manager, Indian Business Services (IT Management)
vi Senior Vice President, Finance and Accounting, Fund Management

more than money'.[vii] Another study found that worker attitudes in China differed depending on the type of organization individuals worked for and whether they were part of the managerial elite. Yan (2003) commented,

> In general, those who work in SOEs [state-owned enterprises] tend to be more conservative and less sensitive to changes in the outside world; this does not necessarily apply to those who hold high positions in these companies, however. In fact, due to the intimate, sometimes kinship-based connections between SOEs and the government, the CEOs [Chief Executive Officers] and managers of these companies have a strong sense of being part of the political as well as the business elite. Many of them regularly travel to Europe and North America, and some have studied abroad. The managerial elites in joint venture and foreign companies are more Westernized than their counterparts in state-owned companies, and many of them have obtained MBAs or other graduate degrees from abroad. ... These people actually promote Western culture in the workplace; for example, in terms of an institutionalized management system or communications and socializing skills.[3]

In our research, employee motives in the private sector in **India** were described mainly in instrumental terms: 'Employee motives are to make money. There is a talent shortage and salaries are rocketing.'[viii] Instrumental motivations did not, however, preclude the wish to grow and develop: 'Everyone has high aspirations; there are no workers content to remain doing the same fairly menial job, as a mechanic, for instance, all their life. They look for growth and a career.'[ix] Neither did their motives preclude a positive attitude to the work: 'They can be motivated by situations; in our start-up, they suffered delayed salary and no bonuses; openness with them kept them working.'[x] A study in the Indian banking sector found that Indian managers possessed achievement orientation in considerable degree and that the highest performers among them were the ones possessing the highest levels of achievement orientation.[4] However, as in China, Indian employees in public sector businesses had different attitudes:

> To the 'senior crowd' [in public sector businesses] who have worked in the company for 20 or 25 years, the organization is the 'be all and end all'. Their vision is narrow – they have had no opportunity to see outside. In the public sector, career growth cannot be accelerated; they have three times the number of employees they need to do the work. They also have a customary way of doing things. There is no room for creativity.[xi]

[vii] Hong Kong, Public Affairs Manager, Hong Kong Utility Company
[viii] Indian, Finance and General Management, Indian MNC (multi-national company) Heavy Industry
[ix] Indian, CEO, Indian subsidiary of a French-owned MNC industrial goods manufacturer
[x] Indian, Product Manager, Indian Business Services (IT Management)
[xi] Indian, Finance and General Management, Indian MNC Heavy Industry

A comparison of Japanese, Indian and American attitudes to work found that **Japan** and **India** were similar: their collectivism meant that the American model of management that attempts to provide meaningful autonomous work and reward to the individual may be grossly insufficient to integrate an Indian or Japanese employee. Equally, 'a focus on clearly delineated roles and responsibilities without visible concern for the well-being of the junior employee and his family would be a relationship doomed to be an alienating one from the beginning.' In other respects, however, the Japanese and Indians were found to have very different work attitudes. In contrast to the Japanese, Indians had very little identification with the work organization or work group. The Japanese drew meaning in life from belonging to a work group and from contributing to the organization; in contrast, Indians drew meaning from the state of their familial relationships. For an Indian, the work organization was 'a place to earn the livelihood of the family and not a place where he or she belongs'.[5]

These differences, it was argued, were based in the different sense of 'self' that was rooted in the cultures. The American psychologist Roland, who studied the Japanese and Indian cultures, concluded that the Indian self was 'familial-jati' while the Japanese was familial-group. In the former the sense of belonging, loyalty and regard was restricted to the extended family, community and caste, while the Japanese quite smoothly transferred such sentiments to extra-familial groups such as local clubs, associations, schools and work groups.[6] The Japanese had a familial self which incorporated the work organization as soon as they went out to work. This extended self included superiors and subordinates as well as peers. On the other hand, the Indian familial self continued to be largely family or jati (sub-caste) centred. As a result, attempts to create family-type features in organizations (for instance, by exercising authority based on affiliation rather than organizational position) underestimated the pull of the actual family, which was away from the organization.

For Indians, aggression had to be suppressed or controlled in the home, and so was displaced onto the work organization, whereas the Japanese controlled aggression at work out of loyalty to the work organization (and Americans suppressed it for the sake of personal achievement).

> Group orientation and high achievement orientation lead the Japanese to commit themselves very intensely to the work organization as well as the whole society. But the strong family-jati orientation, with low concern for social achievement, leads the Indians to...be prone to non-productive expression of aggression and exploitation of work or public systems for personal/family gains at the cost of social good. ... Clinical work with Indians not infrequently elicits bitter, angry feelings about a superior in the hierarchical relationship, although the overt behaviour remains highly deferential, conforming to the expectations of the situation. Or quite frequently the overt attitude is deferential but the actions are less than cooperative.

The Indian self, Roland (1988) argued, was narcissistic (due to prolonged maternal indulgence, especially of boys) and highly accessible, so they resented denial of promotion, rejected negative feedback, indulged in blame of others and might crib, gossip or complain.[7]

Concurring to some degree in this judgement on Indian work behaviour, Budhwar (2003) wrote that Indians brought interpersonal emotional expectations to work, but in a frame of mind that the organization lacked salience. Indians constantly tested and gauged the level of intimacy they had with any person outside of the extended family. Indian managers found it extremely difficult to dismiss an errant employee as, it was felt, 'He too has a family to support.' Rewards were likely to be at least partially governed by relational rather than performance considerations. Family norms emphasizing loyalty to the family authority figure or superior in an organization underlay 'the limited decision-making experience and unfamiliarity with responsibility found in most employees'.[8]

The motivations of employees in the other countries in our sample were mainly attributed to non-material factors, such as self-development or relationships. In **Taiwan**, despite insecurity, more important motives were to have the value of their work recognized, to have learning experiences, faster career paths, and to have it communicated to them what was happening in the wider organization.

> They are attracted to challenging jobs, wanting to be stretched (but it must be possible to succeed). Among managers, there are two kinds of attitudes to their position. Some prefer the status quo, enjoying being a big fish in a small pond; others want to grow faster than is possible within the organization [and so tend to leave to start their own business]. Most take pride in their job title and the status of the organization.[xii]

A Japanese manager working in Taiwan had similar perceptions of the Taiwanese: 'Their motivations are not just money but intrinsic satisfaction, including growth opportunities and careers.'[xiii] An employee attitude survey found that stability was most important, followed by 'room for growth'. In **Japan**, on the other hand, employees 'care more about relationships in the eyes of others than either their career or their financial rewards'.[xiv] 'Individuals' economic motivation is limited – they are as much or more motivated to contribute, to the company or to their boss. (They want to be appreciated by him.)'[xv] Distress was expressed at the thought that Japan might now be shifting towards a 'carrot and stick' approach to work motivation.

---

xii Taiwan, Expatriate banker
xiii Taiwan, Expatriate (Japanese), General Management, Banking
xiv Japanese, Sourcing and Procurement, French MNC Business Services
xv Japanese, Human Resources, Business Service (1)

158 5

INTRODUCTION • THE BUSINESS CULTURES OF FIVE ASIAN COUNTRIES • ANALYSING ASIAN BUSINESS CULTURES • OWNERSHIP, FINANCING AND GOVERNANCE • **ORGANIZATION AND MANAGEMENT** • BUSINESS STRATEGY •

A case study in a Japanese-owned *Hong Kong* megastore revealed significant differences in the work motivations of Japanese and Chinese managers and employees. The Japanese presented themselves as '*kaisha ningen*', company people, devoted to their company; many of the senior local-Chinese staff, disempowered and low in status within the organization, ran their own businesses on the side, using the store's time and resources. In this situation, success in Chinese terms was measured by establishing one's own business and making money, rather than climbing the ranks of an existing corporate hierarchy. This finding was consistent with the pattern established by the overseas Chinese throughout Asia. 'Where they are marginalized or excluded, their response is to set up in business.'[9] Another influence on the attitudes of Hong Kong workers was found to be their state of morale, which could be negatively affected by change. A survey in Hong Kong showed that work restructuring over the previous year reduced workers' intended job performance, attendance and voicing of discontent. These findings held for workers with various characteristics and for restructuring in work outcomes, work processes and staffing, though income and social class strongly influenced reactions.[10]

Although work goals related to personal achievement were not stressed by our Chinese interviewees, Chung-Sheng et al. (2003) reported finding that both mainland Chinese and Taiwanese Chinese students assigned a high importance ranking to them, contrary to predictions based on a preponderance of evidence supporting a divergence in work-goal importance across different cultures. (Because work goals constitute a subset of the personal value system, they are expected to be largely culturally determined.) However, these findings may be affected by the sample population, which for these countries were international students, who may have an atypical value system. More consistent with predictions based on culture was the finding that American students placed a much higher level of overall importance on the 20 work goals used in the study. 'This may be due to these respondents expecting or desiring much more from their jobs than their Eastern counterparts', the researchers surmised.[11]

Working in teams

The Japanese were seen by our interviewees as outstanding team players; there was more doubt about the Chinese, Singaporeans, Indians and Taiwanese. In **Japan** people may take it to an extreme: 'The positive side of our culture is that we are better team players than the Europeans or Americans – I saw it at business school. But we go to extremes. We kill ourselves and contribute ourselves to the team. No one becomes happy but the team is happy.'[xvi] On attitudes to teamwork in **China**, a comparison with people from another Asian country, Malaysia,

---

[xvi] Japanese, Executive Director (Operations) Business Services

was negative: 'Malaysians are very co-operative, good team workers, like a family, have a sense of belonging with their colleagues. This is in marked contrast to China.'[xvii] Other evidence on Chinese lack of team spirit came from a comparison with Westerners:

> " In the West people do not display their personal negative emotions towards colleagues or clients at work, even though they feel them; in China they do. It needs sensitive handling. That applies even to senior managers; the juniors will screw one another. They do not take it so far as to not attend business meetings or be members of a team in a project, but it does affect the work. Dislikes can be based on personality; for instance one person is seen as flashy and not hard working by a colleague; she is always disparaging her work; there is no trust between them.[xviii]

Another interviewee commented, 'People are very motivated to succeed; there can be higher levels of aggression – of competing with colleagues – than in the West.'[xix] A similar competitiveness was reported for *Hong Kong*: 'In Hong Kong there is a lot of within-company competition and fighting at an individual level.'[xx]

In **Singapore**, the lack of team spirit was attributed more to pride than lack of trust. 'Singaporeans are not good team players. As a society, this is very individualistic; Singaporeans will screw you. They are hyper-competitive at an individual level. Everyone thinks they are smarter than everyone else – based on their grades. It is beginning to change, but...'[xxi] In **India**, 'the psyche of the Indian mind, which is jealous and individualistic' was blamed for teamwork problems.[xxii] Even a senior staff member from an Indian bank which was committed to and differentiated itself partly by team work admitted, 'Indians are individualists, so it is difficult to put together a team.'[xxiii] Sinha and Sinha (1990) commented, 'Indians usually work well individually rather than in groups.'[12] In addition to the direct comment by one Taiwanese interviewee that in **Taiwan** people are 'over-competitive... co-operation within companies is a problem; they are not team players',[xxiv] the following comment by a Japanese manager working there was also suggestive: 'Being independent matters more to the Taiwanese than among the Japanese.'[xxv]

---

xvii Singaporean Chinese, Asia Business Development Manager, International MNC, Energy
xviii Mainland Chinese, Partner, International Accounting Firm
xix General Manager, Chinese Chemical SOE and International Energy MNC
xx Hong Kong, Finance and Accounting, Financial Services
xxi Singaporean, Finance and Accounting, Education
xxii Indian, Business Development and Strategy, Indian Engineering and Construction Company
xxiii Indian, Senior Manager, Private Indian Bank
xxiv Senior Vice President, Finance and Accounting, Fund Management
xxv Taiwan, Expatriate (Japanese), General Management, Banking

Weakness of cooperativeness in the broader organization in **China** may be related to Chinese group orientation, which is strongly directed towards the immediate working group and its leadership, because these are the workplace equivalent of the family, the focal social unit in Chinese culture.[13] Chen and Li (2005) reported findings that the Chinese made less cooperative decisions in mixed-motive business situations than did Australians. While the finding that the Chinese were less cooperative is somewhat opposed to the general view of the Chinese that they are more collective and cooperative than people in individualistic cultures, it can be explained by the particular conditions of the business situations presented – there were no formal or informal sanctions for non-cooperation, no prior ties/relationships among the business partners, no communication was permitted and the information about what other business partners might do was extremely limited. In these circumstances, it could have been 'the lack of general trust' of the Chinese that led them to be less likely to cooperate with 'strangers', because the strong family ties in societies such as China's prevent trust from developing beyond the confines of the family.[14] Somewhat confirming these findings was another that groups of Chinese with higher scores on individualism scored higher on cooperation than groups with higher collectivistic scores when the groups were composed of out-group members. In addition, subjects from the more developed coastal area were more individualistic and cooperative than

Table 5.1 **Work behaviour of employees in five Asian countries**

	China	India	Japan	Taiwan	Singapore
Industriousness	High *HKSAR* Very high	High	Quite high (long hours)	High	Quite high
Primary motive	To make money – insecurity *HKSAR* Desire for efficiency	To make money – insecurity	Commitment to the organization	Career; development; learning	
Secondary motive		Career; development; learning			
Team working	Poor	Poor	Very good	Poor	Poor
Cultural underpinning	Collectivist loyalty transferred to work group not the wider organization	Collectivist loyalty to units outside the organization, especially the family	Collectivist loyalty transferred to organization		

subjects from inland China, suggesting that exposure to other influences than traditional Chinese culture increased both individualism and cooperativeness.[15] Another finding that also suggested that outside influence affects Chinese propensities for team working was that cooperative conflict management built confidence in relationships and confidence in the team's interpersonal relationships promoted team effectiveness. This finding, according to researchers Tjosvold et al. (2005) contrasts with traditional theorizing about Chinese values;[16] it may be, however, that the version of Chinese traditional values applied by Tjosvold et al. (2005) ignored the distinction between attitudes to in-group and out-group members that has been noted elsewhere. Table 5.1 summarizes these findings on the work behaviour of employees in our sample countries.

Workplace cultures

How are interpersonal relations at work conducted in different Asian countries? At one extreme, in this case, was the example of **India**, where, 'Culturally people here like to interact. We celebrate birthdays and involve the person's family',[xxvi] and,

> The culture of the workplace is social. People from work form friendships and groups and all get together socially. They get involved with a colleague's family life. Support one another. This applies colleague to colleague, not just the obligation of the superior to the subordinate. For instance our accountant invited everyone (325 staff) to his wedding and was very upset when not everyone attended.[xxvii]

'Within an organization we know people on a friendly basis right across functions',[xxviii] and, 'Have you heard of the train culture? Co-workers have the same compartment, form a group: the devotional compartment (where the ticket collectors don't bother – they assume they are honest); the compartment of women going home who share the preparation of the food for the evening meal.'[xxix] One interviewee did assert that the workplace culture in India was no more sociable than in London, where he had worked, but added, 'The difference is that workplace friends will often include the family.'[xxx]

At the other extreme in Asia from India in terms of sociability, according to our findings, were the Confucian-based cultures. In **China**, 'The workplace culture is not highly social although occasionally, when very good relations are

---

xxvi Indian, Senior Manager, Private Indian Bank
xxvii Indian, CEO, Indian Educational Not-for-Profit
xxviii Indian, Economist, Former Entrepreneur, Senior Academic
xxix Indian, Lawyer, Department Head, Indian Educational Not-for-Profit
xxx Indian, Successful Entrepreneur, Indian internet-based Business Services

established, one might invite a colleague or superior home. Working hours are long – there is not the same work/life balance.[xxxi]

 Locals will not talk to colleagues and will even avoid clients they dislike. Avoidance is such that they will convey messages through a third person, though without making it clear that is what they are doing. You think, 'Why is he saying this to me?' Then you realize it is because he wants you to say it to someone he is not speaking to.[xxxii]

(This suggestion that avoidance is motivated by dislike is worth noting; in the culture literature, collectivist avoidance is attributed to fear of disrupting harmonious relationships, which is a different attribution.) Such behaviour would be extremely rare in **Japan**, where harmony was accounted so 'psychologically rewarding' that it replaced economic motivations for working hard.[xxxiii]

While sociability and competitiveness varied across the region, avoiding overt conflict with colleagues was widespread. Hypothesis-testing research found only limited differences in preferred conflict-handling styles between Japan, Hong Kong, Thailand and Vietnam. In all four countries 'integrating' was the preferred style, although there was less similarity among the nationalities regarding 'competing' and 'avoiding'.[17] From our own research it was reported that in China, although 'Power wins every argument', actually, 'The arguments never happen.'[xxxiv] In Taiwan, where, despite over-competitiveness 'confrontation will be avoided',[xxxv] avoiding overt conflict was important enough to drive strategy: '[The new high technology] businesses have a lack of management skills to manage large numbers of knowledge workers, so spin-offs avoid internal conflict; but links are retained.'[xxxvi] In Singapore, avoiding conflict was blamed for Eastern culture being not very good at cultivating leaders. 'The cultural need for harmony means avoiding conflict – they are not prepared to be disliked, so can't get things done.'[xxxvii] In Japan, 'We see danger in conflict.'[xxxviii]

 Companies are generally cohesive. People, including juniors, are generally attuned to reading atmosphere and context and adapting. Bosses don't quarrel openly, especially not in front of others. However, others may detect that there is hidden conflict and they will try to make it right. Acting maturely, adjusting to atmosphere, used

---

[xxxi] General Manager, Chinese Chemical SOE
[xxxii] Mainland Chinese, Partner, International Accounting Firm
[xxxiii] Japanese, Human Resources, Business Services
[xxxiv] China, Expatriate, Senior Consultant, International Management Consultancy
[xxxv] Taiwan, Expatriate (Japanese), General Management, Banking
[xxxvi] Partner, Taiwanese Venture Capital
[xxxvii] Singaporean, CEO, Thai MNC, Business Services
[xxxviii] Japanese Strategic Management, Business Services

to be considered one of the most important work skills though it is becoming less common now.[xxxix]

Avoidance extended to not giving bad news: it made an American working in Beijing feel that she was not being listened to. 'My assistant won't tell me if there is a problem.'[xl] In India, as Chapter 2 demonstrated, avoiding giving bad news was seen as so pervasive as to be highly detrimental to the efficiency of businesses.

Workplace cultures in **Japan** reflected the overall business culture. A study of the relations among business culture, workplace communication and international human resource management in Japanese firms with a mixture of Japanese and non-Japanese employees, found the strongest correlation (0.66) between business culture and communication; this was as expected, since 'logically, differences in business practices and culture should affect communication between people of different nationalities in the work environment'. This study 'demonstrated the strength of the Japanese business culture and the extent to which it is manifest in workplace communication'.[18]

Organizational structures and processes

Apart from comments on hierarchy, our interviews yielded rather few spontaneous references to organizational structure or role specialization, except in Japan. The impression given was that in the five Asian countries researched, except in Japan organizations generally used functional, divisional or business unit organization and role specialization. In **China**, we were told, 'Structurally, many SOEs are like large Western companies – functional or matrix, or groups of individual divisions that may be legal entities', and, 'Role specialization happens early for most; a few stars are rotated for experience, to groom them for top posts.'[xli] 'Private businesses are moving towards specialization and Western-style value chain integration. The Government is promoting Western management. Chinese business is not likely to converge towards either the Korean or the Japanese model.'[xlii]

One key characteristic of Chinese SOEs was the politicization of the top executive post.

 In China, the CEOs of large SOEs are often government officials who are given the role. Often these are retired generals, who bring in a 'military' culture: that is, one where decisions are executed, not challenged. (Entrepreneurs in private companies are more likely

---

xxxix Japanese Product Manager, Western MNC Pharmaceuticals manufacturer
xl China, Expatriate, Consultant, International Management Consultancy
xli General Manager, Chinese Chemical SOE and International Energy MNC
xlii China, Expatriate, Senior Consultant, International Management Consultancy

to absorb new ideas and listen.) The government appoints these CEOs because if they own it, they should have it headed up by their representative.[xliii]

Lowe (2003) argued, however, that Chinese concepts of organization combined the harmonizing coordination of interrelated parts with *ch'i*, which is the dynamic creativity derived from intuition and subjective or tacit knowledge. The result was a model of organizations which was in stark contrast to Western models on many dimensions. In China, organizations allocated power by ascription instead of achievement, rather than encouraging participation they encouraged following the rules of a patron and paternalism, and they were characterized by high status consciousness rather than a team orientation.[19]

According to Child and Tse (2001) firms in China continuously reformed their organizations under the influence of institutional forces that were more complex and stronger in transitional than in free-market economies.[20] Two institutional forces in particular were noteworthy. One was uneven regional development – initially the coast was developed, later the interior; the other was the continuous expansion of the private sector. Starting in 1979, Sino-foreign joint ventures were introduced to let in foreign financial capital and technology; a few years later, small private firms were allowed to operate; at the same time, former communes were allowed to emerge and operate independently of state control: this led to an explosive growth of millions of town and village enterprises (collectives). By 1989, the total output of the private sector exceeded that of the state-owned firms. From 1993, joint stock firms began to take form, with ownership shared by workers, individual investors, firms and governments. Their status was endorsed in 1999. China also continuously developed two stock exchanges.[21] The 'continuous reform' of organizations described by Child and Tse (2001) is consistent with our finding that the Chinese 'cope well with change'.

In **India**, two specific comments on organizational structure together suggested that there had been too much structural variation over time and between companies for this to be a significant aspect of the business culture there: 'As in the West, Indian companies were previously functionally organized, but are now usually built around business units in order to align with markets, but have functions within them.'[xliv] 'Whether or not there is role specialization varies from company to company. The Tata Group has a pool of managers (the Tata Administrative Service) who are rotated; Reliance is more functionally specialized; Birla develops general management skills.'[xlv]

The most marked difference our research revealed in the ways businesses in Asia were organized and run was in **Japan**. Even its largest corporations

---

[xliii] General Manager, Chinese Chemical SOE and International Energy MNC
[xliv] Indian, CEO, subsidiary of a French MNC, manufacturing
[xlv] Indian, Finance and General Management, Indian MNC Heavy Industry

employed little functional specialization and so developed generalist rather than specialist staff and managers: 'Organizational charts notwithstanding, the actual roles of managers are often unclear; the boundaries are not rigid, the managers (and most full-time permanent employees) are generalists.' Decision-making, wherever it might be located nominally, was really by consensus of key personnel, who were as likely to be involved because of their track record as because of their official position; and status and power were not necessarily co-located.

Decision-making

Table 5.2 summarizes our findings on decision-making, which showed that the dominance of founding families in businesses in many Asian countries strongly influenced decision-making. In private companies in **India**, for example,

> There is a flow of decisions from the owners to the executives without discussion. Not, in the biggest or listed companies, directly but through hand-picked 'experts' – usually in Finance or Purchasing – who constitute an extra layer of direction. They are not company employees. They are known as 'owners' men'. They could be on the board of a holding company. Before a board meeting, the executives of the company will be summoned and told what the decisions will be.[xlvi]

In the words of another interviewee, 'The business remains the founder's business and decision-making is centralized.'[xlvii] On the other hand, there was a suggestion that the presentation of decisions had to make concessions to the Indian employee manager's attitudes in the comment that the 'Jack Welch' style of decision-making – described as high speed and cut-and-dried – would demotivate Indian employees.

Table 5.2 **Decision-making in Asian businesses**

	China	India	Japan
Basis for decision-making	1. *Top down* 2. *Intuition* 3. *Trial and error* 4. *Superstition*	1. Top down 2. Thorough information gathering	1. Consensus 2. Thorough information gathering

[xlvi] Indian, Business Development and Strategy, Indian Engineering and Construction Company
[xlvii] Indian, Consultant, Former CEO Indian subsidiary, US MNC industrial goods manufacturer

166 5

INTRODUCTION • THE BUSINESS CULTURES OF FIVE ASIAN COUNTRIES • ANALYSING ASIAN BUSINESS CULTURES • OWNERSHIP, FINANCING AND GOVERNANCE • **ORGANIZATION AND MANAGEMENT** • BUSINESS STRATEGY •

Business decision-making in **China**, like India, was top down:

> In Chinese companies execution is very good. This is because of the high respect for the team leader which means everybody acts promptly and thoroughly, even if they disagree with the decision. On the other hand, it is risky – the decision is taken by one person without much communication or discussion with others. Subordinates might give suggestions but in general the team leader will have more sense of the business and better access to market intelligence. Once the leader's decision is made it would be impolite – wrong – to challenge it.[xlviii]

Continuing high levels of market regulation in any case meant that 'decision-making is more limited and execution is more important'.[xlix]

A finding that supports ours on Japanese people's still-strong sense of the seniority principle and their cultural preference for consensual decision-making, in contrast to China and India, came from a survey that found that in **Japan** employees under the age of 35 were less willing to take control over decision-making than those over 35; in the USA the percentages were about the same for both age groups.[22]

In relation to how decisions are made (as opposed to by whom), our own research identified a preference in **China** for intuitive decision-making and trial-and-error approaches over systematic and research-based methods. Lowe (2003) contrasted 'rationalistic' Western organizations' decision-making with China's 'intuitive' style: while the Western style relied on analysing information objectively before acting, dividing issues up into measurable variables, employing due diligence and using facts as proof to win arguments, the 'Chinese' style substituted using inductive action to reveal what works best, treating problems as wholes, cultivating unfolding change, discovering 'what works for us' and maintaining harmony and consensus.[23]

Ninan and Pillay (2007) referred to the 'complexities of the values and belief systems of a nonlinear, discontinuous and collective Eastern organisational culture' and their lack of fit with more linear, continuous and individualistic Western decision-making systems.[24] A more extreme finding from an earlier exploratory study even suggested that Chinese business decision-making was influenced by 'superstition', particularly *feng shui*, although there was also evidence that some practitioners experienced cognitive dissonance in using it. Superstition helps Chinese businessmen cope with uncertainty by providing a sense of certainty and alleviating the anxiety associated with uncertainty. Although superstition is often regarded as irrational and unfounded, practitioners try to justify it on

---

[xlviii] General Manager, Chinese Chemical SOE and International Energy MNC
[xlix] Ibid.

the grounds of superstition's substantive validity or instrumental value.' *Feng shui* experts played the roles of expert, provocateur, legitimizer and comforter in strategic decision-making when providing advice to their business clients.[25]

The way that decisions were perceived as being made in **India** was different from the Chinese way: 'Most Indian business leaders will look at a venture for its potential in terms of market leadership, profitability. We research the market in depth, do customer and competitor analysis. It is closer to the Western approach than the Chinese. Business decision-making in India is not based on (national or other) pride alone'.[i] There must be doubt, however, in a society where 'auspiciousness' and its reverse are so implanted in many people's minds, whether such issues never enter business decision-making.

Control

As Table 5.3 shows, our research found that in China and India, information flows were restricted and control was exercised by close supervision; on the other hand, in Japan information was widely dispersed and control was exercised by normative or cultural pressure. Withholding information to gain or maintain power has been described as 'acceptable' in **China**. Openness was often considered a sign of weakness.[26] 'The flow of information is largely in the upwards direction; the flow of decisions downwards.'[li] Communication processes were influenced by Confucian norms of hierarchical relations. The Chinese management style has been described as 'closed door management'.[27] The Chinese leadership style depicts a boss holding information, and thus power, which he hands out to subordinates in small portions, making them more dependent on the leader.[28] The logic behind such practices is that information and the control of information are basic components of power in all organizations. It has been observed that Chinese organizations restrict even vertical communication. The leadership style limited and distorted the communication downwards, while the condemnation resulting from offering opposing views and the sense of powerlessness among middle managers tended to hamper and deform upward communication in the organization.[29] However, a comparison of the approaches to control by overseas Chinese, Japanese, South Korean and Western partners in Chinese joint ventures suggested that whatever their cultural propensities, the overseas Chinese were able to adopt 'appropriate' control measures. They were no more likely than the comparison groups to use personal control rather than structural control, except in the case of labour-intensive firms where they adhered to 'close supervision' methods of control.[30]

Despite the changes in their business environment and in some practices such as lifetime employment, in **Japan** many firms still emphasized cultural control

---

[i] Indian, CEO, Indian subsidiary of a French MNC manufacturer
[li] General Manager, Chinese Chemical SOE and International Energy MNC

Table 5.3   *Information flows and control systems in China, India and Japan*

	China	India	Japan
Information flows and control systems	*Restricted within-company information flows; control by close supervision*	Restricted within-company information flows; *control by close supervision*	Information is widely dispersed; *normative/cultural control systems*

systems in management, rather than output-oriented control systems. As one of our interviewees put it, 'Once [our company] principles are fully understood, everybody should act according to their own judgement. We have autonomous, decentralized management while insisting on the principles.'[lii] Cultural control systems imply that output is controlled by shared norms, that behaviour is guided by the shared philosophy of management, and that performance is not necessarily imposed by an external control system, since employees and managers see performing well as a social obligation. Managers' actions are controlled by training that leads them to act in accordance with accepted standards of behaviour within the company. These company-specific control systems are rooted partly in the way Japanese culture emphasizes trust, loyalty and group identification. (The difficulty of transferring such control systems to non-Japanese employees is considered one reason why Japanese firms generally rely on expatriates to manage foreign affiliates.)[31]

Managerial values

Not surprisingly, perhaps, given the abstract nature of the topic, 'managerial values' received few direct comments in our study. They were, no doubt, implicit in some comments, but our methodology excludes the level of researcher interpretation that would be required to make them explicit. Other studies, using different methodologies, have, however, drawn conclusions set out in this section.

A comparison of the perceptions of middle-level managers in four countries published in 2000 provides a starting point for a comparison of Chinese and Indian values concerning management. The findings for three of the countries are shown in Table 5.4.

With only one 'ability', self-confidence/charisma, rated high and three rated low as determinants of managerial performance by the Chinese managers, there is a suggestion that they had lower overall expectations and beliefs about the role of managers than respondents in the other two countries. The high value Indian

[lii] Japanese, Operations Management, Japanese Manufacturer

Table 5.4 **A comparison of Chinese, Indian and US management values**

Value attached to:	China	India	America
Self-confidence/charisma	High	Intermediate	Low
Educational achievements	Intermediate	Intermediate	Low
Communication skills	Low	High	Intermediate
Past experience	Low	Intermediate	High
Leadership ability	Low	High	Intermediate

Source: Based on Neelankavil, J.P., Mathur, A. and Zhang, Y. (2000) 'Determinants of managerial performance: A cross-cultural comparison of the perceptions of middle-level managers in four *countries*', *Journal of International Business Studies*, **31**(1): 121–40.

managers placed on communication skills and leadership ability corresponds to their paternalistic management culture and to the findings on Indian employees' attitudes to two-way communication and transformational leadership reported in this chapter's section on leadership. The researchers for this study concluded that although modern Indian management practices evolved from the British system, they developed a distinct flavour, reflecting Indian values, as instanced by the way businesses were still run very paternalistically, with personal relationships playing a critical role. The finding that Chinese and Indian managers broadly agreed on the factors that determined their performance but differed on the relative importance of self-confidence/charisma, communication skills, past experience and leadership skills led the researchers to conclude that although certain non-culturally dependent variables relate to managerial success, the relative importance of these factors may be culture-bound.[32]

Lowe (2003) considered that management in **China** was heavily dependent on relationships, with 'fuzzy' accountability and authority based on trust. Fuzzy thinking stresses that structure is temporary and the process of change is immanent. Everything is in the process of changing. This means that rigorous black-and-white Truth is replaced by Virtue, which is contextual, pragmatic, adaptive, dialectic, fuzzy, paradoxical and grey.[33] Similarly, Hill (2007) noted that East Asian lifestyles and management behaviours, many of which conflicted with prevailing globalization trends towards efficiency and competitiveness, were rooted in the region's Buddhist, Confucian and Taoist principles,[34] while Holt (1997) argued that Chinese managers exhibited cultural differences that distinguished them from their international counterparts. They were 'more likely to avoid uncertainty and consequently less likely to exhibit innovativeness or advocate change'. Values associated with self-determination, risk taking and innovativeness were consistently less apparent among Chinese managers. Cultural values operated as constraints to change in China.[35] According to the research of Jenner et al. (1998), Chinese SOEs were 'mired in a culture which seriously impedes effective management and organizational techniques'.[36] 'Chinese traditional culture, especially the

Confucian system, tends to value stability over change, and is more or less static in orientation.' These values, Anderson et al. (2003) argued, acted as obstacles to such modern management techniques as quality function deployment (QFD), which is used to translate customer satisfaction into the engineering language of companies. 'Thus, QFD becomes a potent, multifunctional development tool that allows the voice of the customer to influence a product from its design right through to the manufacturing process. However, such changes lie uneasily alongside management techniques derived from traditional Confucianism.' Similarly, cultural *guanxi* and emphasis on hierarchy impeded the effective implementation of total quality management (TQM). *Guanxi* led managers to

> pay the most attention to their relationships with upper-level authorities. Yet TQM should focus on the involvement and quality-consciousness raising of all workers throughout the organization. ...No one member of a team or group has higher status than any other. ...However, Chinese traditional culture emphasizes hierarchical order, with those at lower levels obeying those at higher levels. Thus, many of the cultural values and behaviour patterns that characterize the Confucian system are still active in Chinese SOEs and COEs (cooperatively owned enterprises), which undermines quality management in the judgement of Anderson et al. (2003).[37]

Studies have reported that not only cultural values, but also traditional socialist ideology and practices influenced Chinese management, acting to constrain them from imposing drastic changes, even as management control was tightened in SOEs. Worker reactions to change depended on the type of change: job satisfaction increased when change involved improved job security or greater mental as opposed to physical workloads.[38] Based on fieldwork in a city in central China, one study showed that with an aggressive implementation of privatization schemes,

> Labour struggles have emerged in which moral economy demands are increasingly permeated by 'class consciousness'. Privatization activates workers' class consciousness, an idea that has become embedded in their minds through several decades' immersion in socialist (and anti-capitalist) ideology. For them, anti-privatization is politically defensible. It provides them with motivation, opportunity and an action-frame for class-conscious mobilization in Chinese factories.[39]

Contrasting with these findings on Chinese management values, Newbury and Yakova (2006) reported an earlier study which concluded that in **India** culture generated a management philosophy that was domineering, leading to labour relations policies that were primarily adversarial and interactions that were predominantly confrontational.[40] Tripathi (1990) found that Indian work organizations displayed a mixed set of values, characteristic of both Western and non-Western societies. 'A belief in Detachment is found to coexist with Materialistic Orientation, Collectivism with Individualism and Humanism with Power Orientation.' The integration of staff ('members') in Indian organizations was related to background factors such as their level of professional education, the family's exposure to work organizations and prior work experience while integration was enhanced by nurturance of subordinates by supervisors, organizational expectations of universalism and peer leadership. These were different sets of factors from those that supported staff integration in an MNC (multinational company) operating in India. Tripathi (1990) argued that indigenous values, such as familism, needed to be synthesized with the values of industrial democracy to make Indian organizations more effective.[41]

Management practices and style

In regard to management style, in our interviews in Taiwan and India a distinction was drawn between different types of businesses – between traditional and new, usually high technology, businesses. In traditional businesses in **Taiwan**, employees usually entered the business when young and there was limited mid-career new blood brought in. 'There used to be a near-Japanese level of lifetime employment, though that has virtually gone in the younger generation.'[liii] 'Promotion is still based on seniority; loyalty rather than ability are rewarded; no shares are given to non-family employees, though there could be a big bonus decided by the whim of the boss. They are hierarchical and stable.'[liv] 'When Taiwanese companies get very big, they become bureaucratic, like government, with formality, regular hours etc.'[lv] High-technology businesses, in contrast, were characterized as dynamic, responding to global competition and changeable. They recruited globally: 'The CEO of ASA is an Italian. There is no loyalty bond and a high staff turnover, especially due to spin-offs. They try to stay lean; the CEO delegates.'[lvi] In both kinds of companies, however, 'The primary need is to enhance communication – Taiwanese managers' communication is one-way.'[lvii] Concurring in this opinion, Lam et al. (1994) stated that in Taiwan, high distance was maintained between superiors and subordinates. The combination of shame as the primary standard for moral behaviour and the highly stereotyped relationships expected between superiors and subordinates were linked to the

---

[liii] Taiwanese, Finance and Accounting, Manufacturing
[liv] Taiwanese, Partner, Taiwanese Venture Capital
[lv] Taiwanese, Finance and Accounting, Manufacturing
[lvi] Taiwanese, Partner, Taiwanese Venture Capital
[lvii] Taiwan, Japanese,

172   5

INTRODUCTION • THE BUSINESS CULTURES OF FIVE ASIAN COUNTRIES • ANALYSING ASIAN BUSINESS CULTURES
• OWNERSHIP, FINANCING AND GOVERNANCE • ORGANIZATION AND MANAGEMENT • BUSINESS STRATEGY •

cultural concern of maintaining 'face'. This concern might require that the patriarch maintain the fiction of his 'correctness' despite contrary evidence: to admit fault could undermine the legitimacy of the patriarch's position. As organizations grew larger and the distance between personal loyalty and intimate personal relations became greater, the premium on orthodoxy and 'face' increased.[42] In smaller Taiwanese organizations, and especially those in less traditional sectors, however, change was perhaps occurring. Wu et al. (2001) investigated the cultural values that influenced Taiwanese PR practitioners and pointed to the significance of a rewarding and supportive work climate, collectivism and joint contribution to the success of the organization, teamwork and cross-tasking.[43]

Management practice in most family businesses in **India** was described as follows:

> To run a tight ship, be directive, and professionalize. They often do well. Their top decision-makers have a stake in the business and may well have technical ability and communication skills. The problem arises on the interpersonal side, which is feudal. The family business system also sets limits to growth because the span of personal control is limited. Plus the system acts as a disincentive to very able people to work there.[lviii]

Management style in India was, however, widely adapted to an employee who was sensitive and whose primary concerns were for family.

> Although Indians are very diverse there are certain common things that will motivate and others that will demotivate most Indians. For example, the Jack Welch style that turned around GE in USA would probably fail in India: the cut and dried decisions, abrasiveness, the seeing things in black and white, not shades of grey, the speed of decision-making, the 'you or me' instead of 'you and me' would impact negatively on many individuals and make them diffident and withdrawn. Relationships mean a lot in any Indian management team. Developing a link with the team is as important as being professional. People do carry their home setting into the working environment. I would tell my staff that an organization is not a family or a club, but I recognized that relationships do impinge on working life also. A person from the same community, caste, language group or town – not really religion any more – would expect a little more camaraderie; not to be treated purely on a merit basis. We have to deal with and communicate about the soft issues. If we ask 'How are you?' it is a genuine question and if the person responds by unburdening himself, we listen, show concern, may get involved in helping.[lix]

[lviii] Indian, Consultant, Former CEO Indian subsidiary, US MNC industrial goods manufacturer
[lix] Ibid.

Sinha and Sinha (1990) found that India's socio-cultural values led to a soft management style that was incompatible with Western work values. As a result an expected shift brought about by the transplant of the Western form of industrial organizations in India from a dependency and personalized work relationship to a contractual one, and from a steeply hierarchical to a reasonably egalitarian authority structure was only partially realized. Instead, technological requirements and job demands at many places were unduly compromised. However, where the social values supported the establishment of *work* as the master value, higher productivity did result from the combination of Western organization and Indian management.[44]

Influenced by US practices, newer businesses in India, unlike those in the public sector or the 'old' private sector, rewarded merit.

> People get promoted over the head of older staff; they are less compartmentalized – people are encouraged to be multi-skilled. An individual or a small team may see a project through from start to finish. In our newly created bank, two thirds of staff are front-end – at the interface with clients; they empower the front end – these staff don't always have to refer back or up for decisions; they use the team concept, even though Indians are individualists, making it difficult to put together a team; they are leaner, with smaller staff to turnover ratios.[lx]

Even in high-technology businesses, however, it was suggested, 'The usual managerial climate is Theory X.' As a result,

> Doing things differently from other managers produces a very positive response. For instance, I would listen and if I needed to refuse a request I would explain the reason. For example there was a woman who wanted to go for training that would cost $3000; when it was found that the same training was available in our own organization, she still wanted to go outside, and was cold towards me. I arranged a meeting with her and explained that that $3000 could be used to send someone – it might be her – to a conference in the USA or for some other unique opportunity; or for business trips to gain the extra business we needed. She accepted and was ok to me after that.[lxi]

The point being made here, in part, was that the method of reasoning with subordinates was atypical for Indian managers.

In contrast to Taiwan and India, in **China**, although different types of businesses were described as having different cultures, this was not brought out in respect of their management style. Instead, a number of general points were made: 'The biggest difference from Western companies is the large number of middle

---

[lx] Indian, Senior Manager, Private Indian Bank
[lxi] Indian, Business Information Technology, business services

level managers, who are happy to work overtime to get results; their urgency drives the top management rather than the other way round.'[lxii] 'Daily execution on the ground is by guidelines rather than detailed procedural manuals; most subordinates self-censor though will occasionally feed an idea in to a boss in such a way that the boss can take the credit. Sometimes the senior managers don't have the experience.'[lxiii]

Chinese management, according to Deloitte (2006), especially in the SOEs, is directed by or towards outside bodies, of which the Party and the central or local bureaucracy are the most important. Since it is still very unusual to reach higher positions without being an honoured member of the Party, pleasing the Party is the main motive and driver of the senior managers of SOEs.[45] For example, senior executives of China's SOEs tended to view organizational innovation from a political perspective. They wanted to show their sponsoring government body their innovative achievement and progress. A case study of a state-owned microelectronics group with approximately 5000 employees showed the problems of these kinds of enterprises. Under the government's control, the business had become a sort of 'small society' with a variety of social operations, including day care, kindergartens, elementary and middle schools, a hospital and community committees. Many of the government's decisions for investment projects at the business were based on political considerations, without due analysis of the products, equipment and market needs. Government policies were continuously changing and frequently put the latecomers at an advantage over the early movers as new, lower tax rates and faster loan-delivery policies were instituted. All technical staff at the SOE had received training from internationally renowned firms, including Toshiba, but employees lacked motivation – the reward system was poor, lacking incentives for innovation, market development and customer servicing. Changing this was not possible, however, because of political and welfare considerations. There was mutual distrust between the SOE and other firms that could or should be in the value chain – a tendency to believe that it could perform better than the others, if only it had additional funds or relevant *guanxi* with the national authorities or the international vendors.[46]

During several periods of the recent past, Party membership and heritage were the only ways to get any kind of skilled work or reach a managerial position. Due to a large power distance culture and the dual hierarchy system – one based on Party membership and the other based on company hierarchy – managers continued to be afraid of workers with Party membership and supervisors to feel uncomfortable about giving them orders. Benefits were mainly distributed according to social ranking in the group, such as Party membership or a seat on the union board.[47]

[lxii] Mainland Chinese, Marketing Manager, Consumer MNC
[lxiii] Mainland Chinese, Consultant, International Management Consultancy

Chinese managers regarded the ability to maintain harmonious relationships with all the people with whom they came in contact in their jobs as the most important reason for their own success, a study found.[48] They were always concerned to intervene to restore harmony when cases of conflict occurred between Chinese employees (although they did show reluctance to deal directly with situations involving foreigners).[49] Rated most important among the people with whom Chinese managers came into contact were not their employees, however, nor clients or customers, but bureaucrats.[50] This is not to say that relations with employees were unproblematic. PRC (People's Republic of China) employees could only be dismissed with elaborate procedures and very solid reasons and, on the other hand, could not easily be promoted over junior colleagues or given substantial financial inducements. Managers had to try to win the support of their subordinates in more subtle ways than outside China. A study on the work of CEOs in state-owned enterprises in Dalian, North China, found that 'patriarchal' affairs concerning housing, the cafeteria, clinic, kindergarten, affiliated schools, and so on, together with party and political work, accounted for approximately 15 per cent of the CEOs' time.[51] (In contrast, in India, where similar levels of corporate welfare provision were commonplace, the work was generally outsourced and took little management time.)

The amount of autonomy and actual power that PRC managers could exercise was 'bounded by local relational obligations'.[52] It depended crucially on the attitude of those who surrounded them: those on whom they were vertically dependent, as well as on the Party Secretary and trade union representative. Despite local variations, the manager in the PRC had one problem managers in capitalist countries are spared: the Communist party's cadres' all-pervading presence, which prevented a manager from exercising much personal individual power. Child and Lu (1990) pointed out that it was the officials in the local industrial bureaus who had the power to appoint directors of enterprises and to approve contracts specifying enterprise performance targets. The bureaus were mainly accountable to the local government, and the support of the enterprise's superior bureau was essential, for instance, if a business wanted to borrow money from the local bank, which was also under the local government. These local regulatory bureaus, which supervised the enterprises, were known colloquially by the Chinese as 'the mothers-in-law'. One of the most vital parts of the job of any manager in the PRC was placating the 'mothers-in-law', which might involve lavish entertaining and other tangible offerings.[53]

Management style in businesses in **Japan** was central to the business culture as perceived by our interviewees and so was described in Chapter 2. As noted there, there was some change and a high awareness of a need to change due to globalization and other pressures, but a strong sense of continuity was also felt. This was apparent to outsiders: an Indian who had close business links with Japan said, 'Its management style has not changed much: it is marked by a strong sense of status hierarchy, a 20 year tradition of low key promotion, egalitarianism.'[lxiv] Rather than MNCs bringing radical change, some subsidiaries of MNCs in Japan adopted the local management style:

> " The [Japanese subsidiary of a Swiss] MNC I work for has lifetime employment which makes staff less aggressive, more loyal. There are both salary men and salary women. Promotion is by seniority. Something like a *ringi* system operates. Japanese companies have an apprenticeship culture. The young don't say their opinion. Leadership is strong, though not verbal; young people consider what older people think. If they are trying to persuade an older person of something, they will gather every item of information beforehand, not just about the proposal but also about the older person's preferences, his thoughts on the area. To do otherwise would be rude. In contrast, when I worked in America, young people made their suggestions as soon as they thought of them and expected to discuss them openly as if they were equal to their boss.[lxv]

Procedures were still learned by word of mouth rather than from manuals.

> " There are manuals but they are thin and only referred to occasionally. Not like General Electric where when you join they give you a thick manual and tell you to get yourself up to speed on it. In Japanese companies there is a two or three month takeover period when someone takes on a new post. This is not just to learn the business, but also to get to know people.[lxvi]

'Companies do have a thin manual but people mostly find out what they need to know by asking other people.'[lxvii]

Business communication style

Past research into work communication in Asia tended to emphasize collectivism as the predominant influence. For instance, Ohbuchi and Takahashi (1994) argued that the Japanese were more concerned than Americans about maintaining a positive relationship with others, because 'for a collectivist culture, maintaining social harmony and relationships is paramount'. Despite the fact that the Japanese in their study thought that engaging with others about problems would be more productive than avoiding, doing so was also seen as very risky – relationships might be damaged and social harmony disrupted. A similar point

---

[lxiv] Indian, General Manager and family member, Indian family shipping business
[lxv] Japanese Product Manager, Western MNC Pharmaceuticals manufacturer
[lxvi] Japanese, Audit, Venture Capital
[lxvii] Japanese Product Manager, Western MNC Pharmaceuticals manufacturer

was made by Bond and Hwang (1986), who argued that, for the Chinese, the most important factor was social order and interpersonal harmony.[54,55]

Lalwani et al. (2006) drew the same 'collectivist/individualist' line, arguing that contrary to the view that collectivists are more likely to engage in deception and socially desirable responding than individualists, both do but in different ways. A study showed that although US and European Americans scored higher on self-deceptive enhancement (the tendency to see oneself in a positive light and to give inflated assessments of one's skills and abilities) than Singaporeans and Asian Americans respectively, the latter scored higher on impression management. Impression management here meant misrepresenting self-reported actions to appear more normatively appropriate and 'so the high scores of the Singaporeans and Asian Americans are consistent with their culturally-influenced outer-directedness.'[56]

From our research, however, a more complex picture emerged: the **Chinese** can be blunt and assertive at work.

> [Harmony] is very important in China, but people are blunter in relation to detailed problems with the work: you can be told, 'That's wrong; fix it.' On the other hand, feedback and appraisal are not really given; even if you go to your manager and ask how you can improve, he [sic] will avoid telling you what your weaknesses are.[lxviii]

'The Chinese are subtle, imputing meanings into how you say things and gestures; they look for hidden meanings, for what's underneath what you say, observe as well as listen. When people confront, or are upfront or blunt, it is taken as meaning the concealment of something they want hidden.'[lxix] An expatriate manager's view, however, was different: 'In China there is a lack of sense of personal space and there is public behaviour that would be unacceptable in the West.'[lxx]

Our research suggested that conflict avoidance was widespread in China, Japan and Taiwan, but less so in India. It also produced the suggestion that avoidance might be motivated by simple dislike rather than support for harmony. Morris et al. (1998) suggested that differences in value orientations underlay two patterns of differences found between US and Chinese managers in conflict management style. Managers in **China** tended towards an Avoiding style, US managers towards a Competing style. These differences in managerial behaviour, they found, reflected underlying differences in value orientations. A Social Conservatism value-orientation, tapping values such as Conformity and Tradition, underlay the tendency of Chinese managers to avoid explicit negotiation of workplace conflicts. An orientation towards Self Enhancement, and

---

lxviii General Manager, Chinese Chemical SOE and International Energy MNC
lxix Hong Kong Chinese, CEO, Chinese Consulting Firm
lxx China, Expatriate, Consultant, Business Services

178   5

INTRODUCTION • THE BUSINESS CULTURES OF FIVE ASIAN COUNTRIES • ANALYSING ASIAN BUSINESS CULTURES
• OWNERSHIP, FINANCING AND GOVERNANCE • **ORGANIZATION AND MANAGEMENT** • BUSINESS STRATEGY •

specifically Achievement, underlay the tendency of US managers to take a competing approach in workplace conflicts. Moreover, the country differences on value dimensions were sharper than the country differences in conflict style. 'This', they argued,

> makes sense given that individuals are more or less free to value what they want, but the role requirements of a manager require use of all of the different conflict management strategies. It is consistent with our argument that values are proximally related to country, and that the influence of country on conflict styles arises through the values into which managers are socialized.[57]

Friedman et al. (2006) found that Chinese managers were much more likely to avoid than Americans, but the difference was smaller in the colleague condition than the boss condition; they also found that while a sizeable subset of Chinese would in fact be just as direct as the Americans, there appeared among the Chinese a set of tactics that were not even considered by Americans. Many focused on a tactic of doing nothing immediately but drawing a lesson for future actions. For these Chinese respondents, there seemed to be less concern than for Americans about the single incident described in the scenario, indicating that a longer time frame for thinking about events (a characteristic of Chinese social culture) influenced their avoiding behaviour. Another approach that the Chinese took, but Americans did not, was to 'support and cooperate'. Here, the approach seemed to be one where an individual's ego was suppressed, and contribution to the greater good was emphasized. This tendency was even stronger in the boss condition, where many Chinese simply wanted to congratulate the boss or try to learn what his or her next action would be. Another Chinese approach involved suppression of one's own ego needs, or emotional self-control. The researchers concluded that the Chinese were more likely to believe that a direct approach to conflict would damage the relationship with the other party and to show concern for the other party. However, no support was found for the proposition that Chinese attitudes to relationships were instrumental – that they cared more about relationships because those relationships, in turn, provided payoffs in terms of *guanxi*, favours, or the potential to be treated as an outsider if a relationship was damaged.[58]

In China, 'Praise is rarely given. Chinese people in general do not believe in offering praises to others, presuming that praise and compliments will make a person become conceited. In fact, a certain embarrassment is a common reaction when Chinese receive a compliment.'[59] Similarly, 'Most Japanese are extremely uncomfortable when you praise them individually; they would rather have their group praised even if they are personally responsible for its success.'[60]

Traditionally, Chinese people did not develop close personal relationships at work. Managers were aloof from subordinates and did not directly reveal their thoughts and feelings. Hierarchy also affected the Chinese approach: research shows that the Chinese, while concerned about maintaining positive relations, were more likely to avoid conflict when the dispute was with someone in a position of authority, 'mainly because avoiding is amplified by hierarchy among Chinese'.[61]

People in **India** 'characteristically place great faith in words', the Indian sociologist Dhirendra Narain observed:

> Indians exhibit a peculiar faith in the efficacy and power of words. With others, language is employed to define issues; we use language to solve issues. Effort, sacrifice, postponement of immediate gratification recede into the background, and the words fill our pages and minds. ... Lofty announcements are made from public platforms, not with a view of implementing them ... but in the naive belief that this is somehow solving the problems and not a mere prelude to the solution.[62]

Face concerns were important in Asia but had varying consequences. 'Face issues mean that Asians generally promise small, deliver big.'[lxxi] Not to deliver what you have promised is to lose face in Japan and some other Asian countries, though in this respect Indians did not seem to have face issues. In other respects, however, face was an issue for Indians: 'Although Indian business has weak governance, borrowers will always try to pay off a personal loan rather than face bankruptcy, because a lot of stigma attaches to it – they will borrow from someone else to pay it off.'[lxxii] In the study by Allen et al. (2007) referred to previously, Indian owners of SMEs (small and medium enterprises), when considering the consequences both of defaulting on a loan and of committing breach of contract, were predominantly concerned with three factors: loss of reputation, loss of personal assets and loss of future business opportunities. Loss of reputation, which is a face issue, was as important as the other two and all three outweighed fear of a court sentence, fears for personal safety or difficulty in funding future projects.[63] 'Face' concerns influenced Japanese companies, as well as individuals. According to Standage (2007), this was one reason why the takeover premium in Japanese mergers and acquisitions was zero, against the American average of 25 per cent. (The takeover premium represents the amount of costs the buyer expects to save.) 'Face' prevented companies achieving cost savings by laying off staff or saving money by replacing two brands with one.[64] For the Taiwanese, face issues were closely aligned to pride.

---

lxxi China and Malaysia, Business Development, International MNC, Energy
lxxii Indian, Senior Consultant, Business Services (Banking Operations and Technology)

180   5

INTRODUCTION • THE BUSINESS CULTURES OF FIVE ASIAN COUNTRIES • ANALYSING ASIAN BUSINESS CULTURES
• OWNERSHIP, FINANCING AND GOVERNANCE • ORGANIZATION AND MANAGEMENT • BUSINESS STRATEGY •

Leadership

When the classic Western types of leadership, people-oriented versus task-oriented leadership, were researched in **China**, it was found necessary to add moral leadership to account for significant variances in the perceived effectiveness of Chinese business leaders. Moral leadership, which is unselfish, righteous and fair to all, was regarded as essential for business leadership in modern China, because of tradition and because the legal system and institutional norms were still evolving. Autocratic leadership was disliked by the Chinese and led to low job satisfaction there. Compliance was the best outcome it produced; rarely commitment.[65] An example given by one of our interviewees concerned a problem leading to the need to call in management consultants. It arose in one private Chinese business:

> " The Chairman had Confucian values – he was the father, the employees the children. This meant that he was free to correct them, punish them by refusing rises (for their own good – to motivate them to try harder), keep them on a tight string, for instance with regard to travel expenses, swear at them and criticize them in front of outsiders. This applied even to the senior management. This culture permeated. The senior managers copied him in treating their subordinates similarly.[lxxiii]

Not surprisingly, perhaps, motivational levels at this company were low.

There is research that suggested that only one style of leadership – the nurturant-task style – was effective in **India**. Sinha (1990) conducted over 40 experimental and field studies on leadership in the Indian context. The findings were that among three models of leadership, participative, nurturant-task and authoritarian, only the nurturant-task leadership model was effective in all contexts. Authoritarian leadership was effective only under stressful conditions and participative leadership was effective only when subordinates were well trained and efficient.[66]

More light is thrown on this question of the 'best' style of Indian leadership by studies that showed leadership style to be related to Indian employees' job satisfaction and perceptions of the fairness of organizational procedures. Two-way communication between leaders and subordinates was clearly related to the subordinates' job satisfaction but did not affect their perceptions of procedural justice. On the other hand, a transformational leadership style was not related to job satisfaction but was related to perceptions that procedures were fair. A possible explanation for these findings on transformational leadership is that

> " the intellectual and emotional demands that transformational leaders make of subordinates may not lead directly to job satisfaction in

---

lxxiii China, Expatriate, Consultant, international management consultancy cultures that are characterized by high power distance. In high power distance cultures such as India, subordinates may feel stressed by the leader's attempts to involve them in coming up with creative solutions to problems.[67]

Although these felt stresses might reduce job satisfaction, the researchers concluded, the association of charismatic/transformational leadership with perceived fairness might derive from the fact that it played an important and positive role in the Indian culture. Together with India's moderately collectivist orientation this might strengthen the transformational leadership-procedural justice relationship (both of which focus on group values) relative to the two-way communication-procedural justice relationship.[68]

Bass (1997) found that concepts of transactional and transformational leadership were universal, but noted that differences in cultural beliefs, values and norms moderated leader–follower relations. For example, whereas in the West, contingent reward for performing better than other members of one's team might be expected as a matter of equity,

> in Japan, it may be a cause for disharmony and loss of face. Pay differentials are small and along with promotions are not by one's immediate superior but by the amorphous company, consistent with its standards, values, history, and traditions. In India, implicit is the preference of many subordinates for a dependent personal relationship rather than a contractual one with their leader.[69]

Human resource management

From our research, one human resource management issue stood out as a concern in Asia – the issue of shortage of talent. Two aspects predominated: a shortage in India and China, possibly caused by the breakneck pace of their growth, and the problem for family businesses of attracting and retaining talent, which was linked to their culture of restricted trust.

A widely recognized problem for businesses in **China** was the lack of managers with international experience. 'Chinese businesses' biggest problem going forward is a lack of international talent – people with international experience.'[lxxiv] This affected not only businesses intending to expand internationally, but also those needing to import methods and standards. In professional firms, for instance, the professional culture was considered to have been progressively diluted as Chinese trained by Chinese took over from Chinese trained by expatriates.[lxxv] There was

---

[lxxiv] China, Expatriate, Senior Consultant, International Management Consultancy
[lxxv] Mainland Chinese, Partner, International Accounting Firm

also a serious shortage of good middle managers with knowledge of modern management techniques and the ability to develop the teamwork and skills needed to raise productivity.[70] Recruitment through *guanxi* was found to be widespread and detrimental to trust relations between management and subordinates, especially when the *guanxi* bases were personal, such as family, rather than distant, such as classmates.[71]

In **India**, talent shortages extended from experienced crane operatives, virtually all construction until recently having been carried out without benefit of mechanization, to engineers with R&D (Research and Development) experience and executives with experience of modern industries such as mass retailing.

> " Indian business's greatest challenge now is talent – to get the right people. If I could get ten more really good people in this 800-strong company I could grow the business an extra 10 per cent. Middle management, which is crucial to success, is in particularly short supply. This sets a cap on growth.[lxxvi]

'There is a shortage of talent in India. We have grown at such a pace. Businesses like ours keep losing talent to the IT companies. It's the fault of the older businesses – we don't pay enough. But they need two where we need twenty. We can't pay the same.'[lxxvii] These shortages were increasingly affecting India's key growth sector of IT (information technology).

> " IT suppliers are having to adopt a business model where they advise in every aspect of the customer's business, then do a feasibility study which leads to the IT. Indian businesses cannot stay in the IT tail end, which is a commodity now. Purchasers have many options for IT as a commodity – Eastern Europe, China etc. So Indian IT companies have to move up, provide more value added by understanding and relating to the customer's business. The problem is that in major sectors of business – retail, life sciences, high technology manufacturing, there are few Indians in the crucial 30 to 40 age group with the 10 or 15 years' experience it takes to be able to advise on strategy. This is because of the stage of economic development – the fact that multiple retailing, for instance, is only just beginning to happen in India.[lxxviii]

Attracting and keeping talent was widely understood as the 'biggest challenge' for family businesses. In Singapore, for instance, SMEs struggle 'to attract professionals, talent without offering them much (eg no options)';[lxxix] Taiwanese

---

lxxvi Indian, CEO, Family-owned business, Advertising
lxxvii Indian, Chairman, Family-owned business group, Indian MNC industrial goods manufacturer
lxxviii Indian, Product Manager (IT), Indian Business Services
lxxix Singaporean, Finance and Accounting, Education

family businesses are not attractive to high flyers because 'Taiwanese only *trust* themselves or their immediate family.'[lxxx] The demotivating effects of the 'ceiling' in Taiwan were thought to make modern human resource management techniques inappropriate: 'The ceiling in family businesses also reduces motivation and so the whole point of appraisal.'[lxxxi] In India, however, some family businesses had modernized their HR (Human Resource) practices:

> Modern business in India has woken up to performance appraisal, 360 degree appraisal, performance-related pay; giving extra reward for extra performance. Where family members occupy leading roles it is because of their competence, not their background. In traditional businesses it depends on whether they 'like your face' or not. Performance counts for less than loyalty.[lxxxii]

More important than company ownership and control were size and type of business:

> We use balanced score card and so on but our HR practices are not as sophisticated as those in companies with 40 to 70,000 knowledge workers; that's a result of our size: we have 250 engineers (and 12,500 workers). Our industry is capital intensive. Human performance is more critical in Infosys, etc where people are the be all and end all. Their key parameters are their attrition rate.[lxxxiii]

Dharwadkar et al. (2006) contended that managing internal labour markets (ILMs) was a key function for organizations in **Japan**.

> ILMs became feasible during the tremendous growth in the Japanese economy in the 1950s and 1960s, which occurred because of the emergence of large Japanese corporations that focused on market share and long-term growth. Eventually, large-scale manufacturing necessitated the use of both simple and complex technologies. By developing ILMs, Japanese firms were able not only to move employees from simple to complex tasks through on-the-job training but also to generate additional savings in skill formation by creating steep ILMs for highly skilled workers and garnering compliance and commitment from their employees. Over time, the ILM system has become institutionalized with comparable staff designations: ordinary company member, team head, subsection head, section head, deputy department head, department head, director, managing director senior

[lxxx] Taiwanese, Senior Vice President, Finance and Accounting, Fund Management
[lxxxi] Ibid.
[lxxxii] Indian, CEO, Family-owned business, Advertising
[lxxxiii] Indian, Senior General Manager and family member, Family-owned business, consumer goods manufacturer

184   5

INTRODUCTION • THE BUSINESS CULTURES OF FIVE ASIAN COUNTRIES • ANALYSING ASIAN BUSINESS CULTURES
• OWNERSHIP, FINANCING AND GOVERNANCE • **ORGANIZATION AND MANAGEMENT** • BUSINESS STRATEGY •

> managing director, vice president, and president. Whereas those ranks up to department head are considered employees, directors and above are classified according to a different legal status. In addition, rank has implications for retirement age and therefore fosters competition.[72]

Our own research suggested, however, that the importance of ILMs may have reduced with the reduction in lifetime employment. For instance, one interviewee reported,

> " HR used to be a key vehicle for corporate policy. It had the right to deploy people around the company. It would consult with line managers but ultimately had the power. This followed from the LTE policy which makes human resources the most important company asset. When the bubble burst, lifetime employment ended, HR lost its power. There is some hire and fire now.[lxxxiv]

Other authors noted a new set of employment relationships coming into play in Japan as the 'iron triangle' of bureaucrats, big companies and unions faded in influence and power.[73] Although some companies permanently abandoned the LTE (life-time employment) system after Japan's financial crisis, the move was controversial and others eventually brought it back (and repurchased the dormitories to house their salary men and women[lxxxv]); the Japanese high levels of risk aversion made such jobs very popular and enabled the companies offering them to attract the best talent. Even in other companies, job mobility was low. Changing jobs was regarded as a lack of allegiance to the company and was disadvantageously evaluated by the next employer.[74]

In the context of HRM (human resource management), Japanese companies have been typified as 'resource accumulators' as opposed to American companies which are 'resource deployers'. The Japanese recruit, develop and retain their core staff in-house instead of hiring personnel with the expertise to fill a needed role. Although Japanese firms hire locals in their international subsidiaries and although employment practices within Japan have changed, with a large increase in the number of part-time and contract workers, and although there are some counter-examples of outside hires to solve problems in the domestic market, resource accumulation remains important for most key roles, especially in larger companies. As interviewees in the present study related, traditionally in Japan job rotation was practised to promote networking among managers and to develop generalists; it was an integral part of the typical Japanese management system. 'Under this HRM system, PCN (Japanese) managers absorb the company culture, and in the process learn to make decisions based on what is acceptable and

---

[lxxxiv] Japanese, Finance and Accounting, Banking
[lxxxv] Japanese, Audit, Venture Capital

expected, what should and should not be done. Essentially, these HRM practices make it possible for Japanese companies to rely heavily on culture-oriented control systems.'[75]

Diversity management

Diversity management and related areas such as discrimination hardly featured in the comments of our interviewees in five Asian countries, apparently because such issues were not considered part of what distinguishes different countries' ways of doing business or managing. In **China**, the only spontaneous comments were made by two expatriate women executives: one expatriate woman entrepreneur had experienced no difficulties in dealing with men across a range of authorities and businesses. 'To them, I am the boss.'[lxxxvi] On the other hand, another woman expat, working for a large international consultancy in Beijing, had experienced,

> difficult working relationships, especially with men over 35, regardless of whether they have overseas experience. They will not address any of my suggestions, long telephone calls show no progress, they never contact me, there is virtually no communication. I have been told they have a comfort hierarchy and foreign women are at the bottom of it, just below young Chinese women.[lxxxvii]

In **India**, in response to questioning we were told, 'All India is proud of the Indian woman CEO of Pepsicola. It will improve women's opportunities within India',[lxxxviii] and, on the other hand, 'Gender discrimination and sexual harassment are serious.'[lxxxix] A woman lawyer commented,

> An older man has problems taking orders from a woman. A woman manager realizes she must be sensitive to this. A site engineer has problems dealing with a woman civil engineer. In law women are pushed towards family or corporate law – away from criminal law. Women will be told, 'It's not meant for women.' Women are excluded from activities that lead to bonding etc. – clubbing is very important in Mumbai.[xc]

In **Japan**, again in an answer to a question, one of only two references was to a damaging corporate incident involving sexual harassment law and the defensive

---

[lxxxvi] China, Expatriate, entrepreneur
[lxxxvii] China, Expatriate, Consultant, International Management Consultancy
[lxxxviii] Indian, General Manager and family member, Indian family shipping business
[lxxxix] Indian, Economist, Former Entrepreneur, Senior Academic
[xc] Indian, lawyer, Educational Not-for-Profit

186   5

INTRODUCTION • THE BUSINESS CULTURES OF FIVE ASIAN COUNTRIES • ANALYSING ASIAN BUSINESS CULTURES
• OWNERSHIP, FINANCING AND GOVERNANCE • **ORGANIZATION AND MANAGEMENT** • BUSINESS STRATEGY •

response of male workers thereafter: 'People [i.e. men] in the organization are afraid to talk to women workers. Two directors were fired because a woman whose father was very powerful – head of the military – accused them of sexual harassment. So they fired them without defending them.'[xci] The other comment was to the difficulties men at work in Japan felt in avoiding locker room humour in the presence of women colleagues. In relation to people with disabilities or ethnic differences there were no comments at all.

For most private sector Asian businesses, diversity management was not a major issue on their agenda. Despite the significance attached in the region to social relationships in business, gender and ethnic relations at work were not considered important factors in employee motivation. If the range of business responses to diversity issues is from reluctantly obeying the law to wholeheartedly embracing diversity for the benefits it can bring (in terms of understanding diverse consumer markets or creative tension in decision-making) then most Asian businesses fell well towards the former end of the range. These facts were clearly reflected in business cultures which ignored these issues and in the labour market effects which are described in Chapter 10.

In **China**, the traditionally inferior status of women in Chinese society, described in Chapter 8, together with a number of legal weaknesses, resulted in discrimination, including preferential treatment of men for employment. As unemployment rates rose following liberalization, unfair hiring practices, such as discrimination on the basis of sex and age, also rose and so did unfair dismissals: for example, in 2003 a case was pending of a childless woman who became pregnant due to failed contraception, was told by her doctor not to have a third abortion after a previous two, was given consent for the child by the neighbourhood planning committee but refused it by her work unit on the grounds that the timing was inconvenient. She was ordered to have an abortion. When she refused, she was penalized and ultimately dismissed. Other discriminatory practices included women receiving an unfair share of redundancies.[76] In many cases women were laid off first by factories and, as one result, increasingly worked in lower-paid, less-valued jobs or had to take work outside the social protection of a regulated formal market. Limited employment opportunities and pressure to send money home could lead to risky occupations such as prostitution, rates of which increased dramatically over the liberalization period.[77] Under the reform of state-owned enterprises, a disproportionate percentage of the millions of workers laid off were women, and female employees were also more likely to be chosen to take pay cuts when a plant or company was in financial trouble. Other unfair practices included earlier retirement ages for women, wage discrepancies and outright sexual harassment.[78] Even in the public sector bureaucracy, according to the United Nations in 2006, women faced more difficulties than men in gaining

---

[xci] Japanese, Strategic Management, Business Services

promotion as, for instance, they were obliged to retire at age 55, five years earlier than men.

The Constitution of **India** guarantees equality of opportunity and status to women; also, in India, important positions in government and industry are regularly held by women, while the tradition and culture of India emphasize recognition and respect for women. These factors probably account for India's higher ranking than China's or Japan's on the United Nations' Gender Empowerment Index. Nevertheless, participation of women in the economy has lagged. Despite all the favourable factors, Devi (1991) found that educated women continued to gravitate towards the 'feminine' professions of teaching and nursing. The proportion of women administrators and managers was 'negligible'. She attributed these findings to the fact that women had always been assigned the nurturing role in Indian society.[79] As late as 2007, fewer than 8 per cent of directors in the top 100 listed companies were women. In the words of the chairperson of the Chamber of Indian Industry National Committee on Women's Empowerment, 'The struggle is ultimately to change hearts and minds, and not just change the law.'[80]

According to Ogasawara (1991), firms in **Japan** traditionally depended on two groups of staff – 'office ladies' and 'salaried men'. Office ladies were women hired to perform relatively simple clerical and office work. Recruited immediately after graduation from high school, junior college or university, they usually had no expectation of receiving promotions. They were typically in their twenties and left their jobs upon marriage or childbirth. Salaried men, in contrast, were hired after graduation from university and then trained to become managers. They enjoyed the well-documented benefits provided by large Japanese employers, including numerous opportunities for cross-functional training, and regular opportunities for promotion. Because the range of duties of salaried men was wide, they depended on office ladies to provide the clerical and administrative support essential to performing those duties effectively. As a result, although an analysis of formal power structures suggests that salaried men wielded a great deal of power in their relationships with office ladies, operationally office ladies exerted substantial power over salaried men, but these women did not receive either rewards or status commensurate with their contribution.[81]

After Japan enacted equal employment opportunity legislation in 1986, women became eligible for these managerial track jobs, but, by 1995, only 6 per cent of first-level managerial positions and less than 1 per cent of top management positions in large Japanese firms were filled by women. The vast majority of Japan's 27 million female workers encountered a system of corporate discrimination based on sex. Many companies relegated women to administration tracks with substandard pay and fewer prospects for promotion, while channelling men into career tracks with greater opportunity for upward mobility and higher compensation.[82]

188   5

INTRODUCTION • THE BUSINESS CULTURES OF FIVE ASIAN COUNTRIES • ANALYSING ASIAN BUSINESS CULTURES • OWNERSHIP, FINANCING AND GOVERNANCE • **ORGANIZATION AND MANAGEMENT** • BUSINESS STRATEGY •

In **Taiwan**, female earnings in 1995 were only 65 per cent of men's, despite the shift from manufacturing to technology-based and service industries, which in other countries had raised the female/male pay ratio. Published evidence on Taiwan provides no support for a widening gender gap in labour force commitment or skills, suggesting that wage discrimination against female workers increased over time.[83] On the other hand, although the number of managerial women in Taiwan was small, they were a highly visible group and more important than their numbers would indicate. The prominence of women managers was promoted by popular magazines and by a few academic surveys that focus on this small minority. Few women, however, became managers. Most highly educated women became professionals. Even if their qualifications were the same, however, women managers did not get managerial positions when they competed with men; they attained managerial positions from either the 'spilled over' category (when there is no qualified man to fill the position) or from the 'new demand' category (where the position is best filled by a woman). Traditional cultural norms defined the home as the woman's responsibility and woman's rightful place as in the home, but free access to examinations and the use of examination outcomes for job advancement has begun to open the doors to women who are both qualified and highly motivated to achieve managerial positions. An exploratory study suggested that work-family conflict and Taiwanese cultural values contributed to the barriers female employees encountered in their climb up the organizational hierarchy and possibly lowered their career ambitions; however, some of the female managers interviewed felt that women's promotional opportunities and their experiences as managers had improved significantly in their generation.[84]

In fields such as advertising and insurance and in positions in MNCs, performance is considered more important and gender less so, thereby proving women with new opportunities to be successful in their careers.[85] An important consideration in evaluating the position of women in Taiwanese business is the point that family members, particularly wives and daughters, who are excluded from direct participation in a family's business may exert an influence on the business far exceeding their official status.[86]

Conclusion

Organization and management practices in Asia are affected by business cultures, but to an extent which varies not only with the country but also with the aspect. With the exception of Japan, the managerial values, styles and practices found by research, including our own, in the Asian countries in our sample, were predominantly top down, with centralized decision-making and restricted information flows. Though it is qualified in China by the tradition of moral leadership and the limits on managerial power imposed by the institutional set-up, especially the

Party bureaucracy, and in India by progressive Westernization and professionalization, the overall picture is one of 'Theory X' management. Such a management approach does not seem to reflect the perceived evaluations of the majority of employees as hard working and motivated towards self-improvement. It therefore seems more likely that it derives from business cultures that embody hierarchy and continuing control by founding families.

On the other hand Human Resource Management issues, such as the talent shortage, seemed more closely linked to stage of economic development than to distinctive business cultures, and HRM practices to the size of the organization and the firm's technology. The low priority given to diversity management in all these countries probably reflects societal values.

References

[1] Quer, D., Claver, E. and Rienda, L. (2007) 'Business and management in China: A review of empirical research in leading international journals', *Asia Pacific Journal of Management*, **24**: 359–84.

[2] Farh, J.-L., Earley, P.C. and Lin, S.-C. (1997) 'Impetus for action: A cultural analysis of justice and organizational citizenship behavior in Chinese society', *Administrative Science Quarterly*, **42**: 421–44.

[3] Yan, Y. (2003) 'Managed globalization: State power and cultural transition in China', in Berger, P.L. and Huntington, S.P. (eds) *Many Globalizations: Cultural Diversity in the Contemporary World*, Oxford: Oxford University Press.

[4] Kunnanatt, J.T. (2008) 'Strategic question in the Indian banking sector: Are Indian bank managers achievement oriented?' *Journal of Management Development*, **27**(2): 169–86.

[5] Gupta, R.K. (2002) *Towards the Optimal Organisation: Integrating Indian Culture and Management*, New Delhi: Excel Books.

[6] Roland, A. (1988) *In Search of Self in India and Japan: Towards a Cross-Cultural Psychology*, Princeton, NJ: Princeton University Press.

[7] Ibid.

[8] Budhwar, P.S. (2003) 'Culture and management in India', in Warner, M. (ed.) *Culture and Management in Asia*, London: Routledge Curzon.

[9] Wong, H.W. (1999) *Japanese Bosses, Chinese Workers: Power and Control in a Hong Kong Megastore*, Richmond, NY.: Curzon Press.

[10] Cheung, C.-K. (2005) 'Rational or demoralized responses to work restructuring in Hong Kong?' *Human Relations*, **58**(2): 223–47.

[11] Chung-Sheng, Y., Taylor, G.S. and Tung, W. (2003) 'A cross-cultural comparison of work goals: The United States, Taiwan, and the People's Republic of China', in Alon, I. and Shenkar O. (eds) *Chinese Culture, Organizational Behavior and International Business Management*, Westport, CT: Praeger.

[12] Sinha, J.B.P. and Sinha, D. (1990) 'Role of social values in Indian organizations', *International Journal of Psychology*, **25**(36): 705–14.

[13] Child, J. and Warner, M. (2003) 'Culture and management in China', in Warner, M. (ed.) *Culture and Management in Asia,* London: Routledge Curzon.

[14] Chen, X.-P. and Li, S. (2005) 'Cross-national differences in cooperative decision-making in mixed-motive business contexts: The mediating effect of vertical and horizontal individualism', *Journal of International Business Studies*, **36**(6): 622–36.

[15] Koch, B.J. and Koch, P.T. (2007) 'Collectivism, individualism, and outgroup cooperation in a segmented China', *Asia Pacific Journal of Management*, **24**(2): 207–25.

[16] Tjosvold, D., Poon, M. and Yu, Z.-Y. (2005) 'Team effectiveness in China: Cooperative conflict for relationship building', *Human Relations*, **58**(3): 341–67.

[17] Onishi, J. and Bliss, R.E. (2006) 'In search of Asian ways of managing conflict: A comparative study of Japan, Hong Kong, Thailand and Vietnam', *International Journal of Conflict Management*, **17**(3): 3–25.

[18] Keeley, T.D. (2001) *International Human Resource Management in Japanese Firms: Their Greatest Challenge*, New York: Palgrave Macmillan.

[19] Lowe, S. (2003) 'Chinese culture and management theory', in Alon, I. and Shenkar, O. (eds) *Chinese Culture, Organizational Behavior and International Business Management*, Westport, CT: Praeger.

[20] Child, J. and Tse D.K. (2001) 'China's transition and its implications for international business', Journal of International Business Studies, **32**(1):5–21.

[21] Lau, C.M., Nan, Z. and Tse, D.K. (2002) 'Institutional forces and organizational culture in China: Effects on change schemas, firm commitment and job satisfaction', *Journal of International Business Studies*, **33**(3): 533–50.

[22] Fuller, M.B. and Beck, J.C. (2006) *Japan's Business Renaissance: How the World's Greatest Economy Revived, Renewed and Reinvented Itself*, New York: McGraw Hill.

[23] Lowe, S. (2003) 'Chinese culture and management theory', in Alon, I. and Shenkar, O. (eds) *Chinese Culture, Organizational Behavior and International Business Management*, Westport, CT: Praeger.

[24] Ninan, A. and Pillay, H. (2007) 'Reassessing the ontology of contemporary organisational decision-making processes for healthier Asian economies', *International Journal of Management and Decision Making*, **8**(2–3): 139–52.

[25] Tsang, E.W.K. (2004) 'Toward a scientific inquiry into superstitious business decision-making', *Organization Studies*, **25**(6): 923–46.

[26] Bjerke, B. (2000) 'A typified, culture-based, interpretation of management of SMEs in Southeast Asia', *Asia Pacific Journal of Management*, **17**: 103–32.

[27] Ibid.

[28] Redding, S.G. and Wong, G.Y.Y. (1986) 'The psychology of Chinese organizational behavior', in Bond, M.H. (ed.) *The Psychology of the Chinese People*, Hong Kong: Chinese University Press.

[29] Selmer, J., Kang, I.-L. and Wright, R.P. (1994) 'Managerial behaviour of expatriate versus local bosses', *International Studies of Management & Organization*, **24**(3): 49–63.

[30] Agarwal, S., Kuen, E.H.K., Hermann, P. and Erramilli, M.K. (2004) 'Does ethnic similarity influence foreign equity position in joint ventures? An empirical analysis of IJVs in China', *Journal of Asia-Pacific Business*, **5**(3): 3–26.

[31] Keeley, T.D. (2001) *International Human Resource Management in Japanese Firms: Their Greatest Challenge*, New York: Palgrave Macmillan.

[32] Neelankavil, J.P., Mathur, A. and Zhang, Y. (2000) 'Determinants of managerial performance: A cross-cultural comparison of the perceptions of middle-level managers in four countries', *Journal of International Business Studies*, **31**(1): 121–40.

[33] Lowe, S. (2003) 'Chinese culture and management theory', in Alon, I. and Shenkar, O. (eds) *Chinese Culture, Organizational Behavior and International Business Management*, Westport, CT: Praeger.

[34] Hill, J.S. (2007) 'Religion and the shaping of East Asian management styles: A conceptual examination', *Journal of Asia-Pacific Business*, **8**(2): 59–88.

[35] Holt, D.H. (1997) 'A comparative study of values among Chinese and U.S. entrepreneurs: Pragmatic convergence between contrasting cultures', *Journal of Business Venturing*, **12**(6): 483–505.

[36] Jenner, R.A., Hebert, L., Appell, A. and Baack, J. (1998) 'Using quality management for the cultural transformation of Chinese state enterprises: A case study', *Journal of Quality Management*, **3**(2): 193–210.

[37] Anderson, J.R., Li, J.-H. and Harrison, R. (2003) 'The effects of firm ownership and culture on Total Quality Management in China', in Alon, I. and Shenker, O. (eds) *Chinese Culture, Organizational Behavior and International Business Management*, Westport, CT: Praeger.

[38] Chiu, C.C.H. (2006) 'Changing experiences of work in reformed state-owned enterprises in China', *Organization Studies*, **27**(5): 677–97.

[39] Chen, F. (2006) 'Privatization and its discontents in Chinese factories', *The China Quarterly*, **185**: 42–60.

[40] Newbury, W. and Yakova, N. (2006) 'Standardization preferences: A function of national culture, work interdependence and local embeddedness', *Journal of International Business Studies*, **37**(1): 44–60.

[41] Tripathi, R.C. (1990) 'Interplay of values in the functioning of Indian organizations', *International Journal of Psychology*, **25**(3–6): 715–34.

[42] Lam, D., Paltiel, J.T. and Shannon, J.H. (1994) 'The Confucian entrepreneur? Chinese culture, industrial organization and intellectual property piracy in Taiwan', *Asian Affairs, an American Review*, **20**(4): 205–17.

[43] Wu, M.-Y., Taylor, M. and Chen, M.-J. (2001) 'Exploring societal and cultural influences on Taiwanese public relations', *Public Relations Review* 27(3): 317–36.

[44] Sinha, J.B.P. and Sinha, D. (1990) 'Role of social values in Indian organizations', *International Journal of Psychology*, **25**(36): 705–14.

[45] Deloitte (2006) 'Management innovation: An imperative for SOE's development in China. A special report for Boao Forum 2006', 21–23 April Hainan Province, China.

[46] Wang, J. and Gupta, V. (2003) 'Post-crisis management: A study of corporate restructuring in Asia', *Journal of the Academy of Business and Economics*, April. URL: http://www.thefreelibrary.com/Post-crisis+management:+a+study+of+corporate+restructuring+in+Asia-a0113563672.

[47] Yao, Y., Shantanu, D., Ilham, I., Li, F. and Tolan, E. (2004) 'Goldman Sachs' China HR challenges', URL: http://papers.ssrn.com/sol13.

[48] Stewart, S. and Delisle, P. (1994) 'Hong Kong expatriates in the People's Republic of China', *International Studies of Management & Organization*, 24(3): 104–18.

[49] Wang, Z.-M. (1998) 'Team management conflict', in Selmer J. (ed.) *International Management in China: Cross-Cultural Issues*, London: Routledge.

[50] Stewart, S. and Delisle, P. (1994) 'Hong Kong expatriates in the People's Republic of China', *International Studies of Management & Organization*, 24(3): 104–18.

[51] Child, J. and Lu, Y. (1990) 'Industrial decision making under China's reform 1985–1988', *Organization Studies*, 2(3): 321–51.

[52] Ibid.

[53] Stewart, S. and Delisle, P. (1994) 'Hong Kong expatriates in the People's Republic of China', *International Studies of Management & Organization*, 24(3): 104–18.

[54] Ohbuchi, K.Y. and Takahashi, Y. (1994) 'Cultural styles of conflict management in Japanese and Americans: Passivity, covertness, and effectiveness of strategies', *Journal of Applied Social Psychology*, 24(15): 1345–66.

[55] Bond, M.H. and Hwang, K.K. (1986) 'The social psychology of Chinese people', in Bond, M.H. (ed.) *The Psychology of the Chinese People*, Hong Kong: Oxford University Press.

[56] Lalwani, A.K., Shavitt, S. and Johnson, T. (2006) 'What is the relation between cultural orientation and socially desirable responding?' *Journal of Personality and Social Psychology*, **90**(1): 165–178.

[57] Morris, M.W., Williams, K.Y., Leung, K., Larrick, R., Mendoza, T.M., Bhatnagar, D., Li, J., Kondo, M., Luo, J.-L. and Hu, J.-C. (1998) 'Conflict management style: Accounting for cross-national differences', *Journal of International Business Studies*, **29**(4): 729–47.

[58] Friedman, R., Chi, S.-C. and Liu, L.A. (2006) 'An expectancy model of Chinese-American differences in conflict-avoiding', *Journal of International Business Studies*, **37**(1): 76–91.

[59] Krone, K.J., Chen, L. and Xia, H. (1997) 'Approaches to managerial influence in the People's Republic of China', *The Journal of Business Communication*, **34**(3): 289–314.

[60] Aggarwal, R. and Mellen, L.E. (1997) 'Perspectives on Japanese finance for portfolio investors', *Review of Business*, **18**, June 22.

[61] Friedman, R., Chi, S.C. and Liu, L.A. (2006) 'An expectancy model of Chinese-American differences in conflict-avoiding', *Journal of International Business Studies*, **37**: 76–91.

[62] Thomas, A.S. and Philip, A. (1994) 'India: Management in an ancient and modern civilization', *International Studies of Management & Organization*, 24(3): 18–27.

[63] Allen, F., Chakrabarti, R., Sankar, D., Qian, J. and Qian, M. (2007) 'Financing Firms in India', URL: http://fic.wharton.upenn.edu/fic/papers/06/0608.pdf.

[64] Standage, T. (2007) 'Going hybrid', *The Economist*, 29 November.

[65] Lau, D.C., Liu, J. and Fu, P.P. (2007) 'Feeling trusted by business leaders in China: Antecedents and the mediating role of value congruence', *Asia Pacific Journal of Management*, 24(3): 321–40.

[66] Sinha, J.P. (1990) 'A model of effective leadership styles in India', in Jaeger, A.M. and Kanungo, R.N. (eds), *Management in Developing Countries,* New York: Routledge.

[67] Pillai, R., Scandura, T.A. and Williams, E.A. (2001) 'Leadership and organizational justice; similarities and differences across cultures', *The Leadership Quarterly*, **12**(1): 31–52.

[68] Ibid.

[69] Bass, B.M. (1997) 'Does the transactional-transformational leadership paradigm transcend organizational and national boundaries?' *American Psychologist*, **52**: 130–9.

[70] Sai-Ching, L.P. and Walters, G.P. (1998) 'Wah Hoi industrial company', *Entrepreneurship: Theory and Practice*, **22**, URL: www.findarticles.com/p/articles/mi_hb6648.

[71] Lau, D.C., Liu, J. and Fu, P.P. (2007) 'Feeling trusted by business leaders in China: Antecedents and the mediating role of value congruence', *Asia Pacific Journal of Management*, **24**(3): 321–40.

[72] Dharwadkar, R., Graen, G., Grewal, R. and Wakabayashi, M. (2006) 'Japanese career progress: An empirical examination', *Journal of International Business Studies*, **37**: 148–61.

[73] Fuller, M.B. and Beck, J.C. (2006) *Japan's Business Renaissance: How the World's Greatest Economy Revived, Renewed and Reinvented Itself*, New York: McGraw Hill.

[74] Intelligence Bridges (2006) *The Characteristic of Japanese People*, URL: http://www.intelbridges.com/japanesedisposition.html.

[75] Keeley, T.D. (2001) *International Human Resource Management in Japanese Firms: Their Greatest Challenge*, New York: Palgrave Macmillan.

[76] Bureau of Democracy, Human Rights, and Labor (2007) 'China (includes Tibet, Hong Kong, and Macau): Country reports on Human Rights Practices 2007', United States State Department, URL: www.state.gove/g/dr/rls/hrrpt/2007/100518.htm.

[77] *China Human Development Report* (2005) United Nations Development Program, URL: www.unchina.org/about_china.html/gender.shtml.

[78] Bulger, C.M. (2003) 'Fighting gender discrimination in the Chinese workplace', URL: www.bc.edu/bc_org/law/lwsch/journals/bctwj/20-2/03_TXT.htm.

[79] Devi, R.D. (1991) 'Women in modern sector employment in India', *Economic Bulletin for Asia and the Pacific*, June/December: 53–65.

[80] *Deccan Chronicle*, 'Women move upwards through the glass ceiling', 2 March 2007.

[81] Ogasawara, Y. (1991) *Office Ladies and Salaried Men: Power, Gender, and Work in Japanese Companies*, Berkeley, CA: University of California Press.

[82] Faiola, A. (2007) 'Japanese working women still serve the tea', *Washington Post*, 2 March.

[83] Zveglich, J., Rodgers, Y. and Rodgers, W. (1995) 'Education and earnings: Gender differentials in Taiwan, 1978–1992', *Development Discussion Paper No. 507*, Cambridge, MA: Harvard Institute for International Development.

[84] Chou, W.-C., Fosh, P. and Foster, D. (2005) 'Female managers in Taiwan: Opportunities and barriers in changing times', *Asia Pacific Business Review*, **11**(2): 251–66.

[85] Cheng, W.-Y. and Liao, L.-L. (1993) 'Women managers in Taiwan', *International Studies of Management & Organization*, **23**(4): 65–86.

[86] Steier, L.P., Chrisman, J.J. and Chua, J.H. (2004) 'Entrepreneurial management and governance in family firms: An introduction', *Entrepreneurship: Theory and Practice*, **28**: 295–303.

6 business strategy

This chapter explores the relations between Asian business cultures, as revealed in our study, and business strategy and its implementation. The institutional perspective makes clear that effective business strategies will normally be tailored to particular institutional contexts. These contexts, as this book has shown, include the business culture, which varies widely within the Asian region. However, strategy is an aspect of business which, according to our analysis set out in Chapter 1 of this book, is only weakly related to business culture in comparison with the subjects covered in the last two chapters, respectively 'ownership, financing and governance' and 'organization and management'. Essentially, in modern businesses concerned with competing, differentiation is often a strategic imperative that argues against following the norms and practices of competitors in domestic markets. Internationally, confronted with different environments and institutions, competitive success depends on adaptation away from cultural norms. Our view concurs with the conclusions from a study of business strategy in Chinese family-owned businesses (CFOBs) that firms 'exercise strategic choice within an environment that predisposes, but does not fix, their behaviour'. Only a small proportion of the variation in business strategies was accounted for by 'CFOB-ness', leaving ample room for human agency.[1]

However, while it is therefore no surprise to find that strategies vary from company to company and industry to industry, some consistencies in the strategic approaches of Asian countries have been noted in the literature. This chapter will attempt to analyse which of these do and which do not correspond to the business cultures we identified in our research.

The following examples illustrate positive relationships between business strategies and business cultures in Asia.

First, as we have seen, the business cultures of **India** and **Taiwan** are ones that accept and hence support the continued influence, amounting in many cases to control, of founding families even in the case of listed companies. In both these countries, many businesses or family-owned business groups exemplify a strategy of unrelated diversification: one Indian example from our research was a group that operated in two sectors – manufacturing and retailing fashion garments for the export market and large-scale wholesaling of edible oils.[i] Another Indian family business in our research had interests in both shipping and viniculture. A bank in Taiwan had diversified into shopping malls and telecoms.[ii] Some, at least, of this diversification is explained by the family setting up units for progeny to run or pursuing the personal interests of family members. For example, in Taiwan one interviewee told us, 'There is a business family with four public companies of which three are high-tech and one is in fashion; when the founder was asked why, he said, "I have four children and one has got a degree in fashion." '[iii] In contrast, in Japan, where the business culture does not support the continuing influence of founding families in listed companies, few businesses adopt strategies of unrelated diversification.[2] Cultural support for founding family control may also be related to the relatively high levels of entrepreneurialism claimed for India and Taiwan: Steier et al. (2004) found that the cultures perpetuated within family firms potentially promoted and sustained entrepreneurial activities, thereby providing them with a strategic advantage over non-family firms. Individualism, external orientation, decentralization and strategic and financial controls on entrepreneurial orientation were all stronger in family firms than in non-family firms.[3]

Second, the availability and strength of specialized intermediary institutions, such as auditors, venture capitalists, market researchers and management consultants are affected by the openness of businesses to outside advice and intermediation. We have seen from our study how the business culture of **China** leads to the roles of auditors and venture capitalists being misunderstood, how Chinese businesses prefer trial-and-error approaches to market research and how management consultants are not given ready access. In turn, the presence or absence of specialized intermediary institutions significantly affect businesses' choices of what activities to perform and how to perform them. 'Institutional voids arise in locations where specialized intermediaries that a firm customarily relies on are absent.'[4] Without these intermediaries to perform certain functions, some strategies are not available. The key fundamentals of competitive strategy – industry analysis, positioning and sustainability – also change in consequence. As Ricart et al. (2004) argued

> Positioning choices are drastically affected by the extent of specialized intermediation. This is easily seen in studies of business groups in emerging economies. These studies show that diversified structures that are believed to be value-destroying in some countries are value-enhancing in others. This is because the internal markets available to diversified entities are relatively more useful when specialized intermediaries are absent and the functioning of external markets is thus compromised.[5]

---

[i] Indian, CEO and family member, Indian family-owned diversified business group
[ii] Taiwanese, Finance and Accounting, manufacturing
[iii] Taiwanese, Product Manager, Taiwanese consumer goods manufacturer

In comparison with China, **India** is relatively well supplied with intermediaries and their use is understood and practised. The Indian business culture is open to outsiders and foreign ideas: one interviewee, from a French-owned MNC (multinational company), considered this demonstrated by his being about to chair a committee of the National Council of the Chamber of Indian Industry.[iv] He also noted

> " For a foreign-owned company to succeed here it is necessary to assemble a team of managers who know the country and are professional but it is not necessary to have a network of contacts initially; that can be developed later. Thus it is not necessary for them to go into a joint venture. The arguments for a joint venture are that the partner company lubricates entry, has business connections, has a distribution channel and has money. Given money, the other factors do not constitute a barrier to successful entry [in India].[v]

Another said explicitly, 'The Indian corporate culture is open – there is little resistance to foreign ideas or ownership.'[vi] As Ricart et al. (2004) commented with regard to financial intermediaries, 'Specialized intermediaries needed to disseminate risk capital to would-be entrepreneurs are far more developed in India than they are in China.' Linked to this and the availability of other types of intermediary was the fact that India's domestically owned private enterprise was far more vibrant than China's, whose economy was characterized by heavy investment by multinational companies. In the absence of suitable intermediaries, including disseminators of risk capital, MNCs are at an advantage compared with domestic businesses, because they generally do not need domestic sources of risk capital as, in their role as cross-border intermediaries, they rely on cash flows from operations around the world.[6]

One business strategy that Indian companies adopted early was outsourcing. The outsourcing industry was well developed in India long before it became a destination for offshoring. In a published interview, the retired chairman of an Indian business group described outsourcing as 'rooted in Indian culture'. As the context makes clear, he was referring to business culture. Drawing on the experience of a cycle-manufacturing joint venture with a British collaborator which lost out to an indigenous competitor, he contended that Indian business style 'needs to be rooted in Indian culture (outsourcing to smaller family enterprises and doing only the final assembly, rather than centralising production in a top-down control environment and seeking economies of scale as the British partners were advising the Indian group to do.).'[7]

[iv] Indian, CEO, Indian subsidiary of a French-owned MNC industrial goods manufacturer
[v] Ibid.
[vi] Indian, Finance and General Management, Indian MNC heavy industry

Business strategy can reflect the attitudes within a country's business culture to innovation. Our research suggested that the business decision-makers of **China** see their country's business culture as weak on innovation. In many industries, strategic advantage is now bestowed by early adoption and effective deployment of advanced technology. The Chinese disadvantage in this area, according to Ahlstrom et al. (2006) is that Chinese firms spend little on absorbing and adapting the technology they acquire.

> In addition, senior executives of many important SOEs [state-owned enterprises] in China do not pursue innovation for strategic purposes, but rather seek to show their sponsoring government body how innovative they are and what they have achieved for the year. ... The low propensity to innovate may hinder indigenous Chinese firms from increasing their faint global footprint and becoming more globally competitive.[8]

Chinese firms involved in software development, telecommunications and automobile parts production, or telephone networks, wireless pagers, mobile phones, motorcycle production, petrochemicals and power generation acquired high technology through partnerships with foreign companies, and failed to invest in research and development or to internalize the technology.[9] Instead of 'properly absorbing the new technology into the product and service production process, providing proper training, and generally modifying the technology to fit their setting', they often rushed new technology into the production process immediately. Throughout the 1990s, large and medium-sized Chinese industrial firms spent only 1 per cent of total industrial technology spending (on equipment) for actually indigenizing that purchased technology, a figure that was well below that of comparable OECD (Organisation for Economic Co-operation and Development) firms.[10] This low spend applies in key sectors such as telecoms equipment, electronics and industrial machinery. This behaviour seems not to correspond with the long-term orientation that has been attributed to Chinese culture by, among others, Hofstede (2007)[11] and Bond (1988)[12]. It does, however, chime with the comments about business culture of our Chinese interviewees that long-term orientation 'is going'.[vii]

This chapter will now examine some aspects of strategy and explore the extent of their links to business culture, beginning with business goals.

Business goals

In some of our sample countries, some business goals were described as central to the business culture and so were outlined in Chapter 2. In **India**, however,

---

[vii] Mainland Chinese, Marketing Manager, Consumer MNC

Table 6.1 **Business goals in four Asian countries**

	China	India	Japan	Taiwan
Business goals	*Goals of SOEs and private business differ, even conflict*	Often to raise personal funds for the founding family; *also 'dynastic goals'; more broadly 'economically rational'* goals	Often not primarily financial returns to shareholders	In older businesses dynastic goals reflect pride in business ownership; in high-technology companies, 'making money and getting out'.

although, as Chapter 2 demonstrated, the personal needs of founding families of family businesses could distort business practice, private sector businesses were also driven by 'goals such as after-tax profit and return on capital employed'.[viii] 'There are certain broad macro-level objectives that drive business worldwide, including in India – profit growth, financial health, strategy, vision.'[ix] 'Businesses in different areas have different priorities: steady growth, planned growth, aggressive growth.'[x] Even in family businesses founded under India's socialist regime between 1947 and 1990, 'Founders aimed for profit maximization',[xi] rather than to serve a wider community. Dynastic goals, too, like those identified in Taiwan, surfaced in India: 'Most have dynastic ambitions – to hand on a flourishing business to the next generation.'[xii] Previous research into the goals of business leaders found that the goals of Indian entrepreneurs differed mainly from those of their British equivalents in exhibiting a more long-term orientation. It showed in a concern for profits in ten years' time and by the addition of a goal of increasing personal wealth, especially that of the family.[13] This orientation was often conservative. As one of our interviewees noted, 'The goal of the traditional businesses is often more to protect what they have than to grow. The entrepreneurial generation has passed and the third or fourth generation is not entrepreneurial.'[xiii]

Except in Japan, where traditionally returns to owners were not the priority, the kinds of business goals ascribed to the private sector in all countries were similar to those described in the paragraph above; in the public sector companies,

---

[viii] Indian, CEO, Indian subsidiary of a French-owned MNC industrial goods manufacturer
[ix] Ibid.
[x] Indian, Chairman, Family-owned business group, Indian MNC industrial goods manufacturer
[xi] Indian, Finance and General Management, Indian MNC heavy industry
[xii] Indian, Chairman, Family-owned business group, Indian MNC industrial goods manufacturer
[xiii] Indian, CEO, Family-owned business, advertising

however, in both China and India, different goals applied. In China, 'SOEs' goals are social stability – profit, yes, but it is more important to maintain employment levels. Welfare considerations predominate.[xiv] 'Maintaining employment levels is the [Chinese] government's main goal, whereas individuals want to make money.'[xv] Indian public sector companies 'are driven by government policy – high level government directives. The decision-making is not primarily commercial'.[xvi] Table 6.1 summarizes our findings on business goals in our sample countries.

Forward planning

In Western concepts, the idea of forward planning is closely linked to business strategy. As Chapter 2 showed, that is also true in Japan, but it is much less the case in China, where private entrepreneurs 'have an idea, and want to try it out. It's a kind of speculation.'[xvii] In **India**, the Indian subsidiaries of US companies were once found to exhibit a greater propensity to undertake the systematic formulation of long-range plans in comparison with locally owned firms; the difference was attributed to the impact of management beliefs and policies imposed by the parent company.[14] However, that was as long ago as 1975. In our research, although there was only one direct reference to forward planning ('Forward planning is done by systems and procedures. Plans would tend to set the broad direction rather than to be detailed and would be modified as circumstances alter and new opportunities emerge.'[xviii]) the context sometimes made clear that 'professionalization', which was frequently mentioned, referred in part to adopting Western management techniques, including planning. However, this in itself indicates that formal planning to date was confined to certain types of business – the listed companies and larger family firms. In **Taiwan**, an absence of forward planning was mentioned, but attributed to economic circumstances rather than to the business culture: 'Taiwanese companies have no power to influence their environment, unlike big Western companies, no sustainable advantage, so they are forced to be opportunistic. This limits the point of forward planning.'

This is not to argue that Asian firms do not look ahead. Chinese companies, such as Lenovo, which took over IBM's PC business in May 2005 for $1.75 billion (with IBM retaining an 18 per cent stake) began around that time looking outside China for growth. Many Chinese companies were cash rich; they were also conscious of the limits of the Chinese market in the short to medium term, and

---

[xiv] Mainland Chinese, Consultant, International management consultancy
[xv] China, Expatriate, Senior Consultant, International management consultancy
[xvi] Indian, Finance and General Management, Indian MNC heavy industry
[xvii] Mainland Chinese, Financial Controller, Chinese venture firm
[xviii] Indian, Finance and General Management, Indian MNC heavy industry

Table 6.2 **Attitudes to forward planning in four Asian countries**

	China	India	Japan	Taiwan
Forward planning	An aversion to forward planning and preference for trial and error	_Used increasingly as family firms professionalize_	Forward planning is thorough but strategic vision may be lacking	_Contingency and opportunism dominate due to the hyper-competitive market_

of their need to develop branding expertise.[xix] Table 6.2 summarizes our findings on forward planning in our sample countries.

Strategy in domestic markets

One strategy is widespread in Asia – the strategy of belonging to a business group. Whitley (1992) noted that 'collective inter-firm commitments' were one of the distinctive characteristics of Japanese business systems, while the Chinese family businesses of Taiwan and Hong Kong were marked by 'personal links between firms'; only in Korea, of the four countries in the sample taken by Whitley (1992) were 'low inter-firm dependence and mutual obligations' characteristic. We found membership of formal and informal business groups to be widespread in India, Japan, Taiwan, Singapore (among SMEs [small and medium enterprises]) and Hong Kong and to be a growing phenomenon in mainland China. Indian business groups generally exhibited not only 'personal links between firms' but also family ties; Japan's links were inter-organizational rather than personal, although the personal ties sometimes continued to support business relationships even after the end of _keiretsu_ membership; Taiwan's groups operated by a combination of family ties and _guanxi_.

In **India**, according to Khanna and Palepu (2002), business groups, although a dominant feature of the economy, were 'simple' in their composition in comparison with some other Asian countries. First, firms were generally members of only one group. Further, marital alliances between families that ran different groups were relatively rarer there. Again, unlike in many other countries, such as Malaysia and Indonesia, a large proportion of groups were publicly traded, so some transparency was present.[15] However, there was a business group phenomenon in India that reduced transparency, our study found. Known as the 'promoter' system, it arose 'because so few had any capital'.

 A family would perhaps sell a piece of land, use the money as seed capital, setting up an SME (small and medium enterprise) business in

---

[xix] China, Expatriate, Senior Consultant, International Management Consultancy

textiles, paper, bicycles, sewing machines or radios. Or they might be in the import or export trades. During the war(s), some made windfall profits. In any case as the family produced sons and grandsons, each would be given something to run; they would be separate legal entities but would be strongly linked in terms of money and control. To expand, borrowing against a future income stream was not available, so they would borrow against assets, leveraging scarce capital. India's many diversified conglomerates are explained partly by the above, partly by the 'joint venture' phenomenon: a family business with connections in Delhi (A) would combine with a family business with access to finance (B) to start a business where they saw opportunities (often because A was able to obtain a licence and so the new venture would benefit from a quasi-monopoly). In many cases, the Industrial Development Corporation or the state government would take a stake in the joint venture.[xx]

Khanna and Palepu (1998) found no evidence that following the shock of the currency crisis and subsequent liberalization of the Indian economy in 1991, Indian business groups significantly reduced their scope of activities. While they exited some peripheral businesses, they continued to be highly diversified and made plans to invest in new lines of business as liberalization opened up new opportunities.[16]

Diversification is a feature of business in India that may be accounted for by 'rational' economic choices, business culture or a combination of the two. Khanna and Palepu (1998) argued that in contrast to the West, in India there were a variety of market failures caused by information and agency problems, which mean that unrelated diversification was a rational strategy. For example, the financial markets were characterized by a lack of adequate disclosure and weak corporate governance and control. Intermediaries such as financial analysts, mutual funds, investment bankers, venture capitalists and the financial press were either absent or not fully evolved. (Later studies, such as that of Ricart et al. [2004], noted earlier in this chapter, disputed the weakness of India's financial intermediaries.) The absence of such intermediaries made it costly for firms to obtain necessary inputs such as finance, technology and management talent. In such circumstances, the scale and scope of diversified business groups enabled them to cost-effectively internally replicate the functions provided by market intermediaries in advanced economies. (It should be noted that the type of diversification discussed by Khanna and Palepu [1998] is different from that described in the example earlier in this chapter from our research, which would not serve to 'replicate the functions provided by market intermediaries in advanced economies'.)

Khanna and Palepu (1998) found that, after 1991, business groups seemed to strengthen their internal structures and processes in ways that would enable

---

[xx] Indian, independent business consultant and academic

them to increase their role as intermediaries in domestic product, labour and capital markets, and in international markets for capital and technology. There was evidence that these activities were associated with an increase in performance.[17] Khanna and Palepu (1998) also reported that the largest and most diversified Indian business groups outperformed their more focused equivalents. This finding supported their hypothesis that the scale and scope of emerging market business groups enabled them to internally replicate the functions provided by stand-alone market institutions in advanced economies. These findings supported the argument that the strategic behaviour of India's business groups was driven by an economically rational adaptation to aspects of their institutional environment, thus suggesting that business culture was not required for an explanation.[18] However, it does not prove that the strategic behaviour adopted by the groups was the only economically rational adaptation possible and so the culturalist explanation of a tendency to enhance what is under the family's ownership and control is still available.

Contradicting the findings of Khanna and Palepu (1998), Kakani (2000) found that the financial performance of large business houses was negatively linked to the extent of diversification of Indian businesses. These findings were obtained for three different economic environments – a period of comparatively low competition (during pre-liberalization), a period of high growth rates for business groups post-liberalization and a third period of still substantial but lower growth, thus suggesting that factors other than economic rationality or profit maximization were influencing their strategy.[19] A further argument, put forward by Kumar (2004) suggests that the culture of treating a business as the private possession of the controlling shareholder did influence group affiliations. A business's ownership structure is crucial in determining the incentive of insiders to expropriate minority shareholders. Debt ratios are also significant for governance, as expropriators often incur more debt to have more resources to use for private interests. Where the controlling shareholder of a firm and the firm's debt providers belong to the same business groups, instead of performing the active monitoring and governance function, debt suppliers could become the centre of corrupted crony systems. From an examination of the link between capital structure and shareholding patterns for more than 2000 publicly traded Indian corporate firms over the years 1994 to 2000, Kumar (2004) found that firms with shareholdings distributed through extensive group affiliations had high debt levels and weak governance. This finding contradicts the argument of Khanna and Palepu (2002) that since emerging market economies like India have poorly functioning institutions, group membership is necessarily beneficial. Although group firms can use their reputation and record of accomplishment to mitigate information problems, and firms affiliated with business groups can benefit from access to internal capital markets, the cost of group affiliation may exceed the benefits of such affiliation due to conflict of interests.[20]

202   6

INTRODUCTION · THE BUSINESS CULTURES OF FIVE ASIAN COUNTRIES · ANALYSING ASIAN BUSINESS CULTURES
· OWNERSHIP, FINANCING AND GOVERNANCE · ORGANIZATION AND MANAGEMENT · **BUSINESS STRATEGY** ·

Businesses in **Japan** tend to

> solve problems by forming a group instead of the Western approach
> by technology. For instance, in the 1980s, Japanese automobile manu-
> facturers reduced their costs by adopting a procurement method
> called '*Kanban Hoshiki* (Price and delivery control system by group-
> ing sub-contractors)' and swept over the US market. In 1990s, the
> US automobile manufacturers developed information technology to
> fight back.[21]

Even aside from membership in horizontal *keiretsu*, which might be declining, Japanese companies developed and nurtured long-term relationships with their channels – relationships that were 'far more intimate than those formed in either Germany or the United States. This is called "*Eigyou*" in Japanese. The *Eigyou* mentality works in Japan because channels – both wholesale and retail – are small and fragmented. Shiseido, the largest cosmetics company in Japan, has over 25,000 retailers'.[22]

The small and medium-sized firms of **Taiwan** are known to be weak organ-izations linked by strong networks,[23] though these are more commonly horizon-tal than vertical.[24] Their networks were described by Chen and Chen (1998) as having a 'unique nature'. 'Networking among Taiwanese firms encompasses non-contractual transactions based on inter-personal links and trust which go beyond pure business relationships.'[25]

In **China**, forming alliances was among a range of strategies that entrepreneurs employed to navigate their 'sometimes hostile and often unpredictable institu-tional environment'. In addition to forming alliances to ensure the presence and enforcement of beneficial industrial standards, regulatory and enforcement regimes and the legitimacy of their industry, these strategies included managing the existing system by co-opting key individuals, locating areas where the entre-preneur could build on existing *guanxi* of their own or others with whom they are aligned and building new sources or relationships through benevolence, often emphasizing one geographic region and one sector for giving.[26] (We found that the last of these strategies had been employed by a small US business which sourced in China: supporting the charitable work of the largest cotton producer in the area where they it was operating led to a good relationship which meant that the cotton producer used her influence with the local authority on their behalf.[xxi])

Chinese businesses may adopt collaborative practices that would be considered contrary to competition codes in other countries. For example, between 1998 and 2005, in the Chinese iron and steel industry, price competition, which was fierce in 1998, settled into a 'well-ordered' mode. This had come about not only due to the strategic perspective adopted by Chinese steel companies after 1998, but also

---

xxi China, Expatriate, entrepreneur

to the existence of an informal platform of communication among competitors, government and trade associations which produced a price-leader/price-follower structure in the industry.[27]

Apart from the strategies of forming or joining business groups or alliances and those set out at the start of this chapter, only a small number of country-specific strategies have been identified, as our logic would predict. In China, research has found an emphasis on price leadership; in Japan on market share, supplier relationships and product churning; in Taiwan, an emphasis on cost leadership and speed of meeting orders through high levels of efficiency.

In **China**, corporate climate (in this context another term for business culture), factor costs and demand conditions accounted for the predominant Chinese market strategy of price leadership, according to Brouthers and Xu (2002). Chinese consumers were highly price sensitive buyers, especially in relation to durable goods, which tended to be paid for out of family savings. Low labour costs also encouraged price leadership strategies. The consequence was that over the years Chinese firms came to adopt price leadership even where it might be less effective than alternative strategies, as in export markets, suggesting that it was a cultural predilection. Thus,

> " China's labour markets, a domestic demand base which is very price sensitive, intense domestic competition in many industries between too many small firms making products which are too similar, and Chinese corporate culture's emphasis on low prices contribute to a national business environment favoring price leadership strategies. Hence, Chinese firms most easily achieve a strategic fit with their home country business environment by pursuing a price leadership strategy.[28]

As Lee et al. (2000) pointed out, firms in **Japan** were 'certainly not all alike', but research showed that they were likely to share some important characteristics. Some of these similarities existed in the area of their approach to strategy. First, market share was always important for Japanese firms; this led to an emphasis on aggressive pricing and the search for economies of scale. Second, supplier relationships were also important factors in Japanese competitive success. Firms made longer-term commitments and reduced the market options they might have in order to take advantage of the close cooperation and coordination of the production process and the fast and flexible development of new products. A survey found that Japanese managers emphasized market share (though to a lesser degree than Korean managers), environmental analysis, especially regarding potential threats from substitute goods/services suppliers, a focus on flexible manufacturing, cooperative relationships with suppliers, information exchange with and closeness to customers and corporate brand/trademark development.[29]

The Japanese system rested, in large part, on the dynamic that drove its consumer product companies perpetually to create and introduce new products. This 'product churning' reflected the Japanese consumer's well-known passion for new products.[30] It also reflected, among manufacturers, the speed-to-market in new product development, in which the Japanese 'completely outclass[ed]' their American or German rivals. In the soft drinks industry, for example, more than 700 new products and brands were marketed each year, but about 90 per cent of them disappeared after only one year in the market. This was a common pattern. Ajinomoto, the largest packaged foods company in Japan, launched between 20 and 35 new frozen food brands each year between 1986 and 1989. Only about half survived for one year, and most had gone entirely from the market by 2005. Such product churning activity was not limited only to packaged goods, but also applied to consumer electronics. Sony launched 182 new products in 1990, almost 1 new product per business day.

Product churning strategies reduce the role of market research and test marketing. In Japan, management focused on sales channels and production technology, not on product market strategy. Rapid product launches were more important for them than understanding the people to whom the new products might actually appeal. Sales plans were based on the salesforce's assessment of how much they could sell to which channel.[31]

The present study suggested that hyper-competitiveness was a characteristic of the business culture of **Taiwan**. Some interviewees attributed this to Taiwan's societal culture. Lam et al. (1994), while agreeing that the marketplace was hyper-competitive and that this was a source of entrepreneurial energy, argued that it was the domination of economic activities by SMEs that caused it. There were numerous suppliers for many goods, and this resulted in a high intensity of competition between firms and pressure on all firms to improve their technology and products over time.[32] The two views can be reconciled within a cultural explanation. We have already seen (in Chapters 2 and 4) that the domination of economic activities by SMEs was itself supported by a culture of pride in business ownership.

In Taiwan, the dominant strategic mindset was concern with speed and cost: 'You are always racing. Any profitable position is temporary. You try to stand in front of the wave. Keep trying for something new. Nothing is sustainable.'[xxii] This approach was, however, closely linked to Taiwanese companies' competitive position and did not preclude a strategic approach:

> Western companies aim for distinctive superiority to compete; for the Taiwanese that is not an option: they cannot beat all the competitors, so they accept being weaker, avoid head-on conflict, keep a low

---

xxii Taiwanese, Product Manager, Taiwanese consumer goods manufacturer

> profile; some go so far as to aim for being 11th or 12th in the market. From 1995–6 on, these companies started to transform their business model. Their strategy is to research and pilot in Taiwan, manufacture in China and have logistical centres all round the world.[xxiii]

Yeh et al. (2006) found that domestic vendors of ERP (enterprise resource planning) in Taiwan perceived themselves to have certain strategic competitive advantages over Western providers although the latter were stronger in software technologies, resources and global market experience. The advantages lay in the area of the ability to meet special requirements, the ability to support the flexibility and speed of domestic small and medium-sized firms, the benefits of direct implementation and the ability to learn from their engagement with local customers. While none of these factors directly refers to culture, the last seems likely to reflect cultural affinity.[33]

International business strategy

All the Asian countries in our sample were, in the early years of the 21st century, placing a strong emphasis on international markets. In general, the explanation was that all their economies needed to gain scale, but there were country-by-country differences in the reasons for this. In the case of China, despite the huge potential of its domestic market, the political need to sustain a growth rate of 10 per cent or more became hard to satisfy from a domestic middle class of under one-fifth of its population. Major product markets had been mature or saturated for ten years or more. Temporary though this situation might be, its influence on Chinese business was substantial. In India's case, the symbolic importance of its offshoring industry, as well as that industry's contribution to growth, made exports of services a focal concern. Japan needed exports to pull the country out of recession, while the small economies were permanently committed to international business to compensate for their limited domestic markets. Varying though the country-by-country reasons for international expansion were, a mixture of economically 'rational' and culturally influenced strategies marked this expansion in the countries we studied, as the model proposed in Chapter 1 would predict.

Many exporters from **China** long pursued a price leadership strategy. Brouthers and Xu (2002) posed the question why they did so. As Lee and Zhou (2000) argued, manufacturers in developed nations were providing high-quality products at reasonably low prices, while other less developed countries' manufacturers seriously challenged Chinese firms by producing similar products at lower costs.

[xxiii] Taiwanese, Product Manager, Taiwanese consumer goods manufacturer

Both trends eroded China's historical cheap labour, price leadership advantage.[34] The answer to the question why Chinese manufacturers nevertheless continued to pursue price leadership appeared to be that the domestic pattern was extended to the international environment: many Chinese firms based their domestic strategies on exploiting the cost savings associated with certain types of labour-intensive manufacturing activities. These firms competed with each other to be price leader, slashing profits in an effort to capture market share in China.[35] They then extended that strategy to export markets. Other possible explanations include that senior managers may not have had the flexibility to change the firm's strategy for political, financial or managerial reasons. Third, many Chinese exporters may have lacked the considerable time and the resources it takes to build a brand. These explanations suggest that a combination of economically 'rational' and cultural factors (conservatism) were operating. A survey of methods used by *Hong Kong* transnational corporations when establishing successful operations within ASEAN (the Association of South East Asian Nations) showed that the methods used corresponded to the personalism and emphasis on business networking of the Chinese business culture. Most used of these successful methods was 'finding a suitable local partner or person to set up the operation' at 25 per cent, followed by 'using personal relations to establish overseas operations' at 18 per cent; 'stimulation, guidance and assistance from local government institutions' came next at 17 per cent, while a technique familiar to Western companies, of 'sending someone over to set up the operation', was fourth at 15 per cent. The cultural tendency to business opportunism found among Chinese businesses was reflected in the low percentage of companies having 'a well-developed corporate procedure to set up overseas operations' – 5 per cent.[36]

In international markets, many Chinese firms suffered the crucial weakness from a strategic management standpoint of a talent shortage. The specificity of Chinese markets and marketing – their difference from other markets – was an impediment to their expanding internationally, where 'the biggest challenge' these enterprises faced was to develop capable managers with international experience. 'The current leaders often have a very China-specific background. They know how to win there because they understand local consumers and businesses very well, but that doesn't necessarily equip them to compete in the global market. Identifying and developing qualified people could take a lot of time.'[37] A survey of Chinese companies in 2008 confirmed that this situation still applied: while 77 per cent expected increased international sales over the next three years, the main barrier they cited was lack of managerial talent, at 44 per cent well ahead of the next most significant barrier, shortage of capital, at 25 per cent.[38]

Many Chinese companies seeking to expand abroad initially pursued an original equipment manufacturing (OEM) strategy, enabling them to build scale quickly without the need for corresponding investments in marketing. From the mid-1990s on, Chinese companies, responding to government pressure, became increasingly motivated to enter international markets with branded products. Their biggest challenge then was to develop marketing strategies for branded goods. Low labour costs made Chinese goods less expensive, and some of the savings could be passed on to Western channel partners and consumers. In addition, China had a large and growing pool of skilled engineers and the money to invest in new products. While many Chinese manufacturers delivered quality that matched that of competitors from other countries, most lacked a comparable marketing expertise. More specifically, most Chinese consumer companies had no overseas distribution channels or service networks, little promotional or advertising know-how and limited pricing skills. It was questionable how quickly these companies could develop a feel for the design and feature preferences of Western customers. Faced with this challenge, some companies found openings by offering value for money to distributors and retailers seeking to differentiate themselves; those that could move quickly found opportunities in the increasingly popular value channels. Some adopted the strategy of learning the ins and outs of selling in developed markets while moving cautiously by making deals with distributors that were able to get leading-edge products in front of consumers without having to invest vast sums on marketing campaigns.[39] It may be that *Hong Kong* firms were leading the way: Davies and Ko (2006) argued that Hong Kong firms were beginning to move away from the traditional Hong Kong business model that kept them in the 'iron fetters' of low-end manufacturing by adopting an up-grading strategy; those that did so were found to enjoy superior performance.[40]

As the offshoring/outsourcing industry, perceived as so important to the economic development of **India**, matured after about 2006, some services became commoditized and threats to its competitive position emerged. For example, some Western utility companies announced the closure of their Indian call centres. These developments provoked a strategic shift towards closer relations with clients. Physical and cultural proximity was important for building closer client relationships, for delivering certain types of services (such as unscripted selling) and for soothing concerns about data security and confidentiality. While cost savings remained the principal motivation to outsource, performance became the main battleground between providers. Vendors attempted to move closer to clients, referring to themselves as partners. As relationships between customers and suppliers deepened, the change was reflected in the increased number of contracts that came to be renewed without the assistance of an adviser.

Faced with competitive threats in their established business process outsourcing (BPO) and software markets, Indian businesses looked to other industries where cost arbitrage and other factors worked in their favour. Examples included medical tourism and clinical research outsourcing. Drug testing, a young industry worth about $118 million a year in 2006, was predicted to be worth $380 million by 2010 as American and European companies looked to India to cut the cost of drug development – particularly the time to market. A three month saving might mean $100 million or $50 million in sales. According to the Head of Indian Pharmaceutical practice for Ernst & Young, a management consultancy, '(India) is becoming a significant player in R&D (research and development) initiatives, manufacturing and licensing as well as clinical trials.' Multinationals were expected to invest further as they gained confidence in India's infrastructure and regulatory framework. A key moment came in 2005 when India signed the GATT (Global Agreement on Tariffs and Trade), for the first time recognizing global patents.[41] Another theme, however, was an emphasis on the personalism that is part of India's business culture. In the words of an Indian marketing manager, 'As production processes and transactions become more commoditized and automated, value with customers lies in hard-to-replicate personal relationships and interactions.'[42]

A number of aspects of **Japan's** international marketing appear to reflect the risk aversion that is part of their business culture. Japanese companies have displayed a preference for entry into mature markets when expanding overseas. These are markets where technology is often available for commercial application, industry standards have emerged and consumer preferences are more predictable. A second example is the way a preference for cooperation over out-of-control competition made Japanese businesses less willing to invest in highly competitive industries abroad and made them very selective in picking new business partners.[43] Japan has been described as having a benchmarking culture, based on risk aversion. In support of this judgement, Henisz and Delios (2001) showed from a sample of 2705 international plant location decisions by listed Japanese multinational corporations across a possible set of 155 countries in the 1990–96 period, that the companies used prior decisions and actions by other organizations to provide legitimization and information to support their decisions in markets where they lacked experience (although the effect did not hold when the uncertainty derived from the structure of a market's policy-making apparatus).[44]

In late 2008, a 'credit crunch' originating in the USA depressed share prices of Western companies at a time when many of the businesses that would otherwise have been considering takeovers were themselves too illiquid or too weakened to take advantage. Japanese companies at this time were 'cash rich' and bought up significant shares in major Western pharmaceutical, electronics, insurance and banking businesses. These purchases were mainly strategic – to add ranges of drugs, complete product lines or enter emerging markets. They were also motivated by the poor prospects in Japan's domestic markets. Nevertheless, the fact that the companies had such a 'surfeit' of unused capital itself points to risk aversion, with its consequences of 'poor governance and fiscal management'.[45]

It has been argued that Japanese firms enjoyed a competitive advantage in the 1980s based on their capacity for tacit information-sharing, another (business) cultural trait, so that the subsequent impact of information and communication

DIMENSIONS OF SOCIETAL CULTURES • SOCIETAL CULTURES REVISITED • POLITICAL CULTURES AND PERCEIVED POLITICAL ENVIRONMENTS • ECONOMIC CULTURES AND PERCEIVED ECONOMIC ENVIRONMENTS • CONCLUDING REMARKS

6   209

technology 'can be considered as one of most important reasons for the apparent erosion of competitiveness of Japanese firms'.[46]

The international business strategy of technological product manufacturers from **Taiwan** is based on a combination of operational efficiency and network linkages. The strategy of globally distributed functions described above,

> means that if Dell, for instance, goes to a Taiwanese manufacturer with a concept, within two months it can be distributed globally. The trick is co-ordination; the companies have to be, and are, fast, efficient and sophisticated. Between 1999 and 2005 almost 70 per cent of Taiwanese FDI [foreign direct investment] was in China. They are interested in it both for manufacturing and as a market. They aim to develop their capability in sales and marketing there. China is a large enough market for branding, unlike Taiwan, and Chinese consumer culture chimes with Taiwanese.[xxiv]

In relation to Taiwan, Chen and Chen (1998) showed that the availability and ease of establishing network linkages were a significant determinant in the locational choice of Taiwanese FDI, independent of firm-specific assets and other locational characteristics of the host country. They also found that inter-firm linkages were preferred over intra-firm linkages, corresponding to the Taiwanese pattern of small linked firms rather than large divisionalized ones. Although Taiwanese FDI in the USA was motivated by strategic linkages, in South East Asia and China, linkages based on existing relations were more important. China was perceived by Taiwanese FDI investors to present the highest contractual risks among the three competing locations of the USA, South East Asia and China. Despite these high perceived contractual risks in China, Taiwanese firms invested there 'due to network linkages'.[47] The benefits of network linkages include effective communication. Effective communications between Taiwanese investors and local Chinese officials who shared common culture and language enabled Chinese government officials to interpret laws and regulations flexibly for Taiwanese investors, accelerating the application process for investment projects and circumventing customs inspection procedures. This flexibility in turn enabled Taiwanese investors to retain their flexibility and speed of operation in serving their export markets from China.[48]

Conclusion

There are elements of the business strategies of firms in Asia which are surprisingly closely linked to the business cultures – surprising in view of the point

---

xxiv Taiwanese product manager, Taiwanese technological goods manufacturer

made in Chapter 1 that differentiation is usually an essential aspect of strategy. Examples of such elements include the diasporic pattern of Asian businesses' overseas expansion, personalism in business-to-business relations and the strategy of business group membership. There are other elements, such as the Chinese price leadership strategy or the Japanese drive for market share, that seem only loosely related to their business cultures and seem to be related more closely to environments and institutions.

References

[1] Davies, H. and Ma, C. (2003) 'Strategic choice and the nature of the Chinese family business: An exploratory study of the Hong Kong watch industry', *Organization Studies*, **24**(9): 1405–35.

[2] Whitley, R. (1992) *Business Systems in East Asia: Firms, Markets, and Societies*, London: Sage.

[3] Steier, L.P., Chrisman, J.J. and Chua, J.H. (2004) 'Entrepreneurial management and governance in family firms: An introduction', *Entrepreneurship: Theory and Practice*, **28**: 295–303.

[4] Ricart, E.J., Enright, M.J., Ghemawat, P., Hart, S.L. and Khanna, T. (2004) 'New frontiers in international strategy', *Journal of International Business Studies*, **35**: 175–200.

[5] Ibid.

[6] Ibid.

[7] Ninan, T.N. (2007) 'Interview with MV Subbiah, former chairman of Chennai-based Murugappa Group', URL: http://www.business-standard.com.

[8] Ahlstrom, D., Nair, A., Young, M.C. and Wang, L.C. (2006) 'China: Competitive myths and realities', *SAM Advanced Management Journal*, **71**(4): 4–10.

[9] Bolt, P. (2002) 'Review of Brown, R.A. (2002) Chinese big business and the wealth of Asian nations', *China Review International*, **9**(1): 71–4.

[10] Gilboy, G.J. (2004) 'The myth behind China's miracle', *Foreign Affairs*, **83**(4): 33–49.

[11] Hofstede, G. (2007) 'Asian management in the 21st century', *Asia Pacific Journal of Management*, **24**: 411–20.

[12] Bond, M.H. (1988) 'Finding universal dimensions of individual variation in multicultural studies of values: The Rokeach and Chinese value surveys', *Journal of Personality and Social Psychology*, **55**(6): 1009–15.

[13] Charles, T.A., Hofstede, G., Mueller, C.B. and Van Deusen, C.A. (2002) 'What goals do business leaders pursue? A study in fifteen countries', *Journal of International Business Studies*, **33**(40): 705–803.

[14] Negandhi, A.R. (1975) *Organization Theory in an Open System*. Port Washington, NY: Kennikat Press.

[15] Khanna, T. and Palepu, K. (1998) 'Policy shocks, market intermediaries, and corporate strategy: The evolution of business groups in Chile and India', Harvard Business School Working Paper, URL: http://ssrn.com/abstract=97809 or 10.2139/ssrn.97809.

[16] Ibid.

[17] Ibid.

[18] Ibid.

[19] Kakani, R.K. (2000) 'Financial performance and diversification strategy of Indian business groups', Indian Institute of Management (IIM) Calcutta, Working Paper Series No. 411/2000. URL: http://ssrn.com/abstract=1021148.

[20] Kumar, J. (2004) 'Debt vs. equity: Role of corporate governance', Eighth Capital Markets Conference, Indian Institute of Capital Markets Paper, URL: http://ssrn.com/abstract=592521.

[21] Intelligence Bridges (2002) 'Characteristics of Japanese people', URL: www.intelbridges.com/japanesedispositionuk.html.

[22] Ohbora, T., Parsons, A. and Riesenbeck, H. (1992) 'Alternate Routes to Global Marketing', *The McKinsey Quarterly Online*, http://www.mckinseyquarterly.com/Alternate_routes_to_global_marketing.1012.

[23] Redding, S.G. (1996) 'Societal transformation and the contribution of authority relations and cooperation norms in overseas Chinese business', in Weiming, T. (ed.) *Confucian Traditions in East Asian*

Modernity: Moral Education and Economic Culture in Japan and the Four Mini-Dragons, Cambridge, MA: Harvard University Press.

[24] Feenstra, R.C., Hamilton, G.G. and Yang, M. (1997) 'Business groups and trade in East Asia: Part 2, product variety', URL: http://papers.ssrn.com/sol3/papers.cfm?abstract_id=225669.

[25] Chen, H. and Chen T.-J. (1998) 'Network linkages and location choice in foreign direct investment', *Journal of International Business Studies*, **29**(3): 445–67.

[26] Ahlstrom, D. and Bruton, G.D. (2002) 'An institutional perspective on the role [of] culture in shaping strategic actions by technology-focused entrepreneurial firms in China', *Entrepreneurship: Theory and Practice*, **26**(4): 53–69.

[27] Zhilong, T., Yuanqiong, H., Changxu, Z. and Guangxi, Y. (2005) 'The pricing behavior of firms in the Chinese iron and steel industry', *Asia Pacific Journal of Marketing and Logistics*, **17**(3): 67–88.

[28] Brouthers, L.E. and Xu, K. (2002) 'Product stereotypes, strategy and performance satisfaction: The case of Chinese exporters', *Journal of International Business Studies*, **33**(4): 637–55.

[29] Lee, J., Roehl, T.W. and Choe, S. (2000) 'What makes management style similar and distinct across borders? Growth, experience and culture in Korean and Japanese firms', *Journal of International Business Studies*, **31**(4): 631–52.

[30] Intelligence Bridges (2005) 'The Japanese Consumer', URL: http://www.intelbridges.com/japaneseconsumer.html.

[31] Ibid.

[32] Lam, D., Paltiel, J.T. and Shannon, J.H. (1994) 'The Confucian entrepreneur? Chinese culture, industrial organization and intellectual property piracy in Taiwan', *Asian Affairs, an American Review*, **20**(4): 205–17.

[33] Yeh, C.-T., Miozz, M. and Vurdubakis, T. (2006) 'The importance of being local? Learning among Taiwan's enterprise solutions providers', *Journal of Enterprise Information Management*, **19**(1): 30–49.

[34] Lee and Zhou (2000) 'Quality management and manufacturing strategies in China', *International Journal of Quality & Reliability Management*, **17**(8): 876–99.

[35] Brouthers, L.E. and Xu, K. (2002) 'Product stereotypes, strategy and performance satisfaction: The case of Chinese exporters', *Journal of International Business Studies*, **33**(4): 637–55.

[36] Yeung, H.W.-C. (1998) 'Business networks and transnational corporations: A study of Hong Kong firms in the ASEAN region', *Economic Geography*, **73**: 1–25.

[37] Orr, G.R. (2005) 'What executives are asking about China', *The McKinsey Quarterly Online*, **3**, URL: www.mckinseyquarterly.com/article.

[38] Competition from China: Two McKinsey Surveys (2008) *The McKinsey Quarterly Online*, URL: http://www.mckinseyquarterly.com/Competition_from_China_Two_McKinsey_Surveys_2147.39 Gao, P. and Woetzel, J. (2003) 'Can Chinese brands make it abroad?' *The McKinsey Quarterly Online*, URL: www.mckinseyquarterly.com/article.

[40] Davies, H. and Ko, D. (2006) 'Up-grading and performance: The role of design, technology and business strategy in Hong Kong's electronics industry', *Asia Pacific Journal of Management*, **23**(3): 255–82.

[41] *The Times*, 9 October 2006 'India's new outsourcing remedy', p. 49.

[42] Tippu, S. (2006) 'India and China economic powerhouses by 2020', India Wire, URL: www.itwire.com.au/content/view/4744/945/.

[43] Pan, Y. (1996) 'Influences on foreign equity ownership level in joint ventures in China', *Journal of International Business Studies*, **27**(1): 1–26.

[44] Henisz, W.J. and Delios, A. (2001) 'Uncertainty, imitation and plant location: Japanese multinational corporations, 1990–96', *Administrative Science Quarterly*, **46**(3): 443–75.

[45] *The Economist*, 'The Japanese are coming (again)', 4 October 2008.

[46] Aoki, M. (2006) 'Whither Japan's Corporate Governance?' Stanford Institute for Economic Policy Research Discussion Paper No. 05–14, URL: http://siepr.stanford.edu.paper/pdf/05-14.pdf.

[47] Chen, H. and Chen T.-J. (1998) 'Network linkages and location choice in foreign direct investment', *Journal of International Business Studies*, **29**(3): 445–67.

[48] Hsing, Y.T. (1998) *Making Capital in China: The Taiwan Connection*, Oxford: Oxford University Press.

212   6

INTRODUCTION • THE BUSINESS CULTURES OF FIVE ASIAN COUNTRIES • ANALYSING ASIAN BUSINESS CULTURES • OWNERSHIP, FINANCING AND GOVERNANCE • ORGANIZATION AND MANAGEMENT • **BUSINESS STRATEGY** •

7 dimensions of societal cultures

This and the following chapter analyse aspects of the societal cultures of some Asian countries and investigate possible links to the business cultures of those countries. This chapter considers the dimensional approaches that have predominated in Western cultural research; the next chapter presents a more nuanced and descriptive view. As a preliminary to both these chapters, it may be useful to consider some theoretical arguments about culture, first clarifying what 'societal culture' is, then discussing the question of whether societal culture influences business and finally presenting the case for and against using nations as the main cultural units.

The term 'societal culture' here approximates to the concept of culture as applying to an entire society within some geographical boundary, most usually a country. In other sources, the term 'social culture' is used to refer to this concept, but we reserve 'social culture' to mean the culture of any group, including, for instance, the members of a church or the inhabitants of a village. Thus a societal culture is the social culture of a whole society, usually a country. The term 'societal culture' is distinguished from business culture in applying to a wider community (the whole of society, not just its business component) and both societal culture and social culture refer to a wider set of behaviours, values and ideas than business culture (including, for example, marriage practices such as dowry which are not generally part of business culture). Social culture can be defined as 'an imperfectly shared system of interrelated understanding, shaped by its members' shared history and experiences',[1] or as 'patterns, explicit and implicit, of and for behaviour acquired and transmitted by symbols, constituting the distinctive achievement of human groups including their embodiment in artefacts, whose essential core consists of traditional (that is, historically derived and selected) ideas and especially their attached values',[2] or in a number of other ways.

Societal culture may be a stronger influence in some countries than in others. In the words of Thompson (1996), 'There are some general indications that *social influences* are stronger in many Asian societies than in the West. In many Asian countries, expectations about behaviour often emphasize communal or group responsibilities rather than individual rights compared to most Western countries.'[3] The implication here is that the beliefs of individualistic cultures themselves weaken the impact of those cultures on behaviour, instead encouraging people to 'do their own thing', whereas Asia's collectivist cultures' beliefs reinforce the influence of culture on how people behave.

On the issue of links between societal culture and business, both our research and the institutional perspective are positive. Our interviews at several points showed that the societal culture and the business culture were linked in the minds of business decision-makers in Asia. Most explicit were the two following statements from Japanese interviewees:

> " The origins of Japan's business culture are in Taoism and to some extent Confucianism. ... History plays a part, too. Only Mongolia ever threatened to attack Japan and even they did not land. So the Japanese became secure in their identity, did not need to compete aggressively, everyone they ever met was like them and so they could assume they understood how others think without it needing to be spelt out. Also with low external threat there was less premium on youth and both the experience of the old and the contribution of the ancestors to the Japanese way of life could be valued. Craftsmanship, too, is highly valued. This is the origin of the apprenticeship and seniority business culture.[i]
>
> Yes, there is such a thing as a distinctive Japanese business culture. It is rooted in our background. Japan is a small island, overpopulated since the 18th century, so ... the interest of the community prevails over that of the individual. Stability is highly valued – no one wants radical change. Attention to detail is characteristic. This culture has largely survived the economic troubles that started in 1990.[ii]

Within the institutional perspective, as Chapter 1 showed, Whitley (1992) acknowledged the importance of societal culture ('cultural preferences and beliefs') for business systems, even though in practice these preferences and beliefs were largely omitted from the analysis;[4] subsequently Redding (2004), commenting on Whitley's (1992) analysis, called for an incorporation of culture at an additional level – that of a prior 'shaping of institutions':

> " Recent reviews have recommended more contextualized analysis of economic systems, and the business systems theory of Whitley is taken as exemplary in this regard. Three slight amendments are proposed to his main framework: acknowledgement of the 'prior' nature of culture in the shaping of institutions; the introduction of the question of rationale as a component of culture; and the mediating role of government in the flow of influence between culture and the formation of institutions. ... The business system is embedded in an institutional fabric, which is in turn embedded in a social culture.[5]

---

[i] Japanese, Marketing Manager, Western MNC (multi-national company) telephony manufacturer
[ii] Japanese, Finance and Accounting, Education

214   7

INTRODUCTION • THE BUSINESS CULTURES OF FIVE ASIAN COUNTRIES • ANALYSING ASIAN BUSINESS CULTURES
• OWNERSHIP, FINANCING AND GOVERNANCE • ORGANIZATION AND MANAGEMENT • BUSINESS STRATEGY •

Given that Redding (2004) accepted Whitley's 'main framework', which included 'cultural preferences and beliefs', it must presumably be the case that societal ('social') culture is considered not only prior to institutions but also as part of the institutional fabric, in the same way as Scott (1995) considered 'cognitive institutions' as one of the three categories of institutions.[6] These three institutional theorists, then, clearly acknowledged the significance of societal culture for understanding business systems.

On the other hand, doubts have at times been expressed about whether the boundaries of social culture are ever as extensive as those of nations, doubts which must be particularly strong in the case of China and India, two countries with huge populations and large land masses and, in India, enormous diversity. For example, Fram and Reid (2005) attributed the failure of some MNCs (multinational companies) in China in part to their using country-wide data, with little attention to regional, social and cultural differences.[7] Despite these doubts, there is support for there being at least some important elements of societal culture that apply throughout each country. For **China**, Peng and Heath (1996) asserted that despite regional variations, 'The culture of China can be viewed as flowing from an institutional environment that is fairly homogeneous and highly tacit.'[8] Chen (2001) considered that Confucian influence remained quite strong throughout China in spite of attempts during the Cultural Revolution to purge it from Chinese consciousness.[9] These arguments were accepted by Ahlstrom and Bruton (2002), even though they acknowledged that regional rivalry and distrust of those outside the local region led the Chinese to erect barriers to commerce between regions.[10] For **India**, Budhwar (2003) referred to a list of writers and researchers who argued that despite the heterogeneity of languages, dialects and customs in India, there existed common attitudinal and behavioural patterns that knit most of the people together to give a sense of uniformity.[11] As far as the other focal countries in this study are concerned, **Japan** is one of the least ethnically diverse countries on earth and its long history of independence and even isolation raise few doubts as to its cultural homogeneity. **Singapore** is more diverse but its businesses, with the exception of multinational companies, are all largely in the control of people of Chinese ethnicity; **Taiwan** business is also largely ethnically Chinese.

The rest of this chapter will outline the main dimensional approaches to culture and explore their links to the patterns of business decisions in Asia.

Dimensions of Asian societal cultures

In most dimensional approaches to culture an emphasis on values is central. In general use, there are several research-based systems providing data for comparing Asian cultural values: Hofstede's (1981),[12] Schwartz's (1994),[13] Bond's (1988) Chinese Values Survey[14] and the series of World Values Surveys.[15]

Drawing on the writings of earlier scholars, Tinsley and Pillutia (1998) provided an explanation of the link between values and culture that is helpful at this point.

> 'Values are desirable goals that serve as guiding principles in people's lives.'[16] Cultural values are those that are shared across cultural group members.[17] Although values may technically reside in the individual as part of his or her cognitive structure, these values are not merely influenced by culture, but 'thoroughly culturally constituted'[18]. Shared values represent a culture's solutions to fundamental questions of human survival, such as coordinating social interaction.[19,20]

For the individual, conforming to the culture's values is socially rewarded and decision-making is simplified. In response to these motivations, members of the culture tend to act in accordance with their culture's values. Socialization, which rewards conforming, leads new members of the culture to internalize cultural values. For the society, 'shared values create a social environment that directs members to select ... behaviours that "fit", that is, lead to outcomes that are socially desirable'.[21]

Hofstede's values dimensions

The five cultural value dimensions that, according to Hofstede's (1981, 2007) well-known research into IBM staff, distinguish national cultures, are individualism-collectivism, power distance, uncertainty avoidance, masculinity/femininity and long-term or short-term orientation.[22,23] Briefly, these can be understood as follows:

• People in individualist cultures value autonomy, choice and the right not to be imposed on by others, while people in collectivist cultures value interdependence, reciprocal obligation and the right to receive support from others. In collectivist cultures, relationship prevails over task; in individualist cultures, the reverse is the case. Church (2000) summarized the major features of collectivist cultures as a focus on contexts more than on internal processes in predicting the behaviour of others, lower consistency in individual behaviours across situations and greater predictability of behaviour from norms and roles than from attitudes. The reverse of these are found in individualist cultures.[24]
• Power distance refers to the extent to which people value egalitarianism or alternatively expect and accept that power is distributed unequally. In organizations, the difference is marked by whether hierarchies are steep or flat, rigid or flexible, and whether information flows are predominantly vertical or horizontal.

- High uncertainty avoidance refers to a societal norm in which people avoid ambiguous situations and prefer to resolve uncertainty by following rules and procedures; in low uncertainty avoidance societies, people tolerate more uncertainty and value the freedom not to be closely regulated in their behaviour. At work, common sense and generalists are valued in low uncertainty avoidance cultures.
- Masculinity describes a high achievement orientation in contrast to a feminine relationship orientation. In the language of the discipline of organizational behaviour, this translates as task versus maintenance orientation.
- A long-term time orientation refers to a willingness to delay returns or rewards. It was originally termed Confucian dynamism (by Bond, 1988)[25] because both at the positive and at the negative pole it reminded of the teachings of Confucius: it opposed future-oriented, dynamic Confucian values to present and past-oriented, static Confucian values. Hofstede renamed it as long-term orientation because the term would be more widely understood. This dimension opposed many Asian countries to most of the rest of the world, in the sense that the Asian countries scored long-term and the others medium or short-term. The top long-term scorers were China, Hong Kong, Taiwan, Japan and Korea. These were followed by Brazil but then again by Asian countries: India, Thailand and Bangladesh.[26]

On Hofstede's value dimensions, the relative rankings of the five focal countries in our study can be compared, while their scores can be compared with one another and the world as a whole. A first point to note is that rather wide differences were found within Asia on these values, with the exception of long-term orientation, thus to some degree undermining any suggestion that 'Asian values' are responsible for economic patterns in Asia.

Hofstede (1981, 2004) made it clear that he believed that these values permeate all aspects of society and so affect business as well as, for instance, family life, happiness, health and schooling. A good many studies have endorsed the links of these values to behaviour. An example published in 2007 is evidence from a study in 58 countries that nearly all of Hofstede's cultural dimensions are linked to nations' internet penetration, either as main effects or as interactions with countries' educational levels.[27]

Hofstede's (1981) values constitute a starting point for comparing our interviewees' accounts of the business cultures of their countries with the literature on dimensions of culture. This comparison shows up some similarities but also some quite marked differences from those that the Hofstede values would predict.

For Asia as a whole, the Hofstede findings were that in comparison with the world average Asia was very low on individualism (high on collectivism), slightly high on power distance, close to the world average on uncertainty avoidance, somewhat high on masculinity and very high on long-term orientation. This pattern would predict business cultures where trust is extended mainly to familiar or related others, where authority figures are respected but not obsequiously obeyed, where rules and procedures have their place but are used flexibly, where task orientation prevails over relationship orientation but not to a great degree and where patient waiting for results is the norm. It may well be that this is a characterization of the average Asian business culture, if there is such a thing. However, both Hofstede's findings and the results of the present study show very substantial variation within Asia. I turn now to compare predictions based on Hofstede's findings with the reports on business cultures for the three largest countries in the present study.

Hofstede's research showed **China** as having an extremely high long-term orientation, well above both Asian and global levels. Murphy and Wang (2006) suggested that this long-term orientation of Chinese culture provided a possible explanation for a finding of theirs. The stakeholder marketing performance of 2 Chinese businesses investigated was in line with the 57 Western businesses in the benchmark stakeholder-performance appraisal database. Stakeholder marketing performance reflects the delivery of long-term economic, social and environmental value to customers, suppliers, community and shareholders. Since stakeholder performance is linked to sustainability, or being in business for the long-term by being responsible stewards of resources, the findings might be hard to explain for businesses in China's stage of economic development and rush to modernize, except in terms of its cultural long-term orientation.[28]

Our interviewees, however, described the mainland Chinese as 'sometimes cutting corners'[iii] and as having currently a short-term orientation, shown by the rush to IPO (raise capital by issuing shares in an initial public offering) by entrepreneurs;[iv] one interviewee attributed the failure of his internet advertising business to Chinese retailers having 'a short-term view of their businesses and so not being willing to spend on advertising'.[v] Another interviewee said specifically, 'Time orientations have shrunk as the quickly expanding economy brings opportunities for early promotion; this changes expectations.'[vi] One consequence for Chinese businesses, in the perception of this interviewee, was a partial setting aside of the seniority principle:

> " For instance, CNPC (China National Petroleum Company) is the most profitable company in Asia. Its CEO (Chief Executive Officer) is appointed by the government, but the CEO of CNPC International is a man in his 30s who got there by merit. Sinopec (China Petroleum and Chemical Corporation) is in the Fortune Top 20 for size, but is largely led by young people.[vii]

[iii] Hong Kong Chinese, Banker, International Bank
[iv] Ibid.
[v] Hong Kong Chinese, Failed entrepreneur in China, Financial Controller, International Consumer Goods Company manufacturing in China
[vi] China, Expatriate, Asia Product Manager, International Oil Company
[vii] Ibid.

(The Chinese business community of **Taiwan** was also considered oriented towards the short-term: 'Short-termism is marked, partly due to the China threat, though fear levels are low',[viii] and, 'Politics are unstable. This leads to short-termism; so does the predominance of SMEs', were two comments in Taiwan.[ix]) There are also published findings such as that 'Chinese investors have a short-term speculative mindset for funds, trading actively on the basis of prevailing market sentiment.'[29]

Leong et al. (2007) noted that the unique historical experience of *Hong Kong* people in living in a place that was contractually committed to be returned to another sovereignty led them to develop a very short-term orientation, with a preference for short-term measures and quick profit. Self-reliance and risk-taking behaviour were typical characteristics of Hong Kong Chinese. Although still influenced by Chinese values such as humility, patience, persistence and hard work, Hong Kong business people were also well versed about Western values. Research indicated that many individuals in Hong Kong saw themselves as possessing a blend of Chinese and Western values and practices. The phenomenon was still more pronounced among Hong Kong business managers, many of whom had been educated abroad or had graduated from Hong Kong business schools which emphasized Western business principles.[30] Some superficially short-termist behaviours, however, may be manifestations of a long-term orientation. For instance, as Lam et al. (2001) pointed out, overseas Chinese often quickly establish a joint venture (JV) in China without careful negotiation and contracting. 'With their long-term perspective, they consider JVs the first step in building lasting relationships. They will rely on this rapport later to solve the problems resulting from lack of feasibility studies or clear contracts.'[31]

A high long-term orientation, according to Hofstede and Hofstede (2004), would predict main work values of learning, honesty, adaptiveness, accountability and self-discipline, a low value attached to leisure time, a business focus on market position, placing high value on profits ten years hence, a sharing of workers' and managers' aspirations, a low tolerance for wide social and economic differences and investment in personal networks.[32] Apart from the investment in personal networks (*guanxi*) these descriptions do not obviously apply to the Chinese business culture that was described to us. For example, even aside from the taken-for-granted awareness of corruption mentioned in Chapter 2, the importance attached to honesty in business was explicitly questioned: 'The downside of no religion is no morality. This does not mean routine dishonesty, but everyone for himself. Consensus, especially public consensus, is important; you must not make anybody look bad to other people; but underneath it's dog eat dog.'[x] 'It's the Wild West out there.'[xi] 'Chinese society has no religious stance

---

[viii] Taiwanese, Senior Vice President, Finance and Accounting, Fund Management
[ix] Taiwan, Expatriate (Japanese), Human Resource Management, Banking
[x] China, Expatriate, General Manager, Energy MNC
[xi] China, Expatriate, Consultant, International Management Consultancy

on business.[xii] 'The only thing that keeps the "Wild West" businesses honest, is the knowledge of the astonishing speed the government can move at when it has made up its mind.'[xiii] As another example, the low value attached to leisure time is hard to reconcile with the reported low work ethic of mainland Chinese, compared with Hong Kong Chinese, which one interviewee attributed to the after-effects of communism. 'When your reward would be the same whether you worked a lot or a little, it made sense to do less.'[xiv] As a third example, a statement such as, 'In SOEs [state-owned enterprises] there is little or no accountability' does not support an attribution of accountability as an important work value.[xv]

One possible explanation for these contradictions between the picture of the Chinese business culture that emerged from our research and the country's societal long-term values orientation is that under certain conditions, business cultures and societal cultures diverge. If that hypothesis is right, economies such as China's, which are in transition from anti-capitalism to capitalism, might well be examples of the conditions in which a short-term orientation might override its core culture in its business culture. Another possible explanation is that the Chinese idea of short-term diverges from the Western idea: that when our interviewees spoke of 'short-term' it was in Western terms relatively long-term. This explanation, though, conflicts somewhat with the examples given: not being willing to spend on advertising, or rushing to IPO a two-year-old business, for instance, count as short-term anywhere.

In contrast to the dubious fit of its business culture with long-term orientation, China's high power distance is clearly reflected in its business culture in the emphasis we found on deference and hierarchy, which also corresponds to the country's Confucian legacy. The five Confucian cardinal relations (*wu-lun*) – emperor–subject, father–son, husband–wife, elder–younger, and friend–friend – are all constructed in hierarchical dyads. In each case, the senior member is accorded a wide range of prerogatives and authority with respect to the junior. Prescriptions for these relations are asymmetric, in that the behaviour expectations of the role with less power (for instance, the subject, the son, the wife) is specified in much more detail than those of the role with greater power. Much more stringent requirements and restrictions are imposed on the less powerful role, and as a result, people in those roles have been 'greatly underprivileged'.[33]

China's individualism relative to both Asia and the world was very low, a value that is reflected in the importance of *guanxi* to the business culture although not in the 'selfishness' deplored by our interviewees when speaking of the younger members of the urban workforce. As noted by Goodall et al. (2007),

xii Mainland Chinese, Financial Controller, Chinese Venture Firm
xiii China, Expatriate, Senior Consultant, International Management Consultancy
xiv Mainland Chinese, Consultant, International Management Consultancy
xv Mainland Chinese, Financial Controller, Chinese Venture Firm

this deviation from traditional values has an explanation in the exposure of the younger generation of Chinese people to new economic and social forces such as increased consumerism, access to the internet (albeit government controlled) and contact with foreign companies and their staff. Hofstede himself (1981) noted a positive correlation between increased individualism and growth in per capita GNP (gross national product). One of the most distinctive changes in Chinese values may, therefore, be increased individualistic tendencies, especially among the younger generation.[34]

According to Lu Le (2003), individualism in Chinese culture is still equated to egoism and is translated as such (*ge ren zhu yi*). 'Only recently has the translation been rendered into terms similar in concept and in connotation to its source version (*ger ti zhu yi*), and then only after much controversial discussion.'[35] However, consistent with the comments of our interviewees, Ralston et al. (1999) found that individualism was higher among Chinese managers under the age of 40, who grew up in the era of social reform, and that collectivism and Confucianism were lower amongst managers aged 41 to 51 than among older managers. (The research treated individualism, collectivism and Confucianism as separate values.)

> Thus Chinese managers under the age of 40 are more likely to act independently and take risks in the pursuit of profits, even when these actions conflict with traditional ways. They are more mobile. Compared with Western managers, younger Chinese managers retain relatively high Confucian values and collectivist tendencies, but these are lower than those of earlier generations of managers.[36]

Chinese uncertainty avoidance was slightly low, a finding which corresponds to the descriptions that Chinese are 'tolerant of lack of system, creative, try to approach a problem in many different ways, sometimes cut corners, clever',[xvi] 'pragmatic people',[xvii] 'flexible and easy to do business with as shown by how easy it is to get a sample made up'.[xviii]

The IBM study found **India** to be somewhat high on power distance and long-term orientation by world standards, and somewhat low on uncertainty avoidance; on masculinity and individualism-collectivism it was close to the world average. The combination of somewhat high power distance and low uncertainty avoidance could account for the Indian business culture which, we found, combined relative informality and sociability even across levels in the hierarchy with firmly top-down decision-making. (In Japan, where the reverse of India's values were found by Hofstede – that is, high uncertainty avoidance and relatively low

---

[xvi] Hong Kong Chinese, Banker, International Bank
[xvii] China, Expatriate, General Manager, Energy MNC
[xviii] China, Expatriate Entrepreneur

power distance – the business culture also exhibited the reverse characteristics – deference and formality combined with consensual decision-making.)

India's somewhat low uncertainty avoidance, according to Hofstede and Hofstede (2004), would predict

> " more changes of employer, shorter service; an emotional need for as few rules as possible; hard working only when needed; time as a framework for orientation; tolerance for ambiguity and chaos; belief in generalists and common sense; top managers not concerned with day-to-day operations; more new trademarks; focus on decision process; freedom for intrapreneurs; large numbers of self-employed; better at invention, worse at implementation; motivation by achievement or esteem and belonging.[37]

Several of these characteristics, but not all, do correspond to what our research revealed about India's business culture. Confirming the prediction, high staff turnover rates quickly became the norm in the fast-growing computer-based industries and, in fact, more widely once graduate unemployment reduced: 'Until recently, firms hired graduates on the basis that they would stay for life. That made it worthwhile to train up technically qualified but non work-ready graduates for up to two years before they became fully effective. Now high staff mobility has changed all that.'[xix] On the other hand, neither working hard only when needed nor a strong time orientation corresponds to India's business culture as revealed by our research.

Although in the middle of the global range of Hofstede's scores on individualism, of the five countries in our study India scored highest. In our research, a sense that Indians considered their culture too individualist for them to be good team workers came through strongly. In a published interview the retired chairman of the Chennai-based Murugappa Group stated, 'Indians don't work well in teams.' He argued that Indian success in software and pharma research results from the fact that in both areas, 'People can work on their own, figuring out algorithms or molecular structures.' In the view of Chaudhuri and Majumdar (2006), India was experiencing major shifts in her socio-cultural structure. Thus, a society that has been known traditionally as 'collectivist' in nature was gradually showing increased evidence of individualism. They commented, 'It is possible that the search for a distinct self-identity has already begun in India', but cautioned, '[India] is a highly heterogeneous country with multiple languages, myriads of cultural practices, and differential rates of urbanization and religious influences.'[38]

Japan was found by Hofstede's research to be extremely high by both Asian and world standards in masculinity and uncertainty avoidance, close to the Asian average (and therefore above the world average) on long-term orientation, above

---

[xix] Indian, Chairman and family member, family-owned business group, Indian MNC industrial goods manufacturer

the Asian average and close to the world average on individualism and close to both the world and the Asian average on power distance.

According to Hofstede, workplaces in high masculinity cultures will usually exhibit decisive and aggressive management, conflict resolution by letting the strongest win, reward based on equity, a preference for larger organizations, living to work, preference for more money over more leisure time, fewer working women in professional jobs, humanization of work by job content enrichment and a specialization in competitive manufacturing and bulk chemistry.[39] Of these characteristics, only living to work, few working women in professional jobs and humanization of work by job content enrichment (a possible description of the absence of a role culture in Japan) correspond to what either our interviewees or other sources have depicted as the Japanese work culture. Japan's consensual decision-making, its avoidance of overt conflict, reward based on seniority and low value placed on economic motivations for work, all contrast with the predicted effect of high masculinity scores.

There is a greater correspondence with organizational behaviours predicted on the basis of high uncertainty avoidance and the Japanese business culture, although it is still far from one to one. Few changes of employer, long service, an emotional need for rules, an inner urge to work hard, being worse at invention and better at implementation, and motivation by security and esteem or belonging, all have a degree of fit, as does the need for precision with the Japanese emphasis on detail; however, a predicted need for formalization seems to be contradicted by a culture in which procedural manuals are thin and rarely consulted and there are no firm boundaries around what people do: 'When I joined Matsui, I didn't know whether I would be a marketer or a finance guy.'[xx] 'Ours is not a silo culture.'[xxi] Similarly, the *ringi* system, which allows non-specialists to make suggestions about any aspect of the business, sits ill with a predicted 'belief in experts and technical solutions'.

Schwartz's values dimensions

Schwartz (1994) put forward a set of seven 'new' cultural values based on a survey of teachers and students in nearly 50 countries. These seven values were conservatism, affective autonomy, intellectual autonomy, hierarchy, mastery, egalitarian commitment and harmony. Conservatism included values primarily concerned with security, conformity and tradition; affective autonomy emphasized stimulation and hedonism; intellectual autonomy placed an emphasis on self-direction; hierarchy stressed the legitimacy of hierarchical role and resource allocation;

[xx] Japanese, Audit, Venture Capital
[xxi] Japanese, Operations Management, Japanese Manufacturer

mastery accentuated active mastery of the social environment through self-assertion; egalitarian commitment emphasized the transcendence of selfish interests in favour of others' welfare; harmony laid emphasis on harmony with nature.[40] These dimensions have been found to predict cultural differences in locus of control, the sources of guidance that managers rely on[41] and capital structure.[42]

Schwartz further condensed these seven value types into two broad cultural dimensions, affective and intellectual autonomy versus conservatism and hierarchy and mastery versus egalitarian commitment and harmony with nature. The autonomy-conservatism dimension focused on the extent to which society views the individual as an autonomous entity or as embedded in a social group. Conservatism occurs in societies where values such as harmony and propriety in person-to-group relations are favoured. Values such as moderation, social order, security, tradition and the reciprocation of favours are seen as crucial in conservative societies. Great importance is placed on the maintenance of the status quo. Also important is the maintenance of harmonious relationships not only within the group but also within society. On conservatism, the scores for the four of our sample countries included in Schwartz's study were China 3.97 out of 5 (*HKSAR* 4.04) Japan 3.87, Singapore 4.38 and Taiwan 4.38. These can be compared with a score of 3.90 for the USA.

Possibly the only surprise in these conservatism scores and the only score that conflicts with our findings on business culture is the low score for Japan – lower even than the USA's. Since the fieldwork for Schwartz (1994) took place in the early 1990s, the score may, however, reflect the fact that Japan had entered the start of its long recession and possibly the need for change, which was reported in our study, was beginning to be felt.

The second culture-level dimension contrasted mastery and hierarchy with egalitarian commitment and harmony. This dimension examined whose interests within society take precedence, those of the individual or those of the group. Mastery encompassed values such as being independent, ambitious, successful and choosing one's own goals. Hierarchy reflected wealth, social power and authority; it was concerned with the use of power to promote individual versus group interests. The scores on mastery for the four of our sample countries included in Schwartz's study were 4.73 for China (4.18 *HKSAR*), 4.27 Japan, 3.93 Singapore and 4.11 Taiwan. The USA scored 4.34.

On the mastery scores it is China's that surprise and are somewhat inconsistent with the country's low score on individualism in Hofstede (1981), although there is a correspondence with the views on the young in our study of China's business culture. Once again, the country's transitional economic situation may be reflected in this score.

Research has established links between 22 countries' scores on conservatism, mastery and business financing. Chui et al. (2002) found from data on 5591 firms that firms in countries with high scores on conservatism used less debt in their

224   7

INTRODUCTION • THE BUSINESS CULTURES OF FIVE ASIAN COUNTRIES • ANALYSING ASIAN BUSINESS CULTURES
• OWNERSHIP, FINANCING AND GOVERNANCE • ORGANIZATION AND MANAGEMENT • BUSINESS STRATEGY •

capital structures. The explanation was that conservatism leads to placing greater importance on harmonious working relationships and social harmony, preserving public image, and security, conformity and tradition. Chui et al. (2002) also found that managers in countries with high scores on mastery tended to use less debt financing; this was because they placed more emphasis on control and individual success.[43] For the Asian countries in the Chui et al. (2000) sample the pattern was as shown in Table 7.1, with the figures for the USA given for comparison.

The results for individual countries display some discrepancies from the broad theory – for example, Hong Kong, with a higher score on Conservatism than Japan's, had a lower debt ratio. However, there is some correspondence in the rankings, as shown in Table 7.2. This is particularly so if the rankings omit Japan, whose score on Conservatism in the original Schwartz results may be anomalous.

Schwartz and Sagiv (1995) delineated another set of values, this time of four higher-order cultural values, arrayed as two sets of opposing dimensions. The

Table 7.1 **Corporate debt ratios of four Asian countries and the USA compared with their scores on conservatism and mastery**

Country	Mean corporate debt ratio	Conservatism	Mastery
China	0.42	3.97	4.73
HKSAR	0.48	4.04	4.18
Japan	0.61	3.87	4.27
Singapore	0.49	4.38	3.93
Taiwan	0.42	4.31	4.11
USA	0.47	3.90	4.34

Source: Based on Chui, A.C.W., Kwok, C.C.Y. and Lloyd, A.E. (2002) 'The determination of capital structure: Is national culture a missing piece to the puzzle?' *Journal of International Business Studies*, 33(1): 99–128.

Table 7.2 **Corporate debt ratio rankings of four Asian countries and the USA compared with their rankings on conservatism and mastery**

	Mean corporate debt ratio ranking	Conservatism	Mastery (reverse ranked)
China	4/5	4	5
HKSAR	2	3	3
Singapore	1	1	1
Taiwan	4/5	2	2
USA	3	5	4

Source: Based on Chui, A.C.W., Kwok, C.C.Y. and Lloyd, A.E. (2002) 'The determination of capital structure: Is national culture a missing piece to the puzzle?' *Journal of International Business Studies*, 33(1): 99–128.

first set opposed self-enhancement and self-transcendence. This set is conceptually similar to individualism-collectivism, although in accordance with recent research, self-enhancement and self-transcendence were treated as separate dimensions. Self-enhancement (individualism) emphasizes the pursuit of one's own success. Individuals are independent, autonomous entities, capable of directing their own future. Self-enhancement is measured with values such as independence, choosing one's own goals and capability. Self-transcendence (collectivism) emphasizes the embeddedness of the individual, and thus socio-centric rather than egocentric values. Self-transcendence is measured with values such as social order, belonging and social recognition.[44] Research found the USA higher than Hong Kong Chinese on self-enhancement, and the Hong Kong Chinese higher than the USA on self-transcendence.[45]

On measures of self-transcendence, self-enhancement, conservation and openness to change, Chia et al. (2007) found that China had the same values orientation as Hong Kong and South Korea and had two differences in values from Taiwan (on self-transcendence and openness to change).[46]

The Chinese Values Surveys

In the 1980s, Michael Bond undertook a study of 21 cultures called the Chinese Values Survey (CVS), which identified two variables that may be particularly relevant to Asian culture. One was social integration versus cultural inwardness: social integration refers to pro-social virtues that enhance cohesiveness with others in general – the factor captures 'a decidedly Chinese focus on harmony in interpersonal relations'; cultural inwardness, in contrast, refers to loyalty to more narrowly defined groups (family, culture) along with their defining habits and customs. Social integration involves the sense of valued tradition itself. According to Bond (1988) this dimension is 'invisible to Westerners, constrained as they are by their individualistic cultural agendas'.[47] The second factor was reputation versus social morality. Reputation is concerned with establishing or maintaining one's standing in society – it is related to the domain of social power; social morality, in contrast, reflects a principled approach to life – it is related to domains of maturity and perhaps restrictive conformity. Results on these factors for the Social integration (+) / Cultural inwardness (–) dimension showed Japan as strongly positive at 4.97, Singapore and Hong Kong (standing in for China) slightly less so at 3.09 and 2.53 respectively and India in negative territory at −1.83.

In these findings, the contrast between India and the other Asian countries on social integration-cultural inwardness calls for comment, corresponding as it does with the divide between Asian countries with a Confucian heritage and the one in this sample without it. The values characterizing the societies of East

Asia may not really match the South Asian context. As Sen (1999) pointed out, ancient Indian traditions and values contrast those of the Sinitic societies to the East.[48] Other writers have referred to the narrow bounds of Indian familism: by comparison with other Asians, Indians appear to be culturally inclined more to a narrow sense of self, a factor that can strongly influence business behaviour.[49] On the second factor, all the Asian countries were shown as high in social morality – that is, as being more influenced by principles than maintaining one's standing in society, whereas the USA, for instance, showed the opposite result. (India's score was −2.72, Japan's −1.50, Singapore's −1.68, Hong Kong's −2.47 and the USA's 1.20, where a positive score indicated a higher value placed on reputation and a negative score a higher value attached to social morality.) These findings are intriguingly different, not only from the emphasis by interviewees in all five countries of the present study on 'maintaining one's standing' in business society but also from the conventional understanding of the meaning of collectivism. It is beyond the scope of this book to explore the possible reconciliation of these findings, except to note that in relation to Japan, Macintyre (1990) argued that the Western distinction between society and the self is meaningless, an argument that carries the implication that the distinction between 'maintaining one's standing in society' and a 'principled approach to life' would also be meaningless.[50]

The Chinese Values Survey (CVS) found no factor that correlated with Hofstede's Uncertainty Avoidance. According to Lowe (2003),

> The CVS showed that Truth and its concomitant scientific rationalism are an intrinsic and tacit cultural element in the West and in most of the rest of the world, but not in China and East Asia. Uncertainty Avoidance (a search for Truth in uncertain contexts) can no longer be regarded as a universal etic value dimension since it has been shown to be irrelevant for the Chinese and East Asians, who constitute nearly one fifth of the world's population and who, by their orientation toward Virtue respond to the uncertain environment differently from the rest of mankind.[51]

The World Values Surveys

The World Values Surveys of people in 62 countries (Fourth Wave) found that 2 dimensions explained more than 70 per cent of the cross-national variance in a factor analysis of 10 indicators; each of these dimensions was strongly correlated with scores of other important orientations. The two dimensions were traditional/secular-rational values and survival/self-expression values. According to the researchers,

> The traditional/secular-rational values dimension reflects the contrast between societies in which religion is very important and those in which it is not. A wide range of other orientations are closely linked with this dimension. Societies near the traditional pole emphasize the importance of parent-child ties and deference to authority, along with absolute standards and traditional family values, and reject divorce, abortion, euthanasia and suicide. These societies have high levels of national pride, and a nationalistic outlook. Societies with secular-rational values have the opposite preferences on all of these topics.

In relation to survival/self-expression, the researchers stated

> A central component of this emerging dimension involves the polarization between Materialist and Postmaterialist values, reflecting a cultural shift that is emerging among generations who have grown up taking survival for granted. Self-expression values give high priority to environmental protection, tolerance of diversity and rising demands for participation in decision making in economic and political life. These values also reflect mass polarization over tolerance of outgroups, including foreigners, gays and lesbians and gender equality. The shift from survival values to self-expression values also includes a shift in child-rearing values, from emphasis on hard work toward emphasis on imagination and tolerance as important values to teach a child. And it goes with a rising sense of subjective well-being that is conducive to an atmosphere of tolerance, trust and political moderation. Finally, societies that rank high on self-expression values also tend to rank high on interpersonal trust.

On these dimensions, the surveys found that China, Japan and Taiwan were all high in secular-rational values and about the mid-point in survival/self-expression values. India, in contrast, was below the mid-point on secular-rational/traditional values and similarly on survival/self-expression values.[52] A selection of findings from the surveys is shown in Table 7.3.

The changes reported in Table 7.3 for **India** between 1990 and 2001 seem to suggest that the country might have been moving rather rapidly through some value changes linked to modernization, an implication that would correspond with the views expressed by some interviewees in our own research. A drop in the importance of family and religion, and an increase in the importance of work, all point to this conclusion; equally an increase in prejudice and decrease in trust are consistent with the effects of the early stages of exposure to urbanization and alienation. The results for **China** are harder to interpret. Relative stability in the importance of family (despite a substantial drop in unconditional respect for parents), friends and prejudice suggest a smaller shift towards modern values than

Table 7.3 **Shifts in values in China, India and USA found by the World Values Surveys between 1990 and 2001 (USA 1999) (Percentage agreeing)**

	China (1990)	China (2001)	India (1990)	India (2001)	USA (1990)	USA (1999)
Family very important	61	61	84	77	94	92
Friends very important	21	21	34	30	58	54
Work very important	57	64	83	86	59	62
Religion very important	2	1	53	49	55	53
Respect and love for parents regardless	85	75	86	84	76	74
Races would not like as neighbours – none mentioned	87	88	62	65	92	92
Most people can be trusted (versus 'You can't be too careful')	57	60	38	35	45	52

Source: Based on European Values Study Group and World Values Survey Association (2006) *European and World Values Surveys Four-Wave Integrated Data File 1981–2004* v.20060423.

in India's case. The increase in the importance of work, however, does imply a modernization of values, as does an increase in generalized trust, which is consistent with China's documented increase in urbanization between 1990 and 2001. Alternative interpretations here are that China's lower scores on the importance of family and friends and higher scores on generalized trust compared with India's reflect a more 'advanced' stage of modernization than India's at the start of the period, that is, in 1990. This would correspond to the earlier date for China in comparison with India for the start of economic liberalization (China 1978, India 1990). Similarly, China's lower score on 'prejudice' compared with India's may reflect a more tolerant set of cultural values or alternatively the lower exposure of China's people to individuals from other 'races', because its society is quite homogeneous while India's is diverse.

Critique

The limitations of dimensional approaches generally were noted in Chapter 1. Dichotomous individualism-collectivism research in particular has been widely criticized. Most influential was the call by Oyserman et al. (2002) for a rethink on individualism and collectivism, based on findings that European Americans were not more individualistic than African Americans or Latinos, and not less collectivistic than Japanese or Koreans, while among Asians, only the Chinese showed large effects, being both less individualistic and more collectivistic. Commenting on these and other limitations of the individualism-collectivism model of culture, Oyserman et al. (2002) wrote, 'Concern is warranted; but it is clear that, depending on situational requirements, both individualism- and collectivism-focused strategies are adaptive; thus, it is likely that human minds have adapted to think both ways.'[53]

More recent dimensional research into values has been criticized as perhaps adding little to our overall understanding of culture. A 2005 review of the literature on culture and international business, after describing the leadership-culture research of House[54] (House et al. 2002) and the GLOBE project, concluded,

> " Despite the use of different items to identify cultural dimensions, the results are consistent with previous results and most of the cultural dimensions identified are related conceptually and correlated empirically with Hofstede's dimensions. Assertiveness Orientation and Gender Egalitarianism are related to Hofstede's construct of Masculinity-Femininity, Institutional Collectivism and Family Collectivism to Individualism-Collectivism, Power Distance and Uncertainty Avoidance to the two Hofstede dimensions with the same labels, and Future Orientation to Long-term Orientation.

Two 'new' dimensions emerged from the research of House et al. (2004): Performance Orientation, which 'seems conceptually related to McClelland's (1953)[55] concept of need for achievement' and Humane Orientation, which 'seems conceptually related to the Human nature is Good vs Bad dimension of Kluckhohn and Strodtbeck (1961)[56]'. This review by Leung et al. (2005) speculated that Performance Orientation and Humane Orientation may be negatively related to close supervision. However, in the view of the present author, in Asia the widespread cultural preference for close control may imply that close supervision is unrelated to whether human nature is perceived as good or bad.[57]

More recently, commenting on a dispute between Hofstede and the researchers from the GLOBE project, Smith (2006) took a balanced view: 'The legacy of Hofstede's work has been that almost all subsequent contributors to the field accept that national culture may be operationalized by aggregating the self-descriptive responses obtained from individuals drawn from a series of different national samples. ... The time-series evidence linking economic growth with change in national values is impressive, but ... such evidence does not preclude the reciprocal contribution of other aspects of culture to economic growth,' and added, 'The viability of nation-level analyses is reinforced.'[58]

From a different point of view, that of the relevance of culture to economic behaviour, Peerenboom (2002) commented, 'The rise of rational choice theories and institutional explanations of behavior have, in some cases, pushed cultural factors to the margins if not completely out of the picture.' However, Peerenboom (2002) concluded, 'It would be a mistake in the opposite direction to totally discount cultural factors and values. At the end of the day, values do matter, though how much, when, which ones, and why all require detailed context-specific studies.'[59]

In the specific context of Asia, doubts have been raised whether the range of variables included in the globally applied dimensional approaches is sufficient. For example, according to Yashimura and Anderson (1997), the behaviour of people from **Japan** is shaped by four variables not so important elsewhere: context, learning from models, avoiding embarrassment and a focus on process. 'Context' links to the high-context/low-context communication model of culture; 'avoiding embarrassment' presumably links to 'face'; but the other two are 'outside of all current cross-cultural models'. Yashimura and Anderson (1997) added that the Japanese defined situations differently from people from other cultures and that this explained much that seemed strange to outside observers of their culture.[60]

The judgements set out in this section suggest that dimensional analyses of culture can be useful. Nevertheless, calls for more context-specific, nuanced, process-oriented and richly descriptive analyses continue, rightly, to be heard.

Conclusion

This chapter has outlined a number of dimensional approaches to societal culture and where possible compared their predictions with the findings of our research into Asian business cultures and other researchers' findings on Asian business behaviour. We have identified both consistencies and inconsistencies. While it could be argued that the inconsistencies imply errors and weaknesses in our findings, we would suggest that the case is not so simple. Not only have criticisms of dimensional approaches been widespread, as noted in Chapter 1 and earlier in this chapter, but logic would also suggest that however valid a set of dimensional descriptions, to use them to predict patterns of business behaviour in some detail is to over-simplify. Leung, Bond and Schwartz (1995) emphasized that there are only moderate links between values and specific behaviours.[61] Smith et al. (2002), arguing for the usefulness of the concept 'sources of guidance' commented as follows:

> " Focusing on sources of guidance is expected to provide a more precise basis than do generalized measures of values for understanding the behaviors that prevail within different cultures. Values are strongly predictive of reliance on those sources of guidance that are relevant to vertical relationships within organizations. However, values are less successful in predicting reliance on peers and on more tacit sources of guidance. Explaining national differences in these neglected aspects of organizational processes will require greater sensitivity to the culture-specific contexts within which they occur.[62]

While we believe that the dimensional approaches have greatly advanced the study of comparative culture and business systems, we do concur in the view that 'values' approaches have limitations. Specifically, we argue that in some contexts business cultures, which are in part the mentally embedded observations by the members of a business community of patterns of business behaviour, are rather likely to provide better predictions.

References

[1] Very, P., Lubatkin, M. and Calori, R. (1998) 'A cross-national assessment of acculturative stress in recent European mergers', in Cardel, M.G., Soderberg, A.M. and Torp, J.E. (eds) *Cultural Dimensions of International Mergers and Acquisitions*, Berlin: Walter de Gruyter.

[2] Kroeber, A.L. and Kluckhohn, C. (1952) *Culture: A Critical Review of Concepts and Definitions*, Cambridge, MA: Harvard University Press.

[3] Thompson, A.G. (1996) 'Compliance with agreements in cross-cultural transactions: Some analytical issues', *Journal of International Business Studies*, 27(2): 375–90.

[4] Whitley, R. (1992) *Business Systems in East Asia: Firms, Markets, and Societies*, London: Sage.

[5] Redding, G. (2004) 'The Capitalist business system of China and its rationale', *Asia Pacific Journal of Management*, 19: 2–3.

[6] Scott, W.R. (1995 and 2001) *Institutions and Organizations*, Thousand Oaks, CA: Sage.

[7] Fram, E.H. and Reid, D.M. (2005) 'Consumer behavior in China: An exploratory study of two cities', *Journal of Asia-Pacific Business*, 5(4): 25–42.

[8] Peng, M.W. and Heath, P.S. (1996) 'The growth of the firm in planned economies in transition: Institutions, organizations, and strategic choice', *Academy of Management Review*, 21: 492–528.

[9] Chen, M. (2001) *Inside Chinese Business*, Boston, MA: Harvard Business School Press.

[10] Ahlstrom, D. and Bruton, G. (2002) 'An institutional perspective on the role of culture in shaping strategic actions by technology focused entrepreneurial firms in China', *Entrepreneurship Theory and Practice*, 26(4): 53–69.

[11] Budhwar, P.S. (2003) 'Culture and management in India', in Warner, M. (ed.) *Culture and Management in Asia*, London: Routledge Curzon.

[12] Hofstede, G. (1981) *Cultures and Organizations: Software of the Mind*, London: Harper Collins.

[13] Schwartz, S.H. (1994) 'Beyond individualism/collectivism: New cultural dimensions of values', in Kim, U., Triandis, H.C., Kagitcibasi, C., Choi, S.-C. and Yoon, G. (eds) *Individualism and Collectivism: Theory, Method and Applications*, Newbury Park, CA: Sage.

[14] Bond, M.H. (1988) 'Finding universal dimensions of individual variation in multicultural studies of values: The Rokeach and Chinese value surveys', *Journal of Personality and Social Psychology*, 55(6): 1009–15.

[15] Inglehart, R. and Baker, W. (2000) 'Modernization, cultural change and the persistence of traditional values', *American Sociological Review*, 65: 19–51.

[16] Rokeach, M. (1973) *The Nature of Human Values*, New York: Free Press.

[17] Kluckhohn, F.R. and Strodtbeck, F.L. (1961) *Variations in Value Orientation*, Evanston, IL: Row Peterson.

[18] Markus, H.R., Kitayama, S. and Heiman, R. (1997) 'Culture and "basic" psychological principles', in Higgins, E.T. and Kruglanski, A.W. (eds) *Social Psychology: Handbook of Basic Principles*, New York: Guilford.

[19] Schwartz, S.H. (1994) 'Beyond individualism/collectivism: New cultural dimensions of values', in Kim, U., Triandis, H.C., Kagitcibasi, C., Choi, S.-C. and Yoon, G. (eds.) *Individualism and Collectivism: Theory, Method and Applications*, Newbury Park, CA: Sage.

[20] Tinsley, C. and Pillutia, M.M. (1998) 'Negotiating in the United States and Hong Kong', *Journal of International Business Studies*, 29: 711–27. (Internal references are omitted).

[21] Malinowski, B. (1944) *A Scientific Theory of Culture and Other Essays*, Chapel Hill, NC: University of North Carolina.

²² Hofstede, G. (1981) *Cultures and Organizations: Software of the Mind*, London: Harper Collins.

²³ Hofstede, G. and Hofstede, G.J. (2004) *Cultures and Organizations: Software of the Mind*, 2nd edition, New York: McGraw Hill.

²⁴ Church, A.T. (2000) 'Culture and personality: Toward an integrated cultural trait psychology', *Journal of Personality*, **69**: 651–703.

²⁵ Bond, M.H. (1988) 'Finding universal dimensions of individual variation in multicultural studies of values: The Rokeach and Chinese value surveys', *Journal of Personality and Social Psychology*, **55**(6): 1009–15.

²⁶ Hofstede, G. (2007) 'Asian management in the 21st century', *Asia Pacific Journal of Management*, **24**: 411–20.

²⁷ Gong, W., Li, Z.G. and Stump, R.L. (2007) 'Global internet use and access: Cultural considerations', *Asia Pacific Journal of Marketing and Logistics*, **19**(1): 57–74.

²⁸ Murphy, B. and Wang, R. (2006) 'An evaluation of stakeholder relationship marketing in China', *Asia Pacific Journal of Marketing and Logistics*, **18**(1) 17–18.

²⁹ *The McKinsey Quarterly Online*, 3 November 2007.

³⁰ Leong, J.C.T., Bond, M.H. and Fu, P.P. (2007) 'Perceived effectiveness of influence strategies among Hong Kong managers', *Journal of Asia Pacific Management*, **24**(1): 75–96.

³¹ Lam, K., Li, J. and Qian, G. (2001) 'Does culture affect behavior and performance of firms? The case of joint ventures in China', *Journal of International Business Studies*, **32**(1): 115–32.

³² Hofstede, G. and Hofstede, G.J. (2004) *Cultures and Organizations: Software of the Mind*, 2nd edition, New York: McGraw Hill.

³³ Farh, J.-L., Earley, P.C. and Lin, S.-C. (1997) 'Impetus for action: A cultural analysis of justice and organizational citizenship behavior in Chinese society', *Administrative Science Quarterly*, **42**: 421–44.

³⁴ Goodall, K., Li, N. and Warner, M. (2007) 'Expatriate managers in China: The influence of Chinese culture on cross-cultural management', *Working Paper Series 01/2007*, Cambridge: Judge Business School.

³⁵ Lu Le (2003) 'Influences of Confucianism [and Taoism] on the market economy of China', in Alon, I. and Shenkar, O. (eds) *Chinese Culture, Organizational Behavior and International Business Management*, Westport, CT: Praeger.

³⁶ Ralston, D., Egri, C.P., Stewart, S., Terpstra, R.H. and Kai-Cheng, Y. (1999) 'Doing business in the 21st century with the new generation of Chinese managers: A study of generational shifts in work values in China', *Journal of International Business Studies*, **30**(2): 415–27.

³⁷ Hofstede, G. and Hofstede, G.J. (2004) *Cultures and Organizations: Software of the Mind*, 2nd edition, New York: McGraw Hill.

³⁸ Chaudhuri, H.R. and Majumdar, S. (2006) 'Of diamonds and desires: Understanding conspicuous consumption from a contemporary marketing perspective', *Academy of Marketing Science Review*, **11**, URL:http://www.amsreview.org.articles.chaudhuri09-2006.pdf.

³⁹ Hofstede, G. and Hofstede, G.J. (2004) *Cultures and Organizations: Software of the Mind*, 2nd edition, New York: McGraw Hill.

⁴⁰ Schwartz, S.H. (1994) 'Beyond individualism/collectivism: New cultural dimensions of values', in Kim, U., Triandis, H.C., Kagitcibasi, C., Choi, S.-C. and Yoon, G. (eds.) *Individualism and Collectivism: Theory, Method and Applications*, Newbury Park, CA: Sage.

⁴¹ Smith, P.B., Peterson, M.F. and Schwartz, S.H. (2002) 'Cultural values, sources of guidance, and their relevance to managerial behavior', *Journal of Cross-Cultural Psychology*, **33**(2): 188–208.

⁴² Chui, A.C.W., Kwok, C.C.Y. and Lloyd, A.E. (2002) 'The determination of capital structure: Is national culture a missing piece to the puzzle?' *Journal of International Business Studies*, **33**(1): 99–128.

⁴³ Ibid.

⁴⁴ Schwartz, S.H. and Sagiv, L. (1995) 'Identifying culture-specifics in the content and structure of values', *Journal of Cross-Cultural Psychology*, **26**(1): 92–116.

⁴⁵ Tinsley and Pillutia, M.M. (1998) 'Negotiating in the United States and Hong Kong', *Journal of International Business Studies*, **29**: 711–27. (Internal references are omitted).

⁴⁶ Chia, H.-B., Egri, C.P., Ralston, D.A., Fu, P.P., Kuo, M.-H. C., Lee, C.H., Li, Y. and Moon, Y.-L. (2007) 'Four tigers and the dragon: Values differences, similarities, and consensus', *Asia-Pacific Journal of Management*, **24**: 305–20.

⁴⁷ Bond, M.H. (1988) 'Finding universal dimensions of individual variation in multicultural studies of values: The Rokeach and Chinese value surveys', *Journal of Personality and Social Psychology*, **55**(6): 1009–15.

[48] Sen, A. (1999) *Development as Freedom*, New York: Anchor.

[49] Gupta, R.K. (2002) *Towards the Optimal Organisation: Integrating Indian Culture and Management*, New Delhi: Excel Books.

[50] Macintyre, A. (1990) 'Individual and social morality in Japan and the United States: Rival conceptions of the self', *Philosophy East and West*, **40**(4): 489–97.

[51] Lowe, S. (2003) 'Chinese culture and management theory', in Alon, I. and Shenker, O. (eds) *Chinese Culture, Organizational Behavior and International Business Management*, Westport, CA: Praeger.

[52] Inglehart, R. and Baker, W. (2000) 'Modernization, cultural change and the persistence of traditional values', *American Sociological Review*, **65**: 19–51.

[53] Oyserman, D., Coon, H.M. and Kemmelmeier, M. (2002) 'Rethinking individualism and collectivism: Evaluation of theoretical assumptions and meta-analyses', *Psychological Bulletin*, **128**(1): 3–72.

[54] House, R.J., Javidan, M., Hanges, P.J. and Dorfman, P.W. (2002) 'Understanding cultures and implicit leadership theories across the globe: An introduction to project GLOBE', *Journal of World Business*, **37**(1): 3–10.

[55] McClelland, D. (1953) *The Achievement Motive*, New York: Appleton Century Crofts.

[56] Kluckhohn, F.R. and Strodtbeck, F.L. (1961) *Variations in Value Orientation*, Evanston, IL: Row Peterson.

[57] Leung, K., Bhagat, R.S., Buchan, N.R., Erez, M. and Gibson, C.B. (2005) 'Culture and international business: Recent advances and their implications for future research', *Journal of International Business Studies*, **36**(4): 357–78.

[58] Smith, P.B. (2006) 'When elephants fight, the grass gets trampled: The GLOBE and Hofstede projects', *Journal of International Business Studies*, **37**(6): 915–21.

[59] Peerenboom, R. (2002) 'China's Long March toward the rule of law', Boston, MA: Cambridge University Press.

[60] Yashimura, N. and Anderson, P. (1997) *Inside the Kaisha: Demystifying Japanese Business Behavior*, Boston, MA: Harvard Business School Press.

[61] Leung, K., Bond, M.H. and Schwartz, S. (1995) 'How to explain cross-cultural differences: Values, valences, and expectancies', *Asian Journal of Psychology*, **1**: 70–5.

[62] Smith, P.B. (2006) 'When elephants fight, the grass gets trampled: The GLOBE and Hofstede projects', *Journal of International Business Studies*, **37**(6): 915–21.

234 7

INTRODUCTION • THE BUSINESS CULTURES OF FIVE ASIAN COUNTRIES • ANALYSING ASIAN BUSINESS CULTURES • OWNERSHIP, FINANCING AND GOVERNANCE • ORGANIZATION AND MANAGEMENT • BUSINESS STRATEGY •

8 societal cultures revisited

This chapter considers several aspects of the societal cultures of five Asian countries and their possible links to business cultures and business decisions. As explained at the start of Chapter 7, a societal culture is the social culture of a whole society.

Worldviews

A more nuanced approach to cultures than the dimensional analyses described in Chapter 7 is available through an understanding of world view. Scholars have emphasized some fundamental differences between Western and Asian worldviews, differences which impact on the thinking processes of people from these parts of the world.

In the words of Lowe (1998), 'Western logic is binary – predisposed to focusing on the measurable, bivalent terms of Truth and to ignoring the holistic greyness of plurivalent phenomena. ... This reduces phenomena to bivalent categories, one of which is privileged as "subject" and the other denigrated as "object".'[1] Within Western rationalism, truth is 'found' rather than made through socially constructed imagination. It is presumed to be found through factist rationalism and is universalistic and uniform rather than pluralistic and multiform. In practice, however, 'Both logical and factual Truth trade accuracy for the simplicity of a black-and-white bivalent "scorecard"'. The culture of **China**, in contrast, 'is oriented toward virtue rather than an absolute truth'. Action is not decided by identifying what is 'true' and proven, but by a consensus about what is acceptable and what 'we' can work with. Taoism involves a multivalued, fuzzy, 'shades of grey' and non-linear worldview that sees contradiction and paradox as normal, common sense and often experienced.[2]

One common theme is the wisdom of patience and deferred gratification. In a Taoist story of a farmer and his horse, a farmer's neighbours alternately condole with him (for instance, on the loss of his horse and an injury to his son) and congratulate him (for instance, on the return of his horse accompanied by six wild horses). The farmer's only reply each time is 'Maybe'. Chinese culture leads people to think in terms of effectiveness, emergence, unpredictability and wholeness. The focus is on the whole as a system of related and interdependent parts. For example, there is a saying, 'No egg is unbroken when a nest is overturned.' Relationality rather than the self, therefore, is the principal source of identity within the Chinese holistic worldview.[3] Taoism encourages an unscientific approach, lacking the use of precision, quantification, analysis, logic and norms. The best-known quotation by Lao Zi, the founder of Taoism, is this: 'The Way (Rule) that can be told of is not an Unvarying Way; the names that can be named are not unvarying names.'[4] In other words, nothing can be pinned down, because everything is changing.[5]

The worldview of **India**, however, different from China's because of its religious foundation, shares the characteristic of holism. De Riencourt (1961), an early analyst of both cultures, is worth quoting at length:

> " It must always be kept in mind that Indians, just as Chinese or other Asians, do not look upon the world as we Westerners have done since the Renaissance. Their world outlook, whatever it may be, is an *all-inclusive* one, a coherent picture of which no part is detachable without entailing the destruction of the rest. We tend to see science, philosophy, religion, ethics, literature and every other segment of human culture as separate, autonomous compartments independent of one another. The West has become culturally atomised and assumes this temporary historical condition to be a normal and permanent one. But India, like China, had gone through such a phase several centuries before Christ and had overcome it. And no more than China did India as a whole succumb to the dangerous lure of Western cultural atomism. It is therefore essential to keep in mind that, however regressive the cultural revolt of India against Western influence, the revolt was justified on a sound basis: it was an instinctive revolt that few Indians could rationalize intellectually, but that was essential for the psychological health of India, whose soul would have been destroyed utterly if Indians had given in without reservation. It was not only an effort to preserve or recover India's forgotten culture; it was an instinctive urge to retrieve a monistic, all-inclusive *Weltanschauung* [worldview] which they could not discover in Western culture.

Beyond this profound difference from a Western worldview, however, India and China diverge. 'The basic cultural orientation of India is rooted in Buddhism, Vedantic and Yogic psychology, derivative epic and Pauranic literature. The Indian value system is set within the framework of transcendent ideology (such as "Chitta-shuddhi" or purification of the mind; self-discipline and self-restraint; renunciation and detachment).'[6] In contrast, the Chinese worldview is nonmystical, 'humanistic, ethical, sociological and historical'. 'The greatest psychological characteristic of the Chinese is their close relationship with the earth and the molding of their energy on the normal pattern of nature.'[7]

What are the implications of these similar and yet different Asian worldviews for their business cultures? This potentially vast topic is too large for a full discussion here, and, consistently with the lack of attention given to business cultures has not been widely considered elsewhere, but a few points can be noted. Since Weber's (1947) attribution of America's economic dynamism to the Protestant work ethic,[8] it has been commonplace to link religion or widely accepted social philosophy to economic performance. Weber himself, in a view now often discredited, attributed the low economic development of his time in the countries influenced by Confucian philosophy to that philosophy's hierarchical values. Others have commented on the disdain for wealth and the low status of merchants, the predecessors of today's business executives, in traditional Confucian societies.

Religion, or in several cases its absence, was an aspect of worldview linked to business culture in our interviewees' perceptions. In one of the five focal countries, India, the religion-based worldview was seen as significant for its business culture and so for business. In China, including Hong Kong, the absence of religion was seen as important for morality and work attitudes. In Japan, the historical residues of religion played a part, but more recently the society's secularism left a gap filled by loyalty to the corporation.

In **India,** our research found, an accommodation was accepted between what to the West are separate worlds. A software engineer in Hyderabad would telephone to alter the date of a job interview once he or she had a reading of his or her horoscope for the interview date. In Bangalore, a software designer would perform a puja (act of worship) to his or her computer. From ice cream stalls to multi-storey office blocks, the opening ceremonies for new business premises were conducted by a priest.[i] Popular Hinduism recognizes multiple gods and has no written doctrine. As one interviewee explained,

> This makes for flexibility but also means there are no rules. The flexibility allows subordinates to 'manage' their bosses. Because the caste system, which is based in Hinduism, means that people are always playing social roles, always doing drama, never asserting their own personality, individuals can bend with the wind, fit in and suppress their own opinions.[ii]

More generally, reconciling their religion with business is not problematic. 'Broadly speaking, for Indian society the cultural framework is "Hinduism", which provides a comprehensive philosophy rather than "merely" a religion; ... it is embedded in an all-encompassing worldview. Within this worldview, commerce, trade,

---

[i] India, Expatriate, CEO MNC, internet-based business services
[ii] Indian, Economist, Former Entrepreneur, Senior Academic

and other sources of accumulating wealth are recognized as being in conformity with the religious doctrines.'[9]

Thomas and Philip (1994), however, contended that religion was a major determinant of organizational functioning in India. Although India was a secular country without an official state religion, 'Indians have always been deeply spiritual and religion plays an important role in everyday life.' Roughly 85 per cent of the population was Hindu, and 10 per cent Moslem. The other major religions of the country included Christianity, Sikhism, Jainism, Zoroastrianism, Buddhism and Judaism. One example of the consequences for business of India's religious diversity and spiritualism was the large number of public holidays, many with dates that could not be determined until shortly beforehand.

> " In addition to New Year's Day, Republic Day (January 26), Independence Day (August 15), Mahatma Gandhi's birthday (October 2), and Christmas Day, there are forty-nine other national, religious, and regional holidays. Since most Indian festivals are based on lunar or religious calendars, the dates of their occurrence vary from year to year. While not all holidays are observed nationally, a certain number are declared central government holidays at the beginning of each year. Others may only be observed by a particular religious community. The governments of each state also announce their own holiday lists.[10]

This analysis, however, relates only to the superficial aspects of 'organizational functioning'. As Sen (2005) explained, at a deeper level,

> " Despite the veritable flood of religious practices in India, there is also a resilient undercurrent of conviction across the country that religious beliefs, while personally significant, are socially unimportant and should be politically inconsequential. Ignoring the importance – and reach – of this underlying conviction has the effect of systematically overestimating the role of religion in Indian society.[11]

In **China**, including *Hong Kong*, traditional values were largely based on Confucianism, which is a social philosophy rather than a religion. In this regard, the following comparisons with the West were made: 'Western capitalism is based on values derived from religion. The Chinese have no such underpinning';[iii] 'China is unlike the West, with its link between the Protestant ethic and business.'[iv] Some interviewees believed, moreover, that the influence even of Confucianism was limited: 'Confucianism still influences the private world but is set aside in the business world.'[v] The absence of a religious underpinning for business in China had both

---

[iii] Mainland Chinese, Partner, International Accounting Firm
[iv] China, Expatriate, Consultant, International Management Consultancy
[v] Mainland Chinese, Senior Manager, Human Resource Management, Chinese SOE (state-owned enterprise)

positive and negative effects: 'For development, Chinese lack of democracy and religion are both pluses.'[vi] On the other hand, 'The downside of "no religion" could be no morality.'[vii] At the start of the 21st century, there was evidence of a resurgence of religious or quasi-religious activity across China even in the cities where Party ideology was traditionally stronger. This Chinese resurgence encompassed ancient folk religions and ancestor worship, along with the organized religions of Buddhism, Taoism, Islam (among ethnic minorities) and, most strikingly, given its foreign origins and relatively short history in China, Christianity. Whether a religious resurgence would have much impact on Chinese business culture was, however, doubtful. Au and Tse (2001) found that Chinese managers of SMEs (small and medium-sized enterprises) who had religious beliefs were not necessarily more ethical than those who did not.[12]

In post-Confucian societies such as *Hong Kong*, according to Chan and Lee (1995) there was a revival of folk beliefs and even superstitions. At the same time there took place a progressive extension of the sphere of scientific reason that came with the onset of modernity. 'Ritualistic practices still constitute a great part of the spiritual life of the populace. These range from the age-old custom of ancestral-worship, the observing of festivals and the lunar year cycle, all the way to mundane prohibitions or taboos that articulate superstition within the framework of everyday life.' While beliefs of this kind could influence business practice, particularly in the timing of events according to astrological predictions, people from Asian cultures generally found little difficulty in reconciling them with modern business approaches.[13]

As in India, one version of the impact of religion in **Japan** emphasized the link between having multiple gods (actually, in Japan's case, multiple religions) and flexibility.

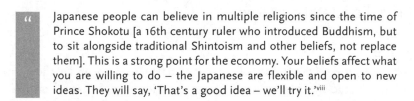

> Japanese people can believe in multiple religions since the time of Prince Shokotu [a 16th century ruler who introduced Buddhism, but to sit alongside traditional Shintoism and other beliefs, not replace them]. This is a strong point for the economy. Your beliefs affect what you are willing to do – the Japanese are flexible and open to new ideas. They will say, 'That's a good idea – we'll try it.'[viii]

A contrasting but not conflicting view was that the Japanese had no belief in any religion and so elevated their employer to a godlike status.

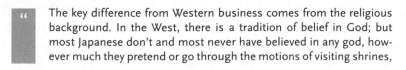

> The key difference from Western business comes from the religious background. In the West, there is a tradition of belief in God; but most Japanese don't and most never have believed in any god, however much they pretend or go through the motions of visiting shrines,

---

[vi] China, Expatriate, General Manager, Energy MNC (multi-national company)
[vii] Ibid.
[viii] Japanese, Finance and Accounting, Banking

etc. Western people make a compact with God; we make a compact with our company, not a god, family or the nation.[ix]

(Of course, many Westerners will dispute this stereotype of Western people; but that may not be to deny some underlying truth in the statement so far as Japanese people are concerned.)

Japanese Confucianism, imported from China, during the 700 years when a military culture dominated in the country came to deviate from the original Confucianism of ancient China, which regarded *ko* (filial piety, or giving back to one's parents) as the most important concept. Japanese Confucianism instead stressed *chu* (loyalty to the dominator or superior). In combination with the tendency for people to bind themselves to their ascribed groups, this meant that for men primary loyalties were to their companies, while for women and children, it was to their homes and schools, respectively.[14]

We were not able to include in our research any country whose main religion was Islam, but some comments were made by interviewees who had worked in Malaysia, suggesting that religion was an important influence on the business culture there:

> Malay culture is strong through Islam – they are a brotherhood. A colleague expressed his link to his Malay colleagues in those terms – 'We went to the mosque together and now we are brothers.' Thus there is a religious basis for who is in their ingroup, who they 'do business' with. The Chinese in Malaysia also cling together – 'do business together' – because they are marginalized.[x]

Traditional societal cultures

Collectivism

The most conspicuous characteristic of the traditional societal cultures of the Asian countries in this study (and most others beside) is collectivism, but it takes different forms in different countries. For example, while the major similarity between Japanese and Indian 'selves' is that they 'are not individualized but familial', 'the major difference lies in the boundary of the familial self. The primary family is the common in-group for the Japanese as well as Indian, but their extensions beyond the family differ.'[15] Thus, while Japanese employees easily transferred their loyalties to their organizations, for Indians there was a permanent conflict between the demands of work and family – a conflict which, as Chapter 2 showed, was often resolved through businesses accommodating to the needs of the family.

[ix] Japanese Strategic Management, Business Services
[x] Singaporean Chinese, Asia Business Development Manager, International MNC, Energy

Although the nuclear family was increasingly evident in urban **India**, as late as 2002 Gupta wrote,

> In Indian society, with all its enormous heterogeneity, the pervasive dominance of the extended family ... is a constant. ... Languages use specific terms for highly complex kinship relationships. ... This is in contrast to American urban society where peer groups and various other extra familial social contexts assume an ever increasing importance vis a vis family relationships. [In India] individuals are used to the idea that their parents will choose their career path, their spouse, where they will live and so on.[16]

The American psychologist Roland, whose comments on the contrasting organizational behaviours of Indians and Japanese were mentioned in Chapter 5, noted,

> Occupational and other major life decisions are rarely left to the individual. ... The Indian self is one whose ego boundaries encompass others of the extended family. ... The Indian self develops to be deeply identified with family and *jati* [subcaste]. ... Relationships, to the Indian psyche, are usually far more important than issues.[17]

Collectivism in **Japan** worked differently, Roland (1988) concluded. Because Japanese non-inheriting sons had to find their human network elsewhere, they were less closely tied to their human group and their common ancestors than inheriting Japanese sons or most members of other Asian societies, such as the Chinese. However, Japanese culture provided alternatives through the institution of *iemoto*. This was a kind of apprenticeship or mentoring in which 'disciples' owed allegiance to a master: they also owed their master their art and skill and most of whatever they might acquire. The master in turn, owed the disciple livelihood, instruction, justice and social responsibility. 'This relationship and its characteristic ideas are not economic, nor militaristic nor religious. They can be applied to any field of endeavour, whether it be running a bean paste shop, an army or a university.' All ties in the *iemoto* were couched in pseudo-kinship terms. From this point of view, each *iemoto* could grow into a 'giant kinship establishment', with the closeness and inclusiveness of its interpersonal links but without the kinship limitations on its size.[18] For many modern Japanese, the 'giant kinship establishment' where they found their 'human network' was the organization they worked for.

Hierarchy

Our study showed hierarchy to be an important element in several Asian business cultures. Hierarchy was emphasized by both Chinese and Indian societal traditions, though the kinds of hierarchy differed between the two societies. In **China**, hierarchy and inequality applied to the relations between dyads such as father–son and husband–wife. In **India**, although such dyadic power imbalances were certainly widespread and culturally endorsed, hierarchy and inequality were particularly shown by the unequally placed caste groups. 'These inequalities have become persistent and resulted in equilibrium because of the organic linkages and interdependence of the different socio-economic groups. The psychology of the vast majority of Hindus is still fundamentally a caste psychology, whatever radical changes have affected their outward lives', the anthropologist R. Lannoy wrote in 1971.[19] As late as 2005, an obituary of R. K. Narayanan (the only Dalit President of India to that date) noted the tenacity of the caste system. As Narayanan put it in 1998, 'The march of society, of social change, has not been fast enough, nor fundamental enough, so far.'

Personal networks

As Chapters 2 and 3 demonstrated, personal networks are very important in most Asian business cultures. They also function more broadly in the social life of some Asian countries, especially those with a Chinese tradition. *Guanxi*, or the 'set of personal connections which an individual may draw upon to secure resources or advantage when doing business *or in the course of social life,* ... is an important asset for an individual'[20] (Present author's italics). Redding et al. (1993) interpreted *guanxi* to mean 'a network of personally defined reciprocal bonds',[21] while Tsui and Farh (1997) described it as 'interpersonal relationships based on particularistic criteria or ties'.[22] Participants in social *guanxi* cemented their ties through exchanges not only of material objects or special favours but also of respect and affection. *Guanxi* could enable individuals to secure tangible resources on better terms, gain access to information in an information-poor society, obtain official permissions without the need for bribery and be protected to some degree from arbitrary state intervention. These were not, however, free goods: the applicant would be obligated to reciprocate at some time, and both the applicant and the granter had to consider the impact of approval or refusal on their *mianzi* (face). Tsui and Farh (1997) argued that various terms related to *guanxi* showed its greater prevalence than in the West: for example, *la guanxi* (literally, to 'pull' *guanxi*) meant to get on someone's good side, to store political capital with them, and carried no negative overtones; *meiyou guanxi* ('without' *guanxi*) had become an idiom meaning, 'It doesn't matter'; *guanxi wang* ('*guanxi* net') meant the whole network through which influence was brokered.[23] The persistence of *guanxi* was suggested by a survey which found that 90 per cent of the residents of Shanghai, arguably China's most modern megacity, said connections were important in daily life and the majority preferred to use them rather than formal channels.

Societal groups

Societal divisions enter into the mindset of people within a society and in this way form part of their culture. While it is important to bear in mind the caution of Ng and Lau (1990) that by attending too much to collective social behaviours, it is possible to produce biased generalizations that ignore the individual and the interaction within and between groups,[24] there is little debate over the proposition that both membership in and awareness of societal groups do influence conduct. Categories of societal groups include those based on ethnicity, gender, religion, class, income or wealth, age or generation, (dis)ability and location (urban/rural, North/South). Of these, in the context of Asian business, age and generation were most emphasized by our respondents, while gender and disability received little attention.

Age and generation

Contrary to the European preoccupation with the effects of population aging, in our study this problem only asserted itself in Japan. Instead, it was the shifting attitudes of the young that attracted attention, especially in **China**, where what might be described as a loss of collectivist values among the young was foremost in interviewees' minds. 'The one child policy has reared a generation unused to sharing.'[xi] 'In China, the young believe that money and power are all that count.'[xii] 'In China, the younger generation tend to believe only in themselves. For instance, the theme of a successful advertising campaign here was, "I am obedient, but only to myself".'[xiii]

The effects in the Chinese workplace were evident in an accountancy firm:

> " Most staff were born after China opened up and were raised in 'one child' families. They are spoilt. They expect wealth to come easily. They always know someone who worked for a business that did an IPO [Initial Public Offering] and who became very rich. They don't care for anybody, have no sense of responsibility and are self-centred. For example, I surveyed 300 assistant managers, who joined the firm three years ago and they all said then that they intended to make their career with our firm; in the survey, after they had worked here for three years, only one in 300 intended to stay. Their reasons were that working here involves too much work, too long hours, to become a partner takes too long (it takes ten to 14 years), they want to enjoy life (which means to go shopping) and their ambition is to work in a company that will IPO soon.[xiv]

[xi] Mainland Chinese, Senior Manager, Human Resource Management, Chinese SOE
[xii] Mainland Chinese, Partner, International Accounting Firm
[xiii] Mainland Chinese, Marketing Manager, Consumer MNC
[xiv] Mainland Chinese, Partner, International Accounting Firm

In **India**, the shift in the attitudes of the young was very recent and less extreme. 'Real exposure to Western influences has happened only in the last two or three years. After 1991 we spent eight years feeling our way, resisting the MTV generation; now in the 16 to 25 age group the gap with the West is quite narrow.'[xv] In the broader society, especially in urban India where the changes were most strongly felt, they were creating strains. 'There is a paradigm shift. The generation of people in their forties is failing to cope in many aspects of life. As parents they can't cope with the shift from within-family authoritarianism of the father, which is disappearing together with the joint family system.'[xvi] In the Indian workplace, however, at least in high-technology businesses, the attitudes of the staff, who were mainly young, were seen more positively than in China: 'They welcome innovation. They respond to solid reasoning. They are often committed to self-development and self-improvement.'[xvii] Loyalty to the organization was, nevertheless, low – staff turnover rates were up to 100 per cent a year and there was intense competition over 'packages'. This, however, might be caused less by a shift in attitudes between the generations than in China, as earlier generations in India were strongly aware of high levels of graduate unemployment. There was no indication that loyalty to their employing organizations, as opposed to individual managers, was ever very strong in India.

In **Japan**, traditionally, 'As a nation, we are community-oriented.'[xviii] 'The interest of the community prevails over that of the individual.'[xix] By the early 21st century, however, there was some change in the younger generation in how community-minded people were and in company loyalty.

> Many have foreign experience or have studied abroad and realize that the global norm is different; there is a generation gap – the young are not as loyal as previous generations. Possibly it may be because of a change in the approach to education: previously teachers, for instance, received respect automatically; now it depends on their perceived capability or performance.[xx]

Another Japanese interviewee said, 'There is a new attitude in the younger guys', as he contrasted the way that 'younger ones' can be dealt with on the job with the need to treat older employees with careful consideration for their feelings.[xxi]

[xv] Indian, General Manager and family member, Indian family shipping business
[xvi] Indian, CEO, Indian Educational Not-for-Profit
[xvii] Indian, Successful Entrepreneur, Indian internet-based business services
[xviii] Japanese, Strategic Management, Business Services
[xix] Japanese, Finance and Accounting, Education
[xx] Japanese, Human Resources, Business Services
[xxi] Japanese, Operations Management, Japanese Manufacturer

The desire for lifetime employment was, however, still strong among the young in Japan.

> " Life-time employment was so important for employees that they would accept any treatment by employers. This still applies, *especially* to the younger generation. Japanese children are reared nearly exclusively by their mothers; the present generation's mothers had mothers who suffered most in the period after WWII. Therefore they instil a strong motivation to obtain security in their children. You can see it on the trains or other public places. Japanese mothers never scold their children, whatever they do. This is to compensate the child for being under enormous pressure to achieve at school and so to get into the kind of university that will give them a chance of a life-time employment job. There has been a swing back following the [19]90s recession. Formerly mothers would discipline their children because for a few years they were putting them under less pressure to study.[xxii]

This desire for security or increased risk aversion among the young was also observed in **Singapore**.

> " The older generation is risk averse, the younger even more. Recent measurements show a two or three percentage point drop [in risk tolerance]. This increase can be explained because Singapore is a well-planned society, comfortable for the individual – people are more concerned about losing what they have than gaining more and also there are many MNCs (multi-national companies) which need educated young people, who lose the hunting spirit.[xxiii]

The shifting attitudes and capabilities of the young created a generation gap in Asia that was perceived as important in the business cultures of all these Asian countries, although the precise aspect emphasized varied, with professionalization of businesses, IT (information technology) skill levels and attitudes to work being most often mentioned.

In **India**, the generation gap was described mainly in the context of family businesses. One interviewee who was a family member from such a business explained,

> " There is a generation gap. Our family business is run on a day-to-day basis by my generation – the 40 year olds. But my father aged 74 and my uncle aged 68 still pull the strings. For instance, recently we were in line for a contract to bring oil to shore from rigs in the Bay of Bengal. My generation wanted to buy a new, bigger ship to enable us

---

[xxii] Japanese, Strategic Management, Business Services
[xxiii] Singaporean Chinese, Asia Business Development Manager, International MNC, Energy

> to take such contracts. My father and uncle were very nervous about the investment – fearful. They said, 'Suppose we don't get the contract, what will we do with the ship?' We answered, 'We'll bid for contracts off Nigeria, or in the North Sea or in Venezuela or Malaysia.' They were horrified. They have both travelled a great deal – go regularly to London, for instance. But the idea of managing a contract in the North Sea had never occurred to them and they could not see how it could be done. In the end we persuaded them and the ship is being built. But it shows the generation gap.[xxiv]

In the view of another interviewee from an Indian family business, 'In family businesses, conservatism is a generational thing. Our company, for instance, was debt free for a long time.'[xxv]

In **Singapore** (and Hong Kong) professionalization of traditional family businesses was seen as an extremely important aspect of the generation gap. In Singapore, 'The second generation are different; thus many of these traditional family businesses [where only obviously practical knowledge was valued formerly] are being professionalized.'[xxvi] '[Singaporean] entrepreneurs are afraid that if they teach their employees too much, they will leave and increase the competition, but their successors, the "new generation", are more open minded.'[xxvii] In *Hong Kong*, where in traditional businesses, the main control 'remains with family members as is shown in close monitoring of all processes and subordinates', the younger generation do delegate 'as a result of professionalization'.[xxviii] IT skill levels created a generation gap in **Taiwan** and **Japan**: 'The generational difference is great, especially in terms of IT literacy.'[xxix] 'The new hires (following the ten-year recruitment gap) are much more highly IT-oriented than the older staff – they are known as the game culture generation.'[xxx]

Gender

Gender, so often of concern in Western society and business, received very little attention from the interviewees in the present study. The explanation might lie in evidence that in cultures where gender differences are most powerful, they can be so unquestioned as to be 'invisible'.[25] According to the United Nations' Gender Empowerment scores, the position of women varied in Asia in 2006, though only Hong Kong, in 9th position, ranked anywhere near the top of the United Nations'

[xxiv] Indian, General Manager and family member, Indian family shipping business

[xxv] Indian, Senior General Manager and family member, Family-owned business, consumer goods manufacturer

[xxvi] Singaporean, Finance and Accounting, Education

[xxvii] Singaporean, Human Resources, Business Services

[xxviii] Hong Kong Chinese, Finance and Accounting, Financial Services

[xxix] Taiwan, Expatriate (Japanese), Human Resources, Banking

[xxx] Japanese, Human Resources, Business Service

Gender Empowerment ranking. Japan, at 42nd, for instance, was ranked lowest among developed countries. (Singapore was placed 18th, India 26th and China a remarkably low-ranked 63rd.)

In regard to Asian societies, there is evidence that culture is a strong influence on gender relations. According to a United Nations report in 2005, gender relations in **China** generally improved after the communists came to power in 1950 and equal opportunity legislation took effect, but then when the country's economic reforms began in 1978, differential treatment in practice began to increase. Women experienced low political participation, especially at the village and township levels; rural women, who made up 60 to 70 per cent of the agricultural work force and undertook much of the primary farm work, were nevertheless prevented by traditional male-oriented cultural values from access to and control over land, credit, technology, information and training. Legal protection for the rights of women to contract lands and other resources was inadequate. Many women and girls still suffered disproportionately from low levels of health and malnutrition as a result of lack of access to health care and parental gender-based negligence. Female foeticide was a serious problem in China, as in India. Although the percentage of girls in primary schools was equal to their share of their age cohort, rates dropped off quickly at higher educational levels.[26]

Traditionally, women in China were perceived as housebound, submissive, second-class citizens. This view was reinforced by Confucian doctrines such as, 'The virtue of a woman lies in the three obediences: obedience to the father, husband and son.' Chinese women could be bought and sold by their husbands and fathers. After marriage, a woman 'belonged' to another family and so was lost as an asset to her parents in their old age. 'Even today in China, the birth of a daughter is seen as a misfortune by many rural families.'[27] In this inferior position, women were assessed by their chastity, fertility and housekeeping ability. After the 1980s and China's adoption of its Open Door policy, societal norms and values related to sex and marriage changed considerably. This was partly because of increased Western influence (music, films, and so on.) and contacts but was also due to the breaking up of the traditional Chinese extended family, the population movements from the countryside to the cities, the change to living in small nuclear families in urban apartments and the resulting loss of social control. Even though the 1950 Marriage Act stated that men and women were to have equal rights, however, thousands of years of 'feudalism' left attitudes in the population that were highly resistant to change. Even among those responding to the government pressure to marry late, and so marrying at 28 (men) or 25 (women), 41 per cent of women had a traditional arranged marriage or modified traditional marriage. Both men and women faced relentless social pressure to marry, as any achievement or advancement in the family or work unit depended on it.

A study that compared the gender-role attitudes of women and men in **China** and **Taiwan** found that in both countries, the strongest predictor of egalitarian gender-role attitudes in both sexes was having been educated to at least senior high school level. (Earlier studies found that women's paid employment would direct them to egalitarian attitudes towards gender roles but not that they were necessarily seeking gender equality.) It also found that the Chinese were less egalitarian than the Taiwanese in their attitudes towards the general gender division between private and public spheres and towards husbands sharing housework with wives. In China, women who had lived or did live in urban areas were more liberal in their gender-role attitudes, though not towards the sharing of domestic work; Chinese men were less influenced by rural or urban experience in their gender attitudes than Chinese women. Also in China, the general idea of gender roles inside or outside of the family varied according to their occupations. For example, women farmers tended to be more traditional towards whether women were better than men to take care of the family. Employment experience was more important for the China sample than the Taiwan sample. Neither age nor family structure was significantly related to Chinese women's gender attitudes. In Taiwan, egalitarian gender-role attitudes were more prevalent among men whose wives were employed and who themselves were employed in professional or skilled occupations, though there was even less difference between the attitudes of urban and rural males in Taiwan than in China. In comparison with Chinese women, Taiwanese women were less affected in their gender-role attitudes by whether or not they had urban living experience.[28]

The social culture of *Hong Kong* has been described as 'utilitarian familism'; this is highly patriarchal, with consequences for the position of women, many of whom were in the past compelled to work to help earn a living for their families or to pay the educational expenses of their male siblings. The patriarchal family was thus an important force that controlled women's labour and dictated their life chances. While women's economic contributions earned them more power and autonomy in terms of domestic decision-making and marriage choice, they were 'not accorded privileges and power commensurate with their contributions'. However,

> women's status within the family has changed substantially in the past decades. The rise of the nuclear family, the decrease in the birth rate, and the higher age of first marriage, all persistent trends since the 1970s, are demographic signs that the traditional patriarchal family has lost its integrity. Patriarchal institutions do, however, remain intact in various spheres. As the results of a recent major territory-wide survey on gender equality show, substantial gender inequality still exists in the household division of labour, employment, and community and political participation.[29]

In **India**, one interviewee commented on the social aspects of gender. A woman lawyer explained, 'It is very difficult for husbands to accept a higher-earning wife. ...There are many decisions that my husband makes and I cannot question. ...Drivers dislike taking instructions from a woman. They will ask for the man of the family to give the instructions.'[xxxi] In a group meeting, professional women pointed out that in order to work they needed their husbands' consent (for social, not legal, reasons) and that the best way to get it was to persuade gently rather than to demand.[xxxii] Bhan (2001) noted that the position of women in India was strongly affected by the religious aspect of societal culture and by politics. 'Increasing economic inequities, the feminization of poverty, and the changing role of the State within a liberal economy, in addition to changing notions of caste, religion, and social mores, have individual and combined effects on understandings of gender in India today.'[30] Despite the fact that India's 60-year-old Constitution required gender equality, 'Notions of women's empowerment come [came] into question when female members of the [2001] Hindu right-[wing] government urged Indian women to return to their home and fulfil their roles as wives, mothers and nothing else.' Women's societal and economic status in India was affected by their role in their religious communities. Among both the numerically dominant Hindus and the Muslims, there were restrictions on women's public and private roles in the name of religion. In addition, among the 70 per cent of the population that was rural, 'Parents have several incentives for not educating their daughters.' Educating girls would bring no returns to their parents as their future lay in the household of their in-laws, their role would be largely domestic and reproductive and their labour was needed on the farm to replace the boys who were increasingly receiving an education. 'In addition there are fears for the protection of the girl's virginity if she attends a school with male teachers and fellow students.'[31] In contrast, in the urban areas, educating girls received a boost from the practice of dowry, as an Indian headmaster explained, saying, 'Education is at least equally important for a girl as it reduces the size of the necessary dowry.'[xxxiii]

Agnihotri et al. (1998) showed that female labour participation significantly reduced prevalent masculine biases in India. This was reflected in the sex ratios of those castes where women's participation in the labour force was high – for example, among the Dalits and scheduled castes. Overall sex ratios in India – the ratio of females to males in a population – were affected by an anti-female prejudice which led to the abortion of female foetuses and 'passive killing' of girl children. Whereas in Western countries, which are taken to have the 'natural' ratio, the sex ratio in 2001 was 105 female to 100 male, in India it was reversed at 933:1000 and fell by nearly 1 per cent at each ten-year interval after 1931. However, among the Dalits and scheduled castes, where women generally worked, even though

---

[xxxi] Indian, lawyer, Educational Not-for-Profit
[xxxii] Indian, publishing professionals.
[xxxiii] Indian, CEO, Indian Educational Not-for-Profit

their employment was concentrated in casual labour, sex ratios were found to be more favourable to women. Additionally, nearly as many Dalit girls as boys were enrolled in school, unlike other sections of the population, where this gap was pronounced.[32]

Spousal decision-making in India may be related to broader social phenomena, such as the way the extended family system works in the modern era. As pointed out by Webster (2000),

> India is an interesting culture in which to explore the antecedents of marital power because its societal and intellectual grains operate in ways vastly different from those the West takes for granted. For instance, unlike Western culture, where the nuclear and neo local families are both the ideological and factual norm, the joint family has been and continues to be an important element of Indian culture.

The complexity of the factors typical to the Indian social environment includes the prevalence of a joint/extended family system, gifts of durables as dowry, large rural markets, and so on.

> Individuals ... in India subscribe to an extended family system, and enter into – and exit from – an extended household according to their needs and requirements throughout life. Extension in family is generally sought for meeting childcare requirements and exit is sought at the time of seeking a job. In India, wives have been seen to exercise covert influence in domestic decisions on critical matters.

Webster (2000) suggested that as women increasingly assumed roles as partial 'breadwinner for the family', they might come to express themselves more openly and their husbands might increasingly accept their wife's informal power.[33]

Around the turn of the millennium a 'new generation' of women in India arose with more positive attitudes to their opportunities and capabilities. Many of these women were found working in the technology sector. For example, Radhakrishnan (2007) quoted a woman whose 'viewpoint provides a stark contrast to an older popular conception of India as a culture and a place that endures all, rather than a place that moves with the times'. The woman's 'own ability to carry out her IT job with a high level of competence and dedication while still being flexible enough to do something entirely different with her life tomorrow is a reflection of a new India.'[34]

In **Japan**, according to Goff (1995), an 'emphasis on maintaining social harmony' had specific implications for Japanese women. Early in their social development, Japanese women developed a keen sensitivity to peer opinion and pressure: 'This tendency is often expressed by the phrase *nagare ni mi o makaseru* (in today's idiom, "Go with the flow").'[35] Japanese society considered making choices

250   8

INTRODUCTION · THE BUSINESS CULTURES OF FIVE ASIAN COUNTRIES · ANALYSING ASIAN BUSINESS CULTURES · OWNERSHIP, FINANCING AND GOVERNANCE · ORGANIZATION AND MANAGEMENT · BUSINESS STRATEGY ·

that maximize harmony among peers, including deferring to others, desirable behaviour, especially among women. A survey on gender equality released by the Japanese Prime Minister's Office in 2002 claimed that only a minority of Japanese showed support for traditional gender roles, though few husbands actually participated in household chores.

> Forty-seven per cent of Japanese back the traditional roles of men as breadwinners and women as housewives, down 11 percentage points from five years ago, ... but only a slight increase was seen in husbands taking part in doing household chores; only 3.9 per cent of husbands take charge of cleaning but 82.4 per cent of wives do so. In Japan, there is a close link between women's status and their position at work.

In fact, Japanese commentators, such as Mitsuko Yamaguchi, head of the women's group Fusae Ichikawa Memorial Foundation, argued, the roots of gender inequality in the society generally was Japan's male-dominated business climate.

These attitudes towards gender relations in the Asian societies that we have researched generally also affected gender relations in business and at work, as Chapter 5 revealed.

Class and caste

Of the five countries in the present study, the one with the most conspicuous and unique social divisions was India. **China**, while it possessed a hierarchical culture, and exhibited some discrimination against its ethnic minorities, lacked long-established categorical divisions, in part due to the more than 50 years of equality imposed by the communists. 'There is no feudalism. There are no class divisions. There is a division between Party cadres and the rest, but Party members are very few.'[xxxiv] **Japan** was ethnically homogeneous and had a long tradition, which was culturally strongly endorsed, of internal egalitarianism. As Kawasaki (1994) explained, Japanese society before industrialization was divided into four societal classes: the warriors and artisans class (5 per cent); the merchant class (10 to 15 per cent); the farmer class (70 to 80 per cent); and the underclass (2 to 3 per cent). In such a class-divided society, class differences determined many other social differences. However, the historical conditions that prevented the Japanese from developing individualism and social reforms enjoying middle-class support, also encouraged the growth of egalitarianism: this condition was the shared catastrophe of losing the Second World War, which gave rise to the notion of 'community of fate'.[36] Taiwan, too, though there were ethnic minorities, displayed few social divisions among the majority who were of Chinese descent.

[xxxiv] China, Expatriate (British), General Manager, Energy MNC

In **India**, caste continued to create significant social divisions, especially in rural areas. Caste social organization meant that rewards were given in accordance with hierarchical status and not related to the 'economic' value of the services rendered, even if such a scale of values or prices was established on the open market.[37] As noted in Chapter 2, some of our interviewees considered that caste divisions were perpetuated by the reservations system, which provided quotas for Dalits and 'other backward classes' (OBCs) in higher education and public sector jobs and which in the early years of the 21st century was being extended into the private sector in some Indian states. The growth of the caste-based parties was coming to dominate politics in some of India's biggest states. A leading political scientist resigned from a government commission over the issue of reservations in 1998, fearing that this would ensure that India remained entrapped in the caste paradigm.

A contrary view, that class had largely replaced caste as the primary societal division apart from gender in India, was put forward by Chaudhuri and Majumdar (2006); however, these authors agreed that acceptance of the superiority of some and inferiority of others remained widespread.

> India has always had a very hierarchy- and status-conscious society, which began with the caste system and has now evolved into more of a class-based system. Inequalities arising out of differences in power or wealth are seen as legitimate, though aspirations were severely restricted during the most of the 20th century, first by a predominant frugality-oriented Gandhian value system, then by socialism.[38]

Sheth (1999) argued that the idea of upward social mobility, 'motivates people of all castes ... the quest today is not for registering higher ritual status; it is universally for wealth, political power and modern lifestyles'.[39] While new routes to earning wealth evolved, benefiting self-employed professionals such as doctors, whose income jumped 20-fold after 1990, it was the English language rather than caste that continued to control access to specialized, professional training; 'It is linked to economic benefits and it reproduces and maintains cultural privilege.'[40]

The effects of caste in business, and of business on caste, were discussed by Khanna (2008) as follows:

> Caste in India is both less important and more important than it used to be. In some sense business is a great leveler. In the cities a low-caste person may earn a lot more than a high-caste person. Business cares about the bottom line. It doesn't care whether you are in caste A or caste B if you can produce a product, manage a sales force, or produce the capital.[41]

A contrary view here is that of Taeube (2000), who argued that caste played an important role in the success of Indians in the global IT industry. The Vaishnavas caste, once dominant among entrepreneurs, had not retained its customary share in business in the evolving software industry, which was largely staffed and controlled by Brahmins. The software industry, a knowledge-based industry, was one suited to the traditional specialization of Brahmins in learning.[42]

Norms

Business behaviour and expectations in all societies are influenced by social norms. Among the most important of these in Asia are equality norms, or their absence, and ethical norms.

Equality norms

The four largest countries in this study all attempted to institutionalize egalitarianism in the second half of the 20th century: China under its communist regime after 1950, India under socialism after 1947 and Japan after its defeat in the Second World War and occupation by the USA up to 1948, while Taiwan introduced democracy. Gini coefficients are an index of the ratio of the income or consumption share of the richest 10 per cent of the population to that of the poorest, where 0 equals perfect equality and 100 perfect inequality. Japan's Gini coefficient of 24.9:1 implies that it is the third most equal country in the world, behind only Denmark and Azerbaijan. China, at 44.7:1, Hong Kong at 43.4:1 and Singapore at 42.5:1 are in the middle of the global range, though more unequal than most Western countries. India, at 32.5:1, is less unequal than the UK or Germany. In the case of **Japan**, egalitarianism seemed to become embedded as reflected in its Gini coefficients – its relatively low measured inequality in income or expenditure. It was also reflected in the comments of interviewees about Japan: 'People ... value equality, so that there are no very rich or very poor; [they] respect those who help the weak, criticize power-seekers and the rich. Everyone is taught to think they are equal; most people hate elites.'[xxxv] In **Taiwan**, too, equality was a norm: 'No one is allowed to be much above or below average. There is a real social fear of difference.'[xxxvi]

In contrast, inequality in **China** climbed rapidly in the years following economic liberalization in 1978, to reach a point above that of Singapore and Hong Kong, and that of **India**, too, rose after its economy was partially deregulated in 1990. This may suggest that the equality norm, which was somewhat imposed in China and India, conflicted with the core value of high power distance in those countries, and in India also with the religious-based notion of an inherent inequality rooted in caste.

[xxxv] Japanese, Finance and Accounting, Education
[xxxvi] Taiwanese, Senior Vice President, Finance and Accounting, Fund Management

Leung (1997) reviewed several empirical studies concerned with the way resources are distributed. He concluded that in general, in equal status situations, equality was preferred in collectivist and equity in individualist cultures. Equal distribution is associated with solidarity, harmony and cohesion, so it fitted with the values of people in collectivist cultures. Equity is compatible with productivity, competition and self-gain, so it fitted with the values of people in individualist cultures. Some people in collectivist cultures even showed a generosity rule when exchanging with in-group members. That is, they used equality even when their contribution was clearly higher than that of other members.[43] However, the growth in inequality and its apparent acceptance in cultures which have been shown to be among the most collectivist in the world suggest that a more complex set of variables should be taken into account.

Ethical norms

Many areas of business decision-making can involve making moral choices. Marketing, with its scope for deceiving large numbers of people, is a well-known one. Management involves ethical issues about the treatment of employees. Finance involves moral hazard and agency problems because decisions are being made about someone else's money or resources. As Aggarwal and Mellen (1997) noted, how these moral hazard problems are resolved depends on the culture and what is considered appropriate ethical behaviour.[44] The question that arises in the context of this book is which culture or combination of cultures is evoked by business decision-makers in cases of moral hazard. While the societal (social) culture is one that may be relevant, so is the business culture and the two may coincide or conflict. Even when ethical considerations all point in the same direction, however, other factors may influence behaviour. For example, female financial-sector employees in China showed high levels of risk aversion compared with their male counterparts; this reduced the likelihood that they would report unethical work practices. The degree of risk and its effect on moral choice depended on the interaction of age, education and employment status. Attitudes towards supervisors, and the existence of instrumental work environments also influenced moral choice.[45] Nevertheless, underlying societal (social) ethics undoubtedly do influence business cultures and work behaviour.

In **China** and other countries with a Confucian heritage, according to Davies et al. (2003), the moral law had a different content from that of the West. For example, people had a moral duty to help family and friends. What in the West would be regarded as nepotism, and so unethical, carried a positive moral weight. People who failed to help their friends and relatives, for example, to obtain a job where they have relevant influence, would not only sacrifice *guanxi* but also be criticized on moral grounds.[46] A second facet of Chinese morality was a deep-rooted belief in retribution; research in Hong Kong found that the more strongly people believed in retribution, the higher their work-related ethical standards.[47] Third, to Chinese people an unfair act might still be a morally acceptable one, if longer-term or wider considerations applied; to Westerners that was not so. The Chinese asked whether a long-term pattern of behaviour was ethical or unethical rather than focusing on any particular action. The Chinese equivalent of fairness was *gong ping*, in which *gong* means public and *ping* means balance.[48]

In 2003, Lu Le asserted with examples and quotations that Confucian principles still governed the everyday lives of Chinese people. Alongside a set of five hierarchical relations, Confucian principles include five norms: goodness, rightness, ritual, wisdom and credibility. Goodness is the key norm; it is exclusively concerned with relations between people and includes tolerance, forgiveness, deference, filial obedience (to parents), faithfulness (to a master), wisdom and honesty. Rightness is also concerned with relations between people, but especially those of friendship and fraternity. Ritual, which carries the connotation of moral force, is advocated as the best way to govern people, rather than by compulsion, which gains obedience but at the cost of the self-respect of those governed. Wisdom is linked to knowledge; this concept underpins the Chinese respect for education.[49] Credibility involves doing what you say you will do and may be linked to the point made in an interview that Asians 'promise small, deliver big'.[xxxvii]

Despite this clear-cut social morality, Chinese researchers themselves have concurred in the judgement of one Chinese interviewee in the present study that the Chinese have no fixed moral standards in business – 'They are very pragmatic; past exemplars are "remembered for ever" but so far they have none in the field of business.'[xxxviii] Another issue is whether the traditional morality can cope with modernization. 'Chinese heritage sets the elementary behavioral code and moral fabric of everyday interaction, while the imperatives of modernity stretch, break, or add on to the plasticity of this original scaffolding.'[50]

Again, while Confucianism was highly compatible with Chinese Marxist theory and its moral view that it was unethical to think of making profit for yourself, Confucian morality may present obstacles to the smooth running of a market economy in China. For example, it gives rise to a belief that while resource allocation and distribution are regulated by supply and demand, power manipulates them; again, because of the disdain for merchants inculcated by Confucius and other teachers, in some people's opinions business occupies a very low rung in the moral hierarchy, so those who engage in it are 'damned anyway' and need not observe moral constraints on practices such as bribery.

The approaches to moral issues in **India**, as revealed by Hindu Indians' accounts of the moral status of a variety of actions, led Shweder et al. (1997) to develop a model of cultural differences consisting of community, autonomy and divinity

---

xxxvii Singaporean Chinese, Asia Business Development Manager, International MNC, Energy
xxxviii Mainland Chinese, Financial Controller, Chinese Venture Firm

ethics.[51] Subsequent research, for instance Rozin et al. 1999, provided support for this model. A community ethic makes duties to the community or the societal hierarchy the moral standard, and sets up role-obligation, respect for authority, loyalty, group honour, interdependence and the preservation of the community as criteria. An autonomy ethic establishes harm, rights, justice, freedom, fairness, individual choice and liberty as the criteria for right or wrong and prioritizes the duty not to hurt another person or infringe their rights and freedoms as individuals. Both these ethics relate quite closely to concepts of the person rooted in collectivism or individualism. However, the model put forward by Shweder et al. (1997) contributed a third category of morality – that of divinity. In this category a person's moral duty is to respect the sacredness of God and to avoid impurity or degradation to the self or others. Hindu morality, Shweder et al. (1997) found, prioritized the divine category of ethics. As Rozin et al. (1999) put it,

> Many people in the world believe that maintaining the purity of the body is a moral duty. Such a view is characteristic of Hindu Indians; a major feature of their moral system involves divinity and purity. Unlike the Western system, in which immorality is focused on acts that harm others, in Hindu India, acts of disrespect or impurity are also immoral.[52]

Rather than one common ethical system for everyone, regardless of position and social function, for many Indians there are as many moral codes as appointed stations in life. Hindu morality requires people to perform their duty in their station in life regardless of its consequences. (The *Bhagavad Gita*, which is known to most Indians from early childhood, encapsulates this important aspect of Hindu morality. Addressing Arjuna, the hero, the god Krishna said, 'Toil day and night but sacrifice beforehand the fruits of thy work.') This morality derives from the belief that individuals are bound by the *karma* of their past lives. According to Taeube (2004), *dharma*, perhaps best translated as 'sacred duty' was the most important principle in determining and understanding the behaviour of Hindus. The requirements of *dharma* were determined by an individual's social role, in other words his or her caste or *jati*. Universalistic moral principles, such as fair dealing, had much less significance than the fulfilment of the religious duty prescribed for one's caste or subcaste.[53] Saberwal (1996) argued that Indian morality is non-modern because Indians 'lack awareness of, or at least are only weakly committed to', the variety of impersonal rules which have to be accepted implicitly, as second nature, if a complex society is to avoid losing itself in an endless mass of contentiousness. This 'weakness' was attributable to the way Indian society was subdivided into many 'cells', owing to the primacy of caste, community and regional identities.[54]

In regard to morality in Indian business, Kanagasabapathi (2007) differentiated between corporate and local businesses, arguing that in SMEs 'higher human

256 8

INTRODUCTION · THE BUSINESS CULTURES OF FIVE ASIAN COUNTRIES · ANALYSING ASIAN BUSINESS CULTURES
· OWNERSHIP, FINANCING AND GOVERNANCE · ORGANIZATION AND MANAGEMENT · BUSINESS STRATEGY ·

qualities such as help, faith-based business transactions and basic norms' were still important;[55] Gopalkrishnan and Iyer (1999) reported that there was a 'complex interplay' of religion, reputation and repeated transactions among trade and business communities that dominated Indian intermediary markets.[56] In India, corporate social responsibility was traditionally linked to spirituality, while 'respect in the corporate world has been treated on a par with the bottom line'.[57] Indian managers of corporations may experience higher levels of conflict than Westerners between their private norms and those of the business world: tentative findings from a study of the ethical stances of Indian and UK managers included Indian managers being more likely than UK managers to experience ethical tension between their personal espoused stances and those they took at work.[58]

In **Japan**, links between social and business ethics were expressed explicitly by our interviewees. For example, the business norm of 'always deliver' described in Chapter 2 was linked to Taoism: 'Taoism, especially, advocates, "Do before you say." So to be moral you must not show off, you must be humble, respect others as you hope to be respected and outperform your promises.'[xxxix] Scholars have, however, disputed the importance of Taoism in Japan, saying that it was never really accepted there. Instead, according to Wargo (1990), the root of Japanese ethics was Shintoism: 'It seems to me that the basic Shinto conceptual framework has not been destroyed. Quite to the contrary, it is a strong and vibrant force even today.'[59] Within Shintoism, 'What was counted as good or evil depended very much on the specific conditions obtaining, as well as on the nature of the community to which one belonged', and, 'The core concepts, both metaphysically and ethically, are purity and pollution or defilement (*kegare*), not virtue and sin.' There are clear and interesting parallels here with the Indian system of ethics, despite the obvious differences of the religious roots. Most important, though, from the point of view of Japanese business ethics, may be the following two statements of Wargo (1990): 'It (Shintoism) gives rise to an interpretation of the word "responsibility" which is radically different from that which emerges from the Judeo-Christian tradition', and, 'What counted more than anything else were sincerity and courtesy, which meant the eradication of selfish desire. A man [*sic*] of pure heart would automatically act properly and promote harmony in the community.'[60] There are echoes here of the concept of cultural control in organizations which was touched on in Chapter 5.

Modern cultural values

One aspect of the societal culture closely linked with business in our interviewees' minds in all five countries was attitudes to education and the effects of

---

xxxix Japanese, Marketing Manager, Western MNC telephony manufacturer

the educational system. For instance, in **Taiwan**, interviewees spoke of a 'huge emphasis' on education.[xl] As Waldron (2000) put it, '[It is] a society where graduate schools and advanced degrees figure in conversation the way weather does to the British.'[61] 'Especially for boys, they are pushed towards engineering, computers, doctors, business. The choice of a boy's career is a family decision. Girls have more freedom to choose.'[xli] In this way attitudes to education in Taiwan clearly reflected the business culture of the recent past in which Taiwan's economy depended on its engineering industry; they also reflected the collectivist aspect of the culture and partially reflected the division in gender roles. Similarly, in **India**, interviewees emphasized what Indians perceived as giving them a competitive edge: their command of the English language. 'A large percentage of children in English-medium schools are first generation English learners. Our skill in English is what gives us an edge over China.'[xlii] There are other factors in play, though: 'Education, demonstrated by qualifications, is an important part of what give a person high social status in India, together with connections, the right family name, which school, which company; in Bombay where you work or live.'[xliii] 'Middle-class Indian parents are over-ambitious for their children – they pressurize them: "Study; graduate." This is partly because in India a child expects to be supported until he has a job and is married. The cost of education is high.'[xliv] As a result, according to the *McKinsey Quarterly* in 2008, 'Spending on private education is already high among India's middle classes and is expected to show a major increase as the size of the middle class increases from five percent to 40 percent of the population over the next 20 years.'[62] Inequalities and inadequacies in education are obstacles to the country's economic future: 'It is as important to reduce disparities by encouraging a common school system and expanding the open learning system, as it is important to nurture latent talent. Industry should be encouraged to continue to strengthen the education sector both from a curriculum and access-to-education perspective.'[63]

In **Japan**, however, a different attitude to education was implied: 'In general, people don't study much at university. They study hard in school because it is hard to get in to university. But once there, the university tries to turn out a rounded human being. This is still true.'[xlv] The educational system of Japan was seen as a carrier of the moral culture, as the following remark made explicit: 'Japanese moral behaviour is based in upbringing and education.'[xlvi] A similar attitude to

---

[xl] Taiwanese, Finance and Accounting, Manufacturing

[xli] Ibid.

[xlii] Indian, CEO, Indian Educational Not-for-Profit

[xliii] Indian, Senior Consultant, Business Services (Banking Operations and Technology)

[xliv] Indian, CEO, Indian Educational Not-for-Profit

[xlv] Japanese, Audit, Venture Capital

[xlvi] Japanese, Banking

258   8

INTRODUCTION • THE BUSINESS CULTURES OF FIVE ASIAN COUNTRIES • ANALYSING ASIAN BUSINESS CULTURES • OWNERSHIP, FINANCING AND GOVERNANCE • ORGANIZATION AND MANAGEMENT • BUSINESS STRATEGY •

the role of education was expressed in **China**, but there the system was depicted as failing:

> The schools do not teach any ethics or social responsibility. Competitiveness is encouraged by a pressurising system that publishes results and rankings. They are encouraged to be self-disciplined but not to share. This is in contrast to the old system, which elevated the public interest over the private. 'Look after others and you will be looked after.' Mao quotes and examples all conveyed this message.[xlvii]

This change in the approach to education was described as partly responsible for a change in the work attitudes of the younger generation of Chinese, which was referred to earlier in this chapter.

As well as attitudes to education, educational levels and style may affect business. The impact of educational level on corporate cultures was illustrated by the history of a Chinese company. Founded 20 years before to distribute liquid petroleum gas, it started very small but grew very fast, achieving double-digit growth each year. It diversified into related fields. It had been started by its owner with friends who had only primary education but were committed, hard working and cohesive. It grew both organically and by mergers and acquisitions. As it grew, the founder had to recruit people with more education as senior managers. Both the growth by acquisition and the recruitment of 'outsiders' as senior managers diluted the culture; employees started asking for more money and increasingly questioned the top-down decision-making and dictatorial management style of the founder.[xlviii] In **Singapore**, although there was an emphasis on educational success,[xlix] and education to a high level went well down the pyramid,[l] many entrepreneurs, who were often immigrants, were 'ill-educated, even illiterate'.[li]

The style of education in all five countries was described as formal, hierarchical, memory-based and examination-based. This style itself, of course, corresponds to deeper levels of societal culture which may be analysed either in terms of values such as power distance, or in terms of an underpinning social philosophy such as Confucianism. As a result of this style, though, 'The emphasis on academic success leads to a lack of entrepreneurial spirit and innovation.'[lii] This view on the link between educational style and low levels of innovation is widespread in the region. As Begley and Tan (2001) noted, efforts to increase innovation in East Asian countries such as Japan, Taiwan and Singapore targeted rote memorization in education as stifling creativity. However, the results of a study by Begley

---

[xlvii] Mainland Chinese, Partner, International Accounting Firm
[xlviii] Chinese, Consultant, International Business Information Technology Consultancy
[xlix] Singaporean, Finance and Accounting, Education
[l] Singaporean, Human Resources, Business Services
[li] Singaporean, Finance and Accounting, Education
[lii] Singaporean, Finance and Accounting, Education

and Tan (2001) on attitudes to entrepreneurialism that was quoted in Chapter 4 hinted at an alternative explanation: cultural systems created beliefs that efforts to innovate lacked feasibility.[64]

Part of the impact of education on creativity was felt through interpersonal style at work. For instance, in **Japan**,

> In the classroom at school and university, you don't speak up. You would go to the teacher after the class with any questions. (When I attended a Western business school, I never felt comfortable raising my hand, so I didn't). We have to say the right thing or nothing. The effect is a lack of brainstorming; creativity is harmed.[liii]

In Japan there was widespread recognition that the educational system needed to change and of the difficulty of changing it against the tide of the overall societal culture.

> The development of innovative ideas was not much needed in the past. Now it is, the education system has to change. There is a debate but older guys are still in charge of education and still believe in the old style which does not mature the individual. Ten years ago there was a move designed to foster creativity by reducing class contact time; it led to a significant drop in exam results. Now the trend is the other way – more class time. People recognize the problem but are conflicted.[liv]

Conclusion

This chapter set out to describe influences that societal cultures, beyond those that can be captured by a set of dimensions, may exert on Asian business cultures and decision-making and to indicate limits of those influences. Influences were found in the areas of worldviews, including religion or social philosophy (or their absence), traditional cultural values, especially the operation of collectivism, hierarchy and intensive personal networks, societal groups and divisions such as age and caste, social norms including egalitarianism, a range of ethical norms and in modern cultural values such as education. Limits that were identified on the influence of societal cultures on business included a partial setting aside of religious belief in India. We interpret the finding that diversity issues are largely ignored by the business cultures of Asia as an indication of the strength, not the weakness, of the influence of societal culture there.

[liii] Japanese Product Manager, Western MNC Pharmaceuticals manufacturer
[liv] Japanese, Banking

260 8

INTRODUCTION • THE BUSINESS CULTURES OF FIVE ASIAN COUNTRIES • ANALYSING ASIAN BUSINESS CULTURES • OWNERSHIP, FINANCING AND GOVERNANCE • ORGANIZATION AND MANAGEMENT • BUSINESS STRATEGY •

References

[1] Lowe, S. (1998) 'Culture and network institutions in Hong Kong: A hierarchy of perspectives. A response to Wilkinson: "Culture, institutions and business in East Asia." – response to Barry Wilkinson, *Organization Studies*, vol 17, p 421, 1996', *Organization Studies*, 9(2): 321–44.

[2] Ibid.

[3] De Riencourt, A. (1961) *The Soul of India*, London: Jonathan Cape.

[4] Hall, D. and Ames, R.T. (2003) *Dao De Jing: A Philosophical Translation*, New York, Ballantine Books.

[5] Lu Le (2003) 'Influences of Confucianism [and Taoism] on the market economy of China', in Alon, I. and Shenker, O. (eds) *Chinese Culture, Organizational Behavior and International Business Management*, Westport, CT: Praeger.

[6] De Riencourt, A. (1961) *The Soul of India*, London: Jonathan Cape.

[7] De Riencourt, A. (1958) *The Soul of China*, London: Honeyglen Publishing.

[8] Weber, M.C.E. (1947) *The Protestant Ethic and the Spirit of Capitalism*, New York: Dover Publications.

[9] Tauebe, F.A. (2004) 'Culture, innovation, and economic development: The case of the South Indian ICT clusters', in Mani, S. and Romijn, H. (eds) *Innovation, Learning, and Technological Dynamism of Developing Countries*, New York: United Nations University Press.

[10] Thomas, A.S. and Philip, A. (1994) 'India: Management in an ancient and modern civilization', *International Studies of Management & Organization*, 24(3): 18–27.

[11] Sen, A. (2005) *The Argumentative Indian: Writings on Indian Culture, History and Identity*, London: Penguin.

[12] Au, A. and Tse, A.C.-B.(2001) 'Marketing ethics and behavioral predisposition of Chinese managers of SMEs in Hong Kong', *Journal of Small Business Management*, 39(3): 272–78.

[13] Chan, H. and Lee, R.P. (1995) 'Hong Kong families: At the crossroads of modernism and traditionalism', *Journal of Comparative Family Studies*, 26(1): 83–99.

[14] Kawasaki, K. (1994) 'Youth culture in Japan', *Social Justice*, 21, URL: http://www.international.ucla.edu/eas/NewsFile/jpnyouth/94summer-sj1.htm.

[15] Gupta, R.K. (2002) *Towards the Optimal Organisation: Integrating Indian Culture and Management*, New Delhi: Excel Books.

[16] Ibid.

[17] Roland, A. (1988) *In Search of Self in India and Japan*, Princeton, NJ: Princeton University Press.

[18] Ibid.

[19] Lannoy, R. (1971) *The Speaking Tree: A Study of Indian Culture and Society*, New Delhi: Oxford University Press.

[20] Davies, H., Leung, T.P., Luk, S.T.-K. and Wong, Y.H. (2003) '*Guanxi* and business practices in the People's Republic of China', in Alon, I. and Shenkar, O. (eds) *Chinese Culture, Organizational Behavior and International Business Management*, Westport, CT: Praeger.

[21] Redding, G.A., Norman, A. and Schelander, A. (1993) 'The nature of individual attention to the organization: A review of East Asia variations', in Dunnette, M.D. and Hough, L.M. (eds) *Handbook of Industrial and Organizational Psychology*, 4: 647–88, Palo Alto, CA: Consulting Psychology Press.

[22] Tsui, A.S. and Farh, J.L. (1997) 'Where *guanxi* matters: Relational demography and *guanxi* in the Chinese context', *Work and Occupations*, 24: 56–79.

[23] Ibid.

[24] Ng, M.L. and Lau, M.P. (1990) 'Sexual attitudes in the Chinese', *Archives of Sexual Behavior*, 19: 373–88.

[25] Buss, D.M., Abbott, M., Angleitner, A., Asherian, A., Biaggio, A. and Blanco-Villasenor, A. (1990) 'International preferences in selecting mates: A study of 37 cultures', *Journal of Cross-Cultural Psychology*, 21: 5–47.

[26] United Nations Research Institute for Social Development (2005) 'Gender equality: Striving for justice in an unequal world', URL: www.unrisd.org/80256B3C005BB128/(httpProjects)/72A65D864B4041EBC1256E4E00575F52?OpenDocument.

[27] Higgins, L.T., Zheng, M., Liu, Y. and Sun, C.H. (2002) 'Attitudes to marriage and sexual behaviors: A survey of gender and culture differences in China and United Kingdom', *Sex Roles: A Journal of Research*, 46(3/4): 75–89.

[28] Tu, S.H. and Liao, P.S. (2005) 'Gender differences in gender-role attitudes: A comparative analysis of Taiwan and coastal China', *Journal of Comparative Family Studies*, **36**(4): 545–66.

[29] Y Lee, E.W. (2004) *Gender and Change in Hong Kong: Globalization, Postcolonialism, and Chinese Patriarchy*, Honolulu: University of Hawaii Press.

[30] Bhan, G. (2001) 'India gender profile: Report commissioned by Sida', *Institute of Development Studies*, University of Sussex, Report No. 2, Brighton, UK.

[31] Ibid.

[32] Agnihotri, S., Palmer-Jones, R. and Parikh, A. (1998) 'Missing women in Indian districts: An entitlement approach', *Economics Research Centre Papers*, Norwich: University of East Anglia.

[33] Webster, C. (2000) 'Is spousal decision making a culturally related phenomenon?' *Psychology and Marketing*, **17**(2): 1035–53.

[34] Radhakrishnan, S. (2007) 'Rethinking knowledge for development: Transnational knowledge professionals and the "new" India', *Theory and Society*, **36**(2): 141–59.

[35] Goff, H.A. (1995) 'Glass ceilings in the land of the rising sons: The failure of workplace gender discrimination law and policy in Japan', *Law and Policy in International Business*, **26**: 193–255.

[36] Kawasaki, K. (1994) 'Youth culture in Japan', *Social Justice*, **21**, URL: http://www.international.ucla.edu/eas/NewsFile/jpnyouth/94summer-sj1.ht.

[37] Lannoy, R. (1971) *The Speaking Tree: A Study of Indian Culture and Society*, New Delhi: Oxford University Press.

[38] Chaudhuri, H.R. and Majumdar, S. (2006) 'Of diamonds and desires: Understanding conspicuous consumption from a contemporary marketing perspective', *Academy of Marketing Science Review* [Online] URL: http://www.amsreview.org/articles/chaudhuri09-2006.pdf.

[39] Sheth, D.L. (1999) 'Secularisation of caste and making of new middle class', *Economic and Political Weekly*, **21** (August): 2502–10.

[40] Ibid.

[41] Khanna, T. (2008) *Billions of Entrepreneurs: How China and India Are Reshaping Their Futures and Yours*, Cambridge, MA: Harvard University Press.

[42] Tauebe, F.A. (2004) 'Culture, innovation, and economic development: The case of the South Indian ICT clusters', in Mani, S. and Romijn, H. (eds) *Innovation, Learning, and Technological Dynamism of Developing Countries*, New York: United Nations University Press.

[43] Leung, K. (1997) 'Negotiation and reward allocations across cultures', in Earley, P.C. and Erez, M. (eds) *New Perspectives on International Industrial and Organizational Psychology*, San Francisco, CA: Lexington.

[44] Aggarwal, R. and Mellen, L.E. (1997) 'Perspective on Japanese finance for portfolio investors', *Review of Business*, **18**, 22 June.

[45] Woodbine, G. (2006) 'Gender issues impact the role of the moral agent in a rapidly developing economic zone of the People's Republic of China', *Journal of Asia-Pacific Business*, **7**: 79–103.

[46] Davies, H., Leung, T.P., Luk, S.T.-K. and Wong, Y.H. (2003) '*Guanxi* and business practices in the People's Republic of China', in Alon, I. and Shenkar, O. (eds) *Chinese Culture, Organizational Behavior and International Business Management*, Westport, CT: Praeger.

[47] Au, A.K.M. and Tse, A.C.E. (2001) 'Marketing ethics and behavioral predisposition of Chinese managers of SMEs in Hong Kong', *Journal of Small Business Management*, **39**(3): 272–8.

[48] Bian, W.-Q. and Keller, L.R. (1999) 'Patterns of fairness judgments in North America and the People's Republic of China', *Journal of Consumer Psychology*, **8**(3): 301–20.

[49] Lu Le (2003) 'Influences of Confucianism [and Taoism] on the market economy of China', in Alon, I. and Shenker, O. (eds) *Chinese Culture, Organizational Behavior and International Business Management*, Westport, CT: Praeger.

[50] Chan, H. and Lee, R.P. (1995) 'Hong Kong families: At the crossroads of modernism and traditionalism', *Journal of Comparative Family Studies*, **26**(1): 83–99.

[51] Shweder, R.A., Much, N.C., Mahapatra, M. and Park, L. (1997) 'The "Big Three" of morality (autonomy, community, divinity) and the "Big Three" explanations of suffering', in Brandt, A. and Rozin, P. (eds) *Morality and Health*, New York: Routledge.

[52] Rozin, P., Lowery, L., Imada, S. and Haidt, J. (1999) 'The CAD triad hypothesis: A mapping between three moral emotions (contempt, anger, disgust) and three moral codes (community, autonomy, divinity)', *Journal of Personality and Social Psychology*, **76**: 574–86.

53 Taube, F.A. (2004) 'Culture, innovation, and economic development: The case of the South Indian ICT clusters', in Mani, S. and Romijn, H. (eds) *Innovation, Learning, and Technological Dynamism of Developing Countries*, New York: United Nations University Press.

54 Saberwal, S. (1996) *The Roots of Crisis: Interpreting Contemporary Indian Society*, Delhi: Oxford University Press.

55 Kanagasabapathi, P. (2007) 'Ethics and values in Indian economy and business', *International Journal of Social Economic*, **34**(9): 577–85.

56 Gopalkrishnan, R. and Iyer, D. (1999) 'The impact of religion and reputation in the organization of Indian merchant communities', *Journal of Business & Industrial Marketing*, **14**(2): 102–17.

57 Sagar, P. and Singla, A. (2004) 'Trust and corporate societal responsibility: Lessons from India', *Journal of Communication Management*, **8**(3): 282–90.

58 Fisher, C.M., Shirolé, R. and Bhupatkar, A.P. (2001) 'Ethical stances in Indian management culture', *Personnel Review*, **30**(6): 694–711.

59 Wargo, R.J. (1990) 'Japanese ethics: Beyond good and evil', *Philosophy East & West*, **40**(4): 499–509.

60 Ibid.

61 Waldron, A. (2000) 'The "Chineseness" of Taiwan', *Policy Review*, August/September.

62 Beinhocker, E.D., Farrell, D. and Zainulbhai, A.S. (2008) 'Tracking the growth of India's middle class', *McKinsey Quarterly Online*, URL: http://www.mckinseyquarterly.com/Tracking_the_growth_of_Indias_middle_class_2032.

63 Ibid.

64 Begley, M. and Tan, W.-L. (2001) 'The socio-cultural environment for entrepreneurship: A comparison between East Asian and Anglo-Saxon countries', *Journal of International Business Studies*, **32**(3): 537–53.

9 political cultures and perceived political environments

Our findings suggested that a business community's business decisions and culture are usually influenced to some degree by the political culture and perceived environment within which the community operates. This chapter attempts to identify links (and their absence) between business cultures and political cultures and environments. Conceptually, political cultures and political environments can be distinguished: the former are at least in part 'in the head' and include taken-for-granted beliefs and values, while the second, although socially constructed, are understood by individuals as external; they affect decisions only as they are consciously perceived. In practice, however, neither our research nor, as far as we know, any preceding research, has distinguished them.

The standing of the findings reported in this chapter differs from that of previous chapters. Chapters 2 and 3 concerned business cultures and so the members of the business communities interviewed were both members of the culture and participant observers of it. The business decision-makers in our study enjoyed 'privileged' access to those cultures. Chapters 7 and 8 dealt with societal cultures and so the same applied – their content reflected both the participant-observed and the experienced aspects of that culture. In this chapter and the next, the interviewees from the business community of a country were in a less 'privileged' position. Business communities are affected by these cultures and environments and contribute to them in varying degrees, but we claim no privileged access for our interviewees.

When our interviews were analysed, they suggested that the following topics concerning politics and government were in the minds of the business decision-makers interviewed: the effects of the political system; media freedom, independence and trustworthiness; the strength or weakness of government control; government policies and cultures; institutional integrity, 'straightness', legal culture and corruption; and the role of government in industry and business. (As noted in Chapter 1, these categories were imposed on the interview data by the researchers in a process that included interpretation.)

The effects of the political system

The impact on business of democracy versus other systems of rule, impersonal versus personal power bases and the location of power were the aspects of political systems that surfaced in our research.

There is great variety in Asia's political systems. Among the five countries where we researched, there were examples of relatively long-established democracies (Japan and India), recently established democracies (Taiwan), a nominal democracy which had been ruled by the same party since independence in 1965 (Singapore) and a one-party dictatorship (China); Hong Kong had an ambivalent status as a recent transfer from being a British colony to being a Special Administrative Region of China. Even within these categories, there were very large differences: in many respects the political systems of Japan and India were more dissimilar than alike. Nevertheless, it was the 'big picture' issues of the location, use and abuse of power in a democracy or a dictatorship that were highlighted by the business executives of our study, as the following quotes reveal: 'Power in **China** is understood to be held by and symbolized by one person, even though that may no longer be fully true. It is part of the Chinese mindset.'[i]

> The current Chinese President is all-powerful, compared to the Deng Xiao Ping period when there were contending factions; he operates according to 'Chinese wisdom', which means you don't know what his agenda is except that he is determined to be the leader. Like others, he got to the top by demonstrating 'loyalty', which is untranslatable but includes reliability, fairness, avoiding mistakes, showing you are capable, massaging the system.[ii]

'There is no impersonal [he said "independent"] system of government in China. It depends on the personality. "A dictatorship depends on the dictator." '[iii]

The effects of being the citizens of a dictatorship were felt in a sense of powerlessness. 'As individuals, [Chinese] people are psychologically very vulnerable. They feel powerless.'[iv] 'Periodic dissent by perhaps 20 million intellectuals is not supported by the 1.3 billion others, so they can be crushed or will compromise.'[v] In China the individual was seen as insignificant in the face of the state, and the leadership regarded part of the population as expendable in its drive to build a rich and powerful country. There was a suggestion that the leadership wanted a cheap, pliable, workforce to enable growth. In Beijing and other big cities,

---

[i] Mainland Chinese, General Manager, international business information hardware manufacturer
[ii] Ibid.
[iii] Hong Kong Chinese, CEO, Chinese consulting firm
[iv] Mainland Chinese, General Manager, international business information hardware manufacturer
[v] Ibid.

the Chinese had access to everything money could buy, and the middle class of over 200 million people accepted this 'deal with the devil'. In **Singapore**, the same sense of powerlessness was felt, but slightly greater press freedom and the long-term success of the economy made this sense more acceptable: 'People do not protest or demonstrate; they feel powerless and think "the decision is not too bad"; their priority is to make a living; politics are not attractive; however, people do voice their opinion in the newspapers and the government does solicit feedback.'[vi]

In the democracies, the frustrations were also strongly felt, though different.

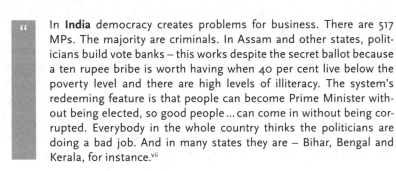

> In **India** democracy creates problems for business. There are 517 MPs. The majority are criminals. In Assam and other states, politicians build vote banks – this works despite the secret ballot because a ten rupee bribe is worth having when 40 per cent live below the poverty level and there are high levels of illiteracy. The system's redeeming feature is that people can become Prime Minister without being elected, so good people … can come in without being corrupted. Everybody in the whole country thinks the politicians are doing a bad job. And in many states they are – Bihar, Bengal and Kerala, for instance.[vii]

Concurring in the view expressed by one interviewee that vote banks were 'pretty much a disaster for the system of governing'[viii] in India, Khanna (2008) asserted, 'Politicians have whipped up caste frenzy. A lot of voting in India happens along caste lines in so-called vote banks. And so politics has become fragmented, with some politicians highlighting caste differences in the electoral process.'[1]

Contrary to this negative view of India's democracy, an outside observer, Luce (2006), argued,

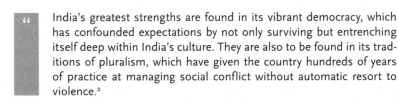

> India's greatest strengths are found in its vibrant democracy, which has confounded expectations by not only surviving but entrenching itself deep within India's culture. They are also to be found in its traditions of pluralism, which have given the country hundreds of years of practice at managing social conflict without automatic resort to violence.[2]

An IMF (International Monetary Fund) paper supported this optimistic view of India's institutions: 'India has very strong political and economic institutions. It is a democracy where the rule of law generally prevails and property rights are protected adequately.'[3] Huang and Khanna (2003) commented in favour of India

---

[vi] Singaporean, CEO, Thai MNC (multi-national company), business services
[vii] Indian, Business Development and Strategy, Indian engineering and construction company
[viii] Ibid.

on the difference between China's and India's political systems and the impact of those differences on their growth patterns:

> China and India are the world's next major powers. They also offer competing models of development. ... At the micro level, India displays every bit as much dynamism as China. Indeed, by relying primarily on organic growth, India is making fuller use of its resources and has chosen a path that may well deliver more sustainable progress than China's FDI [foreign direct investment]-driven approach. ... The fact that India is increasingly building from the ground up while China is still pursuing a top-down approach reflects their contrasting political systems: India is a democracy, and China is not.[4]

Not surprisingly, an Indian government minister also concurred in this more optimistic assessment.

> People no longer ask, 'Have I got a school in my rural area?' They ask, 'Is the quality of the school such that my child has a good chance of getting into a good educational institution?' This is a totally different question. ... That puts pressure on the government to deliver faster, which is on the whole a good thing.[5]

Again, the same politician argued that India's system of government carried the potential to eliminate corruption: 'Corruption is a huge problem – not just in India, but everywhere. However, India's democratic, free-to-criticize atmosphere generates very strong incentives to hold the light up to any kind of wrongdoing. This is one of our strengths. If there's any corruption in India, somebody will draw attention to it.'[6] Nevertheless, as the same minister admitted, India's democracy meant that things were done differently there from in China.

> As China began to integrate with the rest of the world, and also as East Asia began to develop, this benchmarking – if China can do it and East Asia can do it, then India should also be able to do it – became a very important positive factor. Of course, we can't do it the way China does, because they have a totally different political system. The way it's going to be done in India has to be firmly anchored in how a democratic and very diverse society functions.

In **Taiwan**, with its relatively young democracy, some nostalgia for the former clear direction of the economy was expressed (see Chapter 2) but there was also some appreciation of the way democracy had made the system more responsive to popular pressure:

> In 2005 there was a consumer debt crisis – the poor had been encouraged to spend on credit cards with so-called free gifts, etc.

Table 9.1 **Perceived voice and accountability indicators for eight Asian and two comparison countries 2006 (Country's percentile rank)**

	Voice and accountability
China	12
Hong Kong	(44)
India	61
Japan	76
Taiwan	72
Singapore	57
South Korea	66
Malaysia	37
Thailand	32
USA	85
UK	91

Source: Based on Kaufman D., Krasy, A. and Mastruzzi, M. (2007) 'Governance Matters VI: Governance Indicators for 1996–2006' World Bank http://info.worldbank.org/governance/wgi2007/sc_country.asp; © The World Bank.

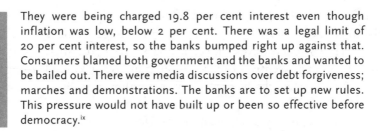

They were being charged 19.8 per cent interest even though inflation was low, below 2 per cent. There was a legal limit of 20 per cent interest, so the banks bumped right up against that. Consumers blamed both government and the banks and wanted to be bailed out. There were media discussions over debt forgiveness; marches and demonstrations. The banks are to set up new rules. This pressure would not have built up or been so effective before democracy.[ix]

The World Bank, defining governance at the level of countries, stated that it was

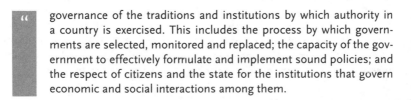

governance of the traditions and institutions by which authority in a country is exercised. This includes the process by which governments are selected, monitored and replaced; the capacity of the government to effectively formulate and implement sound policies; and the respect of citizens and the state for the institutions that govern economic and social interactions among them.

In 2006, the World Bank rated a large number of countries for six governance factors. One of these was Voice and Accountability. The results for eight Asian countries and two Western comparison countries were as shown in Table 9.1. The

---

[ix] Taiwanese, Finance and Accounting, manufacturing MNC

indicators are based on the country's percentile rank among 122 countries: the highest performers are therefore those with a ranking of 100.

Not surprisingly, these findings placed the democracies well in front of the other countries on the Voice and Accountability aspect of political governance, while the flaws in India's democratic system were reflected in its lower rank compared with Japan and Taiwan. In these rankings, which were based on World Bank surveys of opinion leaders and non-governmental bodies based both inside and outside the country, China's extremely low position might have been influenced by its lack of press freedom and its government controls over all information media, which in 2006 and 2007 were extended to the internet.

Media freedom, independence and trustworthiness

Many observers have linked democracy and media freedom in Asia. 'One of the redeeming features of the Indian system of government is the free press.'[x] In comparison with China, India 'not only has more open media, it also has more reliable, if still imperfect, statistical information'. In **China**,

> Caijing and a few other media outlets like it have made some progress, but for the most part credible business media are still scarce. One reason is that Xinhua, China's official news agency, is directly controlled by the Central Committee of the CCP [Chinese Communist Party]. Newspapers that carry a Xinhua story are allowed to rewrite or shorten but not add to or otherwise revise the text. Since Xinhua is the only agency with correspondents based overseas, every other media outlet depends on it for international news. The government control of Xinhua is far from subtle. Typically a working group from the party's propaganda department meets every week to draw up detailed guidelines for what issues Xinhua should cover and how those issues should be presented. Xinhua officials then pass the guidelines along to lower levels. Market information – information gathered by impartial, objective observers in return for monetary compensation – is also scarce in China.

China's government-originated statistics, too, were often misleadingly distorted by political considerations. (The importance of *guanxi* may be linked to the lack of information in China.) By comparison, sources of business information in **India** are considered numerous and reliable.

> As a result of a legal system derived from the common-law tradition, annual reports provide the rudiments of information that Western observers expect, and familiar rules govern corporate disclosure.

[x] Indian-American, CEO, International internet-based business services

> Real-time stock market data are readily available on all publicly traded companies, a result of vigorous competition between the National Stock Exchange (NSE) and the Bombay Stock Exchange (BSE). Private-sector intermediaries in India use business models that include information synthesized from company disclosures and intelligence that they gather from the ground. The Centre for Monitoring [the] Indian Economy (CMIE), for example, is a privately owned clearinghouse for reliable information on publicly quoted companies.

Strong competition among the independent press media, including business magazines, led to intense scrutiny of information released by government-linked bodies such as the Reserve Bank of India and the Planning Commission. India has a Freedom of Information Act.[7]

Despite the perhaps obvious links between democracy and media freedom, the state of media freedom in **Japan** was described by the International Press Institute (IPI), a pressure group for media liberty, as presenting a mixed picture.

> " While significant progress has been made in guaranteeing access for foreign media to official news sources previously monopolized by exclusive local journalists' associations known as '*kisha* clubs', freedom of speech within Japan has suffered setbacks due to acts of violence and intimidation by ultra-nationalist groups, as well as behind-the-scenes pressure from conservative political forces opposed to open discussion of negative aspects of Japan's wartime history.

While this may be a single-issue restriction of freedom, threats have led to self-censorship by journalists, according to the IPI report.[8]

In contrast, a drop in political corruption in **Taiwan** following the introduction of democracy there was attributed by observers to media freedom. Opposition parties exploited newly liberalized media to challenge and alter accepted but corrupt norms of governance.

> " Pillars of the ruling party state, such as its party assets, vote buying and the corrupt patron–client relationships with local factions were until the 1990s either openly or tacitly accepted as legitimate. The Taiwanese opposition parties took a latent political issue, corruption, and progressively broadened the scope of what is publicly acknowledged as corruption.[9]

The strength or weakness of government control

The World Bank Governance survey of 2006 referred to above also rated 8 Asian and 60 other countries on government effectiveness. The findings on government effectiveness for the eight Asian and two comparison countries are shown in Table 9.2.

Table 9.2 **Perceived government effectiveness of eight Asian and two comparison countries 2006 (Country's percentile rank)**

	Government effectiveness
China	46
Hong Kong	(62)
India	53
Japan	86
Taiwan	78
Singapore	100
South Korea	66
Malaysia	81
Thailand	64
USA	91
UK	94

Source: Based on Kaufman, D., Krasy, A. and Mastruzzi, M. (2007) 'Governance Matters VI: Governance Indicators for 1996–2006' World Bank, URL: http://info.worldbank.org/ governance/wgi2007/sc_country.asp; © The World Bank.

As Table 9.2 shows, one Asian country, Singapore, was ranked maximal, above the two Western countries, while Japan was only slightly below. China and India were both given low scores, with China, contrary to the popular outsider view, scoring below India. Although a 1994 survey referred to in Li et al. (2000) indicated that managers in **China** viewed the state regulatory regime as the most influential (as well as the most complex) factor affecting firm performance, the strength of that influence may have diminished thereafter.[10] Our own findings reflected the World Bank survey finding on China: the view of our business decision-makers was that government control was lessening. 'People travel abroad. Peasants come to town.'[xi] 'The government has less and less hold on people's emotions.'[xii] As in other countries, globalization threatened the Chinese government's control of the economy: 'After 1998, richness came unavoidably. The government would probably have preferred that it did not as it threatens to be uncontrollable. But the rest of the world could not be expected to absorb China's production and its consequences indefinitely. So the consumer boom was started.'[xiii] One interviewee saw a balance in the situation:

> The government is now telling businesses to improve standards on safety, environment etcetera. The government is trying to give the right message, but China is more decentralized than Russia. There is

[xi] Mainland Chinese, General Manager, International business information hardware manufacturer
[xii] Mainland Chinese, Consultant, International management consultancy
[xiii] Mainland Chinese, General Manager, International business information hardware manufacturer

also effective bottom up pressure – local action. ... There is, though, also clamping down on protest. They are not told the whole story – for instance about safety figures in industry. Villages have control systems. I think the controls are justified. As far as I can see, it's not like the Stasi.[xiv]

In what might have been a sign of weakness or strength, but in any case showed that the basic political culture had not changed, in 2007 the Chinese government resorted to the 'old-style' storming campaigns with which it dealt with enemies, pests and bottlenecks in the pre-reform period. By 2007, what the Chinese Vice-Premier blamed on lax inspection, weak enforcement and the failure of officials in rival agencies to cooperate had led to the recall of 18 million toys by Mattel, a US toy business. Other export scares hit toothpaste, animal-food ingredients, tyres, eels, seafood and chemicals in cough medicine that killed dozens of people in Panama. 'Shaken by the product scares, China responded with new rules, factory shutdowns, constant news conferences and an old-style campaign to shake up local officials who had often been more focused on economic-growth targets.'[11]

As Chapter 2 explained, our study found that Chinese business decision-makers considered the Chinese government neither so powerful nor so monolithic as its image in the West. Although the Chinese state still had a broad influence over business, the chaotic way this power was exercised contributed to the weakness, not the strength, of Chinese firms. In the power industry some foreign investors withdrew because of the bureaucratic infighting. Chinese government weakness was reflected in a situation which arose with the financing of SOEs (state-owned enterprises). 'In 1981, the Chinese government began to require SOEs to use interest-bearing bank loans instead of interest-free capital appropriations to finance construction projects. The goal was to make firms more cost-sensitive and to force them to choose investments by comparing the cost of capital with expected return. However, this goal was undermined by the persistence of the soft budget constraint and the lax enforcement of loan repayment. Firms were not sensitive to the higher cost of investment because they could offset those costs by negotiating higher profit retention or lower tax rates. They could also postpone loan repayments without difficulty, and if they found themselves in significant economic trouble, they could depend on government grants to bail them out', according to Dodds (1996).[12]

Child and Tse (2001) further noted that by delegating authority to provincial, city and village governments, the central Chinese authority had set up possibilities of systemic conflict.

These 'local' governments are now able to formulate their own policies that attract investment and govern business operations under their jurisdiction, within a general framework set by the central

---

[xiv] China, Expatriate (British), General Manager, energy MNC

272   9

INTRODUCTION · THE BUSINESS CULTURES OF FIVE ASIAN COUNTRIES · ANALYSING ASIAN BUSINESS CULTURES · OWNERSHIP, FINANCING AND GOVERNANCE · ORGANIZATION AND MANAGEMENT · BUSINESS STRATEGY ·

authorities. The process of decentralization has not been smooth. It is common to find frequent changes of policy by the central government and resistance to such policies by local governments.[13]

Political decentralization, despite the consequential uncertainties about policy, might, however, have been beneficial for business. Competition among local governments and bureaucrats from different regions within the same country enabled entrepreneurs to move from region to region to find the most supportive government officials for their private firms. In turn this motivated officials to lend 'helping hands' rather than 'grabbing hands' in the provision of public goods or services, such as the granting of licenses to start-up firms, to prevent an outflow of profitable private businesses from the region.[14]

A negative aspect of the Chinese system, according to Clarke (2003), was that Chinese state control of one sector reduced business efficiency in the entire economy. In fact, Clarke (2003) concluded, the need to provide for the special circumstances of state-sector enterprises ended up 'hijacking' the entire Company Law, so that 'private-sector enterprises are hamstrung by having to follow rules that make sense only in a heavily state-invested economy'. Moreover, the state policy of maintaining a full or controlling ownership interest in enterprises negatively impacted governance in the enterprises it ran. State control of enterprises was used for purposes such as the maintenance of urban employment levels, direct control over sensitive industries or politically motivated job placement; in using its control for purposes other than value maximization, the state 'exploits minority shareholders who have no other way to benefit from their investment'.[15]

A 2006 report on China's investment boom related that the government wanted to cut investment by asking banks to curb their lending, because of worries that too much investment would create industrial overcapacity; however, the same report suggested that recent data implied that slowing the economy would be difficult. Although local government leaders and the state-owned banks were instructed to cut lending, in relation to commercial banks the government resorted to 'pleading'. It is important not to overstate this 'weakness' of the Chinese government, which remained a very strong influence on both people and business, but a correction to the earlier Western view of China's omnipotent state was needed.

Luce (2006) argued that the political culture of **India** was all-enveloping and that the state was very powerful.[16] India's business executives, politicians and judiciary, however, were more conscious of the limits of government power there, perhaps more so because of the comparison with China and other surrounding countries. For instance, a bench of Indian Supreme Court judges, frustrated by the obstacles to stamping out corruption, remarked in court, 'The only way to rid the country of corruption is to hang a few of you on the lamp post. The law does not permit us to do it, but otherwise we would prefer to hang people like you to

DIMENSIONS OF SOCIETAL CULTURES · SOCIETAL CULTURES REVISITED · **POLITICAL CULTURES AND PERCEIVED POLITICAL ENVIRONMENTS** · ECONOMIC CULTURES AND PERCEIVED ECONOMIC ENVIRONMENTS · CONCLUDING REMARKS

9

273

the lamp post.'[17] (In China, officials convicted of corruption had been executed.) A different example is that solving the problems resulting from rapid urbanization in some areas was seen as impeded by government weakness: 'One of India's biggest challenges, modernising its infrastructure to cope with rapid urbanization, is commonly frustrated by the inability of the Indian state to enforce its own decisions, in conjunction with the slow and poor decision-making resulting from confusion of jurisdictions, for instance between municipal and state governments.'[18]

Our own interviewees described a shift in government influence in India somewhat similar to that described for China: liberalization had led to a weakening of central government control. State governments remained important for many industries, but competition among them tended to make them more business-friendly.

> " Previously most businesses depended on government munificence. This meant that business houses geared up to get their piece of the cake and influence government policies; they would have senior managers located in Delhi whose role was an influence peddler. ... After the changes, restrictions were reduced, import quotas raised, duties lowered; the licence raj was removed. India's involvement with the South Asia Free Trade Area and the WTO [World Trade Organization] began. Business became an open field.[xv]
>
> The influence of Delhi is dramatically reduced since liberalization. State governments are more of an issue than the central government now. The deciding power has shifted to them. For example controls over ethyl alcohol are very onerous, because of concerns over adulteration, but they are an essential ingredient for many consumer industries, besides being a key raw material for the chemical industry. The state-level Minister continues to exercise strong arbitrary powers. If you criticize one of them and if he chooses, he can make life difficult for a business – cut off your electricity ('a cable fault'), say you have not paid your sales tax, even engineer a strike.[xvi]

'The state governments have more impact on business than the central government in the ratio 80/20. We [a family-owned conglomerate] have stuck to one state because we didn't want to have to do again everything we had to do, learn everything we had to learn, somewhere else.'[xvii] However, as noted above, business benefited from competition among the states: 'Competition between the states for private sector development led the governments of Gujarat, Andhra Pradesh and other states to adopt pro-business policies.'[xviii]

[xv] Indian, Human Resources Senior Manager, Indian industrial goods manufacturer
[xvi] Indian, Consultant, Former CEO Indian subsidiary, US MNC industrial goods manufacturer
[xvii] Indian, Chairman, Family-owned business group, Indian MNC industrial goods manufacturer
[xviii] Indian, Finance and General Management, Indian MNC heavy industry

274   9

INTRODUCTION • THE BUSINESS CULTURES OF FIVE ASIAN COUNTRIES • ANALYSING ASIAN BUSINESS CULTURES • OWNERSHIP, FINANCING AND GOVERNANCE • ORGANIZATION AND MANAGEMENT • BUSINESS STRATEGY •

As Chapter 3 noted, the business decision-makers we interviewed in **Japan** downplayed the role of government in business there. This contradicted earlier, though recent, sources and may reflect a change resulting from the temporary loss of power by the Liberal Democratic Party (LDP). For decades after the Second World War, one-party rule by the LDP was taken for granted. Under such political stability, triadic coalitions among LDP politicians, interest groups and ministerial bureaucrats were formed in parallel along various industrial, occupational and professional lines, to protect the mutual vested interests of the incumbents.[19] Elite bureaucrats were accounted the driving force behind the economic miracle that took Japan to the position of the second biggest economy in the world. This was despite the fact that the bureaucracy was relatively small so that taxation rates remained low, a factor in itself positive for growth.[20] One of the positive ways in which the Japanese bureaucracy contributed to Japan's high rate of growth was by ensuring a high rate of savings. Most Asian countries did that also, but Japan was particularly successful in generating high levels of savings and in being able to direct those savings into capital investments in targeted industries.[21]

Our research found a high level of acceptance in **Singapor**e for the role of government in business. In a comparison of Singapore and South Korea, Tsui-Auch and Lee (2003) set out to demonstrate that the differing power and policies of the state in those two Asian countries led to differing outcomes when the state tried to loosen family control of businesses after the financial crisis of the late 1990s. Before the crisis these business groups in both countries professionalized their management, but retained family control and corporate rule. The insistence on corporate rule and family control was motivated by the Confucian view of tying the honour of a family to the ownership of family assets and the advantage of exploiting the social capital of family and network ties – it was culturally motivated and endorsed. The crisis increased the pressure on such groups to relinquish family control and corporate rule. Singapore businesses tended to loosen their tight grip on corporate rule by absorbing more professional managers into their upper echelons. In South Korea, in contrast, except for a few chaebol that were on the brink of bankruptcy, the surviving chaebol intensified family control. A significant part of the explanation for these differences was related to the extent of government power in the two countries. The Singaporean government, having single party domination and control of the major media, exerted pressure to bring about professionalism in both management and governance and discourage family control and rule. It restructured the financial sector and criticized reliance on family and network ties in running businesses. The Korean government, however, weakened by democratization in 1987, lost its capacity to discipline the chaebol, except for those that were near to bankruptcy.[22]

The impact of political systems on business is a function not only of the strength or weakness of government control but also by their stability or

Table 9.3 **Perceived political stability and absence of violence indicators for eight Asian and two comparison countries 2006 (Country's percentile rank)**

	Political stability and absence of violence
China	30
Hong Kong	(63)
India	21
Japan	87
Taiwan	72
Singapore	81
South Korea	46
Malaysia	57
Thailand	15
USA	58
UK	65

Source: Based on Kaufman, D., Krasy, A. and Mastruzzi, M. (2007) 'Governance Matters VI: Governance Indicators for 1996–2006' World Bank, URL: http://info.worldbank.org/governance/wgi2007/sc_country. asp; © The World Bank.

instability. In 2007 the World Bank rated eight Asian countries' political stability. The results are shown in Table 9.3 in comparison with two Western countries.

The figures in Table 9.3 relate not only to possible changes in the political system (from dictatorship to democracy, for instance) but also to changes brought about through the intended operation of the political system, as in the switch of government brought about by elections in democracies. Absence of violence was also factored in here. As a result of its turbulent politics and frequent weak coalition governments, therefore, together with having two violent insurgencies (Maoist and Naxalite) operating in some areas and independence movements in some states, India emerged as less politically stable than China, even though its system would by many people be considered more robust in the long term.

The political system in **China** was seen as unstable both by our interviewees – 'One scenario is that the government will stage a revolution, close the borders, return the country to the stone age'[xix] – and by outsiders who concluded from the annual increase in the number of demonstrations taking place in China in the years 2003 to 2005 (50,000 in 2003, 74,000 in 2004 and 87,000 in 2005), that the country's stability was very fragile.

[xix] Mainland Chinese, General Manager, Chinese SOE

Government policies and cultures

The interviews showed that Asian business decision-makers were very aware of government policies. In **Taiwan**, the view was expressed that the switch of power from one party to another was a more important change than the ending of dictatorship.[xx] In **China**, by the early 21st century, the Communist Party claimed to represent not just the worker and peasant masses but entrepreneurs and business leaders, whom it welcomed into its ranks. 'The Party refers to this metamorphosis as the 'three represents': meaning that the party now represents "advanced productive forces" (capitalists); "the overwhelming majority" of the Chinese (not just workers and peasants); and "the orientation ... of China's advanced culture" (religious, political and philosophical traditions other than communism).' Survey data from 1999 and 2005 confirmed that during that period the CCP increasingly embraced not only capitalism but also private sector entrepreneurs. 'The CCP is increasingly integrating itself with the private sector, both by co-opting entrepreneurs into the Party and encouraging current Party members to go into business. It has [even] opened the political system to private entrepreneurs, but still screens which ones are allowed to play political roles.'[23] There were, though, doubts in the business community about how effectively this change had come about. 'Can the leopard change its spots?' was the way one interviewee expressed it. Certainly, more than 30 years after launching its reform programme, the Chinese government continued to pursue 'top down' economic policies that many in the West would regard as flying in the face of the market.[24] For instance, from the late 1990s onwards, the Chinese central state focused on the development of the vast underdeveloped interior areas as a way to bridge regional disparities. In 1999, the 'Great Western Development Strategy (*xibu da kaifa*)' was launched. This was an ambitious top-down effort to steer domestic and foreign investment into the parts of China most in need but least likely to attract aid or business on their own.[25]

India provides an example of government policies that strongly influenced business decision-making for approximately 40 years and had residual influence more than 15 years after they were abandoned. India gained political independence from British rule in 1947. The new democratically elected government was socialist and protectionist, aiming at self-sufficiency and a better standard of living, especially for the poor. Foreign investment and MNCs (multinational companies) were discouraged. The resulting lack of competition hindered the country's own economic and technological development.

> Profits were made by gaining licences and preventing competitors from gaining licences. It also meant there was no focus on improving internal efficiency or developing people; pricing was cost plus; it

---

[xx] Taiwanese, Finance and Accounting, manufacturing

was a seller's market; quality was unimportant; labour management focused on production at any cost — if necessary they would pay a king's ransom. The unions were therefore extremely powerful.[xxi]

As a result of these policies the market was forced to accept local products that were often inferior or old-fashioned. One effect of these policies that persisted after liberalization and was proving hard to eradicate was the increase in and persistence of bribery. Under the 'licence raj', bribery of officials to obtain permits became commonplace.[26] According to our research, it was at that time that it became commonplace to pay 'speed money' and other bribes to everyone from traffic police to government ministers, a form of corruption still prevalent in 2008.

Disputing the standard account that India's growth spurt began with the 1991 liberalization, Rodrik and Subramanian (2005) claimed that the figures showed that a more-than-doubling took place sometime around 1980. 'We argue that the trigger for India's economic growth was an attitudinal shift on the part of the national government in 1980 in favor of private business.'[27] This was a shift focused on raising the profitability of the established industrial and commercial establishments. This shift favoured incumbents and producers. During the 1980s, the government began easing restrictions on capacity expansion for incumbents, removing price controls and reducing corporate taxes.

After the economic crisis in 1990, however, India's central government attempted to introduce market-based policies that favoured new entrants and consumers through trade liberalization, though often impeded by pro-communalist or pro-communist pressures from minority parties. The economy responded very well to these policies, showing an increase in growth rates to 9 per cent by 2007. Business decision-makers spoke positively about such policies. For example, on the vexed question of infrastructure development, one interviewee pointed out,

At last it is happening through private sector involvement. Nine or ten modern new ports have come or are coming into existence, with the roads and so on for onward transport attached. The private sector port operators can turn cargoes round in a tenth the time it took in the public-sector run Mumbai port.[xxii]

In **Japan**, the predominant response to the political situation of the business decision-makers in our study was fear of turbulence because the long-lasting dominance of one party, the LDP, had been brought to an end. 'This revolutionary change [the privatization of a psychologically and economically central business and institution, the Post Office] hammered through by Koizumi [a recent Prime

---

[xxi] Indian, Human Resources Senior Manager, Indian industrial goods manufacturer
[xxii] Indian, Senior Manager, private Indian bank

Minister] destroyed the LDP – factions in favour and against still continue.'[xxiii] Shifts in government policies in Japan following the crisis of the 1990s recession were so extreme as to constitute a 'restructuring [of] its whole society'.[xxiv] The government response to the crisis was to spend lavishly on social welfare and construction; it lent 'huge sums' to the Expressway Corporation, the Housing Loan Corporation and the Urban Renaissance Association, 'an amount equal to GDP [Gross Domestic Product] for several years'.

> " The government borrowed from the Post Office Savings institution. ... There will be [a programme of] privatizations to keep money flowing in. To privatize these heavily indebted corporations (which also have negative equity), the government is injecting money from taxes. They will also be broken up before sale. For the first time they [the government] have to take action that can't be done by balancing.[xxv]

(Usually the Japanese people have preferred to elect 'balancing guys', but the reforming Prime Minister, Koizumi was 'popular because people saw that something had to be done. It was obvious that Japanese society had to change'.)[xxvi]

In contrast to other Asian countries, the government policies of **Singapore** were perceived as having aimed to work with the market: 'The government is open for business. ... Singapore's openness to business stems back three decades and is now a culture.'[xxvii] Tsui-Auch and Lee (2003) concluded from their comparison of the responses to the 1990s Asian currency crisis by businesses in Singapore and South Korea that the state 'matters'; the extent of managerial restructuring of businesses was strongly influenced by the relative strength and weakness of the state in the two countries. Another significant factor, however, was the difference in the political cultures of both government and business leaders in the two countries. Korea was led by ex-military people educated in the military academies of either Japan or Korea who had been exposed mainly to East Asian cultures and organizational models. They had established 'cosy' state-chaebol relationships on the pre-war Japanese model, so the chaebol did not feel the need to gain legitimacy from the state and did not need to seek equity from the international capital market. Furthermore, South Korea had few international companies to compare with. Singapore, on the other hand, was led by a Western-educated elite who had been exposed to Western cultures and organizational models, which they fostered in Singaporean education; also they had few ties with domestic capitalists, adopted a foreign-capital dependent economic development model and enticed multinational companies. Due to the distanced state-capital relationship,

---

[xxiii] Japanese, Finance and Accounting, education
[xxiv] Ibid.
[xxv] Ibid.
[xxvi] Ibid.
[xxvii] Singaporean, Human Resources, business services

businesses in Singapore (except the banks) were left to fend for themselves, which averted the tradition of cronyism and patronage politics in government-business relations. The businesses needed to gain legitimacy in the eyes of the regulatory authorities and the public and hence tended to take the state imperative for professionalism seriously.[28]

Imitation of economic policies successful in one Asian country by another is a common phenomenon. Sometimes, however, the differing economic conditions reduce the chances of success in the imitating country. For example, where China's Special Economic Zones (SEZs) were accounted a success, there were doubts about **India's**. SEZs are enclaves with streamlined procedures, tax breaks and good infrastructure that will lure investors in export-oriented industries. Launching its own SEZs from 2005 on, India's hope was to attract more than $5 billion FDIs by the end of 2007, and private sector investment towards $320 billion-worth of infrastructure. However, there were fears that an absence of a hinterland of labour-intensive manufacturers wanting to start up behind the planned SEZs would mean that the hoped-for benefits would not materialize. There was also opposition to the plans by people arguing that farmers were being forced to sell their land, SEZs were just property deals and the terms were too generous (a five-year tax holiday, exemption from customs and excise and license regulations); there was fear they would just attract investment that would have happened anyway, at huge cost to an Exchequer that was already predicting a fiscal deficit of $38.3 billion by 2011.

Although the shifts in government policy related above are in some cases quite extreme, the concern of Asian business decision-makers over such shifts may not be high by world standards. To ascertain the views of private-sector business entrepreneurs, Brunetti et al. (1999) surveyed more than 3600 entrepreneurs in 69 countries. They found that in South and South East Asia, entrepreneurs rated government-policy related factors as lower obstacles to doing business than the world average of similar entrepreneurs, as Table 9.4 shows. Although 'Large changes in rules and regulations following constitutional changes of government (after elections)' and 'Not having concerns voiced by self or business association taken into account over important changes in laws or policies affecting the business' were named as concerns by 66 per cent and 50 per cent respectively of Asian survey respondents, overall these Asian entrepreneurs were noticeably less negative than the overall 'world' sample about the impact of legal and government policy changes on their business. Asked directly about policy instability, the Asian and South East Asian entrepreneurs rated it as 3.32 as an obstacle to doing business, against an index for the world as a whole of 4.41. South and South East Asia was the only region to experience an overall increase in the predictability of rules and policies.[29]

There appears to be a gap in this area between the business perceptions found by Brunetti et al. (1999) and the historical 'facts', as there is evidence that the

Table 9.4 **Policy-continuity related obstacles to doing business perceived by business entrepreneurs (Percentages)**

Firms fully agreeing, agreeing in most cases or tending to agree (6-point scale) that they were affected by the following obstacles	South and South East Asia	World
Regularly having to cope with unexpected changes in rules, laws or policies which materially affect their business	28	57
The government not sticking to announced policies	12	45
Not being informed when affected by new rules or policies	43	68
Not having concerns voiced by self or business association taken into account over important changes in laws or policies affecting the business	50	78
Fear of retroactive changes of regulations	38	45
Large changes in rules and regulations following constitutional changes of government (after elections)	66	63
Far-reaching policy surprises following unconstitutional changes of government (i.e. coups)	38	49

Note: figures read from a chart in the article, so approximate.

Source: Brunetti, A., Kisunko, G. and Weder, B. (1999) 'Institutional obstacles to doing business: Region-by-region results from a worldwide survey of the private sector', World Bank Policy Research Working Paper No. 1759, Appendix Table 7 – Index of obstacles for doing business – regional averages, URL: http://ssrn.com/abstract=623904; © The World Bank.

considerable shifts in policy environments in the region in the period leading up to 1999 did affect business. As an example, Feinberg and Majumdar (2001) examined the pharmaceutical industry in **India** in the period 1960 to 1994. Both technology and FDI underwent considerable changes during that period. Broadly, policies were liberal in the 1960s but made very stringent in the 1970s; attempts at liberalization were made in the 1980s and then real liberalization took place in the early 1990s. At the same time, the policy environment was characterized by discretionary control and a lack of transparency. This environment had 'profound effects' on the investment and research activities of both MNCs and domestic firms in India. During this time, also, the Indian pharmaceutical sector was subject to a complex and changing mix of sector-specific policies aimed at the objectives of equality of income distribution and self-determination. The policies that affected firms, both foreign and domestic, in the Indian pharmaceutical industry were intended to develop domestic industry and make drugs available to India's poor. However, the policies also had the effect of de-linking firm ownership from ownership of technology and ultimately muting firms' incentives to innovate.[30] Among our interviewees, 'Not having concerns taken into account' was a problem that led to a lack of clarity in legislation, Indians felt. One Group Chief Financial Officer noted that the recommendations of the IT (information technology) industry on clarifications of taxation anomalies were not met. 'This will imply continuance of a litigious environment', he feared.[xxviii]

Similarly, although **China** saw continuity of government, in terms of the same political system and same ruling party throughout, businesses in China had to cope with some quite abrupt changes in government policy during the reform period that began in 1978. For example,

> China's ninth five-year plan, starting in 1996, stated that the policy of mainly relying on preferential concessions to attract foreign capital would be modified in favor of a policy of 'national' treatment, where foreign-invested firms would be treated in the same manner as local Chinese firms in the applicability and enforcement of relevant regulations.

Again, in late 2006, China 'shunned the business community' by introducing Ordinance Ten re-establishing restrictions that had been repealed three years before and obliging Chinese companies to seek government approval before listing overseas. The curb was intended to halt or slow the flood of overseas flotations. The Chinese government had become concerned that it was losing tax revenues because of the favourable treatment of overseas-listed companies and that state-owned companies had been sold too cheaply to foreigners. (A record 19 Chinese companies were listed in London in 2006, bringing the total to 43, including Air China and the construction group Zhejiang Expressway.)[31]

As a result of China's tax changes, after April 1996 foreign joint ventures had to pay taxes on imported machinery, like local firms, which had not been exempted in the past. This raised the cost of such equipment by over 30 per cent. Special deals had also become much more difficult to arrange and taxes on imported raw materials would also be payable in the near future. The authorities in China also took steps to increase the effectiveness of tax collection, and efforts to circumvent Chinese regulations by use of personal connections were more tightly controlled.[32] While changes such as these may be quite logical from the point of view of the economy, they do require rapid and extensive adaptation by businesses and the point made by entrepreneurs in other Asian countries that 'Not having concerns voiced by self or business association taken into account over important changes in laws or policies affecting the business' could well apply even more strongly in China. Interviewees in the present study suggested that expecting such treatment by government was part of the Chinese business culture.

A possible explanation of the difference between the rather positive perceptions of business leaders about policy stability in their country and the kinds of events described here is that business leaders may be more oriented to the current and anticipated situation than to events in the past. Alternatively, the fast-moving

---

[xxviii] Indian, Chief Financial Officer, business information technology

'business, cultural and competitive environments' in at least some parts of Asia have reportedly led to business leaders making strategic decisions intuitively; if they have come to rely on their intuition, concern with 'objective facts' may be generally lower.[33]

Institutional integrity, 'straightness', rule of law and corruption

The World Bank's 2006 indicators for eight Asian and two comparison countries for regulatory quality, rule of law and corruption are shown at Table 9.5.

As Table 9.5 clearly shows, in Japan, Taiwan and Singapore, businesses benefited from a relatively benign political environment by 2006, whereas in both China and India they suffered from serious inadequacies in regulatory quality, rule of law and control of corruption. However, in **China**, although legal protection was perhaps weaker and problems of official corruption worse in the private family business sector than in the state and listed sectors, this did not prevent the private sector from performing well. Reflecting on this anomaly, Allen et al. (2005) contended, 'One of the most effective solutions for corruption for firms in this sector is the common goal of sharing high prospective profits, which aligns interests of government officials with those of entrepreneurs and investors.' Implicit contractual agreements and reputation could act as enforcement mechanisms to ensure that all parties, including government officials, fulfilled their roles to make the firm successful.[34] A more critical perspective on this aligning of

Table 9.5 **Three governance indicators for eight Asian and two comparison countries 2006 (Country's percentile rank)**

	Regulatory quality	Rule of law	Control of corruption
China	48	40	52
Hong Kong	(98)	(84)	(85)
India	35	58	47
Japan	68	83	84
Taiwan	88	78	80
Singapore	100	88	100
South Korea	63	69	58
Malaysia	68	64	66
Thailand	62	57	51
USA	92	90	86
UK	92	93	93

Source: Based on Kaufman, D., Krasy, A. and Mastruzzi, M. (2007) 'Governance Matters VI: Governance Indicators for 1996–2006', URL: http://info.worldbank.org/governance/wgi2007/sc_country.asp; © The World Bank.

the interests of government officials and entrepreneurs is that the two colluded to maintain the political status quo.

> Because of their close personal and professional ties, and because of their shared interests in promoting economic growth, China's capitalists and communist officials share similar viewpoints on a range of political, economic and social issues. Rather than promote democratic governance, China's capitalists have a stake in preserving the political system that has allowed them to prosper, and they are among the Party's most important bases of support.[35]

The data given in Table 9.5 are based mainly on the views of respondents from non-business organizations; from their survey of private sector business entrepreneurs, Brunetti et al. (1999) found that South and South East Asian entrepreneurs rated corruption above crime and theft as well as financing problems as obstacles to doing business but below inflation, an inadequate supply of infrastructure or labour regulations (see Table 9.7); they also rated corruption well below levels for the world sample and were overall less negative about the impact of a government culture of bribery.

Table 9.6 shows the percentage of firms in the region that rated a given corruption-related factor above the median level; a comparison with other factors affecting business is also shown.

Legal environment

Law in the Western sense has not, historically, been central to the experience of Asian countries, except those that were under European colonial rule for long periods. These included India, Hong Kong and Singapore. In the main, the comments of the interviewees in the present study reflected these inter-country differences in historical experience. For instance, 'Singapore is a meritocracy in contrast to China. ... The bureaucracy is transparent and limited. ... The rules are clear, people are aware of them and play by them.'[xxix]

> 'Hong Kong is Westernized in many ways. The legal system, the civil service and the police are all straight. Hong Kong stamped out official corruption, for instance in the immigration department, during the 1970s. The change was brought about through having a free press and one determined Governor, who set up a system of investigation using outsiders (British) and started by tackling the most senior civil servants. It helps that Hong Kong civil servants are well paid.[xxx]

---

xxix Singaporean, Finance, Banking; Entrepreneur, food and beverages
xxx China, Expatriate (British), General Manager, energy MNC

284 9

INTRODUCTION · THE BUSINESS CULTURES OF FIVE ASIAN COUNTRIES · ANALYSING ASIAN BUSINESS CULTURES
· OWNERSHIP, FINANCING AND GOVERNANCE · ORGANIZATION AND MANAGEMENT · BUSINESS STRATEGY ·

Table 9.6 **Percentages of firms rating official corruption-related problems above the median level in comparison with other factors affecting business (Percentages)**

Firms who rated the following problems above the median level on a 6-point scale	South and South East Asia	World
Having to pay some irregular additional payments to get things done	33	43
Predictability of amount of bribe*	50	40
Fear that even after making an 'additional payment' more will be asked for	27	42
Expectation that the service will be delivered after a bribe is paid**	80	70
Ability to get redress if a government agent acts against the rules	65	62
Theft and crime	73	79
Power outages once a week or more often	25	23
Takes less than one month to get a public telephone line connected**	25	23

*Notes: *Predictability of amount of bribe* – This question distinguishes between 'greasing' corruption and 'blocking' corruption. 'Greasing' corruption is predictable and acts like a transaction cost, whereas 'blocking' corruption is highly unpredictable causing large uncertainties. Thus, the SSEA figure is less adverse for business than the World figure; ** A high score on these questions denotes a relatively low obstacle.

Source: Brunetti, A., Kisunko, G. and Weder, B. (1999) 'Institutional obstacles to doing business: Region-by-region results from a Worldwide Survey of the private sector', World Bank Policy Research Working Paper No. 1759, Appendix Table 7 – Index of obstacles for doing business – regional averages, URL: http://ssrn.com/abstract=623904; © The World Bank.

In contrast,

> China does not have rule of law – it has rule by law. A successful entrepreneur or an official in economic control will command a big project to be done and it will be done. In theory his power is limited by law – if, say, he wants to build a high-rise building, there are permitted limits. But he will order his lawyers to find a law that allows what he wants as an exception; or, at the very top, he will promulgate a new law.[xxxi]

Similarly, 'The judicial system in Taiwan is as bad as anywhere, in terms of favouring the powerful, but it is very strict for everyone else.'[xxxii]

Part of the explanation for the differences revealed in our interviews is that China, Taiwan and Hong Kong had different legal systems. Peng (2000) wrote

---

[xxxi] Mainland Chinese, General Manager, international business information hardware manufacturer
[xxxii] Taiwan, expatriate banker

that Hong Kong had a modern Common Law system, although its Company Ordinances were increasingly becoming outdated. Taiwan followed the Civil Law system, and all practitioners and even some government officials admitted that the corporate law was also very archaic. China was reverting to the Civil Law system with a strong emphasis on the 'socialist market economy with Chinese characteristics'. As Dodds (1996) pointed out,

> " Contract systems have a long history of use in China and differ from contracts under modern Western contract law. A Chinese contract system is a general overall agreement between a superior authority and subject where the subject agrees to perform a delegated task and to produce specified results. Under the agreement, the subject has the freedom to manage the task without interference and is entitled to the earnings that remain after turning over a specified amount to the superior authority.[36]

In addition to the foundations of the legal system, bureaucracy and public law administration also differed widely in the three economies. Generally, Hong Kong has been rated as having a far better civil service system than Taiwan and China. In the judgement of Liu (2001) these differences in corporate and administrative law have had profound effects on the state of corporate governance of the respective economies.[37]

In accordance with the views expressed by our interviewees in **China**, Dodds (1996) wrote, 'China's legal system is weak. The rule of law is deficient.' Close ties between the Chinese courts and local communist party officials caused many foreign companies discomfort. 'We're used to a complete divide between the government and the judiciary, which is something that China is nowhere near achieving.' Legal decisions were influenced by local protectionism; intellectual property law enforcement was weak. Peng (2000) noted that until the early 20th century, the concept of law and the notion of the 'rule of law' had not taken root in Chinese society. This was part of the legacy of Confucianism. (There were short periods when a philosophy called 'Legalism' had more influence in China than Confucianism, but Legalism emphasized *fa* or punishment by law but not rule of law – it emphasized state power and control rather than setting up legal standards.) Most Confucian values survived both the introduction of Western civilization into China during the 18th and 19th centuries and the Communists' attempt to replace them with their own ideologies in the 20th century. Thus Confucian values remained embedded in the Chinese people's legal consciousness, expectation of justice and trust in law, with the following consequences:

1. The idea that harmony should prevail between individuals was central to social order: disputes should therefore be dissolved rather than resolved and law was viewed negatively because it was not virtuous to assert one's rights.

Although social and economic changes subsequently mitigated the negative view of law, to engage in a lawsuit was still commonly regarded as to lose face, because it implied a failure to achieve harmony.

2. Confucian thinking also meant that Chinese law was primarily criminal. Civil matters, such as those relating to disputes over business contracts, were either ignored entirely or subsumed under the criminal codes.

3. Confucianism's emphasis on kinship and family meant that the family, not the individual, constituted the unit of the social and political community and the law protected, but also placed obligations on, the family rather than the individual, even to the extent of applying the death penalty to an entire family.

The effects of this legal culture based on Confucianism could be seen, for example, in **Taiwan**, where law was 'marginalized, reflecting the role of traditional legal culture in a modern Chinese society'.[38] Personal connections outweighed legal rights. One consequence was in the realm of intellectual property. Confucianism historically criticized and discriminated against profit seeking and encouraged and praised the copying and imitation of human ingenuity. 'Therefore, Western copyright theory, as codified in the Berne Convention, is on a collision course with Chinese cultural beliefs.' Although the enormous economic benefit generated by its technology industries motivated the Taiwanese government to struggle with different interest groups and fight this long-standing cultural value, without cultural support copyright protection remained relatively weak in Taiwan in comparison with other major information technology producing countries. Another example is the preference shown in the Asia-Pacific Economic Community (APEC) for 'soft' law consisting of a set of commonly agreed skeletal principles stated in broad terms; it is the preferred Asian way. 'For Asians, vague language is often necessary to ensure consensus on sensitive issues. Ambiguity is a useful device, in contrast to the Western view that ambiguity is a weakness.'[39]

In the context of Asia, the legal system of **India** was closest to that of the West. 'It is a democracy where the rule of law generally prevails and property rights are protected adequately.'[40] Nevertheless, one interviewee saw the judiciary as corrupt, 'except for the top ten per cent', while Allen et al. (2007) contended that the difference between protection in practice as opposed to protection in theory by law was the most striking fact about India's legal system.[41] According to Feinberg and Majumdar (2001), India had a weak appropriability environment: its lax patent laws and high import duties created a weak R&D (research and development) appropriability regime for both MNCs and Indian pharmaceutical firms. As a result, knowledge could potentially flow freely, creating spillovers not only between MNCs and Indian firms, but also between Indian pharmaceutical firms that undertook R&D, such as Cipla Pharmaceuticals, Ranbaxy Pharmaceuticals and Dr. Reddy's Laboratories, and 'free riders'.[42]

The role of government in industry and business

From our study we found four aspects of governments' role in business to be present in the minds of Asian business decision-makers: their role in industrialization, modernization and economic reform, government regulation of business, competition from government-owned businesses and the influence of the bureaucracy.

Government's role in industrialization, modernization and economic reform

Studies such as that of Whitley (1992) showed that in East Asia the government's role in the industrialization and modernization of their economies was a central one.[43] In the words of Weiming (2000), 'The presence of the central government in all weighty economic decisions is not only expected but also desired by the business community and the general public.'[44] There was, however, no single model of Asian governments' role in their countries' modernization. As Weiming (2000) noted, 'Government's participation in the economic sphere may take different forms – direct management (Singapore), active leadership (South Korea), informed guidance (Japan), selective interference (Taiwan), or positive non-*interference* (Hong Kong).' In **India**, the governments of the individual states were considered very important by our interviewees. 'Maharashtra is anti-business and so is losing it. Businesses diversify to multiple locations partly for disaster management (the Bombay floods) and partly to insure against the possibility of an anti-business state government being elected. This is despite the fact that it makes management more difficult.'[xxxiii] On the other hand, there was a view that India's political system facilitated adjustment by state governments to business priorities.

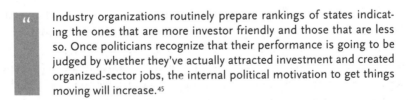

> Industry organizations routinely prepare rankings of states indicating the ones that are more investor friendly and those that are less so. Once politicians recognize that their performance is going to be judged by whether they've actually attracted investment and created organized-sector jobs, the internal political motivation to get things moving will increase.[45]

In **China** after 1979, the steady decentralization of economic initiative to provincial, municipal and even more local tiers of government led to a closer interdependence between local governments and enterprises led by managers or entrepreneurs who were part of the same community.[46] This effective diminution of the role of the central government eventually caused the central authorities to

---

[xxxiii] Indian, Senior Manager, private Indian bank

respond by attempts to counter 'local protectionism' and establish standardization in policy implementation and enforcement by centralizing a growing number of its regulatory bureaucracies up to the provincial level. In the view of Mertha (2005),

> " Thus far this transformation remains imperfect and incomplete. The institutional cleavages and fragmentation that so often give rise to corruption and other pathologies of the state appear to have shifted from horizontal, geographic lines to vertical, functional ones. Moreover, the principal beneficiaries of this shift to centralized management are the provinces, not Beijing, as the institutional mechanisms of personnel and budgetary resource allocations are concentrated at the provincial level. Although this has curbed localism to a degree by transferring power from local governments to the newly centralized bureaucracies, it has also contributed to a situation in which newly strengthened provinces may play a key role in the emergence of a sort of perverse federalism.[47]

As this example shows, contrary to Western beliefs about China's 'monolithic state', the Chinese government often pursued a trial-and-error approach in which significant errors occurred. One source described their policies as 'particularistic' – a series of sometimes unrelated initiatives.[48] One cause, according to our research, was internal government dissension over policy.

> " From the outside, the Chinese government seems unified; from the inside there are many differences, views are fragmented. ... Their think tanks, such as one that supplies the Ministry of Commerce, and so is influential and staffed with bright people from both domestic universities and people trained in overseas universities, lacks technique, analytical tools, system. Also its information base is deficient. Channels are not established. Decisions conflict.[xxxiv]

Consistently with this opinion, Dodds (1996) stated that China's reforms had not followed an overall plan and had been largely ad hoc, dealing with problems as they arose. Nevertheless, Dodds (1996) considered, the reforms were interrelated and exhibited a coherent strategy when examined ex post. Essentially, the strategy was one of 'marketization'. China introduced markets and competition. Without completely relinquishing control over SOEs, it increased enterprise autonomy and gave SOEs incentives to participate in the new markets as profit maximizers.[49] Child and Tse (2001) argued that China's pragmatic approach to reform, which was aimed at balancing the pace of reform with social stability, created uncertainties for both international and local firms as to the exact speed and direction of reform, which included three processes: marketization,

---

[xxxiv] Mainland Chinese, General Manager, International MNC, business information hardware manufacturer

decentralization and privatization.[50] Zhu (2007) characterized Chinese reform as a 'no-theory' 'strategy' that was 'selected' by the Chinese elite, 'accepted' by the Chinese people and 'worked' in the Chinese context, facilitated by a set of historically specific structural factors, factors full of complementarities and tensions that skilled actors were able to exploit to pursue sectional interests. Behind this lay a Confucian philosophy.[51]

Conflicts of interest between the government's concern for social stability and high employment and private individuals' desire to make money were drawn to our attention by an interviewee. 'There are two systems: the government is concerned with social stability and the preservation of communism and so drives the economy to provide employment; individuals want to make money.' Overall, individuals' desire to make money was 'winning'. In the words of an interviewee with extensive international experience, 'It's the most capitalistic system I've ever been in.'[xxxv] There were also conflicts of government logic: 'A conflict between the logic of economic efficiency and political and institutional norms has dominated China's reform experience. Which side prevails, ... determines whether "the future direction of enterprise reform will reflect strategic and operational needs rather than a desire to retain political control and placements." '[52]

Government regulation of business

Apart from a comment that Taiwanese entrepreneurs often invested in China because it was a less regulated environment than Taiwan's, and a complaint that the Japanese authorities would not deregulate medical insurance, there were few signs from our interviews that regulation in our five sample countries was considered burdensome. There were even some signs of approval of increasing regulation aimed at improving governance. From the findings of Brunetti et al. (1999), however, it seems that some labour regulations were a burden for business in South and South East Asia. Table 9.7 gives the regional average of an index for obstacles to doing business for South and South East Asia in comparison with the World average. Labour regulations, regulations for starting a business or new operations and safety or environmental regulations were all rated higher in the region than in the world generally. However, regulations on foreign trade, foreign currency regulations and, significantly, general uncertainty on the cost of complying with regulations were rated as lesser obstacles than the world average. Overall only three out of six top obstacles in this region were regulation-related compared with five out of six in developed countries. While 27 per cent of entrepreneurs in the region stated that they had decided at least once not to make a major investment because of problems relating to complying

---

xxxv China, Expatriate, Consultant, international management consultancy

Table 9.7   Index of regulations as obstacles for doing business compared with other obstacles (1 = no obstacle; 6 = very strong obstacle)

Firms fully agreeing, agreeing in most cases or tending to agree (6-point scale) that they were affected by the following obstacles	South and South East Asia	World
Regulations for starting a business or new operations	3.67	3.12
Regulations on foreign trade (exports, imports)	3.54	3.93
Labour regulations	3.83	2.74
Foreign currency regulations	3.58	3.68
Tax regulations and/or high taxes	4.12	5.12
Safety or environmental regulations	3.32	2.26
Price controls	3.13	3.11
General uncertainty on cost of regulations	3.63	4.21
Inadequate supply of infrastructure	3.91	3.87
Policy instability	3.32	4.41
Inflation	3.87	3.88
Financing	3.60	4.14
Crime and theft	3.37	4.27
Corruption	3.64	4.41
Terrorism	2.38	2.45

Source: Brunetti, A., Kisunko, G. and Weder, B. (1999) 'Institutional obstacles to doing business: Region-by-region results from a Worldwide Survey of the private sector' World Bank Policy Research Working Paper No. 1759, Appendix Table 7 – Index of obstacles for doing business – regional averages, URL: http://ssrn.com/abstract=623904; © The World Bank.

with government regulations, that figure was 38 per cent for the world sample; and only 12 per cent, against a world average of 16 per cent, claimed that more than 50 per cent of senior management time was spent on negotiations with officials about changes and interpretations of laws and regulations. A possible explanation for these low levels of perceived burdens from regulation is that in some Asian countries reform had lessened the burden of regulation in comparison with the relatively recent past.

Competition from government-owned businesses

In many Asian countries the role of government in business extends to government-owned or part-owned businesses being in direct competition with the private sector. In **India** it was claimed that this competition is 'unfair'. 'For many companies there is an eternal battle with government-owned competitors who enjoy an advantage.'[xxxvi] Opinions differed on how effective these companies

---

[xxxvi] Indian, Economist, former entrepreneur, senior academic

were. The view of the Chairman of a family-owned business group was the following:

> They are mostly inefficient. They are not serving their customers, they are serving the government. They are controlled by politicians. There will probably be at least one on their Board. There are one or two exceptions – Indian Oil comes to mind. But even they did not have a level playing field – they had the advantage of an early start before liberalization. Most government enterprises are so slow.[xxxvii]

On the other hand, the CEO (Chief Executive Officer) of a family-owned advertising agency pointed out,

> There are some very good government companies in telecoms, petroleum products and infrastructure development for instance, and they compete with the private sector on a level playing field. Some government companies, such as Indian Oil, would welcome more private competition, because at present they are affected by government price controls which would go if the market were opened up.[xxxviii]

The influence of the bureaucracy

With the exception of Hong Kong, bureaucratic influence over business was strong in the Asian countries of our sample during the early postwar period, but had been weakened since.

As noted in Chapter 5, the power of the bureaucrats in **China** over business at one time was such that they gained the sobriquet 'mothers-in-law' because of their constant and arbitrary interference with enterprise operations. However, serious bureaucratic reforms preceded any economic reforms. A mandatory retirement system for the bureaucracy's cadres was instituted in 1980. It abolished the lifetime tenure cadres had always enjoyed and retired old revolutionary veterans whose political loyalty had been valued more highly than their administrative capabilities, thereby 'moderniz[ing] the contingent of government officials'.[53] A strict retirement age was enforced for government officials, and an education requirement was also introduced at each level of government positions. This first bureaucratic reform resulted in two major consequences. The most direct consequence was that many younger and more-educated bureaucrats replaced the older revolutionary veterans. The second consequence was that the average duration of a bureaucrat's tenure in a government position was reduced and turnover rates increased. One potential negative effect was that cadres would now exhibit more short-termist behaviour. On balance, however, Li (1998) found and provided

---

[xxxvii] Indian, Chairman, family-owned business group, Indian MNC industrial goods manufacturer
[xxxviii] Indian, CEO, family-owned business, advertising

much evidence for the critical role of the changed human capital composition of the Chinese bureaucracy in the successful implementation of economic reforms. Furthermore, as the reform process led to the entry of new businesses which were either partially owned or supported by government, a change took place in the behaviour of Chinese bureaucrats. Officials became de facto shareholders rather than short-termist bribe-takers. Bureaucrats thus began to lobby higher-level agencies for general deregulation on behalf of entrepreneurs in their jurisdiction.[54]

Nevertheless, from a time study of six Chinese enterprise directors in a replication of Mintzberg's (1973) study of US managers, Boisot and Liang (1992) found that although the Chinese enterprise managers in their sample shared many behavioural characteristics with their US counterparts, they did so in an institutional setting that was designed to constrain their managerial behaviour rather than to support them.[55] The study was conducted some years after the start of China's economic reforms. 'Prior to the reforms, managerial activities – to judge from anecdotal evidence – were narrowly technical and primarily concerned with production engineering.' By the time of the study, the weight given to these activities was modest and the managers' concerns appeared to be much broader, with the largest percentages of both received and sent written communication being concerned with general information, while items concerned with the general state of the firm, strategy, production, sales and accounting and finance were all well represented. This did not, however, mean that the managers were given a free hand. 'Nearly 30 per cent of the paper that lands on the desk of our sample originates in the supervising bureaucracy. Much of it will take the form of new detailed instructions or regulations covering all aspects of the firm's activities – purchasing, personnel matters, quality control, energy use, etc.' The relationship between Chinese enterprises and external government agencies, according to Boisot and Liang (1992), was not established by law but by administrative regulations which, in effect, bound them to each other. 'Instructions given by bureaucrats are often conflicting or downright irrational and have the effect of drawing the enterprise manager into a process of perpetual bargaining with his superiors as he seeks to safeguard a minimum measure of managerial freedom of action.'[56]

It is debatable, however, to what extent such managerial autonomy was actively sought by Chinese enterprise directors. In response to the question, as put to them by Child and Lu (1990), Chinese managers certainly claimed to seek greater autonomy. However, Confucian precepts of obedience – 'Emperor-Minister-Father-Son' – remained deeply rooted in the culture. Management as a sphere of activity still enjoyed little institutional legitimacy both in the eyes of the workforce and in those of the supervising bureaucracy. 'A manager is constitutionally required to serve both interest groups and if he shows too strong a concern with autonomy, it will be assumed that he is pursuing his own interests at their expense.'[57,58]

Under British colonial rule up to the 1997 handover to China, the government of *Hong Kong* could more properly be called an administration, and its history was full of examples of the government pursuing administrative reforms to deal with political crises. Nevertheless, the largely laissez-faire policies pursued by the administration meant that the amount of interference with business was limited. After 1997, however, Vickers (2001) used survey and interview material to capture what was described as a reinforced paternalism emerging among the administrative officers, a paternalism that had both Confucian and colonial roots.[59] After Hong Kong reverted to Chinese sovereignty, it was run by a local administration under China's 'one country, two systems' and 'Hong Kong people governing Hong Kong' policies, as a special administrative region (SAR). However, there were subsequent periods when the Hong Kong political structure faced opposition, even to the point of being rejected, by the public, who directed social discontent against the government's incumbent officials. In part, these problems of legitimation arose because the Hong Kong government pursued positive non-interventionism 'only in an arbitrary, ad hoc and instrumental way'; in part, because the democratic 'promise' was not fulfilled.

Although our research did not confirm it, it has been argued that the national bureaucracy was so important in **Japan** that 'rather than a rule of law, a rule of bureaucrats prevails'.[60] Civil servants were considered the most powerful and stable decision-making force in Japan. Politicians and business leaders as well as most other groups' power were much more temporarily defined.

 Law enforcement in the economic sector in the past often took the form of administrative guidance, which meant that the law was equated with whatever policies officials chose to implement. This could result in abuses such as [a ministry's] use of informal enforcement to encourage business enterprises to engage in prohibited anti-competitive conduct.

Mediation systems (*chotei seido*) were another long-standing practice that provided the bureaucrats with discretionary power. Their official purpose was for all disputes to be resolved more rapidly, cheaply and efficiently than in a court, [but] the result was that the bureaucrats who directed the system were able to steer business judgements in accordance with their priorities instead of the law.[61]

In Japan's 'Iron Triangle' between politicians, civil servants and business leaders, contact went beyond professional relations to entertainment and gift-giving. These showings of friendship opened the door to professional trust. A series of reform measures to the bureaucracy, to streamline it and ensure conformity with the National Public Service Law concerned with protecting bureaucratic ethics, were reported to have resulted in an efficient bureaucracy that was more strongly driven by ethical standards, although some of the practices described in the previous paragraph continued.[62]

Despite the reduced power of bureaucrats in some of these Asian countries, businesses continued to have to deal with them. In **India**, 'Government has to be squared – for instance banks employ liaison officers whose job is to square government.'[xxxix] 'It's quite bad. There's a substantial cost to compliance, especially for the smaller companies who can't move files as easily as the big ones.'[xl] An expatriate business leader illustrated the problems by referring to the delay in processing his visa application, which had been forwarded from the local office of the Indian Foreign Service in December 2007 but was still not processed in January 2009.[xli] Another interviewee confirmed the point: 'The bureaucracy is slow, compared to China where all the formalities are done very fast.'[xlii] However, China's new efficiency in its bureaucracy was offset by the ambitions of local governments to develop their area economically: 'If you approach them, they want an ownership stake; it's best not to. The best approach is to have an influential contact intervene on your behalf.'[xliii]

Conclusion

Although the focus of the unstructured interviews in this study was business culture, the responses quite often led to comments on the political cultures and perceived environments of the countries. These responses displayed a substantial measure of agreement within the business communities we researched. It may be that a business culture itself tends to lead its members to perceive their political environment in somewhat similar ways; and this is what our research suggested.

As Tables 9.1, 9.2, 9.3 and 9.5 show, corresponding with the business cultures reported in our study, there were major differences among the five countries we studied on all the six measures of political governance used by the World Bank in 2006. One breakdown of these data places India and China closest together on all the measures except Voice and Accountability while the other three were similar on all measures, with one or two exceptions. (Singapore's ratings on Voice and Accountability were low, for instance.) This breakdown suggests that in Asia factors such as stage of economic development might have been more significant for political stability, government effectiveness, regulatory authority, rule of law and control of corruption in the region than either mode of government (democracy versus one-party rule) or the social culture (Confucianism-influenced versus

---

[xxxix] Indian, Economist, former entrepreneur, senior academic

[xl] Indian , Senior General Manager and family member, family-owned business, consumer goods manufacturer

[xli] India, Expatriate, CEO MNC, internet-based business services

[xlii] Indian, Senior General Manager and family member, family-owned business, consumer goods manufacturer

[xliii] China, Expatriate entrepreneur

Hinduism-influenced). On 'Voice and Accountability', not surprisingly, the three democracies scored significantly higher than the other countries.

Some other things stand out: on almost all measures the smallest countries, Singapore and Taiwan, outperformed the large; China was in the lowest half of countries worldwide except on control of corruption where its recent measures had slightly improved the situation; contrary to widespread beliefs that China's one party rule makes it more effective in government than India, with its clumsy democracy, China scored below India on this measure.

The World Bank measures were obtained from opinion leaders and non-governmental bodies; there are indications both from our own research and from other sources that the members of business communities may perceive the political culture and environments of their countries similarly in some ways but differently in others from such sources. For example, the World Bank measured 'control of corruption' as high in Taiwan, whereas our business interviewees called corruption pervasive and endemic.

References

[1] Khanna, T. (2008) *Billions of Entrepreneurs in China and India: How India and China Are Reshaping Their Futures – and Yours*, Cambridge, MA: Harvard University Press.

[2] Luce, E. (2006) *In Spite of the Gods: The Strange Rise of Modern India*, London: Little, Brown.

[3] Rodrik, D. and Subramanian, A. (2004) 'From "Hindu Growth" to productivity surge: The mystery of the Indian growth transition', *IMF Staff Papers*, **52**, URL: www.imf.org/external/pubs/ft/wp/2004/wp0477.

[4] Huang, Y. and Khanna, T. (2003) 'Can India overtake China?' *Foreign Policy*, June: 74–81.

[5] Zainulbhai, A.S. (2007) 'Clearing the way for robust growth: An interview with India's chief economic planner', *McKinsey Quarterly Online*, http://www.mckinseyquarterly.com/Clearing_the_way_for_robust_growth_An_interview_with_Indias_chief_economic_planner_2067.6 Ibid.

[6] Ibid.

[7] Khanna, T. (2008) *Billions of Entrepreneurs in China and India: How India and China Are Reshaping Their Futures – and Yours*, Cambridge, MA: Harvard University Press.

[8] Horvat, A. (2006) *Japan: 2006. World Press Freedom Review*, URL: http://www.freemedia.at/cms/ipi/freedom_detail.html?country=/KW0001/KW0005/KW0118/

[9] Fell, D. (2005) 'Political and media liberalization and political corruption in Taiwan', *The China Quarterly*, **184**: 875–93.

[10] Li, J.T., Tsui, A.S. and Weldon, E. (2000) *Management and Organizations in the Chinese Context*, New York: Macmillan.

[11] 'Marketing to China's consumers', *McKinsey Quarterly Online*, 24 August 2007.

[12] Dodds, R.F. Jr (1996) 'State enterprise reform in China: Managing the transition to a market economy', *Law and Policy in International Business*, **27**, URL: googlescholar/docid/50004086.

[13] Child, J. and Tse, D.K. (2001) 'China's transition and its implications for international business', *Journal of International Business Studies*, **32**(1): 5–21.

[14] Allen, F., Qian, J. and Qian M. (2005) 'China's financial system: Past, present, and future', *Wharton Financial Institutions Center Working Paper*, URL: http://fic.wharton.upenn.edu/fic/papers/05/0517.pdf.

[15] Clarke, D.C. (2003) 'Corporate governance in China: An overview', URL: http://papers.ssrn.com/sol3/papers.cfm?abstract_id=424885.

[16] Luce, E. (2006) *In Spite of the Gods: The Strange Rise of Modern India*, London: Little, Brown.

[17] *Deccan Chronicle*, 7 March 2007, p. 1 'Supreme remark: Hang the corrupt'.

[18] Mehta, P.B. (2007) 'A bleak urban future', *Center for the Advanced Study of India*, University of Pennsylvania, URL: www.sas.upenn.edu/casi.

[19] Aoki, M. (2006) 'Whither Japan's corporate governance?' URL: http://siepr.stanford.edu/papers/pdf/05-14: 3–10.

[20] Vanoverbeke, D. (2006) 'Driving innovation: On the origin and mechanism of informal bureaucracy in Japan', *XIV International Economic History Conference*, Helsinki, URL: http://www.helsinki.fi/iehc2006/papers2/Vanover.pdf.

[21] Suzuki, K. and Cobham, D. (2005) 'Recent trends in the sources of finance for Japanese firms: Has Japan become a "high internal finance" country?' *Discussion Paper Series*, Heriot-Watt University, 26–9.

[22] Tsui-Auch, L.S. and Lee, Y.-J. (2003) 'The state matters; management models of Singaporean Chinese and Korean business groups', *Organization Studies*, **24**(4): 507–34.

[23] Dickson, B.J. (2007) 'Integrating wealth and power in China: The Communist Party's embrace of the private sector', *The China Quarterly*, **192**: 827–54.

[24] Hutton, W. (2007) 'New China, new crisis', *The Observer*, 6 May.

[25] Qiu, Y. (2005) 'Problems of managing joint ventures in China's interior: Evidence from Shaanxi', *SAM Advanced Management Journal*, **70**(3): 39–46.

[26] Khairulla, D.H.Z. and Khairullah, Z.Y. (2005) 'A study of the extent of Westernisation in Indian magazine advertisements', *Asia Pacific Journal of Marketing and Logistics*, **17**(2): 2–16.

[27] Rodrik, D. and Subramanian, A. (2004) 'From "Hindu Growth" to productivity surge: The mystery of the Indian growth transition', *IMF Staff Papers*, **52**, URL: www.imf.org/external/pubs/ft/wp/2004/wp0477.

[28] Ibid.

[29] Brunetti, A., Kisunko, G. and Weder, B. (1999) 'Institutional obstacles to doing business: Region-by-region results from a worldwide survey of the private sector', *World Bank Policy Research Working Paper No. 1759*, URL: papers.ssrn.com/sol3/Delivery.cfm/SSRN_ID81368_code170891.pdf.

[30] Feinberg, S.E. and Majumdar, S.K. (2001) 'Technology spillovers from foreign direct investment in the Indian pharmaceutical industry', *Journal of International Business Studies*, **32**: 421–37.

[31] *The Times*, 9 October 2006, 'Flotation to beat Beijing crackdown'.

[32] Sai-Ching, L.P. and Walters, G.P. (1998) 'Wah Hoi industrial company', *Entrepreneurship: Theory and Practice*, **22**(3): 87–99.

[33] Haley, G.T. and Tan, C.-T. (1996) 'The black hole of South-East Asia: Strategic decision making in an informational void', *Management Decision*, **34**(9): 37–48.

[34] Allen, F., Qian, J. and Qian M. (2005) 'China's financial system: Past, present, and future', *Wharton Financial Institutions Center Working Paper*, URL: http://fic.wharton.upenn.edu/fic/papers/05/0517.pdf.

[35] Mertha, A.C. (2005) 'China's "soft" centralization: Shifting *Tiao/Kuai* authority relations', *The China Quarterly*, **184**: 791–810.

[36] Dodds, R.F. Jr (1996) 'State enterprise reform in China: Managing the transition to a market economy', *Law and Policy in International Business*, **27**, URL: googlescholar/docid/50004086.

[37] Liu, L.S. (2001) 'Corporate governance development in the Greater China: A Taiwan perspective', in Li, J.T., Tsui, A.S. and Weldon, E. (eds) *Management and Organizations in the Chinese Context*, New York: Macmillan.

[38] Peng, S.-Y. (2000) 'The WTO legalistic approach and East Asia from the legal culture perspective', *Asian-Pacific Law & Policy Journal*, **1**(2): 13–21.

[39] Ibid.

[40] Rodrik, D. and Subramanian, A. (2004) 'From "Hindu Growth" to productivity surge: The mystery of the Indian growth transition', *IMF Staff Papers*, **52**, URL: www.imf.org/external/pubs/ft/wp/2004/wp0477.

[41] Allen, F., Chakrabarti, R., Sankar, D., Qian, J. and Qian, M. (2007) 'Financing firms in India', URL: http://fic.wharton.upenn.edu/fic/papers/06/0608.pdf.

[42] Feinberg, S.E. and Majumdar, S.K. (2001) 'Technology spillovers from foreign direct investment in the Indian pharmaceutical industry', *Journal of International Business Studies*, **32**: 421–37.

[43] Weiming, T. (2000) 'Implications of the rise of "Confucian" East Asia', *Daedalus*, **129**(1) URL: isites.harvard.edu/fs/docs/icb.topic241166.files/EthicsSyl08.doc.

[44] Whitley, R. (1992) *Business Systems in East Asia: Firms, Markets, and Societies*, London: Sage.

[45] Zainulbhai, A.S. (2007) 'Clearing the way for robust growth: An interview with India's chief economic planner', *McKinsey Quarterly Online*, http://www.mckinseyquarterly.com/ Clearing_the_way_for_robust_growth_An_interview_with_Indias_chief_economic_planner_2067.

[46] Boisot, M. and Child, J. (1996) 'From fiefs to clans and network capitalism: Explaining China's emerging economic order', *Administrative Science Quarterly*, 4(41): 600–28.

[47] Mertha, A.C. (2005) *The Politics of Piracy: Intellectual Property in Contemporary China*, Ithaca, NY: Cornell University Press.

[48] Hong, E. and Sun, L. (2006) 'Dynamics of internationalization and outward investment: Chinese corporations' strategies', *The China Quarterly*, 187: 610–34.

[49] Dodds, R.F. Jr (1996) 'State enterprise reform in China: Managing the transition to a market economy', *Law and Policy in International Business*, 27, URL: googlescholar/docid/50004086.

[50] Child, J. and Tse, D.K. (2001) 'China's transition and its implications for international business', *Journal of International Business Studies*, 32(1): 5–21.

[51] Zhu, Z. (2007) 'Reform without a theory: Why does it work in China?' *Organization Studies*, 28(10): 1503–22.

[52] Liu, L.S. (2001) 'Corporate governance development in the Greater China: A Taiwan perspective', in Li, J.T., Tsui, A.S. and Weldon, E. (eds) *Management and Organizations in the Chinese Context*, New York: Macmillan.

[53] Li, D. (1998) 'The Dynamics of institutional change in China: The role of the bureaucracy', *Shorenstein Reports on Contemporary East Asia*, 18, URL: http://ieas.berkeley.edu/shorenstein/1998.03.html.

[54] Ibid.

[55] Mintzberg, H. (1973) *The Nature of Managerial Work*, NY: Harper Row.

[56] Boisot, M. and Liang, X.G. (1992) 'The nature of managerial work in the Chinese enterprise reforms. A study of six directors', *Organization Studies*, 7(2): 135–58.

[57] Ibid.

[58] Child, J. and Lu, Y. (1990) 'Industrial decision-making under China's reform 1985 – 1988', *Organization Studies*, 11(3): 321–51.

[59] Vickers, S. (2001) 'More colonial again? The post-1997 culture of Hong Kong's governing elite', in Cheung, A.B. and Sing, M. (eds) *International Journal of Public Administration*, 24(9) Special issue on Post-transition Hong Kong.

[60] Henderson, D.F. cited in Haley, J.O. (1991) *Authority without Power: Law and the Japanese Paradox*, Oxford: Oxford University Press.

[61] Vanoverbeke, D. (2006) 'Driving innovation: On the origin and mechanism of informal bureaucracy in Japan', *XIV International Economic History Conference*, Helsinki, URL: http://www.helsinki.fi/iehc2006/ papers2/Vanover.pdf.

[62] Ibid.

298   9

INTRODUCTION · THE BUSINESS CULTURES OF FIVE ASIAN COUNTRIES · ANALYSING ASIAN BUSINESS CULTURES
· OWNERSHIP, FINANCING AND GOVERNANCE · ORGANIZATION AND MANAGEMENT · BUSINESS STRATEGY ·

10 economic cultures and perceived economic environments

This chapter considers the possible links between a country's business decisions and culture and its economic culture and perceived economic environment. The same argument that applied in Chapter 9 applies here: we have no way of distinguishing a country's economic culture from the perceived economic environment. It is also the case here as in Chapter 9 that the business culture itself may induce its members to be somewhat alike in how they perceive their environment and again our research supports this possibility.

We derived a number of categories relating to economic culture and environment from our research. They are the following: competitiveness, economic freedom, demographics, income, poverty, wealth and its distribution, savings, investment and consumption, industry structure, markets and institutions, international trade and globalization, economic beliefs and attitudes. (As noted in Chapter 1, these categories were imposed on the interview data by the researchers in a process that included interpretation.) Some economic influences, such as population entrepreneurialism and the role of government in economic affairs, have been discussed earlier in this book and will not be covered here.

Competitiveness

As a conspicuous characteristic of both business and population, competitiveness was highlighted by our interviewees in Taiwan. Conceptually, however, their understanding of competitive, which related to an attitude to doing business, was different from the economic meaning, as a comparison with the Global Competitiveness Report for 2007–08 from the World Economic Forum makes clear. It placed Taiwan in the 14th rank, behind Singapore at 7th and Japan at 8th but ahead of China at 34th (Hong Kong was 12th) and India at 48th.[1] The Report was based on both publicly available data and assessments by business leaders in the countries covered by the Report. A country's overall competitiveness was assessed from 12 'pillars': institutions, infrastructure, macroeconomic stability, health and primary education (the four basics); higher education and training, goods market efficiency, labour market efficiency, financial market sophistication, technological readiness and market size (the efficiency enhancers); and business sophistication and innovation. The greatest strengths of **China**, according to the Report, lay in its macroeconomic stability and market size; its greatest weaknesses in financial market sophistication, higher education and training, institutions and technological readiness. *Hong Kong* was ranked top in the world for goods market efficiency and financial sophistication (which corresponds to the assertions of our Hong Kong interviewees); it was 4th globally for labour market efficiency and 5th for infrastructure; these strengths enabled Hong Kong to be ranked 12th overall, despite rankings in the high twenties for higher and primary education and health and 23rd for innovation. Several past studies found that Hong Kong's economic culture was characterized by economic individualism, as Chapter 7 recorded. People consistently regarded Hong Kong as a land of opportunities and believed that, with ability and effort, everyone had the chance to improve his or her social and economic status.[2]

At 48th, of the five Asian countries in our study **India** was the lowest ranked by the Global Competitiveness Report for 2007–08. Its position had deteriorated six places from 2006, unlike China's, which had improved one rank. India's strengths lay in market size, goods market efficiency, financial market sophistication, business sophistication and innovation; its greatest weaknesses in three basic requirements: infrastructure, macroeconomic stability and health and primary education. (By comparison with China, India had built a sophisticated but partial economy.) Of these factors in competitiveness, it was infrastructure that most impacted on the minds of the Indian business decision-makers in our study, leading to a raised concern with disaster recovery. While India's physical infrastructure, benefiting from the involvement of the private sector, began to improve by 2007, it still lagged China's by a long way. Only one Indian city – Delhi – had an underground railway system and that was a single line. In a country with at least seven cities with population over six million and many others with population of three or more millions, the environmental and efficiency consequences of poor infrastructure could scarcely be overstated.

The competitiveness of **Japan** was ranked 9th in the 2007–08 Global Competitiveness Report, only second to Singapore of the five Asian countries in our study and well ahead of the two other large population countries of China and India. Its position since 2006 had, however, deteriorated by three ranks. Its greatest strengths lay in market size, business sophistication and innovation; its greatest weaknesses in macro-economic stability, financial market sophistication, institutions and health and primary education.

The two smallest economies in our study were closely positioned in the 2007–08 Global Competitiveness rankings, with **Singapore** at 8th and **Taiwan** at 14th. This closeness in the rankings was, however, brought about by different patterns of strengths and weaknesses. Singapore's greatest strengths lay in its goods and labour market efficiency, its institutions, infrastructure and financial market sophistication; whereas Taiwan's lay in its higher education,

Table 10.1 **Competitiveness of five Asian countries**

	China	India	Japan	Singapore	Taiwan
Greatest strengths	1. Macroeconomic stability 2. Market size *HKSAR* 1. Goods market efficiency 2. Financial sophistication 3. Labour market efficiency 4. Infrastructure	1. Market size 2. Goods market efficiency 3. Financial market sophistication 4. Business sophistication 5. Innovation	1. Market size 2. Business sophistication 3. Innovation	1. Higher education and training 2. Health and primary education 3. Innovation	1. Goods and labour market efficiency 2. Institutions 3. Infrastructure 4. Financial market sophistication
Greatest weaknesses	1. Financial market sophistication 2. Higher education and training 3. Institutions 4. Technological readiness *HKSAR* 1. Health and Primary education 2. Higher education	1. Infrastructure 2. Macroeconomic stability 3. Health and primary education.	1. Macroeconomic stability 2. Financial market sophistication 3. Institutions 4. Health and primary education	1. Market size 2. Macroeconomic stability 3. Health and primary education 4. Higher education and training	1. Financial market sophistication 2. Infrastructure 3. Macroeconomic stability 4. Labour market efficiency

Source: Based on The Global Competitiveness Report 2007–2008 © 2007 World Economic Forum.

health and primary education and innovation. Weaknesses for Singapore were market size, macroeconomic stability, health and primary education and higher education and training; and Taiwan had financial market sophistication, infrastructure, macroeconomic stability and labour market efficiency as its greatest weaknesses. The differences have generally been attributed to the different strategies pursued by the two governments during the late 20th century; much of the success of their economies, however, has been ascribed to the similar economic cultures of the populations. Cheng and Liao (1994) attributed Taiwan's economic success to the 'Confucian work ethic' its people shared with the populations of three other East Asian newly industrializing countries or 'four little dragons' – Hong Kong, Singapore and South Korea. 'People in the "four little dragons" share a similar oriental work ethic, labelled the "Confucian ethic" since it promotes "individual and family sobriety, a high value on education, a desire for accomplishment in various skills … and seriousness about tasks, job, family, and obligations".'[3]

Table 10.1 summarizes the competitive strengths and weaknesses of our five sample countries, based on the assessments of the Global Competitiveness Report 2007–08.

Economic freedom

The liberalization of their countries' economies was a topic that arose repeatedly in our interviews in China and India. Perhaps because of the comparison with the recent past, most business decision-makers implied that the level of economic freedom of their country was high; this view, however, conflicts with independent analyses, suggesting a divergence of culture from 'reality'.

On an index of ten economic freedoms,[4] Asia as a whole measured close to the world average in 2007, a position which had only varied slightly over the previous 12 years. Asia included the two 'freest' economies in the world, those of Hong Kong and Singapore, but also countries such as Turkmenistan, Vietnam, Laos, Bangladesh and Burma, all of which were categorized as 'repressed', and North Korea, which had been the world's most economically repressed society for over a decade. Both **China** and **India** were categorized as having 'mostly unfree' economies. China's strengths were low government expenditure and average trade, monetary and labour freedom. Controls on investment, the financial sector, foreign investment, a politicized judicial system and weak property rights accounted for its status as 'mostly unfree'. India's greatest economic freedoms lay in the areas of the labour market, protection of property rights and low government expenditure. Trade freedom was restricted. (India's average tariff in 2007 was 14.5 per cent against China's 4.5 per cent, and non-tariff barriers were severe.) Although

India had a large financial sector, government interference with foreign capital was counted a weakness. Rule of law was impeded by the backlog in the courts.

In terms of our sample countries, China was the weakest in overall economic freedom; at the other extreme was *Hong Kong SAR*, which had only one 'weak' aspect, monetary freedom, due to some price controls; even that was 13 percentage points above the world average in 2007. **Singapore** came a close second to Hong Kong, with high scores on nine out of ten freedoms; the only weak spot in 2007 was financial freedom, which was caused by continuing government control of the banking system. **Japan** at 18th place in the world rankings, and **Taiwan** at 26th (but at 6th and 7th respectively in Asia) both had high scores except in financial freedom for both countries and, for Taiwan, labour market freedom and freedom from corruption.

Demographics

Population pressures were a significant aspect of the mindset of our interviewees in India and China, while the small size of their populations affected attitudes in Taiwan and Singapore and the aging and decline of its population was a concern in Japan.

By the early 21st century, economic forecasts were beginning to factor in demographic projections as major influences on countries' economic prospects. Of the Asian countries in our sample, India, with a population growth rate estimated in 2008 at 1.578 per cent, continued to experience significant population growth, while China's was positive but lower at 0.629 per cent. (Hong Kong's was near to China's at 0.532 per cent.) Japan's was negative at −0.139 per cent. Of the smaller countries, Singapore's was estimated to be growing at a rate of 1.135 per cent, Taiwan's at a close to static 0.238 per cent.[5] In **Japan** the demographic timebomb was creating anxiety; one Japanese interviewee made the following comment: 'Japan is facing an aging society. 120 million will reduce to 60 million by 2050; our fertility rate is 1.2 per woman; people aged 65 plus are living longer – they are up from five per cent of the population to 35 per cent.'[i] In **India**, in contrast, interviewees looked forward to the time when their youthful population would bring a demographic bonus ('India has a younger population than China – China's working age population is predicted to decline after 2015.'[ii]), although continuing anxiety over population density was expressed: 'We are the most densely populated large country in the world. We are not Singapore, which may be more densely populated but can prosper as a niche service provider or manufacturer and import the food it needs. We have to grow a large proportion

---

[i] Japanese, Finance and Accounting, education
[ii] Indian American, Economics, academic

of our own food.'[iii] Singaporeans anticipated that their problems would be solved by the government's policy of encouraging immigration; the Taiwanese perhaps had more pressing concerns and the Chinese were more inclined to discuss the current effects of the (continuing) one child policy.

Income, poverty, wealth and their distribution

In a clear reflection of the 'objective' situation, our study found positive perceptions of growth in all the sample countries except Japan. Concern over inequality was shown mainly in **China**, where it was considered to have the potential to create social instability.

> Our economy is not healthy. It has many pillars but they are all weak. ... A South China garment workers' pay is 200/400 yuan; a graduate earns 1000/3000 yuan; some people in IPOs [initial public offerings] of SOEs [state-owned enterprises] have made ten million. Ordinary people say the old situation was bad but this is worse. There are huge wealth disparities. Ten per cent of the people have 90 per cent of the wealth.

Together with the social costs, which the government did not count ('They are only interested in pumping up the GDP [Gross Domestic Product]'), 'This could lead to social instability. We have no strength to withstand shocks – a global economic crisis, or a national catastrophe in which the army, instead of dealing with matters, went to help their family.'[iv] In a developed economy, it is often perceptions of wealth that matter as much as absolute levels or relative levels compared with poorer countries. One of the factors pinpointed by our interviewees in **Japan** as leading to a widely accepted need for their country to change was this: 'The middle class feels poorer; although prices fell for over ten years and incomes did not drop much, property prices fell exponentially.'[v]

Asia's rapid growth rates, though impressive and constantly quoted, can give a false impression of a country's income and wealth per capita. For example, the per capita income of **India**, despite having grown by 50 per cent in the years from 1999 to 2007, was only a little higher than that of sub-Saharan Africa at the end of the period, and about one-sixth that of Latin America. Twenty per cent of India's population lived on less than $1 a day, which, though down from 50 per cent a few years before, was worse than Pakistan's 17 per cent and Sri Lanka's 6 per cent. These figures do, it is true, ignore both purchasing power parity and the many basic needs which India, in common with many developing countries,

[iii] Indian, Partner, international accounting firm
[iv] Mainland Chinese, General Manager, international business information hardware manufacturing
[v] Japanese, Finance and Accounting, education

subsidizes, including housing, primary health care, education, power and transportation. Nevertheless, poverty levels were very high and malnourishment, especially among young children, was widespread. Our interviewees spoke of the impact on business in India of its poor country environment.

In many Asian countries, wealth distribution was somewhat skewed in 2006. The ratio of the richest 10 per cent of the population by income or expenditure to the poorest 10 per cent was 18.4:1 for China, 17.8:1 for Hong Kong and 17.7:1 for Singapore; in all three it was greater, though not extremely so, than the USA's at 15.7:1.[6] Growth in Asian countries had increased disparities in income and wealth from a base of relative equality. For example, as the economy of **China** grew, its reforms brought about growing inequalities of wealth and income, while effective poverty was increased by a collapse of the welfare system that had functioned up to 1978. Healthcare collapsed, there were water shortages; in many parts of rural China, educational standards fell very low. All schools began to charge fees; state spending on education dropped to less than 2 US cents per capita per annum; later the government announced a $6 billion programme (which worked out at $8 a head per annum). Chinese society came to be judged as 'profoundly unequal'. Despite the marked difference in stage of economic development, a similar pattern of increasing inequality was seen in *Hong Kong*. As its economy became 'post-industrial', income distribution became increasingly unequal. In 1986, the lowest decile group earned only 1.6 per cent of total household income. That figure decreased to 1.1 per cent in 1996. The highest decile group, however, earned 35.5 per cent of total household income in 1986, a figure which increased to 41.8 per cent in 1996.[7]

The egalitarian culture of **Japan**, its maturity as a developed economy and its ethnic homogeneity were reflected in low economic inequality; inequality in **India**, too, was much lower than that of China in 2006, which on this measure would be the obvious comparison. India's greater ethnic, linguistic and religious diversity might predict greater inequality than China's, while its stage of economic development was the same or lower. One possible explanation for the finding that India was less unequal than its giant neighbour is that less time had passed since India moved away from socialism; another that the continuing representation and political pressure of socialist parties in its democratic system meant that it would not move so far, despite its high power distance culture. This was the view in 2007 of the country's Chief Economic Planner. 'Is inequality widening? Marginally perhaps, as often happens in a growth acceleration, but much less than what has happened in China. However, the toleration of gaps is shrinking massively.'[8]

Savings, investment and consumption

By world standards, the populations of all the countries in this study (and many other Asian countries, too) have been savers rather than spenders, a point that was reflected in the comments of our interviewees in China, India and Taiwan. 'The savings rate [in China] is high.'[vi] 'The [Taiwanese] people are hard working, driven by insecurity, (vide the high savings rate) focused on family life.'[vii] 'Indians are savers – in fixed deposits and jewellery, especially gold, which must be 22 carat – the savings of the whole family are often worn about the woman's person';[viii] 'People are no longer averse to using credit as they used to be, but they continue to save – buying jewellery for dowry, for instance.'[ix] Unfortunately, savings worn about the woman's person do not serve an economy well. Only a quarter of India's savings got funnelled to private firms, with an estimated effect on the economy of a percentage point or two of lost growth.

Data for household savings and consumption, though poor in quality, support these beliefs in a positive savings-orientation in Asia. For example, China's savings ratio has been estimated by the World Bank at 44 per cent in comparison with the USA's 1 per cent, Japan's net financial wealth as a percentage of disposable income as over 300 per cent compared with the USA's 150, while India's household saving showed a steady rise from 6.2 per cent in 1950–51 to a (rebased) 22.3 per cent in 2005–06. In 2007, China's private consumption as a percentage of GDP was 35 per cent, Singapore's 40 per cent, Japan's and India's both approximately 55 per cent, compared with the USA's 70 per cent and Britain's 60 per cent. All these statistics, as well as being affected by poor quality data, may well be attributed in part to factors other than economic culture: government policies on interest rates, for instance, although for the period that these figures cover, many Asian countries had very low or negative real interest rates.

Traditionally, most saving in an economy is done by households, most investing by firms. In the years around the turn of the millennium, however, some Asian firms became net savers as their profits exceeded their investments. This was especially true in Japan: burdened with bad debts after a period of massive overinvestment, Japanese firms had been net savers for a decade. The same became true more widely in Asia after its financial crisis of the late 1990s. China was the exception, investing heavily in infrastructure as well as industry but also saving even faster. Nevertheless the Chinese financial system was vulnerable because interest payments were not regular and the debt was rarely repaid.

Industry structure

A sense of where their country's main economic strengths and weaknesses lay in terms of market size, types of industry and size of firm was a basic element in

---

[vi] Mainland Chinese, General Manager, international business information hardware manufacturing
[vii] Taiwanese, Senior Vice President, Finance and Accounting, fund management
[viii] Indian, Senior Consultant, Business Services (banking operations and technology)
[ix] Indian, CEO, Indian educational not-for-profit

306 10

INTRODUCTION · THE BUSINESS CULTURES OF FIVE ASIAN COUNTRIES · ANALYSING ASIAN BUSINESS CULTURES
· OWNERSHIP, FINANCING AND GOVERNANCE · ORGANIZATION AND MANAGEMENT · BUSINESS STRATEGY ·

the business culture, our study showed. For example, in relation to Taiwan, an interviewee said, 'Most industry is for the domestic market. ... Small companies that, for instance hand manufacture moulds, are very important to the Taiwanese economy. ... High tech is slowing down'.[x] A Singaporean said, 'Singaporeans have to go abroad to do business; the market is too small; effectively there is no domestic market.' These kinds of judgements may not always correspond to 'objective' facts, but they are part of the mindset of business decision-makers.

Unlike the smaller countries of East Asia, the manufacturing sector in **India** continued to grow in spite of low-cost competition from China, although its performance was less dramatic than that country's and some industries and businesses suffered: 'Around 1980, our family business got out of textiles – we could not compete with the Chinese. We couldn't even understand how they could do it.'[xi] In the formal manufacturing sector built up under the earlier policy regime, India experienced strong growth from 1980 onwards once the policy stance softened vis-à-vis the private sector, and the 'anti-business' policy regime and its associated controls was dismantled. The modern manufacturing base created under the policy of import substituting industrialization was able to survive and grow in the new conditions.[9]

Although it was the spectacular growth of the Chinese and Indian economies that attracted most attention, the smaller Asian economies underwent what were possibly even greater transformations to adapt to the new regional economic order. For example, the manufacturing base of *Hong Kong*, particularly in textiles, shrank from dominating its economy up to the late 1970s, down to 14 per cent of GDP in 2000 and only 3.5 per cent in 2006. The 'conversion' of the economy to a 'post-industrial' service basis, heavily focused on trade and financial services, was essential to prevent unemployment and negative growth. A demonstration of the flexibility of Hong Kong's business sector in achieving this is found in the clothing industry: 'After the number of clothing factories and work-force peaked in 1984, the industry contracted and demonstrated a slow rate of growth in domestic exports. On the other hand, the re-exports counterpart has shown significant increases since the 1980s and has allowed Hong Kong to maintain its leading trading status with total clothing exports.'[10]

Markets and institutions

Within the institutional perspective, a business's competitive advantage and performance is related to how well it conforms to predominant institutional arrangements such as production factor markets, trade unions and government-business

---

[x] Taiwanese, Partner, Taiwanese venture capital
[xi] Indian, CEO and family member, Indian family-owned diversified business group

relations.[11] As an example, Kshetri and Dholakia (2005) argued that the success of an online seller in the digital world of South Asia was a function of the degree to which the seller could adapt its business models to take account of various institutional pressures. Businesses that were able to re-align and adapt with the environment in South Asia reaped the rewards.[12] The business decision-makers interviewed for our study showed sensitivity to these influences in drawing attention to government-business relations (all five countries), trades unions and labour markets (Japan and India), financial markets (China, especially Hong Kong, India, Singapore) and so on.

Many Asian markets, among them those of **China**, were still under-structured and underdeveloped by the early years of the 21st century. For example, although huge markets opened up in the energy sector in much of Asia, the art of developing or tapping these markets was as yet not well understood. This explains the slow progress that was made in completing many energy-sector projects.[13] Similarly, as Chapter 9 showed, regulatory, political and social institutions functioned imperfectly.

In China, Heilman (2005) observed that pervasive government interference and cronyism in China's financial sector resembled the deficiencies displayed by many other political economies. But in its regulatory efforts, China's government had means at its disposal that were very different – institutional engineering by the Communist Party.

> The rise and demise of the Central Financial Work Commission (CFWC) is an outstanding example of the innovative potential and also the limits of Communist Party institutional engineering in China's economy. The creation of the CFWC was a strategy to arrest the breakdown of hierarchies in the financial industry and to restore central policy decisiveness. By means of Party control over senior financial executives and Party-sponsored institutional reorganization, China's political leadership pushed through a centralization of financial market supervision and a series of regulatory innovations starting in 1998. Leninist institutions provided China's politicians with a reserve capacity for responding to perceived organizational crises and for innovating economic regulation.

The limits of 'Leninist institutions' were, however, exposed, because the government's initiatives were not market-driven and hence did not raise the efficiency of capital allocation. They also proved to be a mismatch with the emerging forms of corporate governance. Therefore the government abolished the CFWC and laid the foundations for national market regulation.[14] (Of two main developments that according to Boisot and Child [1996] stimulated China's growth, one was 'the increasing part played by market transactions, including a growing integration with the world economy'. The other was a shift in industrial ownership and property rights, with the state playing a diminishing role.)[15] Thus the later trend in institutional development in China was towards harmonization with normal market economies rather than more distinctive innovations, 'suggesting that the government accepts that the ingredients for a dynamic market economy are already well known'. Nevertheless, China in 2007 was still far from having all these ingredients in place.[16]

India, on one view 'has very strong political and economic institutions for a country at its income level. Judged by cross-country norms, it ought to have a level of income that is several times higher'. India's strong institutions 'mean that relatively minor changes in the policy environment can produce a large growth impact'.[17] Its financial institutions, however, though advanced by comparison with those of China, were not equal to those of some other developing countries, as the section below on financial infrastructure explains. The other three countries that we studied all had relatively strong markets and institutions, as reflected in their positions on the 'Competitiveness' ranking with which this chapter began.

Labour markets

Most East and South East Asian labour markets saw major restructuring over the last 20 years of the 20th century. For example, in **China**, 30 million people lost their jobs with the closure or running down of state enterprises. In factories that continued working, the company school, hospital and nursery usually closed down and there were many redundancies, reflecting a huge shift in the relationship between labour and business, in which producing units ceased to take responsibility for the welfare of their employees. Data from the China Urban Labour Survey conducted in five large Chinese cities at the end of 2001 showed that employment shocks were large and widespread, and were particularly hard on older workers and women.

> During the period of economic restructuring, unemployment reached double figures in all sample cities and labour force participation declined by 8.9 per cent. Urban residents faced modest levels of wage and pension arrears, and sharp declines in health benefits. Public assistance programmes for dislocated workers had limited coverage, with most job-leavers relying upon private assistance to support consumption, mainly from other household members.[18]

Workers laid off from SOEs who succeeded in re-entering the workforce usually found employment in SMEs (small and medium-sized enterprises), often in locations away from their homes. Migration in search for better paying jobs, virtually prohibited during the Mao era, took off during the 1980s market opening. By the 1990s, nearly 70 million rural people had migrated to the cities for jobs, about two-thirds of them men and one-third women. By 2000, the estimated migrant population exceeded 100 million.[19] 'Everywhere in China you see migrant workers.' Many of these migrants were young female factory workers: their average pay was £80 per week, 'serious money in China'. They lived in single-sex hostels, had no residency rights in the cities and worked 7 days a week, 13 hours a day.

The restructuring of the smaller Asian economies in response to globalization and China's new domination of manufacturing also led to radical change in their labour markets. In *Hong Kong*, the percentage of the labour force in manufacturing shrank from 47 per cent in 1971 to 14 per cent in 1996, and continued to decline. Few capitalist economies have experienced such a rapid decline in the size of their industrial labour force.[20] Japan's labour market, too, began to become more flexible from about the turn of the millennium.

Significant changes in labour market regulations accompanied these changes. The OECD's (Organisation for Economic Co-operation and Development) Economic Survey in 2006 commented, '**China**, with a history of extreme employment security, has drastically reformed its labour relations and created a new labour market.'[21] In China, though, even in 2006, there was a lack of standardization in practice, according to the Index of Economic Freedoms. 'Dismissing a redundant employee can be relatively costly and may require prior consultation with the local labor bureau and labor union. In general, the capacity to end employment varies according to the location and size of the enterprise.' In **India** (as well as Taiwan and even to some degree Hong Kong), regulations made dismissing redundant employees costly and burdensome; the OECD's judgement on India's labour market in 2006 was highly critical, describing its labour laws as inflexible and highly protective; labour reforms to accelerate investment, particularly in industry and export-related sectors, remained 'an unfinished agenda'. There was a marked contrast between the organized sector, which provided too much job security, and the unorganized sector in which 70 per cent or more of Indians worked, which provided almost none. In **Japan** (and Singapore), it was easier to lay off workers, though regulations or the lack of them did not tell the whole story. Dedoussis (2001) argued that what was actually taking place in Japanese management was an ad hoc reshuffle rather than substantial restructuring of internal labour markets.[22] Cultural impediments to laying off salaried staff remained powerful in the larger Japanese corporations, a situation that was eased only by the discriminatory practices described next.

Discrimination in labour markets

According to the UN Human Development Index 2007–08, in 2006 the labour market position of women was disadvantaged in the four of our sample Asian countries for which the United Nations collected data. Even in the best performing country, **China**, women's earnings were on average less than two-thirds of men's, while in Hong Kong they were only 49 per cent and just over half in Singapore.[23]

A World Bank report in 2000 described the laws in China guaranteeing and promoting gender equality as enlightened by any standards and capable of serving as a benchmark for other countries striving for gender equality. Under Chinese law, equal rights for women and men were guaranteed in access to employment, equal pay, compulsory education, political participation, property, marriage and health. Trafficking and kidnapping women and prostitution were prohibited. Affirmative action programs existed to realize gender equality. But, the report continued, 'It is easier to enact laws than to implement them.' Access to the labour market was one of the issues identified by stakeholders as one of the thorniest gender gaps in modern China.[24]

During the communist era, China had achieved greater female participation and gender equality in the workplace than many countries. Women received 80 per cent of the pay men received in the rural industrial sector in 1985 and 88 per cent of men's pay in the state sector in 1987. However, the income gap increased thereafter with deepening labour market liberalization. By 1990, women earned 83 per cent of men's pay and by 1999 only 77 per cent. By 2005, it was down to 64 per cent, which, though the highest of our sample countries, was a significant decline from the earlier ratios. Men consistently occupied most managerial and higher-skilled positions. The share of female administrators and managers was under 12 per cent in 1997.[25] As labour markets liberalized during the transition from a state to a market economy, some changes affected women's labour market position more than men's. These changes included the replacement of the Mao era 'iron rice bowl' with a competitive labour market providing mainly contractual, temporary and informal sector jobs lacking social protection. State affirmative action policies receded, while traditional gender stereotypes and values re-emerged, leading to increased gender discrimination in the labour market. It became harder for women than men to obtain and keep a job. Official statistics showed that in 1998 some 48 females were made redundant for every 40 males.[26]

China had enacted a number of laws that appeared to afford women equal opportunity in employment but the effectiveness of these laws was not apparent. The US State Department identified the Chinese government's overwhelming focus on rapid economic growth as one reason for the government's failure to address open discrimination. A further impediment was an emphasis in Chinese law on protective legislation premised on biological differences between men and women. This resulted in a preference for hiring men. Such protective legislation 'has its roots in traditional patriarchal and hierarchical Confucian principles that define a woman's primary obligation as the perpetuation of the family, or more specifically, producing and wisely raising a male descendent', the State Department's report asserted.[27] In addition, there were barriers and failures within the legal and court systems. The laws enacted to protect women in employment situations contained no enforcement mechanisms.

The employment situation in **India**, as revealed by the limited available data, suggests the presence of discrimination against women at all levels. Women's earnings were on average only 31 per cent of men's in 2007–08. Labour Force Participation Rates (LFPRs) were lower for women than for men, particularly in urban areas. Education has been found to greatly influence wage differentials in many countries, but studies found that the female-male wage ratio in urban India was only 0.82 for female literates (0.59 for female illiterates). Only 22 per cent of the gap in wages could be explained by the lack of female education – 78 per cent of the wage gap, therefore, was due to differential returns to education.[28]

In **Japan**, in 2007–08, women earned much less than men – on average only 44 per cent of men's income, a percentage which had declined from 52 per cent in 2000. As the recession of the 1990s bit, there was a large increase in temporary and part-time employment, with low remuneration and protection, much of which was taken by women. Traditionally, many Japanese women had to quit their jobs when they married or gave birth to their first child. Japan was one of the very few countries where the labour activity rate of women dropped sharply in their late thirties to early forties. In 1999, predicted labour shortages due to the low Japanese birth rate led to legal changes aimed at promoting women's equality. A Basic Law for a Gender Equal Society was passed, directing the government at all levels to take positive action for the promotion of gender equality. Our own research in Japan showed that there was some awareness both of the policy and the reason for it. The following comment was made by a female human resource consultant:

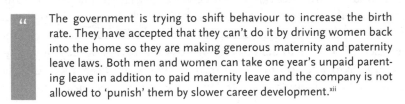

> The government is trying to shift behaviour to increase the birth rate. They have accepted that they can't do it by driving women back into the home so they are making generous maternity and paternity leave laws. Both men and women can take one year's unpaid parenting leave in addition to paid maternity leave and the company is not allowed to 'punish' them by slower career development.[xii]

However, underlying attitudes were reflected in the fact that many companies continued to sidestep these and other weak labour laws, which were undermined by courts continuing to favour private-sector discretion in hiring and promotion practices.

Financial infrastructure

Like many other commentators, Boisot and Child (1996) commented unfavourably on the financial infrastructure of **China** at that time:

> The institutions that characterize a rational-legal system – an effective central bank, macroeconomic levers, enforceable and consistent

---

[xii] Japanese, Human Resources, business service

> laws – remain absent, all official rhetoric to the contrary notwith-
> standing. The freeing up of the financial system, for example, has led
> to the emergence of a sizeable secondary credit sector in which lend-
> ing takes place through direct relationships between firms and other
> bodies at very high interest rates; this sector is beyond the control of
> the monetary and regulatory authorities.[29]

At one time Chinese banks' primary role was to help maintain employment by supporting state enterprises. By 2006, the judgement of one observer was that most banks were performing much better than a few years before, although they were carrying massive amounts of bad debt; they had improved their operating systems and skills, and they had a much stronger risk-management culture. The government-regulated interest-rate spread between deposits and loans was giving banks such as the Construction Bank an enormous margin, one of the largest in the banking world, and they were using it to write off bad debt. Regulators understood the importance of this interest-rate spread, which was intended to remain in place for several years. In addition, favourable market conditions in an economy growing at 9 per cent a year helped a great deal. It was not, however, yet clear whether the improvements in commercial risk management would be robust enough to cope with a weaker economy.[30]

Financing continued to be a headache for Chinese SMEs. Despite the exist-ence of government- or city-sponsored credit guarantee systems, less than 1 per cent of China's SMEs actually qualified and most could only raise money from the local community, family members or retained earnings.

At independence in 1947, **India** had

> arguably the best formal financial markets in the developing world, with
> four functioning stock exchanges ... and clearly defined rules governing
> listing, trading and settlements; a well-developed equity culture, if only
> among the urban rich; an old and established banking system with clear
> lending norms and recovery procedures; and better corporate laws than
> most other erstwhile colonies. The Company's Act of 1956, as well as
> other corporate laws and laws protecting investors' rights, were built
> on this foundation. After independence, however, a decades-long turn
> towards socialism put in place a regime and culture of licensing, protec-
> tion and widespread red-tape, breeding corruption.[31]

By the start of liberalization in 1990,

> Corruption, most severe among the police and judiciary, poor effi-
> ciency and effectiveness of the legal system for contract enforcement
> and poor quality though not quantity of information disclosure were
> undermining the financial infrastructure. Rather than overhauling the
> entire legal system, the government tried to emulate the success of
> China by following the Special Economic Zone approach. Growth of

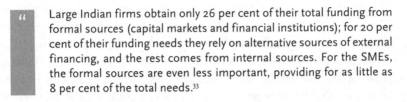

> the markets and banking sector after 2000 notwithstanding, India's financial markets and institutions, relative to the size of its economy, continued smaller than those in many other countries. The country had a lower ratio of market capitalization to GDP than the average of developing economies, while the corporate bond market was 'meager'.[32]

Despite being efficient, India's banking system was not effective in providing capital.

> Large Indian firms obtain only 26 per cent of their total funding from formal sources (capital markets and financial institutions); for 20 per cent of their funding needs they rely on alternative sources of external financing, and the rest comes from internal sources. For the SMEs, the formal sources are even less important, providing for as little as 8 per cent of the total needs.[33]

A 2007 report commissioned by the Indian Ministry of Finance reported that the license-permit-control raj still operated in Indian finance. 'It retards development and sophistication of the financial sector.' The Report identified 28 areas of weakness in India's financial system, including the need to eliminate the Securities Transaction Tax and Stamp Duties, create a bond market and bring forward the liberalization of the financial sector in keeping with commitments to the World Trade Organization Agreement on Trade in Financial Services.[34]

International trade and globalization

Trade within Asia expanded fast in the late 20th and early 21st centuries, within formal groups such as ASEAN (the Association of South East Asian Nations) and SAFTA (the South Asia Free Trade Area), informal configurations such as 'Greater China' and direct cross-border trade such as that between China and India. One characteristic of Asian overseas business ventures was their 'diasporic' pattern, often, as one interviewee expressed it, 'based on family links'.[xiii] In the words of Chatterjee and Nankervis (2006), 'It can be argued that the historic internal migration of Chinese and Indian family entrepreneurs throughout the region, coupled with the effects of and reactions to European colonization, have contributed significantly to the economic resurgence of Asia during the post-Second World War era.'[35]

There is evidence that diasporic South East Asian Indian firms invested to a 'disproportionate' degree in India and Chinese firms in China as well as in Chinese firms in other South East Asian countries. A 2002 finding was that

---

[xiii] Taiwan, Expatriate banker

43 per cent of a sample of Singapore-Chinese businesses venturing abroad did business in China and 66 per cent of the Singapore-Indian businesses turned to India. This diasporic tradition of trans-border ventures was characterized by capital input that was almost exclusively provided by the family and ethnic group.

This pattern was determined in part by regulatory and institutional barriers in the target countries. ASEAN countries (except Singapore) had been hostile towards foreign capital. Nevertheless, cultural affinity played a large part. The social organization of Chinese business outside the mainland emphasized the role of personal and business relationships. For example, even before 1997, coordination and control of networks within Hong Kong transnational companies were most easily and effectively achieved through trusted family members and close associates.[36]

According to Chan (2001), the transnational Chinese economy known as 'Greater China' was made possible by a combination of economic complementarities and cultural ties. One example of the economic complementarities is that while China was eager to gain access to capital, technology and know-how from Hong Kong and Taiwan, and to gain their assistance in penetrating markets in other countries, Hong Kong and Taiwan had an interest in making China their alternative base of production and also in exploiting markets there. The cultural ties among the Chinese societies in terms of their common culture, language, family ties and ancestral roots facilitated these economic complementarities.[37] For example, as one interviewee explained,

> Taiwanese FDIs [foreign direct investments] in USA or Europe are motivated by the wish to acquire marketing know-how. In China, however, they will go into the same business as in Taiwan; even there, however, they are not just seeking low labour costs; they are also, in the longer term, interested in China's market potential. China is the only country where we could develop brand franchises. Chinese culture is easier for us; there, unlike the USA, we can for instance create advertising slogans that ring a bell, have consumer appeal. Taiwanese Chinese is an educated version, spoken by rich people in China, so our natural expressions are sympathetic to them.[xiv]

There is evidence that an increasingly coalescent regional economic grouping emerged in East Asia in the years following the 1997/98 financial crisis. One development was the creation of new mechanisms of regional financial governance by the 'ASEAN Plus Three' (APT) group of countries (Japan, China, South Korea and the ASEAN group), mechanisms such as the Chiang Mai Initiative and the Asian Bond Market Initiative; another was the expansion of bilateral free trade agreements in East Asia and the Asia-Pacific. Both Taiwan and South Asia were excluded from these developments.[38]

[xiv] Taiwanese, Senior Vice President, Finance and Accounting, fund management

Development of trade in East Asia was driven in part by the business culture of one country, Japan, Kojima (1996) argued. While Western FDI was micro-focused and aimed at making profits for individual firms, Japanese FDI was macro-focused and aimed at developing the host economies so that they could supplement the Japanese economy. Thus Japanese FDI was more oriented to promote trade.[39]

At the start of the 21st century, there were signs of an increase in Asian trade decided by 'economic complementarities' rather than cultural ties or culturally influenced business behaviour. Trade between India and China, for example, grew rapidly in that period. Not only were cultural ties between the two countries rather limited – though certainly existent as Sen (2005)[40] argued – but also the economic complementarities clearly dominated in many cases. One example was Chinese companies experienced in the construction of airports, roads, bridges, power stations and telecommunications supplying India as it strove to speed up its infrastructure development. The moves made by China and India towards establishing strategic and cooperative relations instead of the hot and cold wars of the 20th century have been understood as motivated by the wish to trade. Another instance of economic reasons predominating was Singapore's 'new' trans-border strategy of taking business where the opportunities were – in the global market. The Singapore government adopted a regionalization policy designed to create an external economic wing and to assist in the expansion of government-linked companies overseas and prevent the marginalization of SMEs in the Singapore economy. The regionalization policy was judged as fitting well with the Indian government's 'Look East' policy to create synergy for economic collaboration between the two economies.[41] This strategy is distinguished from the strategies of the past in Asia by widely spread cooperative ties and avoidance of dependence on one major sponsor, be it the family, the state or a multinational company (MNC). Insofar as personal networks operated, they consisted of links established during education abroad, with former employers and colleagues, and professional associations (in contrast to traditional Chinese hometown associations).[42] For India, excluded from ASEAN and 'Greater China', seeking global opportunities came naturally once the economy was liberalized. One of its major engines of growth after 2000, its offshoring service industry, was built from the start with the West, especially the English-speaking countries of the USA and UK.[43]

Economic beliefs and attitudes

While the differences and similarities that have been described in this chapter among these five Asian countries have many origins, one is the set of underlying economic beliefs and attitudes accepted in each country – its economic culture. The term economic culture is often used; for instance, Redding (1994) used it as follows: 'The Overseas Chinese have an apparent distinct economic culture that is describable, and the outline of its determinants can be drawn.'[44] Taeube (2004) suggested that economic cultures consist of the informal values and norms which, being shared by a community, allow for cooperation. As examples he gave trust, rationality, religion and the value placed on work.[45]

Although universalist judgements continue to be made about how economies function, for instance that of Castells (2000), 'In spite of a highly diversified social and cultural landscape, for the first time in history the whole planet is organized round a largely common set of economic rules',[46] Lowe (1998) was able to refer to a 'tenuous consensus' on an understanding of there being a link between culture and economy.[47] This 'tenuous consensus' contradicted the resource-based view of economics which argued that rare, specialized and inimitable resources allow corporations to achieve competitive advantage under two assumptions: that resources are heterogeneously distributed across competing firms, and that resources are imperfectly mobile. Instead, it supports the institutional perspective which, as Chapter 1 explained, emphasizes institution-conforming behaviour, such as acting in accordance with predominant norms, traditions and social influence, to achieve competitive advantage and performance. Within the institutional framework, then, there is a consensus that culture influences economics. As the economic sociologist DiMaggio (1993) said, 'Aspects of culture shape economic institutions and affairs ... economic processes have an irreducible cultural component.'[48]

The consensus that cultures and economies are linked, to which Lowe (1998) referred, was of 'a complex indeterminism between influences of pre-modern values, modern values, formal institutional and informal institutional norms, and ideological and political interests (including imperialism and global capitalism)'. Within this understanding is 'the idea that culture is a collective "mental program" which parallels and co-determines a more evident social domain involving structure and action'. However, Lowe (1998) also pointed out, 'The literature on the relationship between culture and economy (work and organization) is often contradictory, reflecting different conceptions of what "culture" is.' One approach (which Lowe called 'anthropological') viewed 'culture and economy' as 'mutually generative and difficult (if not impossible) to distinguish from each other since culture is seen as providing systems of meaning which define actors' interests, so enabling economic action, which in turn generates categories and understanding in an iterative process.'[49] A radically different approach (that of economists) treated economic behaviour and culture as 'analytically distinct' and stressed how culture 'constrains and configures the individuals' economic efforts'. 'In this view, the assumption appeared to be that the relationship between culture and economy was not mutually generative, but involved a dependent and independent variable.'[50]

Lowe's judgement on the question concurs with that of Hofstede (1981) who argued, 'Culture is important enough to be included as an influence (on behaviour) but cultural determinism is a danger to be avoided',[51] and Redding (2004) who suggested, 'It is necessary to reassert that it [culture] is not seen as the dominant cause of economic success, obliterating or ignoring other factors like economic policy. Culture is one of several key features deserving a respectable place in any account.'[52]

Within a perspective that treats culture as a key feature, the social and political aspects of culture must have a place. In the words of Hefner (1998), 'Ultimately the study of economic culture will have to incorporate the cultural ideals that provide the normative guidance to ordinary behavior. To understand an economy, we must also understand the "moral and cultural flora" that guide people's behavior.'[53] One example from Asia that highlights the need for this kind of understanding of an economy attracted attention owing to a study published in 2003 of the Taiwanese organized crime networks, the Heijin. These networks penetrated business and politics – votes were bought, construction bids were rigged, violence and coercion were used by criminals to ensure their political and commercial survival. The three worlds of business, politics and crime were interdependent – in the words of one scholar, they operated symbiotically.[54] A more general example is the case of *Hong Kong*. There is

 emerging evidence that 'modern' East Asian societies like Hong Kong have not developed in the rationalist ideal tradition as epitomized by Weber. ... East Asian societies have not wholly adopted Western values, traditions, norms and institutions. Thus Hong Kong may be described as a modern society with a traditional culture, which, in terms of business values, means a complex combination or convergence and divergence.[55]

Supporting this view, Ralston et al. (1993) found evidence of convergence, divergence and 'crossvergence' between Hong Kong, China and the USA[56] and Tse et al. (1995) found that executives from Hong Kong were influenced by a combination of Western and Chinese cultural norms.[57]

Asian economic attitudes

Survey data from 2005 and 2002 suggested that the attitudes of the populations of China, India and Japan were highly and increasingly in favour of economic liberalism. (Data were not collected for Taiwan or Singapore.) Research by the Pew Research Center used three measures for economic liberalism – attitudes to trade, foreign companies and free markets. In China and India, the samples (which were skewed towards the urban population) were strongly positive on all three measures, yielding an unweighted average support level of 76 per cent for China and 79 per cent for India in comparison with 58 per cent and 66 per cent for the USA and UK respectively. In Japan, while trade was viewed positively, attitudes to foreign companies and free markets were more neutral, resulting in an unweighted average of 58 per cent over the three measures. Positive views of trade increased slightly between 2002 and 2007 in India and China and remained stable in Japan; the percentage saying that the impact of foreign companies was positive increased by 12 percentage points in India, but decreased by the same percentage in China and nearly as much in Japan; while support for free markets increased by 14 percentage points in India, 6 in Japan and 5 in China.[58]

There is evidence that economic attitudes of these kinds fluctuate a good deal over time and are related to the current state of the nation's economy, especially its growth of GNP. We therefore turn to consider the more deep-seated beliefs and values that constitute economic culture. The evidence for our sample countries is rather limited, but some pointers emerge.

Asian economic cultures

Although business cultures and economic cultures are distinct concepts, as Chapter 1 explained, they may have overlapping content. For example, one writer included lifetime employment, management by consensus and the *kereitsu* system as aspects of the economic culture of Japan.[59] While our study found that these were important elements of Japan's traditional business culture, we would not deny that they may also be aspects of its economic culture, accepted by many outside its business community. On the other hand, as the example of China described in the following paragraphs shows, an economic culture can deviate so far from a business culture as to be effectively opposed to it.

There is a lively debate in train about the nature of the economic culture of **East Asia**. On the one hand are arguments that Confucianism is its essential underpinning. On the other hand are some who point to other indigenous cultural forces as well as Western influences such as the Enlightenment. Arguing for the Confucian heritage, Weiming (2000) commented,

> Industrial East Asia since the 1960s and socialist East Asia since the 1980s have experienced a revival of Confucian teaching as political ideology, intellectual discourse, merchant ethics, family values, or the spirit of protest. This is the combination of many factors. Despite tension and conflict rooted in primordial ties, the overall life pattern in East Asia involves consensus formation based on values significantly different from the modern Western emphasis on contractual relationships. ... Economic culture, family values, and merchant ethics in East Asia and in China (including Hong Kong, Macao, and Taiwan) have also expressed themselves in Confucian vocabulary.

The implications of Confucianism in economic culture, Weiming (2000) considered, were six-fold: (1) Government leadership in a market economy was not only necessary but also desirable. (2) Although law was the essential minimum requirement for social stability, 'organic solidarity' could only result from humane rites of interaction. (3) Family as the basic unit of society was the locus from which core values were transmitted. (4) Civil society flourished when it was not an autonomous arena above the family and beyond the state. (5) Education ought to be the civil religion of society. The primary purpose of education was character building. (6) Since self-cultivation was the common root of the regulation of family, the governance of the state, and peace under Heaven, the quality of life of a particular society depended on the level of self-cultivation of its members.[60]

According to Whitley (1992), in **China** (and Korea), where the basis for legitimacy and authority was moral superiority derived from success in the imperial examinations, merchants were for centuries despised and suppressed. Private accumulations of wealth were subject to arbitrary confiscation, 'justified in terms of the ruler's obligation to maintain harmony and frugality. Independent economic power was viewed as extravagant, ethically untenable and punishable. ...This heritage of official hostility to private wealth generated high levels of defensiveness and a preference for personal connections and trust among Chinese business owners.' Even when the Chinese state actively sought expatriate investment for new projects in the 1900s, 'It was still extremely difficult to convince overseas Chinese merchants to invest large sums of money in their homeland ... the fear of mandarin squeeze remained deeply ingrained.'[61]

Qualifying this view, however, Huang (1998) stated that traditional Chinese economic culture was a duality, reflecting two different and parallel modes of production; one was state-controlled commodity production, extraction and distribution through hierarchical bureaucratic structures that emphasized formal morality, loyalty, fairness, benevolence and harmony; the other was characterized by frugality, market competition and even ruthlessness and was the mainstream economic culture of ordinary citizens' lives at least from the time of the Song dynasty over 1000 years before. By concentrating only on the first of these, perhaps because it was better reflected in the official 'account', Western researchers perpetrated the myth that Chinese economic culture consisted only of the Confucian anti-commerce doctrine, which, with the later doctrines of communism, 'consistently obscured Chinese economic culture'.[62]

Based on an analysis of both state-controlled and other production sectors, Willmot (1972) identified four salient features that he considered essential for the Chinese economy's operation. First was the prominent role of the state in economic affairs, such as its monopolistic control of the salt trade, and its various agencies to intervene in and coordinate fragmented regional economic enterprises. The hegemonic power of the state was acknowledged and accepted as normal by citizens. The second was the emphasis on group- or community-based

320   10

INTRODUCTION • THE BUSINESS CULTURES OF FIVE ASIAN COUNTRIES • ANALYSING ASIAN BUSINESS CULTURES
• OWNERSHIP, FINANCING AND GOVERNANCE • ORGANIZATION AND MANAGEMENT • BUSINESS STRATEGY •

collective responsibility for the individual's material well-being. Group affiliation thus defined an individual's basic economic condition. Third was the emphasis on hard work and competition as the avenue for success. And fourth, there was the emphasis on long-term, multi-strained, comprehensive relationships in economic transactions, rather than single-strained, short-term profit maximization.[63] All these 'features' could be characterized as values, and/or as corresponding to taken-for-granted beliefs about how the economic world works, and so as aspects of economic culture.

A literature review by Huang (1998) found that these traditional characteristics of the Chinese economic culture had survived into the modern world. He wrote:

> The ubiquitous role of the state in regulating and monitoring economic affairs, and its critical role in directing societal change, has been clearly delineated from the late Qing to the current regime. Similarly, the cellular nature of Chinese society, including both urban and rural enterprises, the co-opting of individuals by their work units, and the particularistic nature of economic relationships prompted ... the term[s] 'neo-traditionalism' to describe urban enterprises, and 'clientelism' to describe rural economic life. Family-based economic calculation is seen as the driving motivation for individual success in the standard ethnographic portrayal of Taiwan and China. The well-acknowledged gender discrimination against female household members produced a kind of mental complex ... characterized by the filial daughter who, through self-sacrifice, endurance and resilience, provided reliable incomes for struggling families as well as a reliable workforce for new industries in Taiwan. Finally, the use of formal written contracts and the reliance on formal procedures to reach contractual agreements are also ubiquitous in economic transactions in the Chinese world.[64]

In the post-Mao world, China's economic culture comprised 'a lively forum in which we find the interplay, conflation and mutual co-opting of three sets of value orientations'. These were Marxism, which

> shares with Confucian orthodoxy fundamental beliefs in elitist utopianism, this-world orientation, state-controlled economy, and abhorrence of pecuniary concerns, the so-called 'anti-merchant' mentality. And yet this official doctrine also considers Confucianism to be a legacy that is essentially feudalistic, oppressive, and patriarchal, and tries to stamp it out through political campaigns. Similarly, the official doctrine shares with the individually-based economism calculations that are based on materialism and instrumental rationality, and yet it considers unregulated market transactions to be the source of class differentiation and exploitation, 'the tails of capitalism.'

As an example of this interplay, Huang (1998) found the following from an in-depth study of one village in South China:

- A belief in the variability and inequality of abilities, more consistent with Confucianism than Marxism, informed people's job plans for their children and willingness to persist in keeping them in education;
- A belief that there are different categories of work suitable for men and women – repetitive and domestic for women, physically and/or mentally demanding for men – informed the gendered division of labour;
- In the marketplace, where transactions took place impersonally, behaviour was marked by 'negative reciprocity' – competition and exploitation. This was contrary to the ideal Confucian social order, which delineated a well-structured social hierarchy with clearly defined decorum and etiquette among kin and co-workers. This exploitative behaviour was underpinned by a moral code: those with higher ability or greater capability in work *should* command and take advantage of less capable workers.

When, however, the two domains of Confucianism and economic norms were in conflict, Huang's (1998) observations suggested, 'It is the ideal norms that take precedence over the economic norms.' This constituted the fourth assumption in Chinese economic culture, namely that individual short-term economic interests tended to be overshadowed by established relationships. Finally, the last moral tenet in the economic culture Huang (1998) studied seemed to contradict, in a sense, the fourth tenet, in emphasizing the commodification of many different aspects of life: not just goods, services, knowledge and rights, but also human beings themselves.

Huang (1998) argued:

> This analysis sheds light on issues related to current economic problems among Chinese communities in China, Taiwan, Hong Kong, and Southeast Asia: problems such as the prevalence of the *guanxi* networks that permeate legitimate business transactions, the lack of trust between business partners, and the lack of trust in general for authorities in economic affairs. To some extent we may consider these problems as originating from efforts to convert the impersonal, short-term, competitive market transactions into long-term, multi-strained, comprehensive relationships.
>
> Formal Confucian ethics contain well-defined interpersonal relationships with proper decorum specified for interpersonal interactions, and yet the economic reality underscores the murky, capricious, competitive, and manipulative interpersonal transactions in which short-term gains and selfish ends reign.[65]

In **Japan**, according to Whitley (1992), while some of the same Confucian disdain as in China of commercial activities as unproductive and unworthy prevailed, and, unlike in Europe, no capitalist class independent of the prevailing feudal-type social order arose, private concentrations of economic power did develop and merchants provided loans to the country's leaders. They thereby acquired a degree of legitimacy that was denied them in China and Korea and a foundation for impersonal trust relations in business was laid, weaker than in the West but stronger than in the rest of East Asia.

In regard to **India**, studies have concluded that the caste system, with its Hindu religious underpinnings, was sufficiently strong to defeat 'normal' economic forces. Akerlof (1976) showed how the Indian caste system possessed sanctions that could prevent the normal workings of competition from destroying it by undercutting its costly restrictions. A violator, Akerlof (1976) concluded, 'does not gain the profits of the successful arbitrageur but instead suffers the stigma of the outcaste'.[66] Within labour markets, Scoville (1996) argued, cultural factors that possess the characteristics of impermeability, permanence and inevitability create 'almost insuperable transaction costs for labor market competition to exist and produce institutional change'. Illustrating this point by the enduring monopoly of cremation services in Varanasi, India, by the Dom caste, Scoville (1996) noted, 'Religion, especially the focus on impurity, and hereditary occupational castes guarantee impermeability, permanence and single source for service to the dead.'[67]

Osborne (2001) showed that caste neither significantly affected, nor was affected by, economic development. The caste system only facilitated the formation of pressure groups on a government that had many rents to dispense and many factionalized citizens eager to seek them.[68] In the words of Thompson (2001),

> The logic of the power of pre-existing factions in India is quite simple. Once an aggressively interventionist government exists, the choice facing citizens is whether to obtain rents via caste or some other means. Given that caste-membership requires little in the way of organising costs and is easy to verify, so that it is difficult for members of one group to 'pass' as members of another, the continuance of these identities becomes a powerful cultural force in Indian society. What is also evident is that the traditional social cleavages of caste and ethnicity are far more important than economic interests, or class specificity and organization.[69]

As our study showed, although interventionism by India's central government had reduced, it continued in the states, and rents were available at both levels, allowing the continuation of rent-seeking based on caste.

Conclusion

Our research suggested that a country's business culture includes broad beliefs about the economic environment and culture that prevails in the country. We found references to competitiveness, demographics, income, poverty, wealth and their distribution, economic relations between different groups in society, savings, investment and consumption behaviour, industry structure, corporate structure, markets and economic institutions, financial infrastructure, labour markets, the role of the state in economic affairs, international trade and globalization. Other factors, such as productivity and inflation, were not specifically mentioned, but this does not mean that they were not part of the mindset. More research would be needed to delimit the possible influences.

It is not being asserted that all of a country's business decision-makers agree on either the 'facts' or the relative importance of these factors; or that all these factors are evoked each time a decision is made; or even that every business decision-maker is aware of all these factors; nevertheless, we believe that on many of these factors, research would find less variation within the business communities of countries than between them. As noted previously, the business culture itself may tend to influence its members' perceptions of business-relevant variables such as the economy.

The last section of this chapter examined the relationships between economic culture and business in our sample of Asian countries and found one example, China, of a traditionally anti-business economic culture and another, India, where the social culture in some cases conflicted with and undermined a pro-business economic culture.

References

[1] *The Global Competitiveness Report 2007–2008*, World Economic Forum URL: www.weforum.org.

[2] Y Lee, E.W. (2004) 'Introduction', in Y Lee, E.W. (ed.) *Gender and Change in Hong Kong: Globalization, Postcolonialism and Chinese Patriarchy*, Honolulu, HI: University of Hawaii Press.

[3] Cheng, W.-Y. and Liao, L.-L. (1994) 'Women managers in Taiwan', in Adler, N.J. and Izraeli, D.J. (eds) *Competitive Frontiers: Women Managers in a Global Economy*, Oxford: Blackwell.

[4] The Heritage Foundation, *Index of Economic Freedom 2007*, URL: http://heritage.org/Index.

[5] *The CIA World Factbook*, URL: https://www.cia.gov/library/publications/the-world-factbook/rankorder/2127rank.html.

[6] United Nations Development Programme, *Human Development Report 2006*, New York: Oxford University Press.

[7] Lee, K.-M. (2006) 'Citizenship, economy and social exclusion of mainland Chinese immigrants in Hong Kong', *Journal of Contemporary Asia*, **36**(2): 217–42.

[8] Zainulbhai, A.S. (2007) 'Clearing the way for robust growth: An interview with India's chief economic planner', *McKinsey Quarterly Online*, URL: www.mckinseyquarterly.com.

[9] Rodrik, D. and Subramanian, A. (2005) 'From "Hindu Growth" to productivity surge: The mystery of the Indian growth transition', *IMF Staff Papers*, **52**(2), URL: www.imf.org/external/pubs/ft/wp/2004/wp0477.pdf.

[10] Au, K.-F. (1997) 'The current status of the Hong Kong clothing industry', *Journal of Fashion Marketing and Management*, **1**(2): 185–91.

[11] Wad, P. (2001) 'Business systems and sector dynamics: The case of the Malaysian auto industry', in Jakobsen, G. and Torp, J.E. (eds) *Understanding Business Systems in Developing Countries*, London: Sage Publications.

[12] Kshetri, N. and Dholakia, N. (2005) 'E-commerce patterns in South Asia: A look beyond economics', *Journal of Asia-Pacific Business*, **6**(3): 63–79.

324 10

INTRODUCTION · THE BUSINESS CULTURES OF FIVE ASIAN COUNTRIES · ANALYSING ASIAN BUSINESS CULTURES · OWNERSHIP, FINANCING AND GOVERNANCE · ORGANIZATION AND MANAGEMENT · BUSINESS STRATEGY ·

[13] Kumar, R. (1997) 'Learning in understructured environments: Lessons from power sector development in Asia', *The Learning Organization*, 4(5): 211–16.

[14] Heilman, S. (2005) 'Regulatory innovation by Leninist means: Communist Party supervision in China's financial industry', *The China Quarterly*, 181: 1–21.

[15] Boisot, M. and Child, J. (1996) 'From fiefs to clans and network capitalism: Explaining China's emerging economic order', *Administrative Science Quarterly*, 41(1): 600–28.

[16] Sachs, J.D. and Woo, W.T. (1997) 'Understanding China's economic performance', *NBER Working Paper No. W5935*, URL: http://ssrn.com/abstract=225716.

[17] Rodrik, D. and Subramanian, A. (2005) 'From "Hindu Growth" to productivity surge: The mystery of the Indian growth transition', *IMF Staff Papers*, 52(2), URL: www.imf.org/external/pubs/ft/wp/2004/wp0477.pdf.

[18] Giles, J., Park, A. and Cai, F. (2006) 'How has economic restructuring affected China's urban workers?' *The China Quarterly*, 185: 61–95.

[19] Yujia, S. (2005) 'Brief report on the development of the non-state sector of the Chinese economy', *Bulletin of the Swiss-Chinese Chamber of Commerce*, 4(3):22–5, URL: www.sccc.ch/download/bulletin/2005_03.pdf.

[20] Claessens, S., Fan, J.P.H. and Lang, L. (2002) 'The benefits and costs of group affiliation: Evidence from East Asia', *C.E.P.R. Discussion Paper 3364*, URL: http://ideas.repec.org/p/cpr/ceprdp/3364.html.

[21] Organisation for Economic Co-operation and Development (2006) *Economic Survey*, URL: www.oecd.org/document.

[22] Dedoussis, V. (2001) 'Keiretsu and management practices in Japan – resilience amid change', *Journal of Managerial Psychology*, 16(2): 173–88.

[23] United Nations (2008) *Human Development Index 2007–8*, URL: http://hdrstats.undp.org/countries/data_sheets.

[24] Zuckerman, E., Blikberg, A. and Cao, M. (2000) *China Country Gender Review*, Washington, DC: World Bank, URL: www-wds.worldbank.org.

[25] United Nations Development Programme (1997) *China Human Development Report*, New York: Oxford University Press.

[26] Zuckerman, E., Blikberg, A. and Cao, M. (2000) *China Country Gender Review*, Washington, DC: World Bank, URL: www-wds.worldbank.org.

[27] United States State Department (2008) *Country Program Strategic Overview: China*, URL: http://www.state.gov.

[28] Bhan, G. (2001) *India gender profile: Report commissioned by Sida*, Institute of Development Studies Report No. 2. Brighton: University of Sussex.

[29] Boisot, M. and Child, J. (1996) 'From fiefs to clans and network capitalism: Explaining China's emerging economic order', *Administrative Science Quarterly*, 41(1): 600–28.

[30] Orr, G. (2004) 'What executives are asking about China', *Mckinsey Quarterly Online,* URL: www.mckinseyquarterly.com.

[31] Allen, F., Chakrabarti, R., Sankar, D., Qian, J. and Qian, M. (2007) 'Financing firms in India', URL: http://fic.wharton.upenn.edu/fic/papers/06/0608.pdf.

[32] Ibid.

[33] Ibid.

[34] Ministry of Finance, Government of India (2007) *Report of the High Powered Expert Committee on Making Mumbai an International Financial Centre*, URL: www.finmin.nic.in/mifc/fullreport.pdf.

[35] Chatterjee, S.R. and Nankervis, A. (2006) 'Asian management in a changing world', in Chatterjee, S.R. and Nankervis, A. (eds) *Asian Management in Transition*, Basingstoke: Palgrave.

[36] Yeung, H.W.-C. (1997) 'Business networks and transnational corporations: A study of Hong Kong firms in the ASEAN region', *Economic Geography*, 73: 1–25.

[37] Chan, K.-M. (2001) 'Uncertainty, acculturation and corruption in Hong Kong', *International Journal of Public Administration*, 24: 909–28.

[38] Dent, C. (2005) 'Taiwan and the new regional political economy of East Asia', *The China Quarterly*, 182: 385–406.

[39] Kojima, K. (1996) *Trade, Investment and Pacific Economic Integration. Selected Essays of Kyoshi Kojima*, Tokyo: Bunshindo.

[40] Sen, A. (2005) *The Argumentative Indian: Writings on Indian Culture, History and Identity*, London: Penguin.

[41] Yahya, F. (2005) 'State capitalism and government linked companies', *Journal of Asia-Pacific Business*, **6**(2): 3–31.

[42] Dahles, H. (2002) 'Transborder business: The "capital" input in Singapore enterprises venturing in ASEAN and beyond', *Journal of Social Issues in Southeast Asia*, **17**(2): 249–73.

[43] Yahya, F. (2005) 'State capitalism and government linked companies', *Journal of Asia-Pacific Business*, **6**(2): 3–31.

[44] Redding, G. (2004) 'The Capitalist business system of China and its rationale', *Asia Pacific Journal of Management*, **19**(2–3): 221–49. (Internal references omitted).

[45] Taeube, F.A. (2004) 'Culture, innovation, and economic development: The case of the South Indian ICT clusters', in Mani, S. and Romijn, H. (eds) *Innovation, Learning, and Technological Dynamism of Developing Countries*, New York: United Nations University Press.

[46] Castells, M. (2000) *The Information Age: Economy, Society, and Culture*, 2nd edition, Oxford: Blackwell.

[47] Lowe, S. (1998) 'Culture and network institutions in Hong Kong: A hierarchy of perspectives. A response to Wilkinson: "Culture, institutions and business in East Asia." – response to Barry Wilkinson, Organization Studies, vol 17, p 421, 1996', *Organization Studies*, **19**(2): 321–44.

[48] DiMaggio, P. (1993) 'Culture and economy', in Smelser, N. and Swedberg, R. (eds) *The Handbook of Economic Sociology*, Princeton, NJ: Princeton University Press. pp. 27–57.

[49] Lowe, S. (1998) 'Culture and network institutions in Hong Kong: A hierarchy of perspectives. A response to Wilkinson: "Culture, institutions and business in East Asia." – response to Barry Wilkinson, Organization Studies, vol 17, p 421, 1996', *Organization Studies*, **19**(2): 321–44.

[50] Ibid.

[51] Hofstede, G. (1981) *Cultures and Organizations: Software of the Mind*, London: Harper Collins.

[52] Redding, G. (2004) 'The Capitalist business system of China and its rationale', *Asia Pacific Journal of Management*, **19**(2–3): 221–49. (Internal references omitted).

[53] Hefner, R.W. (1998) 'Introduction: Society and morality in the new Asian capitalism', in Hefner, R.W. (ed.) *Market Cultures: Society and Morality in the New Asian Capitalism*, Boulder, CO: Westview Press.

[54] Chin, K.-L. (2003) *HEIJIN: Organized Crime, Business and Politics in Taiwan*, London: M.E. Sharpe.

[55] Redding, S.G. (1994) 'Competitive advantage in the context of Hong Kong', *Journal of Far Eastern Business*, **1**: 71–89.

[56] Ralston, D.A., Gustafson, D.J., Cheung, F.M. and Terpstra, R.H. (1993) 'Differences in managerial values: A study of US, Hong Kong and PRC managers', *Journal of International Business Studies*, **24**(2): 249–75.

[57] Tse, A.C.B., Tse, K.C., Yin, C.H., Ting, C.B., Yi, K.W., Yee, K.P. and Hing, W.C. (1995) 'Comparing two methods of sending out questionnaires: E-Mail versus mail', *Journal of the Market Research Society*, **37**: 441–6.

[58] Pew Research Center (2005) 'World publics welcome global trade – but not immigration', *47-Nation Pew Global Attitudes Survey 2005*, URL: www.pewglobal.org.

[59] Macalister, P. (2000) 'The return of the sun', *Good Returns: The Online Money Management Magazine*, 16 February, URL: www.goodreturns.co.nz.

[60] Weiming, T. (2000) 'Implications of the Rise of "Confucian" East Asia', *Daedalus*, **129**(1) URL: isites. harvard.edu/fs/docs/icb.topic241166.files/EthicsSyl08.doc.

[61] Whitley, R. (1992) *Business Systems in East Asia: Firms, Markets, and Societies*, London: Sage.

[62] Huang, S.-M. (1998) 'Economic culture and moral assumptions in a Chinese village in Fujian', URL: http://www.chineseupress.com.

[63] Willmott, W.F. (1972) 'Introduction', in Willmott, W.E. (ed.) *Economic Organization in Chinese Society*, Stanford, CA: Stanford University Press.

[64] Huang, S.-M. (1998) 'Economic culture and moral assumptions in a Chinese village in Fujian', URL: http://www.chineseupress.com.

[65] Ibid.

[66] Akerlof, G. (1976) 'The Economics of caste and of the rat race and other woeful tales', *Quarterly Journal of Economics*, **90**: 599–617.

[67] Scoville, J. (1996) 'Labor market underpinnings of a caste economy: Foiling the Coase Theorem', *American Journal of Economics and Sociology*, **55**: 385–94.

[68] Osborne, E. (2001) 'Culture, development, and government: Reservations in India', *Development and Cultural Change*, **49**(3): 659–85.

[69] Thompson, H. (2001) 'Culture and economic development: Modernisation to globalisation', *Theory & Science*, **2**(2) URL: http://theoryandscience.icaap.org.

326 10

INTRODUCTION · THE BUSINESS CULTURES OF FIVE ASIAN COUNTRIES · ANALYSING ASIAN BUSINESS CULTURES · OWNERSHIP, FINANCING AND GOVERNANCE · ORGANIZATION AND MANAGEMENT · BUSINESS STRATEGY ·

INTRODUCTION • THE BUSINESS CULTURES OF FIVE ASIAN COUNTRIES • ANALYSING ASIAN
CULTURES • OWNERSHIP FINANCING AND GOVERNANCE • ORGANIZATION AND
MENT • BUSINESS STRATEGY • DIMENSIONS OF SOCIETAL CULTURES • SOCIETAL
CULTURES REVISITED • POLITICAL CULTURES AND PERCEIVED POLITICAL ENVIRONMENTS •
ECONOMIC CULTURES AND PERCEIVED ECONOMIC ENVIRONMENTS • CONCLUDING REMARKS

11 concluding remarks

The main input to this book has been the primary research conducted by means of unstructured interviews in five Asian countries. The main outputs from that research are (1) a theory of relations between business cultures and business decisions (2) a somewhat rich description of the business cultures of five Asian countries (3) indications of the possible influence of the business cultures of the five Asian countries we researched on their business decision-making and (4) indications of the possible relations between the business decisions and business cultures of the five Asian countries and other layers of culture there.

1. A theory of relations between business cultures and business decisions
    a. The central theory generated by the research is that business communities have business cultures that exert an influence on business decision-making. We believe that our research justifies a claim that 71 out of our 75 interviewees subscribed to this theory. (We have taken a conservative view here and allocated the four who specifically asserted that there were different business cultures in different kinds of organization in their country to a 'non-believing' category. Even these interviewees, however, also made generalizations about distinctive values and practices that crossed these boundaries between different types of businesses.) The basis of this claim is the approach we took, which aimed to capture the theories about business and culture in their country held by decision-makers from the business communities of those countries. This approach is further explained and justified in the Appendix.
    Corollaries of this central theory include the following:
        i.   business cultures exist;
        ii. the term 'business culture' is widely understood in an approximately similar sense by a wide range of business decision-makers from different business communities;
        iii. the term 'business culture' can be applied meaningfully at a national level.

327

These statements require some amplification:

i. The definition of 'business culture' which approximates to the understanding of the concept by most business decision-makers is 'a set of business-related values, beliefs, attitudes, meanings and practices shared by a business community'.

ii. The term 'business culture' can be applied at a national level even in a country as populated and diverse as India or one in a transitional condition like China. It can also be applicable to a narrower area, such as a part of a country like 'Maharashtra' or 'the South'; our research suggests that where this is so, it does not imply that no national business culture exists, but that some elements are different in different parts of the country. It is possible, also, that the term business culture can be applied to a wider region than a country, such as South East Asia, but our research provides no evidence on this question.

iii. It is also possible that there exists a phenomenon that might be called 'global business culture', composed of elements of business-related values, beliefs, attitudes and behaviours shared among business communities around the globe but not, necessarily, by other populations. If this phenomenon exists, a question arises about its relationship to national and sub-national business cultures. Our own research is not conclusive on whether it does exist or not.

iv. Our theory that business cultures influence business decisions is somewhat weak according to the Popperian theory of refutability,[1] because to refute the theory would require demonstrating either that business cultures do not exist or that they exist but do not influence business decisions. These refutations are possible but less probable than the refutation of a deterministic theory would be. (Some interviewees did appear to hold a deterministic view of the relationship, but the great majority, we believe, adhered to a weaker view, allowing space for individual agency as well as other institutional variables to exert an influence.)

v. The theory is, however, strong in two non-Popperian senses. It is derived from empirical research and it is new. It suggests the importance of a hitherto neglected concept for understanding business decision-making in different societies and postulates a set of relationships not previously explored.

vi. Given the extent to which business decision-makers are, necessarily, preoccupied with the 'view' from their own organization, and even from their own position within that organization,[2] it is remarkable the degree to which our interviewees were able and willing to formulate and express their theories about the business culture of their country. In itself, this seems to confirm the importance of the concept and the extent to which business culture is seen as influential in business decision-making in the countries studied.

b. We further theorize that the business culture and the broader societal culture may sometimes diverge. We base this on the differences noted in Chapter 7 between predictions about business behaviour and organization founded on dimensional descriptions of societal cultures and our own findings. Business culture is distinguished from societal culture by its narrower range of elements (those concerned with business) and by being confined to a narrower section of society, the business community. It is probable that just as societal culture results from a society's responses to the historical challenges posed by its environment, so the business culture is similarly the response of a business community to the challenges of its environment. This environment includes the societal culture, but also other factors such as the national and international political and economic environments, and, in a globalizing world, global business culture, insofar as that exists. Since the environment of business is notoriously fast-moving, it is therefore no surprise to find indications that elements of business cultures may at times change more rapidly than societal cultures. One such indication is that at the start of the 21st century in much of Asia, but especially in India, the 'skills shortage' was an issue. Shortages of personnel with infrastructure building skills, shortages of in-depth knowledge of management of industries such as multiple retailing which were in their infancy in the subcontinent were seen as hampering the prospects of the Indian software providers in their attempts to add value to their services.[i] Skills shortages would probably not have been in the mindset so strongly a few years before and would not be again or would have assumed a different form a few years later.

Although Chapters 7 to 10 of this book describe various aspects of other cultures and environments (societal, political and economic) which may be linked to business culture, we judge that our research did not provide a basis for a theory asserting what the character of such links are. Undoubtedly, some interviewees held theories about such links, but the links were not sufficiently explored to justify our asserting them. The only direct outcome of our research in this area is the possibility set out above that under certain conditions, business cultures and societal cultures diverge. Where the business culture and the broader societal culture do diverge, it is possible, we believe, that the business culture may be the better predictor of the patterns resulting from business decision-making. If so, this would be a marked departure from the extant dimensional theories that assert rather direct relationships between

---

[i] Indian, Product Manager, Indian Business Services (IT Management)

societal culture and patterns of business decision-making. However, this is one area among many which needs more research.

Our theories locate business cultures within the institutional perspective on economics and organizations. They are important elements of cognitive institutions (Scott 1995),[3] which equate 'to culture defined in terms of socially established structures of meaning that control people's worldviews, what action is possible, and what is less likely to be questioned or even considered'. Business cultures may have their greatest impact on business decision-making by affecting 'what action is [believed] possible and what is less likely to be questioned or even considered'.

2. In addition to theories about business cultures, our research provided a somewhat rich, though admittedly partial, description of the business cultures of five Asian countries and a cross-country comparison of elements of those cultures.

Important differences as well as similarities emerged from our research. In a field where it is still, despite some notable exceptions, common to conflate all Asian countries together, this study and book have helped delineate where there are and where there are not commonalities. As one example among many of difference, at least the following elements of Japan's business culture differ from those in the other four countries in our sample: the prevalence of consensual decision-making, the low priority given to accounting to external bodies, including owners, and the continuing preference for the lifetime employment system, despite the recognition that current conditions render it less viable. As an example of commonality, on the other hand, we believe that our research provides a basis for extending the concept of the 'Chinese family business' to include other Asian family businesses, notably those of India. Although their precise configuration may differ, owing to differences in institutions, there are signs of a fundamental similarity. A more nuanced understanding of Asian cultures emerges. Table 11.1 brings together the tables from Chapters 2 and 3, and Table 11.2 brings together material from the tables in Chapters 4, 5 and 6 to provide a summary of our findings and to allow easier comparison.

We have found no evidence for, and have tried to avoid any suggestion of there being, a broad pan-Asian business culture or set of cultural characteristics. Three possible candidate characteristics are Confucianism, collectivism and state dependence.

i. Confucianism 'fails' because it has no influence in India and many other parts of Asia that were never under China's hegemony. Even within those areas of Asia that were, other strong influences should be taken into account. One of these, Taoism, has been noted by previous writers, but the influence of two Indian and two West Asian religions with their associated moral cultures have not. These are Hinduism, Buddhism, Islam

Table 11.1 *Elements of the business cultures of five Asian countries from Chapters 2 and 3*

	China	India	Japan	Taiwan	Singapore
Personalism in business control and decision-making	High – *guanxi* operates within organizations HKSAR High but changing with incoming professionalization	High familism, some casteism	*High – personal relations outweigh systems*	*High – pride in business ownership is a key value*	*Low – meritocracy except in the small and medium enterprise (SME) sector*
Personalism in employment and work relations	*Mixed, but China not a meritocracy;* *HKSAR meritocratic except in the SME sector where familism prevails*	In traditional businesses, personalism prevails and work relationships are all-embracing; the modern private companies use merit-based systems. 'Soft' culture.	Organizations are communities of their employees. In big companies, appointment is merit-based but promotion is seniority-based.	*High in older companies, low in newer technology-based companies*	*Meritocratic except in the SME sector where familism prevails*
Importance of hierarchy	High – hierarchy very important	Boss–subordinate relations are 'master–servant'	Low power distance – status and power are not co-equivalent	*Medium-high in older companies, lower in newer technology-based companies*	
Deference	High deference to superiors	Extremely high deference to owners; high to superiors	Very high deference to seniors and superiors	*Relatively low*	

Continued

Table 11.1 Continued

	China	India	Japan	Taiwan	Singapore
Entrepreneurialism	High but restricted	Medium – occurs in certain communities; also now sometimes in young not from business backgrounds	Low	High	Low
Attitudes to risk	Some are gamblers; some rational risk-handlers	An individual, not a cultural, matter	Risk averse	Not risk averse and able to handle risk effectively	Singaporean Chinese are risk takers; MNC * employees are not
Innovation and creativity	Low (but fast copiers) HKSAR Low (but highly efficient)	Low (but good problem-solvers)	Low except in technological products; good modifiers	Low (but good at reverse engineering)	Low (but MNCs bring innovation)
Governance	Weak HKSAR Strong	Weak but being seriously addressed by government	Weak	Weak	Strong
Corruption	Official corruption high. HKSAR low	Widespread except in high-technology businesses	Low	Political corruption endemic	Low
Personalism in B2B	B2B depends on personal networks, guanxi	Personal relationships are important but not a guanxi system	B2B relationships even within keiretsu are mainly inter-organizational though	B2B and financing depend on	

			there are elements of personalism	personal networks, guanxi	Role of government central
Business relations with Government	Government not dominant except in SOEs**, not monolithic	*State governments more relevant than central government*	*Minor*	Government previously led business, not now	
Different types of businesses have different cultures	SOEs – 'communist culture'; low-tech private businesses; efficient high-tech businesses	*Public sector businesses 'not primarily commercial'; older private businesses have family business characteristics; high-tech businesses 'modern'*		Some elements of culture vary in different types of business (traditional – banks, real estate – and technology-based)	MNCs international, local businesses Asian
Negotiation style and approach	Holistic, rational, interpersonal, not unfair but there is no 'getting to yes'	*Hard bargaining; the aim is to beat the other side*	*Negotiations are part of a relationship – balanced approach*	A link is a pre-condition The aim is to win; face issues are paramount	
Change		*Globalization reducing impact of traditional culture*	*Need for change – some happening*		

Note: *(multi-national company).
** State-owned enterprise.

Table 11.2 *Elements of the business cultures of five Asian countries from Chapters 4, 5 and 6*

	China	India	Japan	Taiwan	Singapore
Attitudes to business ownership					
Family control important – outsiders distrusted	X	X		X	X
Family control important – financial reasons		X			
Family control important – pride and status of owner				X	
Work behaviour of employees in five Asian countries					
Industriousness	High *HKSAR* Very high	High	Quite high (long hours)	High	Quite high
Primary motive	To make money – insecurity *HKSAR* Desire for efficiency	To make money – insecurity	Commitment to the organization	Career; development; learning	
Secondary motive		Career; development; learning			
Team working	Poor	Poor	Very good	Poor	Poor

Cultural underpinning	Collectivist loyalty transferred to work group not the wider organization	Collectivist loyalty to units outside the organization, especially the family	Collectivist loyalty transferred to organization	
Basis for decision-making	1. Top down 2. Intuition 3. Trial and error 4. Superstition	1. Top down 2. Thorough information gathering	1. Consensus 2. Thorough information gathering	
Information flows	Restricted within-company information flows; control by close supervision	Restricted within-company information flows; control by close supervision	Information is widely dispersed; normative/cultural control systems	
Business goals	Goals of SOEs and private business differ, even conflict	Often to raise personal funds for the founding family; also 'dynastic goals'; more broadly 'economically rational' goals	Often not primarily financial returns to shareholders	In older businesses dynastic goals reflect pride in business ownership; in high-technology companies, 'making money and getting out'.
Forward planning	An aversion to forward planning and preference for trial and error	Used increasingly as family firms professionalize	Forward planning is thorough but strategic vision may be lacking	Contingency and opportunism dominate due to the hyper-competitive market

and Christianity. Of these, Buddhism has been the strongest influence in China itself, where at the start of the 21st century it was experiencing a widespread resurgence, and in Japan. Protestant Christianity, with its work ethic, was also reviving among the educated classes in China who comprised some of the most important business decision-makers.

ii. Collectivism has been found to vary in both strength and type within Asia. India and Japan are both ranked much higher on individualism (lower on collectivism) than the other three countries, though still high on collectivism relative to the Anglo-Saxon countries. Moreover, collectivism in different Asian countries is differently oriented: in broad terms, in Japan collectivism is oriented to the company, in India to the family, *jati* or caste, in China to the *danwei*, in Hong Kong and Taiwan to the kinship or ethnic group.

iii. State dependence appears to have been a temporary phenomenon in most Asian countries and of our sample only continued largely unaltered in Singapore. Economic liberalization ended it for the major part of the economies of India and China, though it survived in pockets; democracy and a change of government reduced it in Taiwan. In Japan, in the postwar period, it was always less marked.

Thus the concept of an overall pan-Asian business culture must be rejected. However, four elements of business culture do seem, but in varying forms, to be found across the Asian countries we researched:

i. There are factors which prevent employment relations from being entirely meritocratic; for example, in Japan there is the *doki* mentality, in India the similar though also different batch mentality, both of which are manifestations of a seniority principle; in China and Taiwan as well as India, loyalty is often valued above performance; while in all five countries there are, in traditional businesses, elements of favouritism based on ethnic or other links rather than ability or performance.

ii. A narrow view is taken on who are the important stakeholders in a business, a view which excludes the wider community. This is also true in many Western countries, but there are different definitions of who the important stakeholders are. In China, including Hong Kong, Taiwan and India the founding families, even of listed companies, are the only really important stakeholders; in China's state-owned enterprises (SOEs) it is the central or local government; in Japan, where previously the most important stakeholders were the core employees, the 'actual' situation has been shifting in favour of shareholders in some large corporations, but this need not mean that the business culture has yet or will soon shift in the same direction. The narrowness of stakeholder definition is closely linked to retention of control of listed businesses by founding families (or government in the case of privatized former SOEs) and the associated replacement of principal-agent conflicts of interest with principal-principal conflicts of interest between majority and minority shareholders.

iii. Network capitalism, in the sense of relying on personal contacts for financing, is widespread, though it may be decreasing as the most appropriate description for the predominant financial systems of India or Singapore. In the words of one interviewee, 'India has had a stockmarket-based economy for fifteen years. The stock market has existed for over fifty years, but the role of equity in family savings and the emergence of mutual funds have made a huge difference since the 1991 liberalization.'[ii] (At the time of writing, precipitous declines in stock markets were occurring globally. Whether this would reverse trends away from network capitalism remains to be seen.)

iv. There is a preference for the personal over the impersonal as the basis for trust.

Our findings begin to complement the work of Whitley (1992)[4] on Asian business systems by identifying elements of the 'currently dominant beliefs, priorities and ways of making judgements' on which ' "rational" and efficient structures and practices' depend and according to which they vary (p. 4). One intriguing possibility is that business cultures, though changing more rapidly than societal cultures, may change less rapidly than some relevant institutions. For example, a change in regulatory and possibly also in normative institutions meant that the Japanese *keiretsu* diminished in importance soon after Whitley (1992) was published, but the business culture which underpinned them, a belief in and preference for cooperative inter-organizational relations over arms-length dealings, survived, our research suggested, and might manifest itself either in a revival of the *keiretsu* or in some other form.

3. As Chapter 1 explained, some types of business decisions are, in logic, more likely than others to be affected by business culture. These are decisions where factors affecting the outcome of decisions and outside the control of decision-makers are weak or slow-acting or both. In such cases, decision-makers may have a range of alternatives, none of which is likely to be proved a mistake in the short or medium term. In cases where such factors are strong and fast-acting, however, behaving in accordance with a set of culturally induced 'prejudices' may often be 'punished' by the market. In Chapter 1 we argued that this logic may suggest that there is a continuum of types of business decisions where the influence of business culture ranges from strong to negligible.

[ii] Indian, Marketing Consultant and Academic

It would be an overstatement to claim that our findings supported this logic, but certainly the types of business decisions most emphasized in the context of business culture by our interviewees were those where 'uncontrollable' factors were relatively weak. These were decisions about ownership, financing, governance, organization and management and some aspects of strategy. As noted in the conclusions of Chapter 4, both the present study and other research show that business ownership and financing patterns in much of Asia reflect the business culture of familism and preference for retaining founder control, a culture which creates major problems for corporate governance. Rules and regulations are often circumvented because founding families feel that they have entitlements that other stakeholders do not, and because this position is supported by the culture. Chapter 5 showed that organization and management practices in Asia are also affected by business cultures. With the exception of Japan, in the Asian countries in our sample centralized decision-making and restricted information flows predominated, despite the fact that managerial evaluations of staff motivations were positive. In a different cultural setting, positive beliefs about staff attitudes would normally lead to 'Theory Y' management. Chapter 6 concluded that some elements of Asian firms' business strategies 'undermine' competitive differentiation. The preferences for joining a business group and expanding overseas through contacts within the same ethnic group are examples of these limits on Asian firms' strategic openness. Finally, we received very few comments or examples that linked business cultures with marketing, although links of marketing to societal cultures, through their impact on consumer behaviour, were made. This was no surprise, as marketing is the area of business where uncontrollable factors are perhaps at their strongest and fastest-acting, and so our logic would predict a low impact of business cultures on marketing decisions.

4. The findings of the present research go to support the concept put forward by Hofstede et al. (1990)[5] that culture is layered, as shown in Figure 11.1. Neither the present research nor any other known to the author permits a judgement on the relative importance of the different layers as influences on business decision-making. Common sense would suggest that it varies from decision to decision. What the present research does permit, however, is the suggestion that 'business culture' as defined in this book (and as understood by practitioners) is one of the important layers for many classes of decision, at least in Asia.

Suggestions for further research

When, as in this case, a claim based on primary research is made that a 'new' or neglected concept has substantial potential in a field, several avenues for research are opened up.

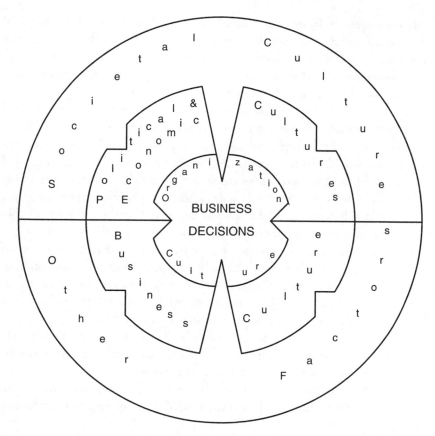

Figure 11.1 **Relations among cultures and business decisions suggested by the findings of the present research**

First it is necessary to ascertain that the concept itself, in this case the concept of 'business culture', is meaningful, and that its definition is appropriate both in the circumstances in which it was first identified and beyond. This process was not, initially, deemed necessary for studies of the relations between societal culture and business, although there has subsequently been some debate on the matter, because the concept of culture was accepted as valid, following the earlier work of anthropologists. The concept of 'business culture' does not, however, enjoy such status, and future developments would be prejudiced unless its validity was established and its application delimited.

It will be remembered that the definition of 'business culture' used here is 'a set of business-related values, beliefs, attitudes, meanings and practices shared by a business community'. Questions that arise are, is this the most functional definition possible? Does it correspond better than any other to the implicit or explicit usage of practitioners? Can it be operationalized effectively for the purposes of quantitative research? If not, what better definition should be used? In the social sciences, questions such as these have often been settled, if at all (they have not been settled for 'culture'), by debate triggered by a proliferation of definitions in use that only serve to confuse and to impede research progress. It would be beneficial if the concept 'business culture' could avoid this fate.

The next stage would be to establish the validity and reliability of the asserted relations between the concept and other variables. In this case that would mean the relations between business cultures and key aspects of business decision-making. This would call for larger-scale hypothesis-testing research. It would need to be conducted in the countries used to generate the theory, as disproving the theory for other countries would only delimit its generalizability, not refute it. For efficiency, however, it might be advantageous to combine testing the theory in the five countries with testing its limits in other countries.

Further exploratory research is also needed. Interesting research questions can be asked about the influence of societal, political and economic cultures on business cultures in, for instance, different European countries in comparison with the USA. There are also possible areas for research in the relative influence of different layers of culture on different kinds of business decisions.

Finally, research is needed to establish whether all business cultures, like societal cultures, have underlying dimensions (which might or might not be values) on which they can be measured, so that these dimensions can be used for comparisons. To meet this need, further qualitative research is needed to identify a set of dimensions, and then these need to be applied in quantitative research.

Practical implications

The practical purpose of cultural research is to enable predictions of behaviour to be made that are more general than those that can be made for individuals, small groups, single organizations or even industries but more specific than those that apply to humanity as a whole. Such predictions are especially needed when the subject of interest is a large entity, such as a country or region. Thus, our conclusion that business cultures affect business decision-making on a country-wide basis gives our study substantial practical applications.

Our findings, if confirmed by further research, have implications for investors in Asia, Asian regulatory authorities and policy-makers, managers, business strategists and those involved in business deals. Investors in Asia may easily establish the facts, for example that overwhelming majority stakes are usually retained in public companies by founding families in India. These facts may well alert them to possible dangers from becoming minority shareholders in such companies. By understanding how deeply embedded and culturally endorsed within the business community are the attitudes that it is 'right' that founding families should continue to profit disproportionately, however, investors can realize more fully that change from outside is likely to be resisted. Similarly, the outcome of a case in Japan in 2008, where foreign investors failed in attempts to increase shareholder representation on major company boards, was always likely in view of Japan's business culture.

Equally, regulatory authorities and policy-makers need to understand the strength of the business culture with which they are dealing when attempting to improve governance. Passing laws or introducing rules to protect minority shareholders has some effect: many companies in Asia are law-abiding, especially if the law is adequately enforced. Nevertheless, we have found evidence that laws and rules are not enough to bring about high standards when they run counter to a strong business culture, such as those of India and Taiwan.

For managers, especially expatriate managers, knowing that employee expectations as well as motivations differ from one business community to the other will enable them to avoid damaging mistakes. The importance of the quality of the (subsidized) food in the staff restaurant or the adequate provision of free transport to work to employee morale in India, for instance, has sometimes been misunderstood in foreign-owned companies, to the detriment of performance and staff retention.

Finally, those seeking to do business in Asia need to take into account the varying levels of preference for a personal versus an impersonal basis for trust.

In all these areas, not only the business culture but also the broader societal culture will have an influence on behaviour. As noted in the previous section of this chapter, we have as yet no knowledge of the relative importance of these influences. Until we do, the wise investor, manager, regulator or business negotiator will try to take both into account.

One way of looking at culture is as a set of embedded attitudes that are widespread in a population. Taking this view leads to the question of the relationship between attitudes and behaviour. Extensive research in the field of consumer behaviour has strongly suggested that attitudes to actions are better predictors of actions than attitudes to related objects: thus attitudes to a product or brand are less predictive of purchase behaviour than attitudes to buying the product or brand. Without overstretching the point, it might be that business cultures more often contain attitudes to business actions than broader societal cultures do.

Objections

There is a case for arguing that those four interviewees (two Chinese and two Indian) who disputed the existence of a national business culture, on the grounds that there existed in their country three types of businesses with different cultures, understood the term 'business culture' to mean something similar to 'organizational culture', and so to implicitly deny or not recognize the concept of a business culture. There are a number of answers to this, if it is seen as an objection to our theory. First, this answer was given by only a very small percentage of our sample – 4 out of 75 interviewees. Second, even these four went on to describe characteristics common to all three types of businesses, such as top-down management, which suggests that they did recognize a common business culture, while simultaneously recognizing that other types of culture may be influential. Third, the particular ways in which these interviewees subdivided businesses and their cultures do not correspond to 'organizational culture' or, indeed, to any other type of culture described in the literature. In both countries, the distinction drawn was between public sector-owned businesses, high-technology 'new economy' privately owned businesses and other private businesses. (There was a difference between the kinds of businesses composing the Indian and Chinese categories of 'other private businesses': in the case of India, it was the traditional family-owned businesses dating back to the pre-liberalization era; in the case of China it was the 'low-technology' private businesses founded since the 1978 liberalization.) This three-fold categorization conflates ownership and technology as a criterion. It is an aspect of our findings which would be worth further research.

Another objection that might be raised is that our respondents were not in complete agreement about the beliefs and practices that constituted their business culture. For example, one interviewee reported the percentage of family businesses in India as 90 per cent, another as 75 per cent. However, we believe it is in the nature of culture to be sometimes fuzzy, to eschew exactitude or accuracy.

A third objection might be that the characteristics that our interviewees perceived as distinguishing the way business is done and organizations are managed in their country are due, not to business culture, but to stage of economic development. Japan, Taiwan and Singapore provide the obvious refutation of this argument, since they are all advanced economically but still retain distinctive organizational and business practices and beliefs.

Another possible objection is that our findings risk the 'proliferation of dimensions that occurs when every country is held to be specific in a different way from every other country'.[6] Clearly our findings do point to the five countries in our sample having overall different business cultures, but though these include one or two country-specific variables, in the main they are made up of a set of variables, larger than that of the dimensional researchers, but not enormous. A further point is that we do not claim that the aspects of business culture that we have labelled 'elements' are dimensions. Since our purpose was to provide rich description, we did not consider reducing these elements to dimensions. It may well be that further research of a less exploratory nature would find a smaller number of underlying dimensions with powerful explanatory value.

Limitations

In addition to the obvious limitation that our work has produced only an untested theory, even if based in primary research, there are other limitations.

We have made no attempt at an internal analysis of business cultures – in other words, to separate out values, beliefs and practices. Our methodology would not allow it. It was clear that the interviewees drew no such distinction; that is, that the terms 'the way business is done and organizations are managed' and 'business culture' evoked a mixed bag of what psychologists and culture scholars would probably analyse out as values, beliefs, attitudes or behaviours.

It is worth reiterating the point made in Chapter 1, but for purposes of exposition set aside elsewhere in the book, that the patterns of ownership, financing, governance, organization and so on described in Chapters 4, 5 and 6 have a dual nature. They are both the consequences of large numbers of individual business decisions influenced by the business culture and practices which manifest the business culture and are part of it. Our research explored only the first of these aspects.

We have not clarified which of the business culture variables that we identified are subject to change, which are enduring, or even whether changeable variables can usefully be considered part of business culture and, if so, what are the lower limits of duration that enables a variable to be counted as part of the culture. In our defence, it must be said that the same limitation applies to all the studies of broader culture so far completed, and we reject the easy but challengeable assertion that cultures are so slow changing that the matter can be set aside. Other kinds of research, in particular longitudinal studies, would be needed to advance understanding on these questions.

In the course of this book and the present study we have identified a large number of characteristics of the way business is conducted and business organizations are managed in five Asian countries. Many of these characteristics cannot easily be accounted for by positive resource-dependence theory but do seem to correspond to the cognitive elements in positive institutional theory. However, whether these characteristics enable the Asian organizations concerned to perform optimally, as some versions of institutional theory would assert, is beyond the scope of this book and study and so no judgement on normative theory is intended or possible here.

Chapters 4, 5 and 6, which respectively deal with business decision-making and its consequences for aspects of how businesses are owned, financed, governed, organized, managed and so on, do not distinguish clearly between the business culture and business decisions. That is, our research method did not distinguish independent and dependent variables. Nevertheless, we believe there is enough evidence in our findings to suggest that business decisions and business cultures are distinct. For example, 'pride in business ownership', which we found to be an element in the business culture of Taiwan, would be compatible with a range of different business decisions regarding financing and governance; it could also influence decisions in a range of distinct business areas and, although in general we found the influence of business culture in marketing to be quite weak, it was considered to influence even marketing communications ('[There is] huge pride in ownership, pride in being a smart businessman, pride in being self-made: it shows in the company name, marketing communications, the tone of ads; it emerges during negotiations.'[iii])

Chapters 7, 8, 9 and 10, which respectively deal with the influences of societal, political and economic factors on business cultures, do not distinguish between cultures and environments; that is, our research does not allow us to distinguish whether an influence is part of the political culture of the country or merely of the political environment in which business in the country operates. The same applies to societal and economic culture and environment, although societal cultures are sufficiently pervasive for it to be likely that many business decision-makers in a country are members of their country's societal culture.

A final word

It is hard to account for the neglect in management research and literature, noted in Chapter 1, of the widely used concept 'business culture'. It seems to lack neither explanatory value nor usefulness. Business cultures would appear to be closer to actual business decision-making and communication than the broader concept of societal culture which has been so extensively explored; their possible influence, on the other hand, is wider than an organizational culture or industry culture and so may be of greater value to those who seek to do business in or with a particular country.

References

[1] Popper, K.R. (1963) *Conjectures and Refutations: The Growth of Scientific Knowledge*, London: Routledge and Kegan Paul.
[2] Guirdham, M. (1982) Individuals' Beliefs and Inter-Organisational Relations, Unpublished PhD thesis, London Business School.
[3] Scott, W.R. (1995 and 2001) *Institutions and Organizations*, Thousand Oaks, CA: Sage.

[iii] Taiwan, expatriate banker

[4] Whitley, R. (1992) *Business Systems in East Asia: Firms, Markets, and Societies*, London: Sage.

[5] Hofstede, G., Neuijen, B., Ohayv, D.D. and Sanders, G. (1990) 'Measuring organizational cultures: A qualitative and quantitative study across twenty cases', *Administrative Science Quarterly*, **35**(2): 286–317.

[6] Aggarwal, R. and Mellen, L.E. (1997) 'Perspective on Japanese finance for portfolio investors', *Review of Business*, **18**, 22 June.

appendix: a note on the methodology of this study

The primary research for this book about culture and business in Asia has been by means of in-depth unstructured interviews with business executives in and from the countries concerned. These interviews were intended to access the beliefs of those interviewed about the topic. We contend that these beliefs are, in fact, theories of a kind that is particularly valuable for understanding links between culture and business.

It has been argued that values, beliefs and norms are rarely observable and hence are difficult to measure. The 'more visible manifestations' of culture are actions, behaviour and actual social practices, which are usually influenced through norms and values.[1] Only behaviourists, presumably, would argue that culture consists *only* of 'actions, behaviour and actual social practices' and their position has long been refuted. Therefore this objection to researching values and beliefs is largely a practical one, as we argue below; on the other hand the objections to confining research into culture to its visible manifestations are more fundamental: what people do cannot be studied, like events in the physical world, in terms which are independent of the intentions of the person concerned. Shotter (1980) put the point in the following way:

> Not only are the naturalistic (common sense) reasons for peoples' conduct very different from the reasons (abstract theories) suggested by scientific, external observers...but...such 'naturalistic' explanations – in terms of motives, beliefs etc. – are the only valid kind of reason in this context; for they are the kinds of reasons in terms of which the people involved are actually conducting their affairs.[2]

A second argument against researching actions alone in studying culture is that people have only partial control of their actions, which are observed as events in the physical world: other variables intervene. For this reason, too, observations of conduct are highly ambiguous about events and states in the human world. If some of the ambiguity can be removed by controlling the conditions, then this reduces the relevance of the study to real-life situations. (This is not to deny that as ordinary people we interpret ambiguous actions with some success, though with some failures, too. However, the criteria for success as ordinary people are different from those for researchers, different in a way which both permits more tolerance of ambiguity and punishes fewer mistakes.) If, in practice, some of the ambiguity of real-life physical events – actions – can be removed by close observation, this in itself is difficult to achieve without affecting the observed phenomena, while one difficulty remains: because of partial non-control we cannot reliably interpret mental states from non-verbal actions.

An approach to our topic confined to culture's 'more visible manifestations' would be based on an assumed possibility of relatively value-free observation by an 'independent' observer, generating objective facts which are neutral to theory. But all facts are theory-laden;[3] what counts as a fact is influenced by theory and the possibility of value-free observation does not exist. Though themselves not value-free observations, the beliefs of our research subjects do enjoy a privileged logical status. If an observer sincerely asserts 'x' is the cause of John doing 'y', then x may or may not be the cause (or even a cause) of John doing y; and that remains the case even if John himself is the sincere observer. But if John sincerely asserts, 'x is my reason for doing y', then that statement enjoys an unchallengeable authority; it *is* his reason for doing y. A similar authority attaches to a person's sincere statements of his or her beliefs and perceptions.[4]

Thus, far from being inferior data to behavioural observations, people's reports of their beliefs are, on two grounds, logically superior to them. If sincere statements of beliefs and reasons are therefore good data, the refusal to admit these phenomena to full status as sources in social research rests on an assumption that people's statements will normally be insincere – that is, what remains now of the inaccessibility argument rests on a distrustful attitude towards other people, which suggests that they will normally be either unable or unwilling to reveal their 'true' beliefs to the researcher. This assumption must be challenged by a researcher who respects people's abilities and control. This respect means that what people tell us, providing we understand their language and meaning, becomes the best kind of material for many studies. The researcher must learn to listen, trusting respondents unless provided with good reason to do otherwise, and respecting respondents as authorities on the subject of the research; often using commonalities and differences in respondents' reports as analysis and explanation. This is not to exempt the researcher from responsibility for the quality of data, since rejecting the idea that respondents are always and systematically unreliable does not commit us to the naïve view that they are always sincere, or that, when statements of cognition are to be interpreted as something more than themselves, for example as evidence of underlying beliefs, there is no possibility of mistake or deceit.

Objections are sometimes raised to researching beliefs (or attitudes) on the reasonable ground that behaviour and beliefs are often inconsistent. This objection only applies, however, when the purpose of accessing beliefs or attitudes is to predict behaviour, as in most consumer-behaviour research. In our research we were not concerned to predict the behaviour of our research subjects, only to ascertain their beliefs about culture and beliefs about behaviour in the form of business decisions.

We argue that the beliefs, or theories, of business executives from a culture have two qualities that do not apply to the theories of outside researchers: first, that as members of the culture themselves, they each have privileged access to at least one member of the culture's beliefs. Even if they are wrong about everybody else, they must be regarded as a trustworthy source (subject to the caveat already made) so far as they themselves are concerned. Second, they are privileged observers of the phenomena under consideration – their exposure is likely to be far greater than that of outside observers. Although in the footnotes listing their status as research subjects, only their present occupation is listed, most of our interviewees had considerable previous and different work experience. Their beliefs about the relations between business and culture were likely to have drawn on all their experience, not just the most recent. Their beliefs (or theories) about the business cultures they spoke about had presumably been based on and proved robust to a range of experiences. Moreover, the subject was likely to be salient to them, since decisions that affected their work and career could follow from their beliefs about it, thus giving them the motivation, even if not in all cases the skill, to pay attention and observe accurately. It is true that raised motivation can lead to distortion but to some extent that is reduced by interviewing a number of different people from different areas of activity about the same phenomena.

If, as might be true, respondents have even greater access to the data from self-reports, which is an alternative method often used for accessing culture, it could also be that their answers would be biased, while getting from self-reports to a theory requires more interpretation from a researcher than reporting and organizing the theories of research subjects themselves. The distortion from our method is likely to be less than that resulting from respondents being led by a series of rating questions in a questionnaire, as is the more common way of researching culture.

Hofstede (1981) and others obtained their cultural dimensions by a process of inference from questions ostensibly about other matters – in Hofstede's case, linked to job satisfaction;[5] this methodology was presumably based on an assumption that culture is not present in people's awareness. This seems likely, when culture is understood in the largely abstract terms that emerged from these researches – it is doubtful whether most individuals could readily have answered whether they or their compatriots had high power distance or uncertainty avoidance. It was also necessitated by the intrinsic comparative nature of cultural descriptions. In large samples it is difficult to ensure that respondents have a basis for comparison. In contrast, by taking a direct approach, we assumed that our interviewees would be able to judge what was *different* about the culture in their country and its relation to the way business was conducted and organizations were managed. In part, this was justified because the topic had moved on. Awareness of culture and cultural difference is much higher than it was in 1980. The increasing internationalization of business also meant that the business decision-makers whose cultures we were researching were more likely to have had some chance of observing at least one alternative country's ways, either by experience or study. By researching in Asia, we also increased this probability, because so many business theories have originated in the West. In the event, this issue turned out not to be a problem. We did receive three or four replies to our request for an interview stating that their experience was limited to working in their own country and so they might not be useful to us; however, we included these respondents and they all proved to have sufficient basis for comparison, based on involvement in international transactions or with foreign-owned businesses in their country.

Although Hofstede and others adopted what was essentially a theory-testing methodology, their research output was theory generation. Subsequent replication has tested some of these theories and found a level of robustness in them, although it is conceivable that the inappropriateness of the methodology for the purpose may explain why Hofstede had to add a dimension afterwards – his methodology did not cast a wide enough net despite the large size of his sample, because of the similarity of the individuals sampled and the range of questions they were asked. In contrast, the approach adopted in this research was a form of qualitative inquiry.

The kinds of data required and the processes involved in qualitative research are quite different from those needed for hypothesis-testing. In fact, as Becker (1996, p. 70) asserted, there are no recipes for ways of doing social research; rather, one has to have 'imagination and ... smell a good problem and find a good way to study it'.[6] Our 'good way to study' the question of links between culture and business in Asia was to use the method of unstructured interviews widely used for qualitative research, to sample as widely as practicable within our population, to 'seek out differences'[7] and to analyse our interview material continuously as it was obtained instead of after data collection was completed. In hypothesis-testing, researchers seek to ensure comparability by exclusion or control of differences which are not being tested, whereas in qualitative studies, researchers are concerned to seek out differences to enhance understanding. In research aimed at testing theory, the sources for independent and dependent variables should be distinct – that is, for example, the theory 'Cultural beliefs on control influence ownership patterns' should not be tested by data provided by the same individuals for both the cultural beliefs on control and the ownership patterns. For qualitative research aimed at understanding, however, this procedure is acceptable.

The elements of our research procedure just described are broadly similar to Glaser and Strauss's (1967) recommendations for generating grounded theory, but our aim was different – to enhance understanding of the field. Glaser and Strauss (1967) and some subsequent researchers advocated using these elements to 'discover' 'grounded' 'theory'. Thomas and James (2006) have criticized these three aspects of the Glaser and Strauss proposals, broadly because they made unsupportable claims for the strength of the kinds of theories that can emerge from induction and because the terms 'discover' and 'groundedness' imply a positivist agenda. In their own words, 'We dispute grounded theory's status as theory, and the assertion that it can be "discovered"; we contest its claim to be consistent with the tenets of qualitative inquiry, and we question its claims to produce better predictive and explanatory outcomes than other methods.' As Chapter 11 stated, we argue that the output of our research is a weak but testable theory – weak in the sense of not being refutable but testable in that hypothesis-testing research could find supporting or non-supporting evidence and could delimit its boundaries. It is also weak in the sense delineated by Thomas and James (2006): '"Middle range," "weak," "protoscientific" or vernacular theories do not explain anything, since ... sophisticated "inference ticket" procedures ... are not present to enable it. Instead, they help us to understand. Understanding is a no less worthy ambition.'[8] We claim that our research has produced a theory that enhances understanding.

The ideal in grounded theory research (GTM) is that all the concepts and their relations, all the categories and their properties are derived directly from the research data. It is doubtful, however, in our view, whether such an ideal is attainable. This 'ideal' demands virtually no researcher intervention in the process by which concepts and categories are generated. Data originating spontaneously with the research subject does not often come in the form of concepts and relations or categories and properties (although, exceptionally, in the case of the present research it sometimes did); instead it usually comes as concrete descriptions and examples. Only interpretation can convert these latter to the former. In the words of Bryant (2003), 'The positivist stance of a neutral observer, gathering data about the world, from which theories somehow emerge is now ... severely discredited.'[9] Not only are there doubts about the attainability of Glaser and Strauss's ideal, however, but also about its desirability. A theory's quality derives, not only from the 'objective' phenomena with which it deals, but also from the imaginative interpretation of those phenomena by human minds. An approach which denies this reality is no more likely to produce good research than one which falls into the opposite error of generating theories at a remote distance from the subject of study.

Our 'weak' theory was developed quite differently from a 'grounded theory' approach. Glaser and Strauss (1967) conveyed the impression that theory emerges by systematically comparing coded units of the research material. In our research, however, what occurred was our recognizing that our research subjects themselves had theories about culture-business relations that revolved around the influence of a national (or occasionally sub-national) business culture on business decisions. In the research, the term 'business culture' emerged from the second interview in response to the opening question, 'What, if anything, makes doing business or managing an organization in [India] different?' The answer given was, 'The business culture of India, like its social culture, comes from the impact of Hinduism – the fact of no fixed ideology, that Hindus are not people of the book; it means they are flexible but there are no rules.' The term itself was also used spontaneously by interviewees in several subsequent interviews. In the larger number where the term itself was not used, the discussion, always in answer to the same opening question, was, we came to recognize, focused on factors that correspond to our definition of a business culture. Interviewees repeatedly answered our question, 'What makes doing business or managing an organization in China/(*Hong Kong*)/India/Japan/Taiwan/Singapore different?' in terms of a business-related set of shared values, beliefs, attitudes, meanings and ways of doing things understood by a business community. To make clear the significance of this, it should be noted that it was open to our interviewees to respond in many different ways – for instance, in terms of exchange rates, natural resources, demand conditions or government controls. Another response, which would be consistent with the resource-dependence view on business decision-making would be that there was nothing distinctive about their country's business practices. Instead, as the analyses in Chapter 11 showed, the answers were overwhelmingly in terms that correspond to a cultural definition.

In effect, therefore, our central theory was neither derived from the data by some quasi-systematic process nor created by the researchers but captured from the theories held by our research subjects, in some cases by simple recording of their statements, in others by interpreting them in the light of our background knowledge derived mainly from earlier interviews. (As noted above, our original intention was not to produce a theory but to enhance understanding.) We make no apology for our acts of interpretation. In the words of Thomas and James (2006), 'Qualitative inquiry is about interpretation.'[10] In the case of our study, however, much of the work of imaginative interpretation was carried out by the research subjects; the researchers interpreted in the sense of recognizing parallel theories in different forms of expression, categorizing, labelling and selecting the significant from the less significant (so importing their own 'values'), but their main role was to stimulate the research subjects to express their theories and to record them.

More interpretation from the researchers was required in our study for ancillary purposes, such as subdividing the material to form this book, than for generating the central theory as set out in Chapter 11. As Chapter 1 noted

> Our interviewees did not neatly partition their observations on what made doing business or managing an organization in their country into categories. These subdivisions [into types of business decisions and types of culture and perceived environments], even the division of the variables composing business cultures from other variables, are based on interpretations by the researchers influenced by Western conventions.

These subdivisions are not fundamental to our findings; they are only a convenient way to present them and relate them to other sources. Although we believe that business culture is a strong influence on business behaviour in Asia, we do not believe that it has clear boundaries.

Sampling

Initially our study was purely exploratory, aimed at identifying possible influences of culture on Asian business decision-makers. The purpose was to begin the process of providing a richer description of Asian culture and Asian culture-business links than the dimensional approaches had so far provided. Our aim, which also required noting cases which appeared not to involve any influence from culture to business, required us to sample as broad a range of Asian business decision-makers as we could. Our sample consisted of business decision-makers in five Asian countries, China, India, Japan, Taiwan and Singapore. Only the initial collection of data was planned. Initially, we sampled business decision-makers in two countries, India and Taiwan. When our analysis of the early interviews suggested that there were important similarities *and differences* in the business cultures and in culture-business relations in the two countries, we added further Asian countries to our sampling frame and extended our interviewing in India to other cities. For practical reasons, only three more countries could be added and our samples were limited to interviewees who could be interviewed in English. However, in the case of qualitative research, this limitation suggests that other factors (cultural influences and cases of non-influence) than those identified may be relevant, not that those identified are invalid. Our selection of individuals relevant to the study was wide enough to delineate some boundaries, such as the relatively weak influence of business culture on consumer marketing.

Data collection

Since the main variables being explored were beliefs, our data could only be obtained from verbal communication, for the reasons given earlier in this Appendix. Although arguments have been advanced in favour of unobtrusive data collection, it is unlikely that any other data can replace a person's own descriptions and stories as source material for understanding his or her beliefs and perceptions. It is true that what an interviewee transmits may include distortions and concealments. These, however, can be reduced if he or she trusts the interviewer and has no reason to see the interview situation as threatening. The openness of discourse met with in the interviews led us to believe that such a situation was generally achieved in this research.

To access those aspects of peoples' perceptions of business–culture relations which they considered important, we decided to rely on their unprompted speech as far as possible. As a check on the stability of beliefs and the interviewer's accuracy in capturing them, the interview notes were submitted to the interviewees for approval. (See below.) This consideration led us to use interviews that were mainly unstructured and that lasted an hour or more as the main data collection method. This approach was consistent with that advocated by Glaser and Strauss (1967): 'At the beginning of the research, interviews usually consist of open-ended conversations, in which respondents are allowed to talk with no imposed limitations of time. Often the researcher sits back and listens, while the respondents tell their stories.'[11] The discussions that the opening question triggered diverged widely, especially in terms of the aspect of business on which the interviewee wished to focus. For some, it was the approach to deal-making, for others to ownership, for others to management style, for others to the workplace culture. These choices tended to reflect the individual's functional background and current position. As the research progressed, we did introduce checklists towards the end of the interviews to cover points raised in earlier interviews.

Unstructured interviews cannot usually yield data on the relative assessed importance of the quoted variables, but our judgement was that most people do not rank or order the elements of their beliefs about relationships or situations. This judgement has, we would assert, been justified by the research findings which suggest that a few people used a simple near-univariate model of influences on business, while for others (the majority of the respondents), multiple variables coexisted in a holistic way, without rank ordering.

Certain difficulties in collecting data are worth mentioning here. One problem concerned the level of subject-interviewer exposure. Our concern was with the meanings of actions and words to the research subjects; this argued for extended exposure, and so did the importance of developing trust between subject and investigator which has been much emphasized by writers on field research. Developing trust calls for an extended time to elapse before the investigation proper begins. On the other hand, since it was important that the subjects' contributions should be as spontaneous as possible, and since our concerns were with their normal perceptions, it was also important not to communicate the focus of our research interests and conceptual bias. This argued for limited exposure of the interviewer. In the event, most subjects showed great freedom in discussing the topic early in the interview after a short email correspondence. This may be because not only were respondents assured in our initial approach that no confidential information was required, but they could also see for themselves that it was not needed in a discussion of the general approach to business and management of their country. Norms of organizational loyalty and issues of confidentiality would not play the same part as in research focused on themselves or their organization.

Another difficulty was to find forms of expression for introductory statements and emails which would be appropriate to the person being interviewed, but would not introduce bias concerning our topic. We tried to hold any bias constant by using a similar form of introduction in all cases.

Data recording

Interviews for qualitative research are usually tape recorded, and certainly that is the expectation in GTM. We decided not to do so, on the basis of initial soundings that suggested that, in China for instance, such methods would substantially increase the rate of refusing to participate and would also reduce interviewee spontaneity. Instead, notes were taken and written up in detail as soon after the interviews as practical, generally within 24 hours. The interviewer found she had acquired a facility for noting down key expressions used by interviewees; this strongly aided recall in cases where the verbal expression seemed important. Most importantly, the interview notes were submitted to the interviewees for approval. In only one case was anything more than minor revisions asked for; the version used for data analysis was the version with these revisions incorporated, on the grounds that what we wanted was not so much an accurate record of the interview (which might have argued for the interviewer's version) but the respondent's actual beliefs. (In the one exceptional case, the interviewee asked for a section describing his company's philosophy to be deleted, because of a fear that the company might be identifiable from that description.)

Clearly there is a loss of detail when interviews are not tape recorded. This loss might be critical when the theory is obscure or obscured to the interviewee. In our case, however, the theories were transparently present and in a sense belonged to, because they were held by, the interviewees.

Data interpretation

The data generated in this research were subjective – beliefs. Subjective data are commonly regarded with suspicion in organizational research, partly because of a history of using subjective data to measure objective variables and partly because of confusion with subjectivity on the part of the researcher.[12] In the present research there is no case to answer on the first objection: beliefs are asserted as legitimate research topics for the reasons already given. On the second point, it is itself a confusion to credit the possibility of objectivity on the part of the researcher or to assert its value if it were attainable.

Data analysis

The method of qualitative analysis recommended by GTM is the 'constant comparison' method in which 'incidents' are coded, sometimes in multiple ways, systematically compared and eventually accumulated to categories and properties of categories. This method has been criticized as 'putting the cart (procedure) before the horse (interpretation)'.[13] However, Glaser and Strauss (1967) and later Glaser (1978; 1992) did not give instructions on how to perform coding. Instead, 'They describe the conceptualisation of coding.'[14] Strauss and Corbin (1998) did make a recommendation of coding by 'microanalysis which consists of analysing data word-by-word' and 'coding the meaning found in words or groups of words'.[15] We decided not to use microanalysis, however; our decision was based on the same reasoning as given by Allen (2003) on the basis of experience with the method: that it would lead to confusion. 'Dividing the data into individual words caused the analysis sometimes to become lost within the minutia of data. So many words being picked over individually led to confusion. There were times when the focus was lost. Doubts were experienced about what it was that we were looking for.'[16]

In the present research, coding in which analysis was processual and intertwined with data collection was undertaken by one researcher out of three; the other two researchers coded independently, using the completed sets of interview notes for each country. However, although the categories derived from coding formed the basis of the analysis, the central theory itself cannot be identified with any such systematic process. It came rather from the beliefs expressed by the interviewees themselves. In some cases, as noted previously, these beliefs found direct expression and the term 'business culture' was used; in others, our interpretation was that the 'incidents' referred to beliefs and values that corresponded to a concept of 'business culture'. Since large numbers of quotations are given in the text, readers can themselves judge whether our interpretations were justified.

To Glaser and Strauss (1967), the integration of concepts and relations exists in vivo, a pattern in the data itself, which can emerge by itself. Although not subscribing to the positivist position which this implies, in the case of our theory, the integration of concepts and relations did exist in the data, in the form of theories held by our interviewees themselves. Thomas and James (2006) criticized the use of the term 'grounded' for the rather superficial reason that 'ground' has 'intimations of solidity and fixity' that do not mix with ' "construction," with its contrasting intimations of the tenuous, the mutable, the interpreted'. However, the article did not provide any alternative term for theories derived from qualitative research, and others, such as 'qualitatively derived theory' or 'inductively derived theory' are clumsy, so we have decided to continue to use the term introduced by Glaser and Strauss (1967). Our theories are 'grounded'.

Once the concept of 'business culture' was recognized as potentially relevant to theory in the area, it became what Allen (2003) termed a Key Point in the interview data; a Key Point is, in the terminology of Glaser and Strauss (1967), a code.

> During the analysis of an interview, the researcher will become aware that the interviewee is using words and phrases that highlight an issue of importance or interest to the research. This is noted and described in a short phrase. This issue may be mentioned again in the same or similar words and is again noted. This process is called *coding*.

Other Key Points were added as the analysis proceeded. Because from very early in the process it was decided not only that business culture and business decisions were Key Points for us, but even our core theory was that the business culture of a business community exerted a considerable influence on a range of business decisions in Asia, a certain redundancy was built into our research by our studies in China, Japan and Singapore. This redundancy could be used to justify treating the theory as tested, following the contention of Allen (2003): 'The resultant theory does not need separate justification and testing because it came from live data.' However, as we did not use a theory-testing methodology, this is not a claim of ours, and in any case we do not subscribe to the logic of the statement. We consider that our output is an untested theory, albeit one that we believe substantially increases understanding. It is more likely to prove robust because it is 'grounded', but the possibility certainly exists that it will be refuted. What would be needed, moreover, is both replication to further delineate the boundaries of the theory and classical hypothesis-testing.

Because the core theory produced from our study was so clearly and firmly held and expressed by most of our interviewees, most coding was concerned with identifying the main characteristics of the business cultures in each country to preserve that richness which is an important virtue of qualitative research. (We also coded and categorized patterns of business decisions that might or might not be influenced by business culture and aspects of societal, political and economic cultures and environments.) To identify variables as elements of a business culture, we needed a criterion number for the minimum number of instances to qualify a variable to be included. The GTM method sets this criterion as follows: 'A single case can indicate a general conceptual category, only a few cases more can confirm the indication.'[17] We therefore adopted a criterion of five instances of spontaneous mention for including a variable as a major element of a country's business culture in our descriptions in Chapter 2. A further reason for adopting this relatively low criterion number was that the topics covered in the interviews were extremely wide-ranging, depending on the interests of the interviewee: an aspect of organizational structure, for instance, would have simply not arisen in interviews concerned with business finance. (In nearly all cases, an 'instance' was a mention by an individual interviewee; in a small number of cases, however, one interviewee would refer to the same variable at different points in the interview from different angles. These cases might lead to one interviewee providing more than one instance.) Some variables that did not meet the criterion of five instances, being either mentioned spontaneously in fewer than five instances in a particular country or only mentioned in response to direct questioning on the point, are included in Chapter 2, but are double asterisked in the text and given in the tables in italics to show their less affirmed status. We justify including them because a position that only variables mentioned in five or more instances are significant cultural elements may be disputed. To take an analogy from market research, both the brands evoked when a product category is named and those recognized on being given their names may be relevant to product recall studies. In the present study, interviewees had an interval between first being alerted to the topic of the research and the interview itself in which to clarify their ideas, so the chances of their omitting variables they considered important were reduced. Nevertheless, extraneous or random factors might still influence what was uppermost in their minds on the day. Clearly, as Chapter 11 noted, further research would be needed to delimit the range of business culture variables more exactly.

A very high level of intercoder reliability was achieved – nearly 90 per cent in the case of Japan, a little lower for the other countries. Differences were reconciled by discussion or in one or two cases by omitting the category, although that meant restricting the richness of the findings.

Research output

Our theory, its corollaries and findings have been described in Chapter 11. The characteristics of the business cultures of five Asian countries that we identified were set out in Chapter 2 and further analysed in Chapter 3.

Research limitations

1. The main constraint imposed by the design of this research concerns the status of its output. It is no more than an untested weak theory, but we believe it is a theory which may add not a little to understanding of culture-business relations as well as drawing attention to a significant but neglected 'layer' of culture.
2. The minimally directive interviewing technique employed entails the consequence that the findings are crucially dependent on two assumptions. The first is that the respondents will normally be willing and able to reveal their opinions and beliefs about the research subject; the non-threatening, salient character of our enquiry minimizes but does not eliminate the possibility that they will not. The second assumption is

that under low-direction conditions respondents will tend to comment on what they perceive as important rather than trivia. This seems plausible, but raises two issues –

  (i) Are the belief patterns in general and the relative importance attached to different factors quite stable over time, or are they closely tied to changing patterns of events? Our research method permits no definitive answer to this question, but a proportion of the interview notes were submitted to interviewees after the lapse of several months with a request for them to check whether their meaning had been properly recorded. It seems likely that if their views had changed, they would record this as a misunderstanding on the interviewer's part, but no identifiable instance of this occurred.

  (ii) Silence, given our research method, is ambiguous. For example, does the silence of all our Japanese respondents on the role of the bureaucracy mean that they had no clear views? That they had views but were unwilling to express them? Or that the direction taken by the discussion chanced to make the expression of their views inappropriate? A similar set of questions applies to our interviewees' silence on issues of diversity management and discrimination.

3. We only interviewed people who could be interviewed in English. While all but one or two were highly fluent in the language, it was for most not their mother tongue and it must be a possibility that some of their thoughts were distorted and others were not expressed because of the impediments caused by using a second language. There is also a possibility that the requirement skewed our findings and that these would have been different had people not able to be interviewed in English been included. We doubt, though, that the central theory would be refuted.

4. We only interviewed people involved in business. It is just possible that had we interviewed people not so involved, the patterns of business decisions would have been so differently attributed that we would have to abandon our theory. As it is, we have presented it in a weak form – business culture as an influence – partly because of our awareness of this limitation and partly because we do not hold a deterministic view. No one factor, whether business culture, social culture, government policy, globalization or individual agency determines most business decisions. Our contribution is to add a significant factor to those usually considered by scholars, not to replace them.

5. Clearly this methodology could only provide a snapshot, not a longitudinal picture, of the perceived business cultures of the focal countries. What was possible, however, was to discover the amount and kind of change perceived and anticipated by the interviewees and this was done.

6. Our interviewees, and so the source of our theories, were 'naive theorists' in psychological terms. Even if some may have had qualifications in psychology, none were practising it. This may help explain the greater emphasis in their theories on practices than values.

Interviewee analyses

Here we give a breakdown of interviewees by function/expertise, (Table A.1) type of industry of employing organization (Table A.2) and type of ownership of employing organization (Table A.3).

Table A.1 **Function/expertise of interviewees**

	China	India	Japan	Taiwan	Singapore	Total
CEO/Senior general management	6	12	1	3	1	23
Entrepreneur	1	2	–	–	2	5
Sales/Marketing	3	4	4	1	–	13
Business strategy and development	–	1	3	–	1	4
Finance and accountancy	3	5	3	1	1	13
Human resource management	1	1	1	1	1	5
Management consultancy	3	1	–	–	–	4
Other*	3	2	2	1	–	8
Total	20	28	14	7	6	75

Notes: *Includes operations management, business information technology, law, banking, publishing and administration.

Table A.2 **Type of industry of interviewees' employing organizations**

	China	India	Japan	Taiwan	Singapore	Total
Consumer manufacturing	2	2	4	3	–	11
Retailing and consumer services	1	1	1	–	2	5
Industrial*	5	8	–	–	1	14
Business services**	4	9	4	–	2	19
Financial services	5	2	3	4	–	14
Management consultancy	3	–	1	–	–	4
Conglomerate	–	2	–	–	–	2
Education	–	4	1	–	1	6
Total	20	28	14	7	6	75

Notes: *Includes industrial manufacturing, engineering and construction and energy production; ** Includes transport, distribution, Japanese trading companies, banking, advertising, market research, sourcing and procurement services, IT services, publishing.

Table A.3 **Type of ownership of interviewees' employing organizations**

	China	India	Japan	Taiwan	Singapore	Total
Private listed	2	7	8	3	–	20
Private unlisted	4	9	1	2	2	18
State-owned enterprise	2	–	–	–	–	2
Listed former state-owned enterprise	2	–	–	–	–	2
Foreign-owned MNC	10	7	4	2	3	27
Not-for-profit	–	5	1	–	1	7
Total	20	28	14	7	6	75

References

[1] Tauebe, F.A. (2004) 'Culture, innovation and economic development: The case of the South Indian ICT clusters', in Mani, S. and Romijn, H. (eds) *Innovation, Learning and Technological Dynamism of Developing Countries*, New York: United Nations University Press.

[2] Shotter, J. (1980) 'Men the magicians; the duality of social being and the structure of moral worlds', in Chapman, A.J. and Jones, D.M. (eds) *Models of Man*, London: British Psychological Society.

[3] Popper, K. (1963) *Conjectures and Refutations: The Growth of Scientific Knowledge*, London: Routledge and Kegan Paul.

[4] Taylor, D.M. (1970) *Explanation and Meaning*, Cambridge: Cambridge University Press.

[5] Hofstede, G. and Hofstede, J. (2004) *Cultures and Organizations: Software of the Mind; Intercultural Cooperation and Its Importance for Survival*, McGraw Hill.

[6] Becker, H.S. (1996) 'The epistemology of qualitative research', in Jessor, R., Colby, A. and Schweder, R. (eds) *Essays on Ethnography and Human Development*, Chicago, IL: University of Chicago Press, 53–71, quoted in Thomas, G. and James, D. (2006) 'Reinventing grounded theory: Some questions about theory, ground and discovery', *British Educational Research Journal*, **32**(6): 767–95.

[7] Glaser, B.G. and Strauss, A.L. (1967) *The Discovery of Grounded Theory*, New York, Aldine.

[8] Thomas, G. and James, D. (2006) 'Reinventing grounded theory: Some questions about theory, ground and discovery', *British Educational Research Journal*, **32**(6): 767–95.

[9] Bryant, A. (2003) 'A Constructive/ist response to Glaser', *Forum Qualitative Sozialforschung/ Forum: Qualitative Social Research* [Online Journal], **4**(1), URL: http://www.qualitative-research.net/ fqs-texte/1-03/1-03bryant-e.htm.

[10] Thomas, G. and James, D. (2006) 'Reinventing grounded theory: Some questions about theory, ground and discovery', *British Educational Research Journal*, **32**(6): 767–95.

[11] Glaser, B.G. and Strauss, A.L. (1967) *The Discovery of Grounded Theory*, New York, Aldine.

[12] Downey, H., Hellriegal, K.D. and Slocum, J. (1975) 'Environmental uncertainty: The construct and its application', *Administrative Science Quarterly*, **20**: 613–29.

[13] Thomas, G. and James, D. (2006) 'Reinventing grounded theory: Some questions about theory, ground and discovery', *British Educational Research Journal*, **32**(6): 767–95.

[14] Allen, G. (2003) 'A critique of using grounded theory as a research method', *Electronic Journal of Business Research Methods*, **2**(1): 1–10.

[15] Strauss, A.L. and Corbin, J. (1998) *Basics of Qualitative research Techniques and Procedures for Developing Grounded Theory*, Thousand Oaks, CA: Sage.

[16] Allen, G. (2003) 'A critique of using grounded theory as a research method', *Electronic Journal of Business Research Methods*, **2**(1): 1–10.

[17] Glaser, B.G. and Strauss, A.L. (1967) *The Discovery of Grounded Theory*, New York, Aldine.

select bibliography

Books

Alon, I. and Shenkar O. (eds) (2003) *Chinese Culture, Organizational Behavior and International Business Management*, Westport, CT: Praeger.

Berger, P.L. and Huntington, S. (2003) *Many Globalizations: Cultural Diversity in the Contemporary World*, New York: Oxford University Press.

Bond, M.H. (1988) (ed.) *The Psychology of the Chinese People*, Hong Kong: Oxford University Press.

Brown, R.A. (2002) *Chinese Big Business and the Wealth of Asian Nations*, New York: Palgrave.

Chen, M. (2001) *Inside Chinese Business*, Boston, MA: Harvard Business School Press.

Davis, H.J., Chatterjee, S.R. and Heuer, M. (eds) (2006) *Management in India: Trends and Transitions*, New Delhi: Sage.

De Riencourt, A. (1958) *The Soul of China*, London: Honeyglen Publishing.

De Riencourt, A. (1961) *The Soul of India*, London: Jonathan Cape.

Fukuyama, F. (1995) *Trust: Social Virtues and the Creation of Prosperity*. New York: Free Press.

Glaser, B.G. and Strauss, A.L. (1967) *The Discovery of Grounded Theory*, New York: Aldine.

Gupta, R.K. (2002) *Towards the Optimal Organisation: Integrating Indian Culture and Management*, New Delhi: Excel Books.

Hofstede, G. (1981) *Cultures and Organizations: Software of the Mind*, London: Harper Collins.

Hofstede, G. (2001) *Culture's Consequences: Comparing Values, Behaviors, Institutions and Organizations*, 2nd edn, Thousand Oaks, CA: Sage.

Hofstede, G. and Hofstede, J. (2004) *Cultures and Organizations: Software of the Mind; Intercultural Cooperation and Its Importance for Survival*, 2nd edn, New York: McGraw Hill.

Kluckhohn, F.R. and Stodtbeck, F.L. (1961) *Variations in Value Orientation*, Evanston, IL: Row Peterson.

Li, J.T., Tsui, A.S. and Weldon, E. (2000) (eds) *Management and Organizations in the Chinese Context*, New York: Macmillan.

Mani, S. and Romijn, H. (eds) *Innovation, Learning, and Technological Dynamism of Developing Countries*, New York: United Nations University Press.

Popper, K.R. (1963) *Conjectures and Refutations: The Growth of Scientific Knowledge*, London: Routledge and Kegan Paul.

Redding, S.G. (1990) *The Spirit of Chinese Capitalism*, New York: Walter de Gruyter.

Rokeach, M. (1973) *The Nature of Human Values*, New York: Free Press.

Scott, W.R. (1995 and 2001) *Institutions and Organizations*, Thousand Oaks, CA: Sage.

Sen, A. (2005) *The Argumentative Indian: Essays on Indian Culture, History and Identity*, London: Penguin.

Warner, M. (ed.) (2003) *Culture and Management in Asia*, London: Routledge Curzon.

Whitley, R. (1992) *Business Systems in East Asia: Firms, Markets, and Societies*, London: Sage.

Yashimura, N. and Anderson, P. (1997) *Inside the Kaisha: Demystifying Japanese Business Behavior*, Boston, MA: Harvard Business School Press.

Articles

Allen, F., Chakrabarti, R., Sankar, D., Qian, J. and Qian, M. (2007) 'Financing Firms in India', *Wharton Financial Institutions Center Working Paper*, URL: http://fic.wharton.upenn.edu/fic/papers/06/0608.pdf

Allen, F., Qian, J. and Qian M. (2005) 'China's Financial System: Past, Present, and Future', *Wharton Financial Institutions Center Working Paper*, URL: http://fic.wharton.upenn.edu/fic/papers/05/0517.pdf

Allen, G. (2003) 'A Critique of Using Grounded Theory as a Research Method', *Electronic Journal of Business Research Methods*, 2(1): 1–10.

Aoki, M. (2006) 'Whither Japan's Corporate Governance?' *Stanford Institute for Economic Policy Research Discussion Paper*, URL: http://siepr.stanford.edu.paper/pdf/05–14.pdf

Boisot, M. and Child, J. (1996) 'From Fiefs to Clans and Network Capitalism: Explaining China's Emerging Economic Order', *Administrative Science Quarterly*, 41(1): 600–28.

Bond, M.H. (1988) 'Finding Universal Dimensions of Individual Variation in Multicultural Studies of Values: The Rokeach and Chinese Value Surveys', *Journal of Personality and Social Psychology*, 55(6): 1009–15.

Child, J. and Tse, D.K. (2000) 'China's Transition and Its Implications for International Business', Chinese Management Centre, Hong Kong, The University of Hong Kong.

Clarke, D.C. (2003) 'Corporate Governance in China: An Overview', URL: http://papers.ssrn.com/sol3/papers.cfm?abstract_id=424885

Dickson, B.J. (2007) 'Integrating Wealth and Power in China: The Communist Party's Embrace of the Private Sector', *The China Quarterly*, 192: 827–54.

Fisher, C.M., Shirolé, R. and Bhupatkar, A.P. (2001) 'Ethical Stances in Indian Management Culture', *Personnel Review*, 30(6): 694–11.

Fiske, A.P. (2002) 'Using Individualism and Collectivism to Compare Cultures – a Critique of the Validity and Measurement of the Constructs: Comment on Oyserman et al. (2002)', *Psychological Bulletin*, 128(1): 78–88.

Giles, J., Park, A. and Cai, F. (2006) 'How Has Economic Restructuring Affected China's Urban Workers?', *The China Quarterly*, 185: 61–95.

Hofstede, G., Neuijen, B., Ohayv, D.D. and Sanders, G. (1990) 'Measuring Organizational Cultures: A Qualitative and Quantitative Study across Twenty Cases', *Administrative Science Quarterly*, 35(2): 286–317.

House, R.J., Javidan, M., Hanges, P.J. and Dorfman, P.W. (2002) 'Understanding Cultures and Implicit Leadership Theories across the Globe: An Introduction to Project GLOBE', *Journal of World Business*, 37(1): 3–10.

Inglehart, R. and Baker, W.E. (2000) 'Modernization, Cultural Change and the Persistence of Traditional Values', *American Sociological Review*, 65: 19–51.

Kanagasabapathi, P. (2007) 'Ethics and Values in Indian Economy and Business', *International Journal of Social Economic*, 34(9): 577–85.

Kisunko, G., Brunetti, A. and Weder, B. (1999) 'Institutional Obstacles to Doing Business: Region-By-Region Results from a Worldwide Survey of the Private Sector', *World Bank Policy Research Working Paper*, No. 1759. URL: papers.ssrn.com/sol3/Delivery.cfm/SSRN_ID81368_code170891.pdf

Kitayama, S. (2002) 'Culture and Basic Psychological Processes – toward a Systems View of Culture: Comment on Oyserman et al. (2002)', *Psychological Bulletin*, 128(1): 89–96.

Leong, J.C.T., Bond, M.H. and Fu, P.P. (2007) 'Perceived Effectiveness of Influence Strategies among Hong Kong Managers', *Journal of Asia Pacific Management*, 24(1): 75–96.

Leung, K., Bhagat, R.S., Buchan, N.R., Erez, M. and Gibson, C.B. (2005) 'Culture and International Business: Recent Advances and Their Implications for Future Research', *Journal of International Business Studies*, 36(4): 357–78.

Lowe, S. (1998) 'Culture and Network Institutions in Hong Kong: A Hierarchy of Perspectives. A Response to Wilkinson: "Culture, Institutions and Business in East Asia." – Response to Barry Wilkinson, *Organization Studies*, vol. 17, p. 421, 1996', *Organization Studies*, 9(2): 321–44.

Markus, H.R., Kitayama, S. and Heiman, R. (1997) 'Culture and "Basic" Psychological Principles', in Higgins, E.T. and Kruglanski, A.W. (eds) *Social Psychology: Handbook of Basic Principles*, New York: Guilford.

Oliver, C. (1997) 'Sustainable Competitive Advantage: Combining Institutional and Resource-Based Views', *Strategic Management Journal*, 18(9): 697–793.

Oyserman, D., Coon, H.M. and Kemmelmeier, M. (2002) 'Rethinking Individualism and Collectivism: Evaluation of Theoretical Assumptions and Meta-Analyses', *Psychological Bulletin* 128(1): 3–72.

Quer, D., Claver, E. and Rienda, L. (2007) 'Business and Management in China: A Review of Empirical Research in Leading International Journals', *Asia Pacific Journal of Management*, 24: 359–84.

Redding, G. (2004) 'The Capitalist Business System of China and Its Rationale', *Asia Pacific Journal of Management*, 19: 2–3.

Sagar, P. and Singla, A. (2004) 'Trust and Corporate Social Responsibility: Lessons from India', *Journal of Communication Management*, 8(3): 282–90.

Schwartz, S.H. (1994) 'Beyond Individualism/Collectivism: New Cultural Dimensions of Values', in Kim, U., Triandis, H.C., Kagitcibasi, C., Choi, S.-C. and Yoon, G. (eds) *Individualism and Collectivism: Theory, Method and Applications*, 85–119, Newbury Park, CA: Sage.

Schwartz, S.H. and Sagiv, L. (1995) 'Identifying Culture-Specifics in the Content and Structure of Values', *Journal of Cross-Cultural Psychology*, 26(1): 92–116.

Smith, P.B. (2006) 'When Elephants Fight, the Grass Gets Trampled: The GLOBE and Hofstede Projects', *Journal of International Business Studies*, 37(6): 915–21.

Smith, P.B., Peterson, M.F. and Schwartz, S.H. (2002) 'Cultural Values, Sources of Guidance, and Their Relevance to Managerial Behavior', *Journal of Cross-Cultural Psychology*, 33(2): 188–208.

Suzuki, K. and Cobham, D. (2005) 'Recent Trends in the Sources of Finance for Japanese Firms: Has Japan Become a "High Internal Finance" Country?', *Discussion Paper Series*, Heriot-Watt University, 26–9.

Thomas, G. and James, D. (2006) 'Reinventing Grounded Theory: Some Questions about Theory, Ground and Discovery', *British Educational Research Journal*, 32(6): 767–95.

Tsui-Auch, L.S. and Lee, Y.-J. (2003) 'The State Matters; Management Models of Singaporean Chinese and Korean Business Groups', *Organization Studies*, 24(4): 507–34.

Wang, J. and Gupta, V. (2003) 'Post-Crisis Management: A Study of Corporate Restructuring in Asia', *Journal of the Academy of Business and Economics*, April.

index

Note: All the *italic* numbers refer to the chapter reference sections.

accountability, 60, 147, 170, 219–20
  political, 268–9, 295–6
  and state-owned enterprises, 36
accountants in China, 37
Adler, N., 5, 29
age, 243–6
Ahlstrom, D., 101, 112, 113, 114, *128*, 197, 215
Allen, F., 116, *130*, 134, 139, 144–5, 146, *151*, 180, 283, 287
Allen, G., 353, 354, *358*
ASEAN, 207, 314, 315, 316
Asia, financial crisis, 134, 141–2, 275
Asian business, 1
  culture(s), 23, 94–127, 330, 336–7
  systems, 8–9, 10, 12, 13, 26, 337
Asian cultures, 2–3
Asian economic attitudes, 318–19
Asian employment relations, 336
Asian values, 217
Asia-Pacific Economic Community, 287
attitudes to work, 338
  in China, 155–6
  in Hong Kong, 44–5
  in India, 53, 157–8
Au, K., 5, 6, 29, 307
autonomy, 255–6
  affective, 223–4
  intellectual, 223–4

Bandyopadhyay, S., 115, *130*
Barton, C., 117, *130*
batch mentality, 52, 336
Begley, M., 26, *31*, 106, 259
Berger, P.L., 15, 29

Bjerke, B., 15, *30*, 97, 113, 125
Boisot, M., 120, *131*, 293, 308, 312
Bond, M.H., 3, 23, *28*, 177, 197, 215, 226
Brown, R.A., 134, 135, *150*
Brunetti, A., 280, 281, 284, 285, 290, 291, 297
Budhwar, P.S., 95, 97, *127*, 158, 215
bureaucracy, influence of, 292–5
  in China, 175, 292–4
  in Hong Kong, 286, 294
  in India, 295
  in Japan, 275, 294–5
  in Singapore, 284
business, regulation by government, 290–1
business communication style, 172, 177–80
  in China, 178–9
  in India, 62–3, 180
  in Japan, 72
  in Taiwan, 172
business community, 14, 16, 17, 19, 20, 329
  Chinese, of Singapore, 107
  of Taiwan, 78
business culture(s), 13–20, 32–93, 94–127, 213–14
  and business strategies, 194–7
  of China, 33–44, 47
  and decision areas, 17–20
  definition, 17
  and environment, 16
  of Hong Kong, 44–7
  of India, 47–64
  influences on, 22–3
  issues, 23–6
  of Japan, 65–77

business culture(s) – *continued*
  links to other types of culture, 213, 235, 264, 299
  of Singapore, 86–91
  and societal culture, 214
  of Taiwan, 77–86
  and values dimensions, 217–23, 224, 231
  variations in, 43–4, 61–2
business decision-makers, 11, 13, 17, 19, 20–1
  and *guanxi*, 35, 42
business decisions, 13, 18, 19, 161
  and business culture, 17–20, 327–9, 330, 337, 339
business environment, 16
business financing, *see* financing of businesses
business goals, 197–9
business governance, *see* corporate governance
business group(s), 110, 118, 136, 143, 194, 195, 200–3
business ownership, 18, 20, 132–8, 150
  attitude to in Taiwan, 78–9, 334
business relations (B2B), 18, 20, 113–18
  in China, 34, 47, 113–15
  in India, 60, 64, 115–17
  in Japan, 77
  in Singapore, 90
  in Taiwan, 78, 85, 117–18
business strategy(ies), 194–7, 200–10
  and business culture, 194–7, 204
  Chinese, 197, 203–4, 206–8
  Indian, 194–5, 196, 200–2, 206, 208–9
  Japanese, 203, 204, 209–10
  Taiwanese, 194, 195, 203, 204, 205, 210
business system(s), 8–9, 10, 12, 13, 26, 214, 215
  in China, 39–40
  in India, 54–5, 61
  in Japan, 76
  in Singapore, 68, 69, 70, 75, 77, 147
  in Taiwan, 10

Casson, M., 5, 10, 29
caste(s), 7, 104, 116, 157, 173, 237, 241, 242, 249, 251–3, 256, 266, 323, 336
  and India's business culture, 56–7, 59, 64
Chakrabarti, R., 146, *152*

Chan, K.-M., 315, *325*
change, 125–7
  India's business culture and, 57
  Japan's business culture and, 66, 72–4
Chatterjee, S.R., 4, *28*, 126, *131*, 314, *325*
Chaudhuri, H.R., 222, *233*, 252
Chen, M., 2, *28*, 215
Chia, H.-B., 24, 25, *30*
Child, J., 114, 121, 122, *130*, *151*, 165, 176, *192*, 272, 289, 293
Chillier, C., 25, *30*
China
  attitudes to change in, 125–6
  attitudes to risk in, 38
  attitudes to work in, 155–6
  bureaucracy, influence of, 292–4
  business communication style in, 178–9
  business culture in, 33–47
  business goals in, 199
  business strategy(ies), 203–4
    in international markets, 206–7
  collectivism in, 121, 221, 336
  competitiveness of, 300, 301
  contracts in, 34, 118–19
  control in, 168
  corporate governance in, 18, 20, 143–6
  corruption in, 112, 283
  counter-cultures in, 104
  culture of, 2
  diversity management in, 186, 187–8
  economic culture of, 320–2
  economic freedom in, 302–3
  economic growth of, 1
  economic inequality in, 304, 305
  entrepreneurialism in, 42, 101–2
  financial infrastructure of, 312–13
  financing of businesses in, 18, 20, 139
  gender relations in, 186, 187, 247
  generation and age effects in, 221, 243
  government
    control by, 271–3
    policies in, 277, 282
    reform and, 288–90
  guanxi in, 34–5 114–15
  hierarchy in, 98–9
  honesty in, 219–20
  human resources management in, 182–3
  innovation in, 197
  institutional voids in, 195

China – *continued*
  labour markets in, 309–10
    discrimination, 310–11
  leadership in, 181
  local government in, 288–9
  management style in, 174–6
  managerial values in, 169–71
  markets in, 309–10
  media in, 269
  modern values in, 259
  morality in, 254–5
  organizational structures in, 164–5
  planning, attitudes to in, 40
  political power in, 264–5
  political stability and, 276
  price leadership strategy, 204
  religion in, 238–9
  rule of law in, 283, 285, 286–7
  short-term orientation and, 218
  socialist ideology and, 171
  societal culture of, 215, 235–6, 238–9,
    242, 247, 253, 254, 259
  teamwork in, 159–60
  values dimensions, 218, 229
  work behaviour in, 154–5
  workplace culture in, 162–3
  worldview, 235–6, 238
Chinese family-owned businesses
    (CFOBs), 77, 85, 100, 114, 125, 194
Chinese Values Surveys, 215, 226–7
Chui, A.C.W., 224, 225, *233*
citizenship behaviour, 155
Claessens, S., 134, 143, *150, 325*
class (social), 251–3
collectivism, 240–1, 336
collectivism-individualism, 177–8, 216
communication at work, *see* business
    communication style
competition, Taiwan, 80–1
competitiveness, 299–302
computer-mediated communication, 26
conflict avoidance, 163–4, 178–9
conflict management style, 179
Confucian relations, 220
Confucian values, 100, 104, 145, 170–1,
    217, 226, 286–7
Confucianism, 214, 238, 240, 255, 319–20,
    321, 322, 330
consensus, importance in Japan, 69

conservatism, 223, 224, 225
consumer marketing, 19
consumption, 299, 305–6
contracts, 34, 114, 118–19
control, 168–9
corporate governance, 142–50
  in China, 35–7
  in India, 49–50, 60
  in Japan, 75
  in Singapore, 87–8
  in Taiwan, 83–4
corruption, 283–8
  see also entries under individual countries
counter-cultures, 104
creativity, *see* innovation
crony capitalism, 115
cronyism, 112–13
cross-shareholding, 133, 136, 137, 148
cultural control, 169
cultural convergence, 23–4
cultural inwardness, 226–7
cultural preferences and beliefs, 12, 13,
    214, 215
  in China, 139
  in Taiwan, 127
culturalist explanations, 5
culture, 5
  economic, 299–324
  layers, 17
  political, 264–96
  social, 213
  societal, 213, 235–60
    values dimensions of, 215–31
  types of, 17
culture-business relations, 3–4, 5–6
cultures, societal, 213–32, 235–60

Dahles, H., 105, 107, *128*
Dana, L.P., 102, *128*, 137
data analysis, 353–5
data collection, 351–2
data interpretation, 353
data recording, 352–3
De Riencourt, A., 236, *261*
decision-making, 166–8, 216, 249, 250
  business, 1, 21–2, 41–2, 140, 254, 283,
    324, 331, 335
  in China, 42, 47, 99, 122,
    125–6, 144

decision-making – *continued*
    in India, 50, 60, 61, 64, 147
    in Japan, 68, 69, 70, 75, 147, 203, 209
    in Singapore, 91
    in Taiwan, 84, 85, 141
  and business culture, 18–20
  government, 39, 289, 294
  personalism in, 47, 94–7
deference, 100–1
  in China, 33
  in India, 50, 101
  in Japan, 67
delivering on commitments, Japan, 71–2
democracy(ies), 265, 266–8, 269
demographics, 299, 303–4
diasporic trade patterns, 314–15
dimensional approaches,
    critique, 229–31
discrimination in labour markets, 310–12
diversification, 194–5, 201–2
diversity management, 186–9
Dodds, R.F., 272, 286, 289, 296

East Asia, 106, 143, 288, 315
  financial crisis in, 23, 134, 315
economic attitudes, 299
economic beliefs, 299, 316–23
economic culture(s), 23, 319–23
  Asian, 319–23
economic development, stage of, 24
economic freedom, 299, 302–3
economy, openness, Singapore, 87
education, 258–60
egalitarian commitment, 223–4
employee expectations in India, 51–3
employee motivation, Japan, 67
employment relations
  in Asia, 336
  in India, 50, 51
  in Japan, 8, 65–6, 177, 185, 245
  in Taiwan, 85
entrepreneurialism, 101–7, 195
  in China, 42–3
  in India, 58–9
  in Japan, 75
  in Singapore, 88
  in Taiwan, 81
environment
  economic, 299–324

legal, 284–7
political, 264–96
equality, importance in Japan, 69
equality norms, 253–4
ethical norms, 254–7
Eyjolfsdottir, H.M., 15, *30*

face concerns, 172–3, 180
  in Taiwan, 79–80, 84
familism, 46, 96–7
  in Taiwan, 78–9
family businesses, 96–7
family control in India, 48–9
family ownership in India, 47–9, 51
Feigenbaum, E.A., 103, 108, *128*
Feinberg, S.E., 281, 287, 297
financial infrastructure, 312–14
financing of businesses, 138–42
Fiske, A.P., 4, *28*
Fukuyama, F., 109, *129*
further research, 338–40

gender relations
  in employment, 310–12
  in society, 246–51
generation, 243–6
Glaser, B.G., 349, 351, 353, 354, *358*
Global Competitiveness Report, 299, 300–2
global credit crunch, 209
globalization, 299, 314–16
GLOBE, 3, 230
goals, *see* business goals
Goodall, K., 220, *233*
governance, corporate
  in China, 35–7
  in India, 49–50, 60
  in Japan, 75
  in Singapore, 39–40, 87–8
  in Taiwan, 47, 83–4
  see also corporate governance
governance, national, 268, 283–4
  of Singapore, 87–8
government
  as competition, 288, 291–2
  control, 270–6
  culture(s), 277–83
  effectiveness, 271
  policies, 277–83
  regulation of business, 288, 290–1

government – *continued*
  relations with business, *see* business,
    regulation by government
  role in industrialisation, 288–90
  role in modernisation, 288–90
gross domestic product (GDP), 24
grounded theory, 349
guanxi, 34–5, 38, 41–2, 113–15,
    171, 200, 219, 242, 322
  in Taiwan, 78
Gupta, R.K., *190, 241, 261*

harmony, 223–4
heijin, 318
Heilman, S., 308, *325*
hierarchy, 98–100, 224, 241–2
  in China, 33–4
  in Taiwan, 100
Hinduism and India's business
    culture, 55–6
Hofstede, G., 3, 13, 15, 16, 17, 23, *28*, 29,
    30, 99, 197, *211*, 215, 216–23, 227,
    230, 317, 338, *345, 348*
Hofstede's values dimensions, 216–23
Hong Kong
  administration of, 294
  attitudes to work in, 159
  business culture, 44–6
  business strategy(ies), 200
    in international markets,
      207, 208
  competitiveness, 160, 301–2
  corporate governance in, 145–6
  corruption in, 112
  economic freedom in, 303
  economic inequality in, 305
  gender relations in, 248
  guanxi in, 113–14
  industry structure of, 307
  labour market in, 310
  short-term orientation in, 219
  worldview, 239
House, R.J., *28*, 230
Hsu, B.F.C., 145, 146, *152*
Huang, S.M., 320, 321, 322, *326*
Human Development Index, 24
human resource management, 15, 182–6
  in Japan, 185
hybrid enterprises, 43

iemoto, 241
income, 2, 304–5
India
  attitudes to change in, 126
  attitudes to risk in, 59
  attitudes to work in, 156, 157–8
  business communication style in, 180
  business culture in, 47–64
  business goals in, 197–8
  business groups in, 200–2
  business ownership in, 135–6
  business strategy(ies), 194–5, 196,
    200–2
    in international markets, 208–9
  caste in, 252–3
  class in, 252
  competitiveness of, 300, 301
  contracts in, 55, 56, 116, 119
  corporate governance in, 110–11, 146–7
  corruption in, 313–14
  cross-shareholding in, 136
  culture of, 2
  decision-making in, 166, 168
  demographics, 303–4
  diversification in, 201–2
  diversity management in, 186, 188
  economic attitudes in, 318–19, 323
  economic freedom in, 302–3
  economic growth of, 1
  economic inequality in, 304–5
  entrepreneurialism in, 102–3
  financial infrastructure of, 313–14
  financing of businesses in, 139–40
  Freedom of Information Act, 270
  generation and age effects in,
    244, 245–6
  gender relations in, 248–50
  government control in, 273–4
  government policies in, 277–8
  hierarchy in, 99, 242
  human resource management in, 183–4
  innovativeness in, 59, 109
  organizational structures in, 165
  individualism in, 222
  institutions in, 309
  labour markets in, 310
    discrimination in, 312
  leadership in, 181–2
  management practices in, 173–4

India – *continued*
   management style in, 173, 174
   managerial values in, 170, 171–2
   manufacturing in, 307
   media in, 269–70
   modern values in, 258
   morality in, 255–7
   obstacles to doing business in, 281
   personalism, 95–6, 97–8
     in B2B, 115–17
   pharmaceutical industry, 281, 287
   planning in, 199–200
   political power in, 266–7
   religion in, 238
   skills shortage in, 329
   societal culture of, 215, 221, 229,
     236, 237–8, 242, 244,
     245–6, 248–9, 252–3,
     255–7, 258
   specialized intermediaries in, 196
   state governments in, 274, 288
   teamwork in, 160
   values dimensions, 221–2, 229
   work behaviour in, 155
   workplace culture in, 162
   worldview, 236, 237–8
Indians, the 'self' of, 157–8
individualism-collectivism, 177–8, 216
industry structure, 299, 306–7
industry-specific view, 10
Inglehart, R., 25, 30
innovation, 108–9, 197
   in China, 38–9
   in India, 60
   in Japan, 71, 108–9
   in Singapore, 88–9
   in Taiwan, 82–3
institutional perspective, 6–12, 214–15,
     307–8, 317, 330, 337
   and East Asia, 8–9
   and economic behaviour, 8–11
   and organisations, 11
   and socialisation, 11–12
institutional voids, 195–6
institutions, 299, 307–14
integrity, 283–7
internal auditors, 149
internal labour markets, 184–5
International Monetary Fund, 266

international trade, 299, 314–16
   diasporic pattern in Asia, 314–15
interviewee analyses, 356–7
   functions/expertise, 357
   organisational ownership, 357
   type of industry, 357
interviews, 351–2
investment, 299

Japan
   attitudes to change in, 65, 66,
     72–5, 126
   attitudes to risk in, 70–1
   attitudes to work in, 157–8, 159
   bureaucracy in, 294
   business communication style in, 72
   business groups in, 203
   business ownership in, 136–8
   business strategy(ies), 203, 204–5
     in international markets, 209–10
   collectivism in, 241
   competitiveness of, 300, 301
   consensus, importance of, 67, 69
   contracts in, 119
   control in, 168–9
   corporate governance in, 111, 147–9
   cross-shareholding in, 148
   culture of, 2
   decision-making in, 68, 70
   deference in, 68
   demographics, 303
   diversity management in, 186–7, 188
   economic freedom in, 303
   economy of, 1
   entrepreneurialism in, 103
   financing of businesses in, 140–1
   gender relations in, 250–1
   generation and age effects in,
     244–5, 246
   global credit crunch and, 209
   hierarchy in, 99–100
   human resource management in, 184–6
   innovation in, 71, 108–9
   labour markets, 310
     discrimination in, 312
     internal, 185
   lifetime employment in, 8, 65–6, 177,
     185, 245
   management style, 66, 176–7

Japan – *continued*
  market relations, 65, 76
  media in, 270
  modern values in, 258
  morality in, 257
  organizational structures in, 67, 165–6
  power in organizations in, 68
  religion in, 239–40
  societal culture of, 69, 214, 215, 222,
      231, 239–40, 241, 244–5, 246, 253,
      257, 258, 260
  teamwork in, 159
  values dimensions, 222–3
  wealth effects, 304
  work behaviour in, 157, 158–9
  work relations in, 65, 66, 74–5, 163
  workplace culture, 164
Japanese, the 'self' of, 157–8

Kakani, R.K., 202, *211*
Keeley, T.D., 15, *30*
keiretsu, 8, 73, 136–8, 141, 200, 319, 337
Khanna, T., 200, 201, 202, *211*, 252, *262*, 266
Kitayama, S., 16, *30*
Kluckhohn, C., 16, *30*
Kroeber, A.L., 16, *30*
Kshetri, N., 308, *324*
Kumar, R., 202, *211*

labour markets, 309–10
  discrimination in, 310–12
Lam, D., 104, *128*, 138, 172, 205, 219
leadership, 181–2
Lee, J., 112, *129*
Lee, S.-H., 99, *128*
Lenartowicz, T., 13, *29*
Leong, J.C.T., 219, *233*
Leung, K., 26, *30*, 230, 231, 234, 254, *262*
lifetime employment, 8, 65–6, 177, 185, 245
  in Taiwan, 172
Liu, L.S., 110, 117–18, 126–7, *130*
London, T., 4, *29*
long-term orientation, 217
Lowe, S., 165, 167, 170, *191*, 227, 235,
      261, 317
Luce, E., 266, 273, 296

Malaysia, business culture, 240
management practices, 172–80

management style, 172–80
managerial values, 169–72
manager-subordinate relations, 50
marketing, business to business, 20
marketing, consumer, 19–20
markets, 299, 307–14
masculinity/femininity, 217
mastery, 224–5
media and political culture, 269–70
modern values, 257–60
modernity, 24–5
Morris, M.W., 25, *30*, 178
multi-national companies, 33, 87
  in Singapore, 245

negotiation(s), 122–3
  in China, 40–1
  in India, 63
  in Japan, 76
  in Taiwan, 78, 80
network capitalism, 337
Newbury, W., 171, *191*
norms, 253–7

obstacles to doing business, 280–1
Oliver, C., 11, 12, *29*
Organisation for Economic Cooperation and
      Development (OECD), 143, 197, 310
organization and management, 18, 20,
      154–90
  in Japan, 65–70
organizational structures and processes,
      164–9
Orr, G.R., 144, *151*
outsourcing, 196
ownership of businesses, 132–8
  distribution of listed companies, 134
Oyserman, D., 28, 229, 230, *234*

Park, S.H., 114, *130*
Peng, M.W., 215, *232*
personal networks, 242
personalism, 337
  in B2B relations, 113–19
  in control and decision-making, 94–7
  in employment and work relations,
      97–8
  in India, 60–1
  in Taiwan, 78

Pew Research Center, 318
planning, 199–200
    attitudes to in China, 40
    attitudes to in Japan, 70
political culture(s), 23, 264
political stability, 275–6
political systems, 264, 265–9
poverty, 299, 304–5
power distance, 216
power in organisations, 67–8
practical implications, 340–1
professional culture, Taiwan, 80
professionalism in India, 49
profit maximisation, 69, 198
pyramid ownership structure, 134, 143

Ralston, D., 25, 30, 221, *233*
Randlesome, C., 16, 22, *30*
recruitment, international, 87
Redding, S.G., 8, 29, 96, 100, 125, *127*, *191*,
    196, 214, 215, 242, *261*, 316, 318
reputation, 226–7
research limitations, 355–6
research methodology, 346–57
research output, 355
resource-dependence theory, 10
resource-dependence perspective, 317 343, 350
risk, attitudes to, 107–8
  in China, 38
  in Japan, 70–1
  in Singapore, 107–8
  in Taiwan, 81–2
Roland, A., 157, 158, *190*, 241
role culture, lack of, Japan, 66
Rozin, P., 256, *262*
rule of law, 283–7

SAFTA, 314
sampling, 351
saving, 299, 305–6
Schwartz, S.H., 3, 23, *28*, 122, *131*, 215, 223,
    224, 225
Schwartz's values dimensions, 223–6
Scott, W.R., 6, 7, 8, 12, *29*, 215, 330
self-enhancement, 225
self-transcendence, 225
Selmer, J., 98, 122, *128*
Sen, A., *28*, 99, 227, 234, 238, 316
Sheedy, E.A., 107, 108, *129*

Sheer, V.C., 4, 5, *29*
Sheth, D.L., 252, *262*
Shintoism, 239, 257
Shotter, J., 346, *358*
Shweder, R.A., 255, 256, *262*
Singapore
  attitudes to risk in, 2–3
  business culture of, 86–91
  competitiveness of, 300–2
  contracts in, 90
  corporate governance in, 149
  culture of, 2–3
  economic freedom in, 303
  entrepreneurialism in, 105–6
  government control in, 275
  government policies in, 279–80
  innovation in, 109
  political power in, 265
  small and medium enterprises in,
    86, 90
  societal culture of, 215, 245, 246, 259
  teamwork in, 160
Sinha, D. 160, 174, *190*
Sinha, J.B.P., 160, 174, 181, *190*, *192*
Smith, P.B., 4, 15, 23, 28, 230,
    231, *233*
social culture, 23
  definition, 213
social integration, 226–7
social morality, 226–7
societal culture(s), 23, 213–32, 235–61
societal groups, 243–53
South Asia, 227, 274, 308
South Korea, 109, 275, 279–80
Special Economic Zones (SEZs), 280
stakeholders, 149–50, 336–7
state dependence, 336
state-owned enterprises (SOEs), 43–4,
    156, 164–5, 197, 199
Steier, L.P., 6, *29*, 97, 195
stereotypes, 123–5
strategy, *see* business strategy
study methodology, 4–5, 32, 346–58
Suzuki, K., 141, *151*

Taiwan, 25–6
  attitudes to change in, 126–7
  attitudes to risk in, 81–2
  business culture of, 77–86

Taiwan – *continued*
  business ownership in, 138
  business strategy(ies), 194–5, 205–6
    in international markets, 210
  competitiveness of, 300–2
  corporate governance in, 149
  culture of, 2
  diversity management in, 189
  economic freedom in, 303
  entrepreneurialism in,
    103–4, 105
  financing of businesses in, 141–2
  gender relations in, 248
  government policies in, 277
  guanxi in, 117–18
  management style in, 172–3
  media in, 270
  modern values in, 258
  networks in, 203
  personalism, 96
    in B2B, 117–18
  planning in, 199–200
  political power in, 267–8
  rule of law, 286, 287
  short-termism, 219
  societal culture in, 215, 219, 246, 247,
    253, 258
  teamwork in, 160
  work behaviour in, 155
  work motives in, 158–9
Taoism, 214, 235–6, 257, 317
Tauebe, F.A., *261*, 317
team working, 159–62
Thomas, A.S., *128*, 238
Thomas, G., 349, 350, 354, *358*
Thompson, A.G., 213, *232*
thoroughness, importance of in Japan, 70
timeliness, in India, 55–6
Tinsley, C., 122, 123, *131*, 216
Town and Village enterprises, 43, 102
traditional societal cultures, 240–2
traditionalism, 24–5
Tsui, A.S., 242, *261*
Tsui-Auch, L.S., 11, *29*, 275, 279

uncertainty avoidance, 217, 227
unions, Japan, 185
United Nations' Gender Empowerment
  Index, 246–7
United Nations Human Development
  Index, 310
US management values, 170
USA, 1, 3, 42, 53, 78, 81, 167, 209,
  225, 229, 305

values
  Chinese Values Survey, 215, 226–17
  definition, 215
  dimensions of, 216–29
    Hofstede's, 216–23
    Schwartz's, 223–6
  modern cultural, 257–60
  secular-rational, 228–9
  self-expression, 228–9
  survival, 228–9
  traditional, 228–9
  World Values Surveys, 227–9
voice, political, 268–9

wealth, 299, 305
Weber, M.C.E., 237, *261*
Western values, in Hong Kong, 219
Whitley, R., 2, 8, 9, 10, 12, 13, 26, 27, *28*,
  109, *129*, 200, 214, 215, 288,
  320, 322, 337
Wilkinson, B., 5, *29*, *261*
work behaviour, 154–62
work relations
  in India, 62–3
  in Japan, 65, 66, 74–5, 163
workplace cultures, 162–4
World Bank, 143, 268, 270–1, 276, 283,
  295–6, 311
World Economic Forum, 299
World Values Surveys, 25, 145, 215, 227–8
worldviews, 235–40

Zhang, J., 101, *128*
Zhu, Z., 290, *298*

8111